"十三五"江蘇省高等學校重點教材 2017-2-097

胡星銘 編著

中國古典哲學原著選讀

[漢英對照]

南京大學出版社

目録 / Contents

前言 / Preface ·· 001
英譯説明 / A Note on Translations ································ 007
致謝 / Acknowledgements ··· 001

一、孝悌 / Part I　Filial Piety ···································· 001

《論語》/ The Analects ·· 002
《孟子》/ Mencius ··· 008
《孝经》/ Classic of Family Reverence ························· 024
《墨子》/ Mozi ·· 026
　　法儀第四
　　Chapter 4　On the Necessity of Standards ············· 026
　　兼愛中第十五
　　Chapter 15　Universal Love II ································ 029
　　兼愛下第十六
　　Chapter 16　Universal Love III ······························· 035
　　節葬下第二十五
　　Chapter 25　Simplicity in Funerals III ······················ 040
《荀子》/ Xunzi ·· 052
　　子道篇第二十九
　　Chapter 29　The Way to Be a Son ························· 052
《韩非子》/ Hanfeizi ··· 054
　　十過第十
　　Chapter 10　Ten Faults ··· 054

奸劫弑臣第十四
Chapter 14　Ministers Apt to Betray, Molest, or Murder the Ruler …… 055
内儲說上七術第三十
Chapter 30　Inner Congeries of Sayings, The Upper Series: Seven Tacts …… 057
外儲說左上第三十二
Chapter 32　Outer Congeries of Sayings, The Upper Left Series …… 058
六反第四十六
Chapter 46　Six Contrarieties …… 059
忠孝第五十一
Chapter 51　Loyalty and Filial Piety: A Memorial …… 059

二、義利 / Part Ⅱ　Righteousness …… 067
《論語》/The Analects …… 068
《孟子》/Mencius …… 070
《墨子》/Mozi …… 081
尚賢下第十
Chapter 10　Exaltation of the Virtuous Ⅲ …… 081
兼愛中第十五
Chapter 15　Universal Love Ⅱ …… 083
天志中第二十七
Chapter 27　Will of Heaven Ⅱ …… 084
非命上第三十五
Chapter 35　Anti-Fatalism Ⅰ …… 093
經說上第四十二
Chapter 42　Exposition of Canon Ⅰ …… 095

三、治亂 / Part Ⅲ　Governance …… 097
《老子》/Laozi or Dao De Jing …… 098
《莊子》/Zhuangzi …… 120

應帝王第七
　　　Chapter 7　The Normal Course for Rulers and Kings ············ 120
《論語》/The Analects ································· 126
《大学》/Great Learning ······························ 133
《荀子》/Xunzi ·· 143
　　王制篇第九
　　　Chapter 9　The Rule of a True King ························· 143
《韓非子》/Hanfeizi ···································· 158
　　主道第五
　　　Chapter 5　The Dao of the Ruler ··························· 158
　　二柄第七
　　　Chapter 7　The Two Handles ······························· 163
　　大體第二十九
　　　Chapter 29　Fundamental Principles ······················· 168
　　五蠹第四十九
　　　Chapter 49　Five Vermin: A Pathological Analysis of
　　　Politics ·· 170
　　顯學第五十
　　　Chapter 50　Learned Celebrities: A Critical Estimate of
　　　Confucians and Mohists ······················· 193

四、心性 / Part Ⅳ　Human Nature ····················· 199
《孟子》/Mencius ·· 200
《荀子》/Xunzi ··· 209
　　禮論篇第十九
　　　Chapter 19　Discourse on Ritual ··························· 209
　　性惡篇第二十三
　　　Chapter 23　Human Nature Is Bad ························· 210

五、名實 / Part Ⅴ　Lauguage ························· 223
《公孫龍子》/Gongsun Longzi ························· 224

　　　　白馬論第二
　　　　Chapter 2　On White and Horse (BAIMA LUN) ············· 224
　　　　堅白論第五
　　　　Chapter 5　On Hard and White (JIANBAI LUN) ············· 227
　　《荀子》/Xunzi ·· 231
　　　　正名篇第二十二
　　　　Chapter 22　Correct Naming ··· 231

六、知行 / Part Ⅵ　Knowledge ··· 237
　　《莊子》/Zhuangzi ·· 238
　　　　逍遙遊第一
　　　　Chapter 1　Wandering Boundless and Free ····························· 238
　　　　齊物論第二
　　　　Chapter 2　The Adjustment of Controversies ························· 240
　　　　大宗師第六
　　　　Chapter 6　The Great and Most Honored Master ···················· 255
　　《荀子》/Xunzi ·· 260
　　　　勸學篇第一
　　　　Chapter 1　An Exhortation to Learning ································ 260
　　　　儒效篇第八
　　　　Chapter 8　The Achievements of the Confucian (Ru) ············ 269
　　　　解蔽篇第二十一
　　　　Chapter 21　Dispelling Obsession ·· 274

七、天人 / Part Ⅶ　Heaven ·· 289
　　《論語》/The Analects ·· 290
　　《孟子》/Mencius ·· 292
　　《墨子》/Mozi ··· 297
　　　　天志上第二十七
　　　　Chapter 27　Will of Heaven Ⅱ ·· 297
　　　　非命上第三十五
　　　　Chapter 35　Anti-Fatalism Ⅰ ··· 297

《莊子》/Zhuangzi ··· 304
    大宗師第六
    Chapter 6　The Great and Most Honored Master ············ 304
《荀子》/Xunzi ·· 312
    天論篇第十七
    Chapter 17　Discourse on Heaven ································· 312

附錄：哲學家小傳 / Appendix：Biographies of Chinese Philosophers ········ 321
  孔子 Confucius ··· 321
  韩非 Han Fei ··· 322
  老子 Laozi ·· 323
  孟子 Mencius ·· 324
  墨子 Mozi ··· 325
  荀子 Xunzi ·· 326
  莊子 Zhuangzi ··· 326

術语 / Glossary ·· 329
參考書目 / Bibliography ··· 331

前 言 / Preface

"中國古典哲學"有廣、狹二義。廣義上的"中國古典哲學"是指從先秦到清代的中國哲學流派的統稱。這種用法在中國大陸比較常見。比如張岱年在《北京大學學報》1957年第8期發表的《中國古典哲學的幾個特點》，就是在廣義上使用"中國古典哲學"一詞。近年出版的著作如郭齊勇《中國古典哲學名著選讀》和馮達文《中國古典哲學略述》都沿用了張岱年的用法。狹義上的"中國古典哲學"與英文"Classical Chinese Philosophy"或"Ancient Chinese Philosophy"相對應，是指從東周初期到秦始皇統一中國之前，在中國本土產生的各種哲學理論。這個用法在港台和海外比較流行。比如台灣大學哲學系日籍教授佐藤將之在台大開設課程"中國古典哲學導論"，美國中國哲學專家万白安（Bryan W. Van Norden）著有《中國古典哲學導論》（Introduction to Classical Chinese Philosophy）。他們講的都是狹義上的"中國古典哲學"。本編採用海外的用法，因爲本編的目的之一是培養本土學生用英文介紹和研究中國哲學的能力，並且本編預設的讀者包括外國留學生。

狹義上的中國古典哲學前後有五百多年歷史（約前770—約前220年）。東周之前，中國已有各種哲學思想，但流傳下來的多是片段，無較爲系統的論述。東周之後，諸子興起，百家爭鳴。歷史學家司馬談（司馬遷的父親）將那時的學説分成陰陽、儒、墨、名、法、道德六家。陰陽家的代表人物是鄒衍；儒家的代表人物有孔子、孟子和荀子；墨家的代表人物是墨子；名家的代表人物是公孫龍和惠施；法家的代表人物是韓非子（荀子被認爲是韓非子的老師，部分是因爲他明確强調了法律的重要性）；道德家（即通常講的道家）的代表人物是老子和莊子。這六派哲學很大程度上塑造了後來的中國文化和歷史。

要理解中國古典哲學，需要弄清楚那時的哲學家所思考的問題，因爲每個哲學理論都是某些哲學問題的回答。中國古典哲學的繁榮時期是中央權威衰敗、舊社會制度瓦解、新社會秩序尚未建立的戰亂時代。那個時代的哲學家主要關心兩個問題：一、如何重建社會秩序（平治天下）；二、如何安身立命。這兩個問題是緊密聯繫的：某種方式的安身立命能夠有助於重建社會秩序，而重建社會秩序最終目的是爲了更好地安身立命。大概言之，儒、墨都認爲，個人的安身立命至少部分體現在對重建社會秩序的努力中。儒家的"士不可不弘毅，任重而道遠"，墨家的"摩頂放踵以利天下"，都強調個人的社會責任。與之相對照，道家則注重清淨無爲，認爲社會之所以亂，個人之所以不能安身立命，都是因爲想要有一番作爲，特別是想要積極地改造社會。所以，道家是比較徹底的批評者，挑戰了儒、墨的共同前提（即，我們應該通過個人的積極行動來重建社會秩序）。法家有調和儒、墨、道三派的傾向，一方面講"寄治亂於法術，托是非於賞罰"，另一方面講"澹然閑靜，因天命，持大體"。

　　此外，深入探討"重建社會秩序"和"安身立命"這兩個問題，必然涉及其他哲學問題。比如，要重建社會秩序，必須要弄清楚什麼樣的社會是好的社會。是"小國寡民"還是"國強民庶"？是"愛有差等"的"老吾老以及人之老，幼吾幼以及人之幼"，還是"愛無差等"的"視人之家若視其家，視人之身若視其身"？國與國之間是"民至老死不相往來"，還是"以至仁伐不仁"，抑或"滅諸侯，成帝業，爲天下一統"？好的社會之所以好，是因爲它是大多數人所嚮往的，還是因爲它是古代聖人所垂範的，還是因爲它符合了天道（或天命或天志），抑或三者兼而有之？如果符合天道是好社會的最終標準之一，那麼我們如何知道天道？此外，要建立一個好的社會，我們應該採取什麼樣的手段？是"道之以德，齊之以禮"，還是以法、術、勢相結合，抑或是"無爲而治"？這又涉及人性問題，因爲何爲最佳方案很大程度上依賴於人性是否爲惡：在"人性惡"這個假設基礎上設計出的方案必定與在"人性善"這個假設基礎上設計出的方案不同。對於這些問題，不同的哲學家給出了大相徑庭的回答，都認爲自己是正確的，別人是錯誤的。這種"百家爭鳴"的現象是不是意味著並沒有一個客觀的真理？還是意味著只有某一個哲學家的看法是正確的，其他都是"蔽於一曲，而暗於大理"？如果並沒有一個客觀的真理，我們應該如何安身立命？如果有一個客觀的真理，我們如何可以知道這些真理？以上都是中國古代哲學家關心的問題。

　　讀者可能注意到：我前面說中國古典哲學主要有六家，但談到中國古典哲學的問題時，只提到儒、墨、道、法四家，沒有提及陰陽家和名家。這是因爲陰陽家和名家直接討論的問題與儒、墨、道、法四家有別。但這並不意味著陰陽家和名家不能納入我上面的敘說框架中。陰陽家和名家的論述表面上與"如何重建社會秩序"或"如何安身立命"的關係的確不大,然而其旨趣却是對這兩個問題的回答。陰陽家鄒衍的"五德終始説"是用木、火、土、金、水這五種元素(即"五德")的循環運轉去解釋歷史變遷和王朝興衰,其本身是一個社會學理論,但它有價值藴涵:要安身立命和重建社會秩序,必須尊重"五德終始"的規律。司馬遷《史記·孟子荀卿列傳》説:"鄒衍睹有國者益淫侈,不能尚德,……乃深觀陰陽消息而作怪迂之變,《終始》《大聖》之篇十餘萬言。其語閎大不經,必先驗小物,推而大之,至於無垠。……然要其歸,必止乎仁義節儉,君臣上下六親。"可見鄒衍最終關心的仍是如何重建社會秩序和如何安身立命這兩個問題。

名家公孫龍以"白馬非馬"和"離堅白"兩個理論知名,其所討論的是抽象的語言哲學和形而上學問題,但《公孫龍子·跡府篇》———篇關於公孫龍的傳記——説他之所以討論這類問題,是因為"欲推是辯,以正名實而化天下焉"。公孫龍在《名實論篇》説:"至矣哉!古之明王。審其名實,甚其所謂。至矣哉!古之明王。"可見,他認為辨明"白馬非馬"和"離堅白"這類關於"名實"的問題,有助於社會秩序的重建。這個思想可以追溯到孔子。在《論語·子路》中,孔子説,要治理好國家,最先要做的是"正名",因為"名不正,則言不順;言不順,則事不成;事不成,則禮樂不興;禮樂不興,則刑罰不中;刑罰不中,則民無所措手足"。後來荀子和韓非子批評公孫龍等名家,其理由也是從政治角度出發的:公孫龍等人的那套"名實"學説,不但不會有助於社會秩序的重建,還會導致社會混亂。

關於中國哲學原著選讀的教材,坊間已有不少。較有影響的有:北京大學中國哲學教研室編《中國哲學原著選讀》(北京大學出版社,具體出版年月不詳,大概在1980年前後,目前市面上已買不到),方克立、李蘭芝編《中國哲學名著選讀》(南開大學出版社,1996年),郭齊勇編《中國古典哲學名著選讀》(人民出版社,2005年),以及洪修平主編《儒佛道哲學名著選編》(南京大學出版社,2006年)。但英譯的教材只有兩本:Wing-Tsit Chan (ed.), A Source Book in Chinese Philosophy (Princeton University Press, 1969)與Philip J. Ivanhoe and Bryan W. Van Norden (ed.), Readings in Classical Chinese Philosophy (Hackett Publishing, 2nd edition, 2005)。中英對照版的只有一本:石俊主編《中國哲學名著選讀》(漢英對照,中國人民大學出版社,1988年)。此書雖重版過但影響較小,市面上已很難買到。

與已有的教材相比,這本選讀有兩個特色。首先,在選材和編排方面,這本選讀試圖突出中國古典哲學中豐富而精緻的論證;缺乏論證性的材料(如陰陽家的論述)一般不選,除非與其他論證性的材料直接相關。有些人認爲,中國古典哲學與古希臘哲學有很大的不同:前者是直覺式、領悟式的斷言,缺乏細膩的邏輯論證,而後者則非常注重邏輯論證。這個說法最早可追溯到著名中國哲學專家馮友蘭。他在其成名作《中國哲學史》的緒論中說:

> 凡所謂直覺、頓悟、神秘經驗等,雖有甚高的價值,但不必以之混入哲學方法之內。無論科學、哲學,皆系寫出或說出之道理,皆必以嚴刻的理智態度表出之。……普通人只知持其所持之見解,而不能以理論說明何以須持之。專門哲學家則不然,彼不但持一見解,而對於所以持此見解之理由,必有說明。……荀子所謂"其持之有故,其言之成理"是也。……中國哲學家之哲學,在其論證及說明方面,比西洋及印度哲學家之哲學,大有遜色。此點亦由於中國哲學家之不爲,非盡由於中國哲學家之不能。

此處馮友蘭有兩個論斷:一、論證是哲學的核心,無論證不成哲學;二、中國哲學在論證方面遠遜於西洋和印度哲學。如果一種哲學在論证方面越高明,其价值就越大,那麼根據馮友蘭的觀點,中國古典哲學的價值遠遠不如西洋和印度哲學。

我同意馮友蘭的第一個論斷——無論證不成哲學,但不同意他的第二個論斷。我認爲中國古代哲學家在論證方面並不比柏拉圖和亞里士多德差。細讀這本選讀的人會發現,墨子、孟子、莊子、荀子和韓非子非常注重論證,其論證技能也是一流的。《老子》和《論語》雖然直接的論證不多,但綜觀全書,它們對一些核心主張是有間接論證的。比如,我們可以在《老子》中找到支持"無爲而治"的理由,也可以在《論語》中找到支持"子女有盡孝之責任"的理由。不可否認,中國古代哲學論證甚少以明確的演繹形式來表述。有人認爲,這表明中國古代哲學家缺乏演繹論證的思維——不懂或不會做演繹論證。我不同意這個看法。在我看來,說孔孟老莊不理解或不會做演繹推理(比如這樣一個演繹推理:"如果一個人向官府舉報自己父母的罪行,那麼他做了一件不孝的事。葉公的老家人向官府舉報自己父母的罪行,因此,葉公的老家人做了一件不孝的事"),是極不厚道的詮釋。事實上,中國古代哲學家的許多論證,像柏拉圖的許多論證一樣,雖然不是以明確的演繹形式來表述,但都可以重構成有效的演繹論證。此外,對於演繹論證與非演繹論證的區分,在邏輯哲學中是有很大爭議的。邏輯哲學中有一派叫演繹主義,認爲一切非演繹論證——包括歸納論證——都可以還原爲演繹論證,無需"歸納有效"這種概念。根據演繹主義,中國古代哲學家所做的每個非演繹論證都可以還原爲演繹論證。

這本選讀的第二個特點是:與已有的選讀不同,它不是以人頭爲單位,而是按照中國古典哲學的幾個核心主題——孝悌、義利、治亂、名實、心性、知行、天人——來組織閱讀材料。按人頭編選的優點是能讓讀者瞭解一個哲學家的體系,知道某個論點在其體系中的位置。缺點是不能突出不同哲學家對同一個問題的不同進路,展現中國古典哲學百家爭鳴的圖景。英美的哲學原著選讀,以人頭爲單位選編的較少,大多數都是以主題爲單位來選編材料,以突出不同哲學家在同一主題上的針鋒相對,方便讀者比較與反思。後一種編選方式之所以比前一種更流行,似乎與英美哲學界對哲學教育之目標的認識有關。他們似乎認爲,哲學教育最重要的目標不是幫助學生理解一個個偉大哲學家的哲學體系,而是幫助學生更好地思考哲學問題,而他們多年的教學實踐表明,以主題爲單位的原著選讀能更有效地幫助學生更好地思考哲學問題。這個觀點是否正確或有爭議,但顯然值得我們去實驗一下,特別是在用英文教授中國哲學這種本身就頗具實驗性的課堂上。

因爲要突出中國古典哲學的百家爭鳴,有些學説(如陰陽家的"五德終始説")雖然有趣,但沒有入選,因爲從流傳下來的文獻看,這些學説在先秦基本上是一家獨鳴而不對他家學説構成挑戰(如儒、墨、道、法等各家的核心理論與陰陽家的"五德終始説"在邏輯上並無矛盾),別家對此學説也幾乎沒有任何直接或間接的嚴肅批評(輕蔑的拒斥不算嚴肅的批評)。入選的幾個主題都是先秦諸子特別注重的辯題。它們與"如何重建社會秩序"和"如何安身立命"這兩個問題緊密相關,涵蓋了"百家爭鳴"的主要領域。以孝悌爲例。在儒家看來,蘊含差等之愛的孝悌既是重建社會秩序的根本,也是安身立命的根本。墨家和法家則不同意儒家的説法。這本選讀挑選了《論語》《孟子》《孝經》《墨子》《荀子》和《韓非子》關於孝悌的主要論述。讀者在讀完這部分文獻後,會對先秦諸子的孝悌觀有一個比較全面深入的瞭解。前幾年,中國學術界圍繞儒家的"親親相隱"展開了一場持久的論戰。論戰的雙方聚焦於《論語》和《孟子》關於孝悌的論述,對於《墨子》和《韓非子》的孝悌觀則沒有深入的討論。這是很遺憾的,因爲《墨子》和《韓非子》關於孝悌有非常精彩的論述。

有人可能認爲,孝悌、義利、治亂這三個主題是形而下的東西,不是哲學重點關注的對象。我不同意這個看法。首先,這三個主題是中國古典哲學家非常關心的、著重討論的。其次,這三個主題在西方哲學屬於倫理學(包含政治哲學)領域,而倫理學和知識論、形而上學並列爲哲學的三個核心領域。西方哲學對於義利、治亂的研究汗牛充棟，不必多説。其對孝悌的研究也可以追溯到柏拉圖，雖然不是顯學，但近些年關於家庭關係的哲學研究越來越多，對於孝悌也很多討論。

　　最後，我想解釋一下這本書的書名。有人可能認爲，本書選編的的材料既然只涉及中國古典哲學幾個主題，沒有面面俱到，稱之爲"中國古典哲學中的若干問題文獻選編"更爲適切；以"中國古典哲學原著選讀"爲書名，有點名不副實。我承認"中國古典哲學中的若干問題文獻選編"是個更爲精確的書名，但任何一本原著選讀都不可能涵蓋中國古典哲學的所有內容，必須有所取捨；不同編者的取捨標準也常常不同。從精確的角度考慮，把已有的以人頭爲單位的選讀稱爲"若干中國古代哲學家關於若干哲學問題之論述的文獻選編"，更爲適當。但這個名稱沒有人採用，因爲它有些累贅。精確是重要的，但也要兼顧簡潔。

2017 年 9 月 28 日於南京大學

英譯説明 / A Note on Translations

這本選讀的中文原文以中華書局的"中華經典藏書"系列爲藍本,英譯文主要基於以下翻譯:

- The Analects, translated by James Legge
- Classic of Family Reverence, translated by James Legge
- Great Learning, translated by James Legge
- Hanfeizi, translated by W. K. Liao
- Xunzi, translated by Burton Watson
- Laozi, translated by James Legge
- Mencius, translated by James Legge
- Mozi, translated by W. P. Mei
- Gongsun Longzi, translated by Ian Johnston
- Zhuangzi, translated by James Legge

以上譯本都是努力忠實原文的"學究式"翻譯,比較可靠。譯者不僅對整個先秦哲學有所瞭解,而且對於後來的註疏有較爲精深的研究(有些翻譯看上去很奇怪,好像是洋人不懂古文引起的,其實是基於中國某些著名學者的註疏)。

但我在編選時並沒有完全複製以上譯本的譯文,而是做了仔細的校對。首先,對於中國人名和地名,我將原譯文中的威妥瑪拼音(Wade-Giles system)全部改成目前通行的漢語拼音,以便讀者辨識。其次,對於晦澀難解或不夠準確的英譯文,我參考了所能找到的其他所有翻譯(書末附有參考書目),按照自己的理解做了一些選擇和刪改,努力使譯文更清楚和準確。以《論語》4.18節爲例：

　　子曰："事父母幾諫，見志不從，又敬不違，勞而不怨。"

　　理雅各（James Legge）的譯文是：The Master said, "In serving his parents, a son may remonstrate with them, but gently; when he sees that they do not incline to follow his advice, he shows an increased degree of reverence, but does not abandon his purpose; and should they punish him, he does not allow himself to murmur." 把"不違"翻譯成"the son does not abandon his purpose"，把"勞"翻譯成"punish"，似乎都欠妥。森舸瀾（Edward Slingerland）的翻譯是：The Master said, "In serving your parents you may gently remonstrate with them. However, once it becomes apparent that they have not taken your criticism to heart you should be respectful and not oppose them, and follow their lead diligently without resentment." 把"不違"翻譯成"the son does not oppose his parents"，把"勞"翻譯成"follow parents' lead diligently"，似乎更好些。

　　但倪培民（Peimin Ni）不贊同森舸瀾的翻譯。倪的譯文是：The Master said, "In serving your parents, remonstrate with them gently. After showing your aspiration, though they do not comply, remain reverent but do not abandon your purpose. Though weary, hold no resentment." 倪繼承了理雅各對"不違"的翻譯。在他看來，森舸瀾把"不違"理解爲"順從父母"，是錯誤的，因爲孔子反對無條件地服從父母（倪援引《孔子家語》爲證據）。此外，倪把"勞"翻譯成"weary"，與理雅各和森舸瀾的翻譯都不同。倪也没説清楚所謂"勞"是指哪一方面。

　　大衛·辛頓（David Hinton）對《論語》4.18節的翻譯是：The Master said: "In serving your mother and father, admonish them gently. If they understand, and yet choose not to follow your advice, deepen your reverence without losing faith. And however exhausting this may be, avoid resentment." 把"不違"翻譯成"without losing faith"，與理和倪的理解較爲接近；把"勞"翻譯成"exhausting"，與倪接近，但比倪更清楚，也比森舸瀾的譯文更圓融（與上下文銜接得更好）。

　　然而，無論是理雅各、倪培民、辛頓，還是森舸瀾，對"無違"的翻譯似乎都是錯誤的。在《論語》2.5節，孔子對"無違"給出一個解釋：

> 孟懿子問孝，子曰："無違。"樊遲御，子告之曰："孟孫問孝於我，我對曰'無違'。"樊遲曰："何謂也？"子曰："生，事之以禮；死，葬之以禮，祭之以禮。"

可見孔子所謂的"無違"，是不違背對待父母的禮節，而非不違背自己或父母的意志。因此在本書中，我將"不違"翻譯成"serve your parents in accordance with rituals"。關於"勞"，我則採用了辛頓的翻譯。於是我將理雅各的譯文改爲：The Master said, "In serving his parents, a son may remonstrate with them, but gently; when he sees that they do not incline to follow his advice, he remains respectful and serves his parents in accordance with rituals. And however exhausting this may be, avoid resentment."我覺得這個譯文最貼切原文的意思，比理雅各的翻譯好很多。

值得注意的是，理雅各的翻譯並非一個外國人望文生義的結果，而是基於大學者朱熹的解釋。在《四書集注》這本名著中，朱熹對"不違"和"勞"給出了如下解釋：

> 見志不從，又敬不違，所謂"諫若不入，起敬起孝，悅則復諫"也。勞而不怨，所謂"與其得罪於鄉、黨、州、閭，寧熟諫。父母怒不悅，而撻之流血，不敢疾怨，起敬起孝"也。

所謂"悅則復諫"，就是"絕不放棄規勸父母的目標"，就是理雅各所說的"the son does not abandon his purpose"，辛頓所說的"without losing faith"。所謂"撻之流血"，即懲罰子女，就是理雅各說的"punish"。因此，如果理雅各的翻譯是錯的，那麼大學者朱熹的解釋也是錯的。我對朱熹有崇高的敬意，但我覺得他對"勞"和"不違"的解釋誤導了理雅各以及後來的一些學者。

除了《論語》外，本書對於其他文本的譯文也有類似細緻的校對和個人詮釋（像《老子》和《莊子》這類比較晦澀的文本，翻譯在很大程度上是譯者的創造性詮釋）。這不是聲稱我在翻譯上有任何原創性貢獻——我只是在不同譯本中選擇了在我看來更清楚、準確的譯文，並在某些字詞方面做了一些改動，絕對算不上原創性貢獻。但如果書中有任何翻譯錯誤，全部責任在我，因爲譯文是我選擇和加工的結果。

對於中文讀者，我希望這本書的英譯文能有助於他們更好地理解中文原文；對於非中文讀者，我希望本書可以幫助他們更準確地理解中國古典哲學；對於專家，我希望這本書沒有讓他們太失望，並希望能得到他們的批評和指教。

2018 年 3 月 22 日於南京大學

致　謝
Acknowledgements

　　感謝白欲曉、陳施羽、陳佩輝、傅新毅、韓林合、胡軍、胡永輝、郝長墀、劉金鑫、溫海明、蕭陽、徐小躍、張亮(按拼音順序)諸位師友，以及編輯施敏和傅裕女士。

一、孝悌 / Part I　Filial Piety

　　對於我們來說，孝敬父母是常識。但如何解釋這個常識的合理性呢？我們應該孝敬父母，僅僅是因爲父母是人，而我們應該給予每個人愛和尊重，並在他們需要的時候予以援手嗎？假設你的父親和一個陌生人同時需要你的幫助，但你只能幫助其中一人，那麼你應該優先幫助你的父親嗎？如果是，爲什麼？如果在你年幼時，你的父母不曾善待你，那麼在他年老多病的時候，你還負有照顧他的義務嗎？如果你的父親犯了錯，或犯了罪，你又該怎麼做？中國古代的哲學家曾激烈地討論過這些問題。

　　閱讀選文時，思考一下這些哲學家對以上問題的回答有何區別。哪個回答是有道理的？爲什麼？

It is common sense that we should love and respect our parents and take care of them when they are in need. How can this common sense be justified? Is it just because our parents are human beings, and we should love and respect every human being and take care of him/her when he/she is in need? Put differently, suppose both your father and a stranger need your help, and you can only help one of them. Should you give priority to your father? If yes, why? What if your father refused to take care of you when you were a kid? Do you then still have an obligation to take care of him when he is old and ill? What should you do when you think that your father makes a mistake or commits a crime? Ancient Chinese philosophers debated heatedly over these questions.

As you read the selections, ask yourself how those philosophers differ from one another in answering these questions. Is any of those theories provided by ancient Chinese philosophers plausible? Why?

《論語》/ The Analects

1.2　有子曰："其爲人也孝弟,而好犯上者,鮮矣;不好犯上,而好作亂者,未之有也。君子務本,本立而道生。孝弟也者,其爲仁之本與!"

1.2　Youzi said, "There are few who, being filial and respectful of their elders, are fond of offending against their superiors. There have been none, who, not fond of offending against their superiors, like to stir up rebellion. The gentleman bends his attention to the roots. Once the roots are firmly established, the Way will grow. Filial piety and respect for elders—are they not the root of all benevolent actions?"[①]

1.11　子曰："父在,觀其志;父没,觀其行;三年無改於父之道,可謂孝矣。"

1.11　The Master said, "While a man's father is alive, look at the bent of his will; when his father is dead, look at his conduct. If for three years he does not alter from the way of his father, he may be called filial."

2.5　孟懿子問孝。子曰："無違。"樊遲御,子告之曰："孟孫問孝於我,我對曰,'無違'。"樊遲曰："何謂也?"子曰："生,事之以禮;死,葬之以禮,祭之以禮。"

2.5　Meng Yizi asked what filial piety was. The Master said, "It is not being disobedient." Soon after, as Fan Chi was driving him, the Master told him, saying, "Just now Meng asked me what filial piety was, and I answered him, 'not being disobedient'." Fan Chi said, "What did you

---

① Youzi was a student of Confucius. Whether Confucius would endorse what Youzi said here is a controversial issue.

mean?" The Master replied, "When your parents are alive, serve them according to the rites; when they pass away, bury them according to the rites and sacrifice to them according to the rites."

2.6　孟武伯問孝。子曰:"父母唯其疾之憂。"

2.6　Meng Wubo asked about filial piety. The Master replied, "Let your parents worry about nothing other than your illness."①

2.7　子游問孝。子曰:"今之孝者,是謂能養。至於犬馬,皆能有養;不敬,何以別乎。"

2.7　Ziyou asked what filial piety was. The Master said, "Nowadays 'filial piety' means simply being able to provide one's parents with nourishment. But even dogs and horses are provided with nourishment. If you are not respectful, wherein lies the difference?"

2.8　子夏問孝。子曰:"色難。有事,弟子服其勞;有酒食,先生饌,曾是以爲孝乎?"

2.8　Zixia asked what filial piety was. The Master said, "The difficulty is with the countenance. When there is work to be done, the young shoulder the burden; when the young have wine and food, they set them before their elders. Yet, does filial piety merely consist of these?"

2.20　季康子問:"使民敬、忠以勸,如之何?"子曰:"臨之以莊,則敬;孝慈,則忠;舉善而教不能,則勸。"

2.20　Ji Kangzi asked, "How can I make the people respectful, loyal, and industrious?" The Master said, "If you preside over them with gravity,

---

① You never commit misdeeds that would worry your parents.

they will show respect for you. If you are filial and kind to all, they will be loyal to you. If you promote the accomplished and teach the incompetent, they will be industrious."

2.21　或謂孔子曰："子奚不爲政？"子曰："《書》云：'孝乎惟孝，友於兄弟，施於有政。'是亦爲政，奚其爲爲政？"

2.21　Someone addressed Confucius, saying, "Sir, why are you not engaged in the government?" The Master said, "What does *The Book of Documents* say of filial piety—'Simply by acting as a filial son and being kind to your brothers, you will be contributing to the smooth running of the government.' Thus, by being a filial son and good brother, one is already engaged in the government. Why do you need to take up a government position?"

4.15　子曰："參乎！吾道一以貫之。"曾子曰："唯。"子出。門人問曰："何謂也？"曾子曰："夫子之道，忠恕而已矣。"

4.15　The Master said (to his disciple Zeng Shen), "Shen, the Way that I advocate has one unifying principle." Zeng replied, "Yes, sir." After the Master left, other disciples asked, "What did the Master mean by that?" Zeng said, "The Way that Master advocates consists simply of loyalty (zhong) and forgiveness (shu)."

4.18　子曰："事父母幾諫，見志不從，又敬不違，勞而不怨。"

4.18　The Master said, "In serving his parents, a son may remonstrate with them, but gently; when he sees that they do not incline to follow his advice, he remains respectful and serves his parents in accordance with rituals. And however exhausting this may be, avoid resentment."

4.19　子曰："父母在，不遠游，游必有方。"

4.19 The Master said, "While his parents are alive, the son may not travel far. If he does travel, he must have a fixed place to which he goes."

4.20 子曰:"三年無改於父之道,可謂孝矣。"

4.20 The Master said, "If the son for three years does not alter from the way of his father [after his father has passed away], he may be called filial."

4.21 子曰:"父母之年,不可不知也:一則以喜,一則以懼。"

4.21 The Master said, "Never forget your parents' age. Though it fills you with dread, it also fills you with joy."

9.16 子曰:"出則事公卿,入則事父兄,喪事不敢不勉,不爲酒困,何有於我哉?"

9.16 The Master said, "In public, to serve the high ministers and nobles; at home, to serve one's father and elder brothers; in all duties to the dead, not to dare not to exert one's self; and not to be befuddled by wine—to what extent do I achieve these things?"

11.5 子曰:"孝哉閔子騫,人不間於其父母昆弟之言。"

11.5 The Master said, "Filial indeed is Min Ziqian! Other people say nothing of him different from the report of his parents and brothers."

11.22 子路問:"聞斯行諸?"子曰:"有父兄在,如之何其聞斯行之!"冉有問:"聞斯行諸?"子曰:"聞斯行之!"公西華曰:"由也問聞斯行諸,子曰:'有父兄在';求也問聞斯行諸,子曰:'聞斯行之'。赤也惑,敢問。"子曰:"求也退,故進之;由也兼人,故退之。"

11.22　Zilu asked whether he should immediately carry into practice what he heard. The Master said, "There are your father and elder brothers to be consulted. Why should you act on that principle of immediately carrying into practice what you hear?" Ran You asked the same, whether he should immediately carry into practice what he heard, and the Master answered, "Immediately carry into practice what you hear." Gongxi Hua said, "Zilu asked whether he should carry immediately into practice what he heard, and you said, 'There are your father and elder brothers to be consulted.' Ran You asked whether he should immediately carry into practice what he heard, and you said, 'Carry it immediately into practice.' I am perplexed, and venture to ask you for an explanation." The Master said, "Ran You is overly cautious; therefore I urged him forward. Zilu is too impetuous; therefore I kept him back."

12.11　齊景公問政於孔子。孔子對曰："君，君；臣，臣；父，父；子，子。"公曰："善哉！信如君不君，臣不臣，父不父，子不子，雖有粟，吾得而食諸？"

12.11　Duke Jing of Qi asked Confucius about governing. Confucius responded, "Let the lord be a true lord, the ministers true ministers, the fathers true fathers, and the sons true sons." The Duke replied, "Well put! Certainly if the lord is not a true lord, the ministers not true ministers, the fathers not true fathers, and the sons not true sons, even if there is sufficient grain, will I ever get to eat it?"

13.18　葉公語孔子曰："吾黨有直躬者：其父攘羊而子證之。"孔子曰："吾黨之直者異於是：父爲子隱，子爲父隱，直在其中矣。"

13.18　The Duke of She informed Confucius, saying, "Among my people, there is an upright man. When his father stole a sheep, he testified against him." Confucius said, "Among my people, those who are upright are different from this. The father conceals the misconduct of the son, and the son conceals the misconduct of the father. Uprightness is to be found in this."

13.20　子貢問曰:"何如斯可謂之士矣?"子曰:"行己有恥,使於四方,不辱君命,可謂士矣。"曰:"敢問其次。"曰:"宗族稱孝焉,鄉黨稱弟焉。"曰:"敢問其次。"曰:"言必信,行必果,硜硜然,小人哉!抑亦可以爲次矣。"曰:"今之從政者何如?"子曰:"噫!斗筲之人,何足算也!"

13.20　Zigong asked, saying, "What qualities must a man possess to entitle him to be called a noble officer?" "The Master said, "He who in his conduct of himself maintains a sense of shame, and when sent on embassies to the four corners of the earth, will not disgrace his sovereign's commission, deserves to be called an officer." Zigong pursued, "May I ask who may be placed in the next lower rank?" And he was told, "He whom the circle of his relatives pronounce to be filial, whom his fellow villagers and neighbors pronounce to be fraternal." Again the disciple asked, "I venture to ask about the class still next in order." The Master said, "In his speech, he insists on being trustworthy, and with regard to his actions, he insists that they bear fruit. What a narrow, rigid little man he is! And yet he might still be considered the next best." Zigong finally inquired, "Of what sort are those of the present day, who engage in government?" The Master said, "Pooh! Those petty functionaries are not even worth considering."

17.21　宰我問:"三年之喪期已久矣!君子三年不爲禮,禮必壞;三年不爲樂,樂必崩。舊穀既没,新穀既升;鑽燧改火,期可已矣。"子曰:"食夫稻,衣夫錦,於女安乎?"曰:"安!""女安,則爲之!夫君子之居喪,食旨不甘,聞樂不樂,居處不安,故不爲也。今女安,則爲之!"宰我出。子曰:"予之不仁也!子生三年,然後免於父母之懷。夫三年之喪,天下之通喪也;予也有三年之愛於其父母乎?"

17.21　Zaiwo asked about the three-year mourning period, saying, "Surely three years is long enough. If the gentleman refrains from practicing ritual for three years, the rites will surely fall into ruin; if he refrains from music for three years, this will surely be disastrous for music. After the lapse of a year the old grain has been used up, while the new grain has ripened, and the four different types of tinder have all been drilled in order to rekindle the fire. One year is surely long enough."

"So," replied the Master, "by now you're content eating fancy rice and wearing fine brocade?" "Yes."

"Well, if you're content, then go ahead. For the noble-minded in mourning, there's no savor in food and no joy in music and there's no contentment in their homes, so they don't eat fancy rice or wear fine brocade. But if you're content, you should go ahead and enjoy yourself."

After Zaiwo left, the Master remarked, "This shows how lacking in Goodness or ren this Zaiwo is! A child is completely dependent upon the care of his parents for the first three years of his life—this is why the three-year mourning period is the common practice throughout the world. Did Zaiwo not receive three years of care from his parents?"

19.18　曾子曰："吾聞諸夫子：'孟莊子之孝也，其他可能也，其不改父之臣與父之政，是難能也。'"

19.18　Zengzi said, "I have heard this from our Master: The filial piety of Meng Zhuangzi, in other matters, was what other men are competent to, but, it is difficult to match the way he refrained from changing the ministers or governmental policies of his father."

《孟子》 / Mencius

3A.5　墨者夷之因徐辟而求見孟子。孟子曰："吾固願見，今吾尚病，病愈，我且往見，夷子不來！"

他日，又求見孟子。孟子曰："吾今則可以見矣。不直，則道不見，我且直之。吾聞夷子墨者，墨之治喪也，以薄爲其道也。夷子思以易天下，豈以爲非是而不貴也？然而夷子葬其親厚，則是以所賤事親也。"

徐子以告夷子。夷子曰："儒者之道，古之人若保赤子，此言何謂也？之則以爲愛無差等，施由親始。"

徐子以告孟子。孟子曰："夫夷子信以爲人之親其兄之子爲若親其鄰之赤子乎？彼有取爾也。赤子匍匐將入井，非赤子之罪也。且天之生物也，使之一本，而夷子二本故也。蓋上世嘗有不葬其親者，其親死，則舉而委之於壑。他日過之，狐狸食之，蠅蚋姑嘬之。其顙有泚，睨而不視。夫泚也，非爲人泚，中心達於面目，蓋歸反虆梩而掩之。掩之誠是也，則孝子仁人之掩其親，亦必有道矣。"

徐子以告夷子。夷子憮然爲閒曰："命之矣。"

3A.5 The Mohist, Yi Zhi, sought, through Xu Bi, to see Mencius. Mencius said, "I indeed wish to see him, but at present I am still unwell. When I am better, I will myself go and see him. He need not come here again."

The next day, Yi Zhi again sought to see Mencius. Mencius said, "Today I am able to see him. But if I do not correct his errors, the Way will not be made apparent. Let me first correct him. I have heard that Master Yi is a Mohist. Now Mo considers that in the regulation of funeral matters a spare simplicity should be the rule, and Master Yi apparently thinks such simplicity can transform all beneath Heaven. So how can he himself denounce it rather than treasure it? However, Master Yi buried his parents in a sumptuous manner, and so he served them in the way that he himself disparages."

Xu informed Yi of these remarks. Yi said, "Even according to the principles of the learned, we find that the ancients ruled 'as if they were watching over an infant'. What does this expression mean? To me it means that one should love without distinctions and that the love begins with parents and extends from there."

Xu reported this reply to Mencius, who said, "Now, does Yi really think that a man's affection for the child of his brother can be exactly the same as his affection for the infant of a neighbor? What is to be approved in that expression is simply this: if an infant crawling about is likely to fall into a well, this is not the fault of the infant (for the infant does not know better). Moreover, Heaven gives birth to creatures in such a way that they have one root, and Yi makes them have two roots. This is the cause of his error.① And, in the most ancient times, there were some who did not bury their parents. When their parents die, they toss them into gullies. Then one day they pass by and see them there: bodies eaten away by foxes and sucked dry by flies. They break into a sweat and can't bear to look. That sweat on their faces isn't a show for their neighbors: it's a reflection of their deepest feelings. They instantly go home, and come back with baskets and spades to cover the bodies over. Burying them is truly right, and filial children and benevolent people also act properly when they bury their parents."

Xu informed Yi of what Mencius had said. Yi was thoughtful for a short time, and then said, "He has instructed me."

3B.9 公都子曰："外人皆稱夫子好辯，敢問何也？"孟子曰："予豈好辯哉？予不得已也。天下之生久矣，一治一亂。當堯之時，水逆行，泛濫於中國，蛇龍居之，民無所定，下者爲巢，上者爲營窟。《書》曰：'洚水警余。'洚水者，洪水也。使禹治之。禹掘地而注之海，驅蛇龍而放之菹，水由地中行，江、淮、河、漢是也。險阻既遠，鳥獸之害人者消，然後人得平土而居之。

"堯舜既没，聖人之道衰，暴君代作，壞宮室以爲汙池，民無所安息；棄田以爲園囿，使民不得衣食。邪説暴行又作，園囿、污池、沛澤多而禽獸至。及紂之身，天下又大亂。周公相武王，誅紂，伐奄三年討其君，驅飛廉於海隅而戮之，滅國者五十，驅虎、豹、犀、象而遠之，天下大悅。……

"世衰道微，邪説暴行有作，臣弒其君者有之，子弒其父者有之。孔子懼，作《春秋》。《春秋》，天子之事也；是故孔子曰：'知我者其惟《春秋》乎！罪我者其惟《春秋》乎！'

"聖王不作，諸侯放恣，處士橫議，楊朱、墨翟之言盈天下。天下之言不歸楊，則歸墨。楊氏爲我，是無君也；墨氏兼愛，是無父也。無父無君，是禽獸也。公明儀曰：'庖有肥肉，廄有肥馬；民有飢色，野有餓莩，此率獸而食人也。'楊墨之道不息，孔子之道不著，是邪説誣民，充塞仁義也。仁義充塞，則率獸食人，人將相食。吾爲此懼，閑先聖之道，距楊墨，放淫辭，邪説者不得作。作於其心，害於其事；作

---

① This is an obscure passage. Scholars disagree on what Mencius means by "one root" and "two roots."

於其事，害於其政。聖人復起，不易吾言矣。

"昔者禹抑洪水而天下平，周公兼夷狄、驅猛獸而百姓寧，孔子成《春秋》而亂臣賊子懼。《詩》云：'戎狄是膺，荊舒是懲，則莫我敢承。'無父無君，是周公所膺也。我亦欲正人心，息邪說，距詖行，放淫辭，以承三聖者，豈好辯哉？予不得已也。能言距楊墨者，聖人之徒也。"

3B.9 Gong Duzi said to Mencius, "Master, the people beyond our school all speak of you as being fond of arguing. I venture to ask why."

Mencius replied, "Indeed, I am not fond of arguing, but I am compelled to do it. A long time has passed since the world came into being, and periods of order have alternated with periods of chaos. In the time of Yao, the waters, flowing out of their channels, inundated the Middle Kingdom. Snakes and dragons occupied it, and the people had no place where they could settle themselves. On the low grounds they made nests for themselves on the trees, and on the high grounds they made caves. It is said in The Book of Documents, 'The flood waters were a warning to us.' Those 'flood waters' were the waters of the deluge. Shun appointed Yu to bring the waters under control. Yu dug out the earth so that the water would flow to the sea. He drove away the snakes and dragons, and forced them into the grassy marshes. Where the water rushed toward the sea, it carved out rivers: the Yangtze and Huai, the Yellow and Han. Obstacles and dangers were rinsed away, and ravaging birds and animals disappeared. Only then could people level farmland and settle down.

"After the death of Yao and Shun, the Way of the sages fell into decay. Oppressive sovereigns arose one after another, who pulled down houses to make ponds and lakes, so that the people knew not where they could rest in quiet; they threw fields out of cultivation to form gardens and parks, so that the people could not get clothes and food. Afterwards, deviant speech and oppressive actions became more prevalent; gardens and parks, ponds and lakes, thickets and marshes became more numerous, and birds and beasts swarmed. By the time of the tyrant Zhou, the kingdom was again in a state of great confusion. The Duke of Zhou assisted King Wu, and destroyed

Zhou. He smote Yan, and after three years put its sovereign to death. He drove Fei Lian to a corner by the sea, and slew him. The states which he extinguished amounted to fifty. He drove far away also the tigers, leopards, rhinoceroses, and elephants. All the people were greatly delighted. ...

"But after them, things began to unravel again, and the Way grew weak. Deviant speech and oppressive actions again became prevalent. There were instances of ministers who murdered their sovereigns, and of sons who murdered their fathers. Confucius was afraid, and so wrote *The Spring and Autumn Annals*. *The Spring and Autumn Annals* is concerned with the affairs of the Son of Heaven. On this account Confucius said, 'Yes! It is *The Spring and Autumn Annals* which will make men know me, and it is *The Spring and Autumn Annals* that will make men condemn me.'

"Once more, sage sovereigns cease to arise, and the princes of the states give the reins to their lusts. Unemployed scholars indulge in unreasonable discussions. The words of Yang Zhu and Mo Di fill the country. If you listen to people's discourses, you will find that they have adopted the views either of Yang or of Mo. Now, Yang's school preaches 'each one for himself', ignoring the interests of the sovereign. Mo's school preaches 'to love all equally', ignoring our special obligations to our father. No father and no sovereign—that's the realm of birds and animals. Gong Mingyi said, 'There's plenty of juicy meat in your kitchen and plenty of well-fed horses in your stable, but the people here look hungry, and in the countryside they're starving to death. You're feeding humans to animals.' If the principles of Yang and Mo are not stopped, and the principles of Confucius not set forth, then those deviant speeches will delude the people and block the path of benevolence and righteousness. When benevolence and righteousness are blocked up, beasts will be led on to devour men, and men will devour one another. I am fearful about this and defend the way of the former sage by resisting Yang and Mo. I drive away their licentious expressions, so that such perverse speakers may not be able to show themselves. If their views spring up in our mind, they would cripple our endeavors and thereby destroy government. If ever great sages arise again, they won't question what I've said.

"In former times, Yu controlled the vast waters of the inundation, and the country was reduced to order. The Duke of Zhou subjugated the barbarous tribes of the east and the north, and he drove away all ferocious animals. So the people enjoyed repose. When Confucius finished The Spring and Autumn Annals, rebellious ministers and thieving sons were filled with fear. It is said in The Book of Odes, 'He smote the barbarians of the west and the north; He punished Jing and Shu; and no one dared to resist us.' These father-deniers and sovereign-deniers[①] would have been smitten by the Duke of Zhou. I also wish to rectify men's hearts, to put an end to those deviant doctrines, to oppose their dangerous actions and banish away their licentious expressions, and thus to carry on the work of the three sages. Do I do so because I am fond of arguing? I just can't see how to avoid it, for only those who speak out against Yang and Mo are true followers of the sages."

4A.18 公孫丑曰:"君子之不教子,何也?"孟子曰:"勢不行也。教者必以正。以正不行,繼之以怒。繼之以怒,則反夷矣。'夫子教我以正,夫子未出於正也。'則是父子相夷也。父子相夷,則惡矣。古者易子而教之,父子之間不責善。責善則離,離則不祥莫大焉。"

4A.18 Gongsun Chou said, "Why is it that the gentleman does not himself teach his son?" Mencius replied, "The circumstances of the case forbid its being done. The teacher must inculcate what is correct. When his students do not practice what is correct, the teacher follows them up with being angry. When the teacher gets angry, the students in turn feel hurt: 'My master inculcates in me what is correct, but he himself does not practice what is correct.' The result of this is, that father and son are offended with each other. When father and son come to be offended with each other, the case is evil. The ancients taught each other's children. In that way, father and son never demand perfect virtue of each other. If they

---

① Mencius thinks that barbarians are father-deniers and sovereign-deniers.

demand perfect virtue of each other, they grow distant. And nothing is more ominous than fathers and sons grown distant from each other."

4A.26　孟子曰:"不孝有三,無後爲大。舜不告而娶,爲無後也,君子以爲猶告也。"

4A.26　Mencius said, "There are three things which are unfilial, and to have no posterity is the greatest of them. Shun married without informing his parents out of concern that he might have no posterity. The gentleman considers that his doing so was the same as he had informed his parents."①

4A.27　孟子曰:"仁之實,事親是也;義之實,從兄是也;智之實,知斯二者弗去是也;禮之實,節文斯二者是也;樂之實,樂斯二者,樂則生矣;生則惡可已也,惡可已,則不知足之蹈之手之舞之。"

4A.27　Mencius said, "The substance of benevolence is serving one's parents; the substance of rightness is following one's older brother; the substance of wisdom is knowing these two things and not departing from them; the substance of the ritual is regulating and adorning these two; the substance of music is infusing these two things with joy. When there is joy, they grow; when they grow, how can they be stopped? When they come to this state that they cannot be stopped, then hands and feet soon strike up a dance of their own."

4A.28　孟子曰:"天下大悅而將歸己,視天下悅而歸己,猶草芥也,惟舜爲然。不得乎親,不可以爲人;不順乎親,不可以爲子。舜盡事親之道而瞽瞍厎豫,瞽瞍厎豫而天下化,瞽瞍厎豫而天下之爲父子者定,此之謂大孝。"

4A.28　Mencius said, "Imagine all beneath Heaven turning to you with great delight. Now imagine seeing that happen and knowing it means

---

①　See 5A.2.

nothing more than a wisp of straw; only Shun was capable of that. He considered that if one could not get the hearts of his parents, he could not be considered a man, and that if he could not reach an accord with his parents, he could not be considered a son. Through Shun's fulfilling the Way of serving his parents, Gusou① came to be pleased, and when Gusou came to be pleased, the world was transformed. When Gusou came to be pleased, the model for fathers and sons was set for all beneath Heaven. This is called great filial piety."②

4B.30　公都子曰："匡章,通國皆稱不孝焉,夫子與之游,又從而禮貌之,敢問何也？"孟子曰："世俗所謂不孝者五：惰其四支,不顧父母之養,一不孝也；博奕好飲酒,不顧父母之養,二不孝也；好貨財,私妻子,不顧父母之養,三不孝也；從耳目之欲,以爲父母戮,四不孝也；好勇鬥很,以危父母,五不孝也。章子有一於是乎？夫章子,子父責善而不相遇也。責善,朋友之道也；父子責善,賊恩之大者。夫章子,豈不欲有夫妻母之屬哉？爲得罪於父,不得近,出妻屏子,終身不養焉。其設心以爲不若是,是則罪之大者。是則章子而已矣。"

4B.30　Gong Duzi said, "Throughout the whole kingdom everybody says Kuang Zhang is unfilial. But you, Master, keep company with him, and moreover treat him with politeness. I venture to ask why you do so."

Mencius replied, "It's common now for people to say there are five ways to be unfilial. Neglecting the care of parents because you're lazy—that is the first. Neglecting the care of parents because you love wine and go—that is the second. Neglecting the care of parents because you love wealth and adore wife and children—that is the third. The fourth is following the desires of one's ears and eyes, so as to bring his parents to disgrace. The fifth is being fond of bravery, fighting and quarreling so as to endanger his parents. Is Zhang guilty of any one of these things? Now between Zhang and his father there arose disagreement, because he reproves his father, urging

---

① Gusou is Shun's father. Literally, "gusou" means the blind old man.
② See 7A.35.

him to do the right thing. Friends may urge each other to do the right thing. But such urging between father and son will destroy the father-son relationship. Moreover, did not Zhang wish to have in his family the relationships of husband and wife, child and mother? Once his father was offended, he wouldn't let Zhang come near him. That's why Zhang sent his wife away, banished his children, and lived his whole life without their loving care. He was convinced that his offense would be even greater if he didn't do that. Such and nothing more is the case of Zhang."

5A.1 萬章問曰:"舜往于田,號泣于旻天。何爲其號泣也?"孟子曰:"怨慕也。"萬章曰:"父母愛之,喜而不忘;父母惡之,勞而不怨。然則舜怨乎?"曰:"長息問於公明高曰:'舜往于田,則吾既得聞命矣;號泣于旻天、于父母,則吾不知也。'公明高曰:'是非爾所知也。'夫公明高以孝子之心爲不若是恝。我竭力耕田,共爲子職而已矣;父母之不我愛,於我何哉?帝使其子九男二女,百官牛羊倉廩備,以事舜於畎畝之中。天下之士多就之者,帝將胥天下而遷之焉。爲不順於父母,如窮人無所歸。天下之士悦之,人之所欲也,而不足以解憂。好色,人之所欲,妻帝之二女,而不足以解憂。富,人之所欲,富有天下,而不足以解憂。貴,人之所欲,貴爲天子,而不足以解憂。人悦之、好色、富貴無足以解憂者,惟順於父母,可以解憂。人少則慕父母,知好色則慕少艾,有妻子則慕妻子,仕則慕君,不得於君則熱中。大孝終身慕父母,五十而慕者,予於大舜見之矣。"

5A.1 Wan Zhang asked Mencius, saying, "When Shun went into the fields, he cried out and wept towards the pitying heavens. Why did he cry out and weep?"

Mencius replied, "He was full of resentment and longing."

Wan Zhang said, "When his parents love him, a son rejoices and forgets them not. When his parents hate him, he suffers but never resents them. So what is it Shun resented so?"

Mencius answered, "Chang Xi asked Gong Minggao, saying, 'As to Shun's going into the fields, I have received your instructions, but I do not know about his weeping and crying out to the pitying heavens and to his parents.' Gong Minggao answered him, 'You do not understand that matter.' Now, Gong Minggao certainly didn't believe a worthy child could be indifferent enough to think 'I work hard plowing the fields. That's all parents can demand of a child. If they don't love me, how could it be my fault?'

"Yao sent his nine sons and two daughters, the various officers, oxen and sheep, storehouses and granaries to help Shun in the fields. Officials throughout all beneath Heaven turned to Shun. Yao designed that Shun should superintend the kingdom along with him, and then to transfer it to him entirely. But because his parents were not in accord with him, Shun felt like a poor man who had nowhere to turn to.

"Everyone wants to have officials throughout all beneath Heaven to rejoice in him, but that wasn't enough to ease Shun's worry. Everyone wants beautiful women, but even Yao's two daughters weren't enough to ease his worry. Everyone wants wealth, but even the wealth of all beneath Heaven wasn't enough to ease his worry. Everyone wants renown, but even the renown of being the Son of Heaven wasn't enough to ease his worry. People rejoicing in him, beautiful women, wealth, renown—all that wasn't enough to ease his worry. Being in accord with his parents—that was the one thing that could ease his worry.

"When we're young we long for our parents. When we begin thinking of beautiful women, we long for the young and beautiful. When we have a wife and family, we long for wife and family. When we're ready to serve, we long for a sovereign and burn with anxiety if we don't find one. Longing for your parents throughout life—that is the mark of a great child. To see a man who still longs for his parents at the age of fifty, I look to Shun."

5A.2 萬章問曰:"《詩》云:'娶妻如之何?必告父母。'信斯言也,宜莫如舜。舜之不告而娶,何也?"孟子曰:"告則不得娶。男女居室,人之大倫也。如告則廢人之大倫以懟父母,是以不告也。"萬章曰:"舜之不告而娶,則吾既得聞命矣。帝之妻舜而不告,何也?"曰:"帝亦知告焉則不得妻也。"萬章曰:"父母使舜完廩,捐階,瞽瞍焚廩。使浚井,出,從而掩之。象曰:'謨蓋都君咸我績。牛羊父母,倉廩父母,干戈朕,琴朕,弤朕,二嫂使治朕棲。'象往入舜宮,舜在床琴。象曰:'鬱陶思君爾。'忸怩。舜曰:'唯茲臣庶,汝其于予治。'不識舜不知象之將殺己與?"曰:"奚而不知也？象憂亦憂，象喜亦喜。"曰："然則舜偽喜者與？"曰："否。昔者有饋生魚於鄭子產，子產使校人畜之池。校人烹之，反命曰：'始舍之圉圉焉，少則洋洋焉，攸然而逝。'子產曰：'得其所哉！得其所哉！'校人出，曰：'孰謂子產智？予既烹而食之，曰："得其所哉！得其所哉！"'故君子可欺以其方，難罔以非其道。彼以愛兄之道來，故誠信而喜之。奚偽焉？"

5A.2 Wan Zhang asked Mencius, saying, "It is said in *The Book of Odes*, 'In marrying a wife, how ought a man to proceed? He must inform his parents.' No one should be a better example of this than Shun. But why did Shun marry without informing his parents?"

Mencius replied, "If he had informed them, he would not have been able to marry. There is a great obligation on a man and a woman to get married and live together. If Shun had informed his parents, he must not only have failed to fulfill this obligation but also made his parents angry. On this account, he did not inform them!"

Wan Zhang said, "As to Shun's marrying without informing his parents, I have heard your instructions; but how was it that Emperor Yao gave him his daughters as wives without informing Shun's parents?"

Mencius said, "Yao also knew that if he had informed them, he could not have married his daughters to Shun."

"Shun's parents sent him to repair the granary," said Wan Zhang, "then they pulled down the ladder and his depraved father set the granary on fire. They sent him to dredge the well, then followed him and sealed him in. His brother Xiang said: 'I'm the one who thought of a way to deal with my brother, the city-building sovereign. You can have his granaries, my parents, and his cattle and sheep. But his shield and spear are mine. His Qin① and bow are mine. And his two wives—they'll offer their comforts in my home now.' Xiang then went to Shun's palace, and there was Shun on

---

① The Qin is a plucked seven-string Chinese musical instrument of the zither family. It has been played since ancient times, and has traditionally been favored by scholars and literati as an instrument of great subtlety and refinement (Wikipedia).

his couch playing his Qin. Xiang said, 'I am here simply because I was worried and thinking of you.' He blushed deeply. Shun replied, 'And I am thinking of my people. Help me govern them.' I do not know whether Shun was ignorant of Xiang's attempt to kill him."

Mencius answered, "How could Shun be ignorant of that? But when Xiang was sorrowful, he was also sorrowful; when Xiang was joyful, he was also joyful."

Wan Zhang said, "In that case, then, did not Shun rejoice hypocritically?"

Mencius replied, "No. Formerly, someone sent a live fish to Zican of Zhang. Zican ordered his pond-keeper to keep the fish in the pond. But the pond-keeper cooked it, then lied to Zican, 'When I first let the fish go, it seemed confused by all that water. In a little while, it seemed to be somewhat at ease, and then it swam away joyfully.' Zican exclaimed, 'It had got into its element! It had got into its element!' The pond-keeper then went out and said, 'Who calls Zican a wise man? After I had cooked and eaten the fish, he said, "It had got into its element! It had got into its element!"' Thus to deceive the gentleman, you must abide by their principles. It's impossible to trap them unless you use their own way. Xiang came in the same loving way that Shun would have come, so Shun was truly pleased. What hypocrisy was there?"

5A.3 萬章問曰："象日以殺舜爲事,立爲天子,則放之,何也？"孟子曰："封之也。或曰放焉。"萬章曰："舜流共工于幽州,放驩兜于崇山,殺三苗于三危,殛鯀于羽山,四罪而天下咸服。誅不仁也。象至不仁,封之有庳。有庳之人奚罪焉？仁人固如是乎？在他人則誅之,在弟則封之。"曰："仁人之於弟也,不藏怒焉,不宿怨焉,親愛之而已矣。親之,欲其貴也；愛之,欲其富也。封之有庳,富貴之也。身爲天子,弟爲匹夫,可謂親愛之乎？""敢問'或曰放'者何謂也？"曰："象不得有爲於其國,天子使吏治其國,而納其貢稅焉,故謂之放。豈得暴彼民哉？雖然,欲常常而見之,故源源而來。'不及貢,以政接于有庳',此之謂也。"

5A.3 Wan Zhang said, "Xiang spent his days trying to kill Shun. When

Shun was made the Son of Heaven, how was it that he only banished him?"

Mencius said, "Shun gave Xiang a noble title and the lands of Youbei. Some called it banishment."

Wan Zhang said, "Shun banished Gong Gong to Youzhou; he sent away Huan Dou to the mountain Chong; he slew San Miao in San Wei; and he imprisoned Gun on the mountain Yu. When the crimes of those four were thus punished, the whole kingdom acquiesced—it was a cutting off of men who were destitute of benevolence. But Xiang was of all men the most destitute of benevolence, and Shun raised him to be the governor of Youbei—what had people of Yubei done to deserve that?! Does a benevolent man really act thus? In the case of other men, he cut them off; in the case of his brother, he gave him a noble title and the lands of Youbei."

Mencius replied, "A benevolent man does not lay up anger, nor cherish resentment against his brother, but only regards him with affection and love. Regarding his brother with affection, he wishes him to be honorable; regarding him with love, he wishes him to be rich. To give his brother a noble title and the lands of Youbei was to enrich and ennoble him. If while Shun himself was the Son of Heaven, his brother had been a common man, could he have been said to regard him with affection and love?"

Wan Zhang said, "I venture to ask what you mean by saying that some called it a banishing of Xiang?"

Mencius replied, "Xiang could do nothing in his state. The Son of Heaven appointed others to govern and collect taxes there. That's why people called it banishment. Do you think Shun would allow him to abuse the people there?" Shun still wanted to see him often, so he came to visit often, as is signified in that expression, "He didn't wait for times of tribute: he welcomed him as the Lord of Youbei."

6B.2 曹交問曰:"人皆可以爲堯舜,有諸?"孟子曰:"然。""交聞文王十尺,湯九尺,今交九尺四寸以長,食粟而已,如何則可?"曰:"奚有於是? 亦爲之而已矣。有人於此力不能勝一匹雛,則爲無力人矣;今曰舉百鈞,則爲有力人矣。然則舉烏獲之任,是亦爲烏獲則已矣。夫人豈以不勝爲患哉? 弗爲耳。徐行後長者謂之弟，疾行先長者謂之不弟。夫徐行者，豈人所不能哉？所不爲也。堯舜之道，孝弟而已矣。子服堯之服，誦堯之言，行堯之行，是堯而已矣。子服桀之服，誦桀之言，行桀之行，是桀而已矣。"曰："交得見於鄒君，可以假館，願留而受業於門。"曰："夫道若大路然，豈難知哉？人病不求耳。子歸而求之，有餘師。"

6B.2　Jiao of Cao asked Mencius, saying, "It is said, 'All men may become saints such as Yao and Shun.' Is it so?"

Mencius replied, "It is."

Jiao went on, "I have heard that King Wen was ten cubits high, and Tang nine. Now I am nine cubits four inches in height. But I can do nothing but eat my millet. What am I to do to realize that saying?"

Mencius answered him, "What has this—the question of size—to do with the matter? It all lies simply in acting as such. Here is a man, whose strength was not equal to lift a duckling—he was then a man of no strength. But today he says, 'I can lift 3,000 catties' weight.' And he is a man of strength. And so, he who can lift the weight which Wu Huo lifted is just another Wu Huo. Why should a man make a want of ability the subject of his grief? It is only that he will not do the thing. To walk slowly and keep behind his elders, is to perform the part of a younger brother. To walk quickly and precede his elders, is to violate the duty of a younger brother. Now, is it what a man cannot do—to walk slowly? It is what he does not do. The course of Yao and Shun was simply that of filial piety and fraternal duty. Wear the clothes of Yao, repeat the words of Yao, and do the actions of Yao, and you will just be a Yao. And, if you wear the clothes of Jie, repeat the words of Jie, and do the actions of Jie, you will just be a Jie."

Jiao said, "I shall be having an interview with the prince of Zou, and can ask him to let me have a house to lodge in. I wish to remain here, and receive instruction at your gate."

Mencius replied, "The way of truth is like a great road. It is not difficult to know it. The evil is only that men will not seek it. Do go home and search for it, and you will have abundance of teachers."

6B.3　公孫丑問曰："高子曰：'《小弁》，小人之詩也。'"孟子曰："何以言之？"曰："怨。"曰："固哉，高叟之爲詩也！有人於此，越人關弓而射之，則己談笑而道之；無他，疏之也。其兄關弓而射之，則己垂涕泣而道之；無他，戚之也。《小弁》之怨，親親也。親親，仁也。固矣夫，高叟之爲詩也！"曰："《凱風》何以不怨？"曰："《凱風》，親之過小者也；《小弁》，親之過大者也。親之過大而不怨，是愈疏也；親之過小而怨，是不可磯也。愈疏，不孝也；不可磯，亦不孝也。孔子曰：'舜其至孝矣，五十而慕。'"

6B.3　Gongsun Chou asked about an opinion of the scholar Gaozi, saying, "Gaozi observed, '"Xiaopan" is the ode of a petty man.'"

Mencius asked, "Why did he say so?"

"Because of the murmuring which it expresses," was the reply.

Mencius answered, "How stupid was that old Gao in interpreting the ode! Suppose a man from Yüeh drew his bow and shot someone: I might tell the story with a smile because the man's a stranger to me. But suppose my brother drew his bow and shot someone: then I'd be in tears when I told the story because he's my own flesh and blood. The resentment expressed in "Xiaopan" comes from loving one's family members, and that love shows benevolence. Stupid indeed was old Gao's interpretation of the ode."

Chou then said, "How is it that there is no resentment expressed in 'Kaifeng'?"

Mencius replied, "The parent's fault referred to in 'Kaifeng' is small; that referred to in 'Xiaopan' is great. If you don't resent a parent's fault when it's serious, you're treating parents like strangers. And if you resent a parent's fault when it's slight, you're treating parents with abandon. Treating them like strangers, treating them with abandon—either is no way for a child to honor parents. Confucius said, 'Shun was indeed perfectly filial! When he was fifty, he was full of longing for his parents.'"

7A.20　孟子曰："君子有三樂，而王天下不與存焉。父母俱存，兄弟無故，一樂也；仰不愧於天，俯不怍於人，二樂也；得天下英才而教育之，三樂也。君子有三樂，而王天下不與存焉。"

7A.20 Mencius said, "The gentleman delights in three things, and to be the ruler of the world is not one of them. To have parents alive and brothers well—this is the first delight. To face Heaven above and people below without any shame—that is the second delight. To attract all the finest students beneath Heaven, and to teach and nurture them—that is the third delight. The gentleman delights in three things, and to be the ruler of the world is not one of them."

7A.35 桃應問曰:"舜爲天子,皋陶爲士,瞽瞍殺人,則如之何?"孟子曰:"執之而已矣。""然則舜不禁與?"曰:"夫舜惡得而禁之? 夫有所受之也。""然則舜如之何?"曰:"舜視棄天下,猶棄敝蹝也。竊負而逃,遵海濱而處,終身訢然,樂而忘天下。"

7A.35 Tao Ying asked, saying, "Shun being sovereign, and Gao Yao chief minister of justice, if Gusou (i.e. Shun's father) had murdered a man, what would have been done in the case?" Mencius said, "Gao Yao would simply have apprehended him." "But would not Shun have forbidden such a thing?" "Indeed, how could Shun have forbidden it? Gao Yao had received the law from a proper source." "In that case what would Shun have done?" "Shun would have regarded abandoning the kingdom as throwing away a worn-out sandal. He would privately have taken his father on his back, and retired into concealment, living somewhere along the sea coast. There he would have been all his life, cheerful and happy, forgetting the kingdom."

7B.7 孟子曰:"吾今而後知殺人親之重也:殺人之父,人亦殺其父;殺人之兄,人亦殺其兄。然則非自殺之也,一間耳。"

7B.7 Mencius said, "From this time forth I know the heavy consequences of killing a man's family members. If you kill his father, he'll kill your father; if you kill his brother, he'll kill your brother. There's precious little difference between that and killing your father or brother with your own hands."

《孝经》/ Classic of Family Reverence

1. 仲尼居，曾子侍。子曰："先王有至德要道，以順天下，民用和睦，上下無怨。汝知之乎？"曾子避席曰："參不敏，何足以知之？"子曰："夫孝，德之本也，教之所由生也。復坐，吾語汝。身體髮膚，受之父母，不敢毀傷，孝之始也。立身行道，揚名於後世，以顯父母，孝之終也。夫孝，始於事親，中於事君，終於立身。……"

1. Confucius was unoccupied, and his disciple Zeng was sitting by in attendance on him. The Master said, "The ancient kings had a perfect virtue and all-embracing rule of conduct, through which they were in accord with all under Heaven. By the practice of it, the people were brought to live in peace and harmony, and there was no ill-will between superiors and inferiors. Do you know what it was?" Zeng rose from his mat and said, " I am not intelligent enough to understand such things." The Master said, "It was filial piety. Now filial piety is the root of [all] virtue, and [the stem] out of which grows [all moral] teaching. Sit down again, and I will explain the subject to you. Our bodies—to every hair and bit of skin—are received from our parents, and we must not injure or wound them. This is the beginning of filial piety. When we have distinguished ourselves via following the Way, made our names famous in future ages, and thereby glorified our parents, this is the end of filial piety. It commences with serving parents; it proceeds to serving the ruler; it is completed by distinguishing oneself. ..."

2. 子曰："愛親者，不敢惡於人；敬親者，不敢慢於人。愛敬盡於事親，而德教加於百姓，刑於四海。蓋天子之孝也。……"

2. The Master said, "He who loves his parents will not dare [to incur the risk of] being hated by any man, and he who reveres his parents will not dare [to incur the risk of] being contemned by any man. When the love and

reverence [of the Son of Heaven] are thus carried to the utmost in serving his parents, such conduct will educate and transform (dejiao) the common people, serving as exemplary in all corners of the world. This is the filial piety of the Son of Heaven. ..."

15. 曾子曰:"……敢問子從父之令,可謂孝乎?"子曰:"是何言與,是何言與!昔者天子有爭臣七人,雖無道,不失其天下;諸侯有爭臣五人,雖無道,不失其國;大夫有爭臣三人,雖無道,不失其家;士有爭友,則身不離於令名;父有爭子,則身不陷於不義。故當不義,則子不可以不爭於父,臣不可以不爭於君;故當不義,則爭之。從父之令,又焉得爲孝乎!"

15. The disciple Zeng said, "... I would venture to ask if [simple] obedience to the orders of one's father can be called filial piety." The Master replied, "What on earth are you saying?! What on earth are you saying?! Anciently, if the Son of Heaven had seven ministers who would remonstrate with him, although he had not right methods of government, he would not lose his possession of the kingdom. If the prince of a state had five such ministers, though his measures might be equally wrong, he would not lose his state. If a great officer had three, he would not, in a similar case, lose [the headship of] his clan. If a lower official had just one friend who would remonstrate with him, he was still able to preserve his good name. And the father who had a son that would remonstrate with him would not behave reprehensively. Thus, if confronted by reprehensible behavior on his father's part, a son has no choice but to remonstrate with his father, and if confronted by reprehensible behavior on his ruler's part, a minister has no choice but to remonstrate with his ruler. Hence, remonstrance is the only response to immorality. How could simply obeying the commands of one's father be deemed filial?"

17. 子曰:"君子之事上也,進思盡忠,退思補過,將順其美,匡救其惡,故上下能相親也。……"

The Master said, "The gentleman serves his ruler in such a way that, when at court in his presence, his thought is how to discharge his loyal duty to the utmost, and when he retires from it, his thought is how to amend the ruler's errors. He carries out with deference the measures springing from the ruler's excellent qualities and takes steps to remedy what the ruler has messed up. It is in this way that those above and below are able to appreciate each other. …"

《墨子》/ Mozi

法儀第四
Chapter 4　On the Necessity of Standards

子墨子曰：天下從事者不可以無法儀，無法儀而其事能成者無有也。雖至士之爲將相者，皆有法，雖至百工從事者，亦皆有法，百工爲方以矩，爲圓以規，直以繩，正以縣。無巧工不巧工，皆以此五者爲法。巧者能中之，不巧者雖不能中，放依以從事，猶逾己。故百工從事，皆有法所度。

Mozi said: To accomplish anything whatsoever one must have standards. None have yet accomplished anything without them. The gentlemen fulfilling their duties as generals and councilors have their standards. Even the artisans performing their tasks also have their standards. The artisans make square objects according to the square, circular objects according to the compasses; they draw straight lines with the carpenter's line and find the perpendicular by a pendulum. All artisans, whether skilled or unskilled, employ these five standards. Only the skilled workers are accurate. Though the unskilled laborers have not attained accuracy, yet they do better by following these standards than otherwise. Thus all artisans follow the standards in their work.

今大者治天下，其次治大國，而無法所度，此不若百工，辯也。然則奚以爲治法而可？當皆法其父母奚若？天下之爲父母者衆，而仁者寡，若皆法其父母，此法不仁也。法不仁，不可以爲法。當皆法其學奚若？天下之爲學者衆，而仁者寡，若皆法其學，此法不仁也。法不仁，不可以爲法。當皆法其君奚若？天下之爲君者衆，而仁者寡，若皆法其君，此法不仁也。法不仁，不可以爲法。故父母、學、君三者，莫可以爲治法。

Now, the government of the empire and that of the large states do not observe their standards. This shows the governors are even less intelligent than the artisans. What, then, should be taken as the proper standard in government? How will it do for everybody to imitate his parents? There are numerous parents in the world but few are magnanimous (ren or benevolent). For everybody to imitate his parents is to imitate the unmagnanimous. Imitating the unmagnanimous cannot be said to be following the proper standard. How will it do for everybody to follow his teacher? There are numerous teachers in the world but few are magnanimous. For everybody to imitate his teacher is to imitate the unmagnanimous. Imitating the unmagnanimous cannot be taken as following the proper standard. How will it do for everybody to imitate his ruler? There are many rulers in the world but few are magnanimous. For everybody to imitate the ruler is to imitate the unmagnanimous. Imitating the unmagnanimous cannot be taken as following the right standard. So then neither the parents nor the teacher nor the ruler should be accepted as the standard in government.

然則奚以爲治法而可？故曰莫若法天。天之行廣而無私，其施厚而不德，其明久而不衰，故聖王法之。既以天爲法，動作有爲必度於天，天之所欲則爲之，天所不欲則止。然而天何欲何惡者也？天必欲人之相愛相利，而不欲人之相惡相賊也。奚以知天之欲人之相愛相利，而不欲人之相惡相賊也？以其兼而愛之、兼而利之也。奚以知天兼而愛之、兼而利之也？以其兼而有之、兼而食之也。

What then should be taken as the standard in government? Nothing better than following Heaven. Heaven is all-inclusive and impartial in its activities, abundant and unceasing in its blessings, and lasting and untiring in its guidance. And, so, when the sage-kings had accepted Heaven as their standard, they measured every action and enterprise by Heaven. What Heaven desired they would carry out, what Heaven abominated they refrained from. Now, what is it that Heaven desires, and what is it that it abominates? Certainly Heaven desires to have men benefit and love one another and abominates to have them hate and harm one another. How do we know that Heaven desires to have men love and benefit one another and abominates to have them hate and harm one another? Because it loves and benefits men universally. How do we know that it loves and benefits men universally? Because it claims all and accepts offerings from all.

今天下無大小國，皆天之邑也。人無幼長貴賤，皆天之臣也。此以莫不犓羊、豢犬豬，絜爲酒醴粢盛，以敬事天，此不爲兼而有之、兼而食之邪！天苟兼而有食之，夫奚說以不欲人之相愛相利也！故曰愛人利人者，天必福之；惡人賊人者，天必禍之。曰殺不辜者，得不祥焉。夫奚說人爲其相殺而天與禍乎！是以知天欲人相愛相利，而不欲人相惡相賊也。

All states in the world, large or small, are cities of Heaven, and all people, young or old, honorable or humble, are its subjects, for they all graze oxen and sheep, feed dogs and pigs, and prepare clean wine and cakes to sacrifice to Heaven. Does this not mean that Heaven claims all and accepts offerings from all? Since Heaven does claim all and accepts offerings from all, what then can make us say that it does not desire men to love and benefit one another? Hence those who love and benefit others Heaven will bless. Those who hate and harm others Heaven will curse, for it is said that he who murders the innocent will be visited by misfortune. How else can we explain the fact that men, murdering each other, will be cursed by Heaven? Thus we are certain that Heaven desires to have men love and benefit one another and abominates to have them hate and harm one another.

昔之聖王禹湯文武，兼愛天下之百姓，率以尊天事鬼，其利人多，故天福之，使立爲天子，天下諸侯皆賓事之。暴王桀紂幽厲，兼惡天下之百姓，率以詬天侮鬼，其賊人多，故天禍之，使遂失其國家，身死爲僇於天下，後世子孫毀之，至今不息。故爲不善以得禍者，桀紂幽厲是也；愛人利人以得福者，禹湯文武是也。愛人利人以得福者有矣，惡人賊人以得禍者亦有矣。

The ancient sage-kings, Yu, Tang, Wen, and Wu, loved the people of the world universally, leading them to reverence Heaven and worship the spirits. They benefited the people a lot. And, thereupon Heaven blessed them, establishing each of them the Son of Heaven; and all the feudal lords of the empire showed them respect. [On the other hand] the wicked kings, Jie, Zhou, You, and Li, hated all the people in the world, seducing the people to curse Heaven and ridicule the spirits. Great were their injuries to the people. Thereupon Heaven brought them calamity, depriving them of their empire and their lives; and posterity condemned them to this day. Jie, Zhou, You, and Li, then, are those that committed evil and were visited by calamities. And Yu, Tang, Wen, and Wu are those that loved and benefited the people and obtained blessings. Thus we have those who obtained blessings because they loved and benefited the people as well as those who were visited by calamities because they hated and harmed the people.

兼愛中第十五
Chapter 15　　Universal Love Ⅱ

子墨子言曰："仁人之所以爲事者，必興天下之利，除去天下之害，以此爲事者也。"然則天下之利何也？天下之害何也？子墨子言曰："今若國之與國之相攻，家之與家之相篡，人之與人之相賊，君臣不惠忠，父子不慈孝，兄弟不和調，此則天下之害也。"

Mozi said: The purpose of the magnanimous (ren or benevolent) is to be found in procuring benefits for the world and eliminating its calamities. But what are the benefits of the world and what are its calamities? Mozi said: Mutual attacks among states, mutual usurpation among houses, mutual injuries among individuals; the lack of grace and loyalty between the ruler and the ruled, the lack of affection and filial piety between father and son, the lack of harmony between elder and younger brothers—these are the major calamities in the world.

然則崇此害亦何用生哉？以不相愛生邪？子墨子言："以不相愛生。今諸侯獨知愛其國，不愛人之國，是以不憚舉其國以攻人之國。今家主獨知愛其家，而不愛人之家，是以不憚舉其家以篡人之家。今人獨知愛其身，不愛人之身，是以不憚舉其身以賊人之身。是故諸侯不相愛則必野戰，家主不相愛則必相篡，人與人不相愛則必相賊，君臣不相愛則不惠忠，父子不相愛則不慈孝，兄弟不相愛則不和調。天下之人皆不相愛，強必執弱，富必侮貧，貴必敖賤，詐必欺愚。凡天下禍篡怨恨，其所以起者，以不相愛生也，是以仁者非之。"

But whence did these calamities arise? Did they arise out of want of mutual love? Mozi said: They arose out of want of mutual love. At present, feudal lords have learned only to love their own states and not those of others. Therefore they do not scruple about attacking other states. The heads of houses have learned only to love their own houses and not those of others. Therefore they do not scruple about usurping other houses. And individuals have learned only to love themselves and not others. Therefore they do not scruple about injuring others. When feudal lords do not love one another, there will be war on the fields. When heads of houses do not love one another, they will usurp one another's power. When individuals do not love one another, they will injure one another. When the ruler and the ruled do not love one another, they will not be gracious and loyal. When father and son do not love each other, they will not be affectionate and filial. When older and younger brothers do not love each other, they will not be harmonious. When nobody in the world loves any other, naturally the strong will overpower the weak, the many will oppress the few, the wealthy will mock the poor, the honored will disdain the humble, and the cunning will deceive the simple. Therefore all the calamities, usurpations, complaints, and hatred in the world have arisen out of want of mutual love. Therefore the benevolent disapproved of this want.

既以非之,何以易之?子墨子言曰:"以兼相愛、交相利之法易之。"然則兼相愛、交相利之法,將奈何哉?子墨子言:"視人之國,若視其國,視人之家,若視其家,視人之身,若視其身。是故諸侯相愛則不野戰,家主相愛則不相篡,人與人相愛則不相賊,君臣相愛則惠忠,父子相愛則慈孝,兄弟相愛則和調,天下之人皆相愛,強不執弱,衆不劫寡,富不侮貧,貴不敖賤,詐不欺愚。凡天下禍篡怨恨,可使毋起者,以相愛生也,是以仁者譽之。"

Now that there is disapproval, how can we have the condition altered? Mozi said it is to be altered by the way of universal love and mutual aid. But what is the way of universal love and mutual aid? Mozi said: It is to regard the state of others as one's own, the houses of others as one's own, and the bodies of others as one's own. When feudal lords love one another there will be no more war; when heads of houses love one another there will be no more mutual usurpation; when individuals love one another there will be no more mutual injury. When the ruler and the ruled love each other they will be gracious and loyal; when father and son love each other they will be affectionate and filial; when older and younger brothers love each other they will be harmonious. When all the people in the world love one another, then the strong will not overpower the weak, the many will not oppress the few, the wealthy will not mock the poor, the honored will not disdain the humble, and the cunning will not deceive the simple. And it is all due to mutual love that calamities, strife, complaints, and hatred are prevented from arising. Therefore the benevolent exalt it.

然而今天下之士君子曰:"然。乃若兼則善矣,雖然,天下之難物於故也。"子墨子言曰:"天下之士君子,特不識其利,辯其故也。今若夫攻城野戰,殺身爲名,此天下百姓之所皆難也,苟君說之,則士衆能爲之,況於兼相愛,交相利,則與此異。夫愛人者,人必從而愛之,利人者,人必從而利之,惡人者,人必從而惡之,害人者,人必從而害之。此何難之有!特上弗以爲政,士不以爲行故也。

But the gentlemen of the world would say, "So far so good. It is of course very excellent when love becomes universal. But it is only a difficult and distant ideal." Mozi said: This is simply because the gentlemen of the world do not recognize how it can benefit the world, nor do they appreciate the arguments for universal love. Now, to besiege a city, to fight in the fields, or to achieve a name at the cost of death—these are what men find difficult. Yet when the superior encourages them, the multitude can do them. Besides, universal love and mutual aid are quite different from these. Whoever loves others is loved by others; whoever benefits others is benefited by others; whoever hates others is hated by others; whoever injures others is injured by others. Then, what difficulty is there with it (i.e. universal love)? It is just that the ruler did not embody it in his government and the ordinary man in his conduct.

"昔者晉文公好士之惡衣,故文公之臣,皆牂羊之裘,韋以帶劍,練帛之冠,入以見於君,出以踐於朝,是其故何也?君說之,故臣爲之也。昔者楚靈王好士細要,故靈王之臣,皆以一飯爲節,脇息然後帶,扶牆然後起。比期年,朝有黧黑之色,是其故何也?君說之,故臣能之也。昔越王句踐好士之勇,教馴其臣和合之,焚舟失火,試其士曰:'越國之寶盡在此!'越王親自鼓其士而進之。士聞鼓音,破碎亂行,蹈火而死者,左右百人有餘,越王擊金而退之。"

Formerly, Lord Wen of the state of Jin (about 630 B.C.) liked the uncouth uniform of the soldier. And so all his ministers and officers wore sheepskin jackets, carried their swords in leather girdles, and put on silk-spun hats. Thus attired, they attended the lord when they went in and paced the court when they stayed out. What was the reason for this? It was that what the ruler encourages the ruled will carry out. And Lord Ling of the state of Chu (about 535 B.C.) liked slender waists. And so all his ministers and officers limited themselves to a single meal per day. They tied their belts after exhaling, and could not stand up without leaning against the wall. Within a year the court looked grim and dark [due to starving themselves]. What was the reason for this? It was that what the ruler encourages the ruled will carry out. Again, Lord Goujian of the state of Yue (about 480 B.C.)

liked the warrior's courage, and trained his subjects accordingly. He had his palace boat set on fire. To test his soldiers, he proclaimed that all the treasures of the state were contained therein. And he beat the drum himself to urge them on. Upon hearing the drum, the soldiers rushed on in disorder. More than a hundred strong perished in the flames. Thereupon the lord beat the gong to let them retreat.

是故子墨子言曰："乃若夫少食惡衣，殺身而爲名，此天下百姓之所皆難也，若苟君說之，則衆能爲之。況兼相愛、交相利，與此異矣。夫愛人者，人亦從而愛之，利人者，人亦從而利之，惡人者，人亦從而惡之，害人者，人亦從而害之。此何難之有焉，特君不以爲政，而士不以爲行故也。"

Therefore Mozi said: Now, things like scanty diet, coarse clothing, and the achievement of a name at the cost of death are those in which people find difficulty. Yet when the ruler encourages them the multitude can stand them. Besides, universal love and mutual aid are different from these. Whoever loves others is loved by others; whoever benefits others is benefited by others; whoever hates others is hated by others; whoever injures others is injured by others. Then what difficulty is there with it (i.e. universal love)? It is just that the ruler failed to embody it in his government and the ordinary man in his conduct.

然而今天下之士君子曰："然，乃若兼則善矣，雖然，不可行之物也，譬若挈太山，越河濟也。"子墨子言："是非其譬也。夫挈太山而越河濟，可謂畢劫有力矣，自古及今，未有能行之者也。況乎兼相愛、交相利，則與此異。古者聖王行之。何以知其然？古者禹治天下，西爲西河漁竇，以洩渠孫皇之水，北爲防原泒，注後之邸，呼池之竇，灑爲底柱，鑿爲龍門，以利燕代胡貉與西河之民，東爲漏大陸，防孟諸之澤，灑爲九澮，以楗東土之水，以利冀州之民，南爲江漢淮汝，東流之，注五湖之處，以利荊楚干越與南夷之民。此言禹之事，吾今行兼矣。昔者文王之治西土，若日若月，乍光於四方於西土，不爲大國侮小國，不爲衆庶侮鰥寡，不爲暴勢奪穡人黍稷狗彘。天屑臨文王慈，是以老而無子者，有所得終其壽，連獨無兄弟者，有所雜於生人之閒，少失其父母者，有所放依而長。此文王之事，則吾今行兼矣。昔者武王將事太山隧，傳曰：'泰山，有道曾孫周王有事，大事既獲，仁人尚作，以祇商夏，蠻夷醜貉，雖有周親，不若仁人，萬方有罪，維予一人。'此言武王之事，吾今行兼矣。"

Nevertheless, gentlemen say, though it would be an excellent thing if love can be universalized, it is something quite impracticable. It is like carrying Mt. Tai and leaping over the Ji River. Mozi said: This is a false analogy. Of course to be able to carry Mt. Tai and leap over the Ji River would be an extreme feat of strength. Such has never been performed from antiquity to the present time. But universal love and mutual aid are quite different from this. And the ancient sage-kings did practice it. How do we know they did? When Yu was working to bring the deluge under control, he dug the West River and the Youdou River in the west in order to let off the water from the Qu, Sun, and Huang Rivers. In the north he built a dam across the Yuan and Gu Rivers in order to fill the Houzhidi (which is a basin) and the Huzhi River. Mt. Dizhu was made use of as a water divide, and a tunnel was dug through Mt. Lungmen. All these were done to benefit the people west of the [Yellow] River and various barbarian tribes, such as Yan, Dai, Hu, and Ho of the north. In the east he drained the great Plain and built dykes along the Mengzhu River. The watercourse was divided into nine canals in order to regulate the water in the east and in order to benefit the people of the district of Ji. In the south he completed the Yangtze, Han, Huai, and Ru Rivers. These ran eastward and emptied themselves into the Five Lakes. This was done in order to benefit the people of Jing, Qi, Gan, Yue, and the barbarians of the south. All these are the deeds of Yu. Thus it is possible for us to universalize love in conduct.

When King Wen was ruling the Western land, he shone forth like the sun and the moon all over the four quarters as well as in the Western land. He did not allow the big state to oppress the small state, he did not allow the multitude to oppress the singlehanded, and he did not allow the influential and strong to take away the grain and live stock from the farmers. Heaven visited him with blessing. And, therefore, the old and childless had the wherewithal to spend their old age, the solitary and brotherless had the opportunity to join in the social life of men, and the orphans had the support for their growth. This was what King Wen had accomplished. Thus it is possible for us to universalize love in conduct.

When King Wu was about to do service to Mt. Tai, it was recorded thus, "Blessed is Mt. Tai. Duke of Zhou by a long descent is about to perform his duty. As I have obtained the approval of Heaven, the magnanimous (ren or benevolent) arise to save the people of Shang Xia as well as the barbarians [from the tyranny of Emperor Zhou]. Though [Emperor Zhou] has many near relatives, they cannot compare with the magnanimous. If there is sin anywhere, I am solely responsible." This relates the deeds of King Wu. Thus it is possible for us to universalize love in conduct.

是故子墨子言曰:"今天下之士君子,忠實欲天下之富,而惡其貧,欲天下之治,而惡其亂,當兼相愛、交相利,此聖王之法,天下之治道也,不可不務爲也。"

Therefore Mozi said: If gentlemen sincerely desire the world to be wealthy and dislike to have it poor, desire to have it orderly and dislike to have it chaotic, they should practice universal love and mutual aid. This is the way of the sage-kings and the way to order for the world, and it should not be neglected.

兼愛下第十六
Chapter 16　Universal Love Ⅲ

……

然而天下之士,非兼者之言猶未止也。曰:"即善矣！雖然,豈可用哉?"子墨子曰:"用而不可,雖我亦將非之,且焉有善而不可用者? 姑嘗兩而進之。誰以爲二士,使其一士者執別,使其一士者執兼。"是故別士之言曰:"吾豈能爲吾友之身,若爲吾身,爲吾友之親,若爲吾親。"是故退睹其友,飢即不食,寒即不衣,疾病不侍養,死喪不葬埋。別士之言若此,行若此。兼士之言不然,行亦不然。曰:"吾聞爲高士於天下者,必爲其友之身,若爲其身,爲其友之親,若爲其親,然後可以爲高士於天下。"是故退睹其友，飢則食之，寒則衣之，疾病侍養之，死喪葬埋之，兼士之言若此，行若此。若之二士者，言相非而行相反與？當使若二士者，言必信，行必果，使言行之合猶合符節也，無言而不行也。然即敢問，今有平原廣野於此，被甲嬰胄將往戰，死生之權未可識也，又有君大夫之遠使於巴越齊荊，往來及否未可識也。然即敢問，不識將惡也，家室，奉承親戚，提挈妻子，而寄託之？不識於兼之有是乎？於別之有是乎？我以為當其於此也，天下無愚夫愚婦，雖非兼之人，必寄託之於兼之有是也。此言而非兼，擇即取兼，即此言行費也。不識天下之士，所以皆聞兼而非之者，其故何也？

...

Still, there are other objections. It is asked, "It may be a good thing, but can it be of any use?" Mozi replied: If it were not useful then even I would disapprove of it. But how can there be anything that is good but not useful? Let us consider the matter from both sides. Suppose there are two men. Let one of them hold to partiality and the other to universality. Then the advocate of partiality would say to himself: How can I take care of my friend as I do of myself, and how can I take care of his parents as my own? Therefore when he finds his friend hungry he would not feed him, and when he finds him cold he would not clothe him. In his illness he would not minister to him, and when he is dead he would not bury him. Such is the word and such is the deed of the advocate of partiality. The advocate of universality is quite unlike this both in word and in deed. He would say to himself: I have heard that to be a superior man one should take care of his friend as he does of himself, and take care of his friend's parents as his own.

Therefore when he finds his friend hungry he would feed him, and when he finds him cold he would clothe him. In his sickness he would serve him, and when he is dead he would bury him. Such is the word and such is the deed of the advocate of universality. These two persons then are opposed to each other in word and also in deed. Suppose they are sincere in word and decisive in deed so that their word and deed are made to agree like the two parts of a tally, and that there is no word but what is realized in deed. Then let us consider further. Suppose a war is on, and one is in armor and helmet ready to join the force, life and death are not predictable. Or suppose one is commissioned a deputy by the ruler to such far countries as Ba, Yue, Qi, and Jing, and the arrival and return are quite uncertain. Now [under such circumstances] let us inquire upon whom one would lay the trust of one's family and parents. Would it be upon the universal friend or upon the partial friend? It seems to me, on occasions like these, there are no fools in the world. Even if he is a person who objects to universal love, he will lay the trust upon the universal friend all the same. This is verbal objection to the principle but actual selection of it—this is self-contradiction between one's word and deed. It is incomprehensible, then, why people should object to universal love when they hear it.

然而天下之士,非兼者之言猶未止也。曰:"意可以擇士,而不可以擇君乎?"姑嘗兩而進之,誰以爲二君,使其一君者執兼,使其一君者執別。是故別君之言曰:"吾惡能爲吾萬民之身,若爲吾身!此泰非天下之情也。人之生乎地上之無幾何也。譬之猶馳駟而過隙也。"是故退睹其萬民,飢即不食,寒即不衣,疾病不侍養,死喪不葬埋。別君之言若此,行若此。兼君之言不然,行亦不然,曰:"吾聞爲明君於天下者,必先萬民之身,後爲其身,然後可以爲明君於天下。"是故退睹其萬民,飢即食之,寒即衣之,疾病侍養之,死喪葬埋之。兼君之言若此,行若此。然即交若之二君者,言相非而行相反與? 常使若二君者,言必信,行必果,使言行之合猶合符節也,無言而不行也。然即敢問,今歲有癘疫,萬民多有勤苦凍餒,轉死溝壑中者,既已衆矣。不識將擇之二君者,將何從也? 我以爲當其於此也,天下無愚夫愚婦,雖非兼者,必從兼君是也。言而非兼,擇即取兼,此言行拂也。不識天下所以皆聞兼而非之者,其故何也?

Yet the objection is not all exhausted. It is objected: Maybe it is a good criterion to choose among ordinary men, but it may not apply to the rulers. Let us again consider the matter from both sides. Suppose there are two rulers. Let one of them hold to partiality and the other to universality. Then the partial ruler would say to himself: How can I take care of the people as I do of myself? This would be quite contrary to common sense. A man's life on earth is of short duration; it is like a galloping horse passing by. Therefore when he finds his people hungry he would not feed them, and when he finds them cold he would not clothe them. When they are sick he would not minister to them, and upon their death he would not bury them. Such is the word and such is the deed of the partial ruler. The universal ruler is quite unlike this both in word and in deed. He would say to himself: I have heard that to be an upright ruler of the world one should first attend to his people and then to himself. Therefore when he finds his people hungry he would feed them, and when he finds them cold he would clothe them. In their sickness he would minister to them, and upon their death he would bury them. Such is the word and such is the deed of the universal ruler. These two rulers, then, are opposed to each other in word and also in deed. Suppose they are sincere in word and decisive in deed so that their word and deed are made to agree like the two parts of a tally, and that there is no word but what is realized in deed. Then let us consider further. Suppose, now, that there is a disastrous pestilence, that most people are in misery and privation, and that many lie dead in ditches. [Under such circumstances] let us inquire: if a person could choose one of the two rulers, which would he prefer? It seems to me on such occasions there are no fools in the world. Even if he is a person who objects to universal love, he will choose the universal ruler. This is verbal objection to the principle but actual selection of it—this is self-contradiction between one's word and deed. It is incomprehensible, then, why people should object to universal love when they hear it.

……

然而天下之非兼者之言猶未止。曰："意不忠親之利,而害爲孝乎?"子墨子曰:"姑嘗本原之孝子之爲親度者,吾不識孝子之爲親度者,亦欲人愛利其親與?意欲人之惡賊其親與?以說觀之,即欲人之愛利其親也。然即吾惡先從事即得此?若我先從事乎愛利人之親,然後人報我以愛利吾親乎?意我先從事乎惡人之親,然後人報我以愛利吾親乎?即必吾先從事乎愛利人之親,然後人報我以愛利吾親也。然即之交孝子者,果不得已乎?毋先從事愛利人之親者與?意以天下之孝子爲遇，而不足以爲正乎？姑嘗本原之先王之所書，《大雅》之所道曰："無言而不讎，無德而不報，投我以桃，報之以李。"即此言愛人者必見愛也，而惡人者必見惡也。不識天下之士，所以皆聞兼而非之者，其故何也？

......

Yet the objection is still not exhausted. One might ask, "If one does not put one's parents' interest before others', can we still call it filial piety?" Mozi replied: Now let us inquire about the plans of the filial sons for their parents. I may ask, when they plan for their parents, whether they desire to have others love or hate them? Judging from the whole doctrine [of filial piety], it is certain that they desire to have others love their parents. Now, what should I do first in order to attain this? Should I first love others' parents in order that they would love my parents in return, or should I first hate others' parents in order that they would love my parents in return? Of course I should first love others' parents in order that they would love my parents in return. Hence those who desire to be filial to their parents, if they have to choose, had best first love and benefit others' parents. Would any one suspect that all the filial sons are stupid and incorrigible [in loving their own parents]? We may again inquire about it. It is said in Da Ya among the books of the ancient kings, "No idea is not given its due value; no virtue is not rewarded. When a peach is thrown to us, we would return with a plum." This is to say whoever loves others will be loved and whoever hates others will be hated. It is then quite incomprehensible why people should object to universal love when they hear it.

......

"故兼者聖王之道也，王公大人之所以安也，萬民衣食之所以足也。故君子莫若審兼而務行之。爲人君必惠，爲人臣必忠，爲人父必慈，爲人子必孝，爲人兄必友，爲人弟必悌。故君子莫若欲爲惠君、忠臣、慈父、孝子、友兄、悌弟，當若兼之，不可不行也，此聖王之道，而萬民之大利也。"

......

Therefore, universal love is really the way of the sage-kings. It is what gives peace to the rulers and sustenance to the people. The gentleman would do well to understand and practice universal love; then he would be gracious as a ruler, loyal as a minister, affectionate as a father, filial as a son, courteous as an elder brother, and respectful as a younger brother. So, if the gentleman desires to be a gracious ruler, a loyal minister, an affectionate father, a filial son, a friendly elder brother, and a respectful younger brother, universal love must be practiced. It is the way of the sage-kings and the great blessing of the people.

節葬下第二十五
Chapter 25　Simplicity in Funerals Ⅲ

子墨子言曰：仁者之爲天下度也，辟之無以異乎孝子之爲親度也。今孝子之爲親度也，將奈何哉？曰：親貧則從事乎富之，人民寡則從事乎眾之，眾亂則從事乎治之。當其於此也，亦有力不足，財不贍，智不智，然後已矣。無敢捨餘力，隱謀遺利，而不爲親爲之者矣。若三務者，孝子之爲親度也，既若此矣。

Mozi said: The magnanimous (ren) ruler takes care of the empire, in the same way as a filial son takes care of his parents. But how does the filial son take care of his parents? If the parents are poor, he would enrich them; if the parents have few grandchildren, he would increase them; if the members [of the family] are in confusion, he would put them in order. Of course, in doing this, he might find his energy insufficient, his means limited, or his knowledge inadequate. But he dares not allow any energy, learning, or means unused to serve his parents. Such are the three interests of the filial son in taking care of his parents.

雖仁者之爲天下度，亦猶此也。曰："天下貧則從事乎富之，人民寡則從事乎眾之，眾而亂則從事乎治之。"當其於此，亦有力不足，財不贍，智不智，然後已矣。無敢捨餘力，隱謀遺利，而不爲天下爲之者矣。若三務者，此仁者之爲天下度也，既若此矣。

And the same is true of the magnanimous ruler in taking care of the empire: if the empire is poor he would enrich it; if the people are few he would increase them; if the multitude are in confusion he would put them in order. Of course in doing these he might find his energy insufficient, means limited, or knowledge inadequate, but he dares not allow any energy, learning, or means unused to serve the world. And such are the three interests of the magnanimous ruler in taking care of the empire.

今逮至昔者三代聖王既没，天下失義，後世之君子，或以厚葬久喪以爲仁也，義也，孝子之事也；或以厚葬久喪，以爲非仁義，非孝子之事也。曰二子者，言則相非，行即相反，皆曰："吾上祖述堯舜禹湯文武之道者也。"而言即相非，行即相反，於此乎後之君子，皆疑惑乎二子者言也。若茍疑惑乎之二子者言，然則姑嘗傳而爲政乎國家萬民而觀之？計厚葬久喪，奚當此三利者？我意若使法其言，用其謀，厚葬久喪，實可以富貧衆寡，定危治亂乎，此仁也，義也，孝子之事也，爲人謀者，不可不勸也。仁者將興之天下，誰賈而使民譽之，終勿廢也。意亦使法其言，用其謀，厚葬久喪，實不可以富貧衆寡，定危理亂乎，此非仁非義非孝子之事也，爲人謀者不可不沮也。仁者將求除之天下，相廢而使人非之，終身勿爲。

When the sage-kings of the Three Dynasties had passed away, and the world had become ignorant of their principles, some of the gentlemen in later generations regarded elaborate funerals and extended mourning as magnanimous and righteous, and a duty of a filial son; while others held them to be not magnanimous, not righteous, and not a duty of the filial son. These two groups condemn each other in words and contradict each other in deed, and yet both claim to be followers of the way of Yao, Shun, Yu, Tang, Wen, and Wu. But since they disagree in word and oppose each other in deed, people doubt the assertions of both. Now that the assertions of both are doubted, it will be well to turn to the government of the country and the people and see how elaborate funerals and extended mourning affect the three interests. In my opinion, if in adopting the doctrine and practicing the principle, elaborate funerals and extended mourning could enrich the poor, increase the few, remove danger, and regulate disorder, they would be magnanimous, righteous, and a duty of a filial son. Those who are to give counsel could not but encourage them. And the magnanimous [ruler] would seek to have them flourish in the empire and establish them so as to have the people praise them and never disregard them in their life. [On the other hand,] if in adopting the doctrine and practicing the principle, elaborate funerals and extended mourning really cannot enrich the poor, increase the few, remove danger, and regulate disorder, they will not be magnanimous, righteous, and a duty of the filial son. Those who are to give counsel cannot but discourage them. And the magnanimous will seek to have them abolished in the empire and abandon them so as to have the people condemn them, never to practice them in their life.

且故興天下之利,除天下之害,令國家百姓之不治也,自古及今,未嘗之有也。何以知其然也？今天下之士君子,將猶多皆疑惑厚葬久喪之爲中是非利害也。故子墨子言曰:然則姑嘗稽之,今雖毋法執厚葬久喪者言,以爲事乎國家。此存乎王公大人有喪者,曰棺椁必重,葬埋必厚,衣衾必多,文繡必繁,丘隴必巨;存乎匹夫賤人死者,殆竭家室;乎諸侯死者,虛車府,然後金玉珠璣比乎身,綸組節約,車馬藏乎壙,又必多爲屋幕。鼎鼓几梴壺濫,戈劍羽旄齒革,挾而埋之,滿意。若送從,曰天子殺殉,眾者數百,寡者數十。將軍大夫殺殉,眾者數十,寡者數人。

It has never happened, from ancient times to the present day, that by elaborate funerals and extended mourning, benefits are procured, calamities are averted for the world, and disorder among the people of the country is regulated. How do we know? For even at the present the gentlemen of the world are still doubtful whether elaborate funerals and extended mourning are right and beneficial. Mozi said: I have examined the sayings of those who uphold elaborate funerals and extended mourning. If they should be taken seriously in the country, it would mean: when a lord dies, there would be several inner and outer coffins. He would be buried deep. There would be many shrouds. Embroidery would be elaborate. The grave mound would be massive. So, then, the death of a common man would exhaust the wealth of a family. And the death of a feudal lord would empty the state treasury before his body would be surrounded with gold, jade, and pearls, and the grave filled with carts and horses and bundles of silk. Further, there should be plenty of canopies and hangings, dings, drums, tables, pots, and ice receptacles, spears, swords, feather banners, and hides, all to be carried along and buried. Not till then are the requirements considered fulfilled. And, regarding those who were to die to accompany their lord, for the emperor or a feudal lord there should be from several hundred to several tens, and for a minister or secretary there should be from several tens to several.

處喪之法將奈何哉？曰哭泣不秩聲翁，縗絰垂涕，處倚廬，寢苫枕塊，又相率強不食而爲飢，薄衣而爲寒，使面目陷㢴，顏色黧黑耳目不聰明，手足不勁強，不可用也。又曰上士之操喪也，必扶而能起，杖而能行，以此共三年。若法若言，行若道使王公大人行此，則必不能蚤朝，五官六府，辟草木，實倉廩。使農夫行此。則必不能蚤出夜入，耕稼樹藝。使百工行此，則必不能修舟車爲器皿矣。使婦人行此，則必不能夙興夜寐，紡績織絍。細計厚葬。爲多埋賦之財者也。計久喪，爲久禁從事者也。財以成者，扶而埋之；後得生者，而久禁之，以此求富，此譬猶禁耕而求穫也，富之說無可得焉。

What are the rules to be observed by the mourner? He must weep without restraint and sound as if he is choking. Sackcloth is worn on the breast and hat of flax on the head. His tears and snivel are not to be wiped away. The mourner is to live in a mourning hut, sleep on a coarse mat of straw, and lay his head on a lump of earth. Then, he would be obliged to abstain from food in order to look hungry, and to wear little in order to look cold. The face and eyes are to look sunken and as if in fear, and the complexion is to appear dark. Ears and eyes are to become dull, and hands and feet to become weak and unusable. And, also, if the mourner is a high official, he has to be supported to rise, and lean on a cane to walk. And all this is supposed to last three years. Adopting such a doctrine and practicing such a principle the ruler cannot come to court early [and retire late]; the officials cannot attend to the five offices and six posts and encourage farming and forestry and fill the granaries; the farmers cannot start out early and come in late to cultivate the land and plant trees; the artisans cannot build boats and vehicles and make vessels and utensils; and the women cannot rise early and retire late to weave and spin. So, then, in elaborate funerals, much wealth is buried, and in extended mourning, abstention from work is prolonged. Wealth already produced is carried away into the grave. Child-bearing is postponed. To seek wealth in this way is like seeking a harvest by prohibiting farming. The way to wealth then is not here found.

是故求以富家,而既已不可矣,欲以眾人民,意者可邪？其說又不可矣。今唯無以厚葬久喪者為政,君死,喪之三年；父母死,喪之三年；妻與後子死者,五皆喪之三年；然後伯父叔父兄弟孽子其；族人五月；姑姊甥舅皆有月數。則毀瘠必有制矣,使面目陷陬,顏色黧黑,耳目不聰明,手足不勁強,不可用也。又曰上士操喪也,必扶而能起,杖而能行,以此共三年。若法若言,行若道,苟其飢約,又若此矣,是故百姓冬不仞寒,夏不仞暑,作疾病死者,不可勝計也。此其為敗男女之交多矣。以此求眾譬猶使人負劍,而求其壽也。眾之說無可得焉。

Now that the practice of elaborate funerals and extended mourning has failed to enrich the country, perhaps it can yet increase the population? Again it is powerless. For if elaborate funerals and extended mourning are adopted as the rule, then upon the death of the emperor there will be three years' mourning, upon the death of a parent there will be three years' mourning, and upon the death of the wife or the eldest son there will be three years' mourning. There will be three years' mourning for all five [relations]. Besides, there will be one year for uncles, brothers, and the other sons; and five months for the near relatives, and also several months for aunts, sisters, nephews, and uncles on the mother's side. Further, there are set rules to emaciate one's health: the face and eyes are to look sunken and as if in fear, and the complexion is to appear dark. Ears and eyes are to become dull, and hands and feet are to become weak and unusable. And, also, if the mourner is a high official, he has to be supported to rise and lean on a cane to walk. And this is to last three years if such a doctrine is adopted and such a principle is practiced. Being so hungry and weak, the people cannot stand the cold in winter and the heat in summer. And countless numbers will become sick and die. Sexual relations between husband and wife are prevented. To seek to increase the population by this way is like seeking longevity by thrusting one's self upon a sword. The way to dense population is not here found.

欲以治刑政，意者可乎？其說又不可矣。今唯無以厚葬久喪者爲政。國家必貧，人民必寡，刑政必亂。若法若言，行若道，使爲上者行此，則不能聽治；使爲下者行此，則不能從事。上不聽治，刑政必亂；下不從事，衣食之財必不足。若苟不足，爲人弟者求其兄而不得，不弟弟必將怨其兄矣。爲人子者求其親而不得，不孝子必是怨其親矣。爲人臣者求之君而不得，不忠臣必且亂其上矣。是以僻淫邪行之民，出則無衣也，入則無食也，内續奚吾，並爲淫暴，而不可勝禁也。是故盜賊衆而治者寡。夫衆盜賊而寡治者，以此求治，譬猶使人三睘而毋負己也，治之説無可得焉。是故求以治刑政，而既已不可矣。

Now that it has failed to increase the population, perhaps it can yet regulate jurisdiction? Again it is powerless. For, adopting elaborate funerals and extended mourning as a principle in government, the state will become poor, the people few, and the jurisdiction disorderly. Adopting such a doctrine and practicing such a principle, the superiors cannot give attention to administration, and the subordinates cannot attend to their work. When the superiors are unable to give their attention to administration there will be disorder. When the subordinates are unable to attend to their work, the supply of food and clothing will be insufficient. When there is insufficiency, the undutiful younger brother will ask his older brother for help, and when he does not receive it he will hate the elder brother. The unfilial son will turn to his father for help and when he does not receive it he will spurn his father. And the disloyal minister will turn for help to his lord and when he does not receive it he will mock his lord. And vicious and immoral people will commit evil and immorality beyond control when they are without clothing outside and without food at home. So, bandits and thieves will be numerous but law-abiding people few. Now, to seek order by multiplying the bandits and thieves and diminishing the law-abiding people is like demanding of a person not to present his back to you while making him turn around three times. The way to order is not here found.

欲以禁止大國之攻小國也，意者可邪？其說又不可矣。是故昔者聖王既沒，天下失義，諸侯力征，南有楚、越之王，而北有齊、晉之君，此皆砥礪其卒伍，以攻伐並兼爲政於天下。是故凡大國之所以不攻小國者，積委多，城郭修，上下調和，是故大國不耆攻之。無積委，城郭不修，上下不調和。是故大國耆攻之。今唯無以厚葬久喪者爲政，國家必貧，人民必寡，刑政必亂。若苟貧，是無以爲積委也；若苟寡，是城郭溝渠者寡也；若苟亂，是出戰不克，入守不固。此求禁止大國之攻小國也，而既已不可矣。

Now that it has failed to regulate jurisdiction and government, perhaps it can yet prevent the large states from attacking the small states? Again it is powerless. For since the ancient sage-kings have passed away and the world has become ignorant of their principles, the feudal lords resort to attack by force. On the south there are the kings of Chu and Yue, and on the north there are the lords of Qi and Jin. All of them show favors and encouragement to their warriors and soldiers, making it their business in the world to attack and absorb [others]. There are some small states that, however, they do not attack, and this is because these small states are well stored with supplies, their inner and outer city walls are kept in good repair, and in them the superiors and the subordinates are harmonious. Therefore the large states would not want to attack them. Those which are not well stored with supplies, whose inner and outer city walls are not in good repair, and in which the superiors and the subordinates are not harmonious, the large states would want to attack. Adopting elaborate funerals and extended mourning in government, the state will become poor, the people few, and jurisdiction disorderly. Since the state is poor, no surplus goods can be stored. Since its numbers are few, there will be few workmen to keep the city walls and moats in good repair. Since it is disorderly, a state will not be victorious in attack or strong in defense.

欲以幹上帝鬼神之福，意者可邪？其說又不可矣。今唯無以厚葬久喪者爲政，國家必貧，人民必寡，刑政必亂。若苟貧，是粢盛酒醴不淨潔也；若苟寡，是事上帝鬼神者寡也。若苟亂，是祭祀不時度也。今又禁止事上帝鬼神，爲政若此，上帝鬼神始得從上撫之曰："我有是人也，與無是人也，孰愈？"曰："我有是人也，與無是人也，無擇也。"則惟上帝鬼神降之罪厲之禍罰而棄之，則豈不亦乃其所哉！

Now that it has failed in preventing the large states from attacking the small states, perhaps it can yet procure blessing from God and the spirits. Again it is powerless. For, adopting elaborate funerals and extended mourning as a principle in government, the state will become poor, the people few, and the jurisdiction disorderly. When the state is poor the cakes and wine will be unclean. When the people are few the worshippers of God and the spirits will be reduced in number. And when jurisdiction is in disorder the sacrifice will not be made according to season. Moreover, the worship of God and the spirits is now even prohibited. When the government is run like this, God and the spirits would deliberate from on high, saying, "Which is better, to have these people exist or not to have them exist? It really makes no difference whether they exist or not." Therefore God and the spirits will send judgment upon them and visit them with calamities and punish and desert them. Is not this quite in place?

故古聖王制爲葬埋之法曰："棺三寸，足以朽體，衣衾三領，足以覆惡。以及其葬也，下毋及泉，上毋通臭，壟若參耕之畝，則止矣。死者既以葬矣，生者必無久哭而疾而從事，人爲其所能，以交相利也。"此聖王之法也。

Therefore the ancient sage-kings authorized the code of laws regarding the burial of the dead thus: The coffin shall be three inches thick, sufficient to hold the body. As to shrouds there shall be three pieces adequate to cover the corpse. It shall not be buried so deep as to reach water and neither so shallow as to allow the odor to ascend. Three feet in size shall be big enough for the mound. There shall be no extended mourning after burial, but speedy return to work and pursuit in what one can do to procure mutual benefit. Such are the laws of the sage-kings.

今執厚葬久喪者之言曰：厚葬久喪，雖使不可以富貧、衆寡、定危、治亂，然此聖王之道也。子墨子曰：不然。昔者堯北教乎八狄，道死，葬蛩山之陰。衣衾三領，穀木之棺，葛以緘之，既淝而後哭，滿坎無封。已葬，而牛馬乘之。舜西教乎七戎，道死，葬南己之市。衣衾三領，穀木之棺，葛以緘之。已葬，而市人乘之。禹東教乎九夷，道死，葬會稽之山，衣衾三領，桐棺三寸，葛以緘之，絞之不合，通之不埳。土地之深，下毋及泉，上毋通臭。既葬，收餘壤其上，壟若參耕之畝，則止矣。若以此若三聖王者觀之，則厚葬久喪果非聖王之道。故三王者，皆貴爲天子，富有天下，豈憂財用之不足哉？以爲如此葬埋之法。

Those who uphold elaborate funerals and extended mourning say, "Although elaborate funerals and extended mourning cannot enrich the poor, increase the few, remove danger and regulate disorder, yet they were a principle of the sage-kings." Mozi replied: Not at all. Anciently, Yao went north to instruct the eight tribes of Di. He died on the way and was buried in the shade of Mt. Qiong. Of shrouds there were three pieces. The coffin was of soft wood, and sealed with flax linen. Weeping started only after burial. There was no mound; only the pit was filled up. After burial, oxen and horses plodded over it. Shun went west to instruct the seven tribes of Rong. He died on the way and was buried in the market place of Nanji. Of shrouds there were three pieces. The coffin was of soft wood and sealed with flax linen. After burial the people in the market place walked over it. Yu went east to instruct the nine tribes of Yi. He died on the way and was buried at Mt. Guiji. Of shrouds there were three pieces. The coffin was of tong wood and sealed with flax linen. It did not crush when bound, and it did not sink in when pressed. The pit was not deep enough to strike water and not so shallow as to allow the odor to ascend. When the coffin had been buried, the remaining earth was gathered on it, and the mound was three feet high and no more. So, to judge according to these three sage-kings, elaborate funerals and extended mourning were really not the way of the sage-kings. These three sage-kings held the rank of Sons of Heaven and possessed the whole empire, yet they authorized their burial in this way. Was it because of any fear of lack of means? No. It is because they think this is the appropriate way of funeral and mourning.

今王公大人之爲葬埋，則異於此。必大棺、中棺，革闠三操，璧玉即具，戈劍、鼎鼓、壺濫、文繡、素練、大鞅、萬領、輿馬、女樂皆具，曰："必捶涂差通，壟雖凡山陵。"此爲輟民之事，靡民之財，不可勝計也。其爲毋用若此矣。

The way in which the present rulers are buried is quite different from this. There are the outer and the inner coffins, and then the three layers of hide and embroidered covers. When the stones and jade are all collected, there are yet to be completed the spears, swords, dings, pots and ice receptacles, and ten thousand of decorated reins and yokes, and the carriages, horses, and the chorus girls. Then, there must be building the tunnel to reach under the tomb which is as high as a hill. This interferes with people's work and wastes people's wealth to such a great extent. How indeed is this to be avoided?

是故子墨子曰：鄉者吾本言曰，意亦使法其言，用其謀，計厚葬久喪，請可以富貧、衆寡、定危、治亂乎？則仁也，義也，孝子之事也。爲人謀者，不可不勸也。意亦使法其言，用其謀，若人厚葬久喪，實不可以富貧、衆寡、定危、治亂乎？則非仁也，非義也，非孝子之事也。爲人謀者，不可不沮也。是故求以富國家，甚得貧焉；欲以衆人民，甚得寡焉；欲以治刑政，甚得亂焉；求以禁止大國之攻小國也，而既已不可矣。欲以干上帝鬼神之福，又得禍焉。上稽之堯、舜、禹、湯、文、武之道，而政逆之。下稽之桀、紂、幽、厲之事，猶合節也。若以此觀，則厚葬久喪，其非聖王之道也。

So Mozi said: I have already said that if in adopting the doctrine and practicing the principle, elaborate funerals and extended mourning really could enrich the poor, increase the few, remove danger and regulate disorder, they would be magnanimous, righteous, and thus a duty of the filial son. Those who give counsel could not but encourage them. [On the other hand,] if in adopting the doctrine and practicing the principle, elaborate funerals and extended mourning really cannot enrich the poor, increase the few, remove danger and regulate disorder, they are not magnanimous, righteous, and thus not a duty of the filial son. Those who are to give counsel cannot but discourage it. Now, [we have seen] that to seek to enrich a country thereby brings about poverty; to seek to increase the people thereby results in a decrease; and to seek to regulate government thereby begets disorder. To seek to prevent the large states from attacking the small ones by this way is impossible on the one hand, and, on the other, to seek to procure blessing from God and the spirits through this way only brings calamity. When we look up and examine the way of Yao, Shun, Yu, Tang, Wen, and Wu, we find it diametrically opposed to [these]. But when we look down and examine the regimes of Jie, Zhou, You, and Li, we find the way they followed agrees with these like two parts of a tally. So, judging from these, elaborate funerals and extended mourning are not the way of the sage-kings.

今執厚葬久喪者言曰：厚葬久喪，果非聖王之道，夫胡說中國之君子爲而不已、操而不擇哉？子墨子曰：此所謂便其習而義其俗者也。昔者越之東，有輆沐之國者，其長子生，則解而食之，謂之宜弟；其大父死，負其大母而棄之，曰鬼妻不可與居處。此上以爲政，下以爲俗，爲而不已，操而不擇。則此豈實仁義之道哉？此所謂便其習而義其俗者也。楚之南，有炎人國者，其親戚死，朽其肉而棄之，然後埋其骨，乃成爲孝子。秦之西，有儀渠之國者，其親戚死，聚柴薪而焚之，熏上謂之登遐，然後成爲孝子。此上以爲政，下以爲俗，爲而不已，操而不擇，則此豈實仁義之道哉？此所謂便其習而義其俗者也。若以此若三國者觀之，則亦猶薄矣。若以中國之君子觀之，則亦猶厚矣。如彼則大厚，如此則大薄，然則葬埋之有節矣。故衣食者，人之生利也，然且猶尚有節；葬埋者，人之死利也，夫何獨無節於此乎？

Those who uphold elaborate funerals and extended mourning are saying, "If the elaborate funerals and extended mourning were not the way of the sage-kings, why then do the gentlemen of the Middle Kingdom practice them continually and follow them without discrimination?" Mozi said: This is because habit affords convenience and custom carries approval. Anciently, east of the state of Yue there was the tribe of Kaishu. Among them the first-born son was dismembered and devoured after birth and this was said to be propitious for his younger brothers. When the father died, the mother was carried away and abandoned, and the reason was that one should not live with the wife of a ghost. By the officials this was regarded as a government regulation and by the people it was accepted as a commonplace. They practiced it continually and followed it without discrimination. Was it then the good and the right way? No, this is really because habit affords convenience and custom carries approval. South of Chu there was a cannibal tribe. Upon the death of the parents the flesh was scraped off and thrown away, while the bones were buried. And by following this custom one became a filial son. West of the state of Qin there was the tribe of Yiqu. Upon their death the parents were burned on a bonfire and amidst the smoke, and this was said to be ascension to the golden clouds. In this way one became a filial son. The officials embodied it in the government regulations and the people regarded it as a commonplace. They practiced it continually and followed it without discrimination. Is it then the good and the right way? No, this is really because habit affords convenience and custom carries approval. Now, the practice of these three tribes is too heartless and that of the gentlemen of the Middle Kingdom is too elaborate. This being too elaborate and that being too heartless, then there should be rules for funerals and burials. Even regarding clothing and food, which are the necessities of life, there are rules. How then can there be none regarding funerals and burials, which are the necessities of death?

子墨子制爲葬埋之法，曰：棺三寸，足以朽骨；衣三領，足以朽肉。掘地之深，下無菹漏，氣無發洩於上，壟足以期其所，則止矣。哭往哭來，反從事乎衣食之財，佴乎祭祀，以致孝於親。故曰子墨子之法不失死生之利者，此也。

Outlining the rules for funerals and burials, Mozi said: The coffin shall be three inches thick, just sufficient to hold the rotting bones. Of shrouds there shall be three pieces just to be enough to hold the rotting flesh. The pit shall be dug not so deep as to strike water, and not so shallow as to allow the odor to ascend. The mound shall be just high enough to be identified [by the mourners]. There may be weeping on the way to and from the burial. But upon returning they shall engage in earning the means of livelihood. Sacrifices shall not be neglected in order to express one's filial piety to parents. Thus the rules of Mozi neglect the necessities of neither the dead nor the living.

故子墨子言曰：今天下之士君子，中請將欲爲仁義，求爲上士，上欲中聖王之道，下欲中國家百姓之利，故當若節喪之爲政，而不可不察此者也。

Hence, Mozi said: If the gentlemen of the world really want to practice righteousness and magnanimity, and to seek to be superior men, desiring to attain the way of the sage-kings on the one hand and to procure blessings for the people on the other, they cannot afford to neglect the principle of Simplicity in Funeral in government.

《荀子》/Xunzi

子道篇第二十九
Chapter 29　The Way to Be a Son

入孝出弟，人之小行也；上順下篤，人之中行也；從道不從君，從義不從父，人之大行也。若夫志以禮安，言以類使，則儒道畢矣。雖舜不能加毫末於是矣。

To be filial at home and to be fraternal away from home is lesser conduct. To be compliant to one's superiors and devoted to one's inferiors is middle conduct. To follow the Dao and not one's lord, to follow righteousness (yi) and not one's father is the greatest conduct. If one's intentions are at ease in ritual, and one's words are put forth in accordance with the proper classes of things, then the Dao of Confucianism (ru) is complete. Even Shun could not improve any more.

孝子所不從命有三：從命則親危，不從命則親安，孝子不從命乃衷；從命則親辱，不從命則親榮，孝子不從命乃義；從命則禽獸，不從命則脩飾，孝子不從命乃敬。故可以從而不從，是不子也；未可以從而從，是不衷也；明於從不從之義，而能致恭敬、忠信、端愨、以慎行之，則可謂大孝矣。傳曰："從道不從君，從義不從父。"此之謂也。故勞苦、彫萃而能無失其敬，災禍、患難而能無失其義，則不幸不順見惡而能無失其愛，非仁人莫能行。《詩》曰："孝子不匱。"此之謂也。
……

There are three cases in which the filial son does not follow his parents' orders. When following orders will endanger his parents, but not following orders will make them safe, then the filial son will not follow orders, and this is having scruples. When following orders will disgrace his parents, but not following orders will bring them honor, then the filial son will not follow orders, and this is being righteousness (yi). When following orders requires a beastly act, but not following orders requires cultivation and good manners, then the filial son will not follow orders and this is being respectful. If one may follow one's parents' orders but refuse to do so, one is unfilial. If one follows orders when it is not permissible to do so, one lacks any scruples. If one understands the proper purposes of following and not following orders, and if one can be reverent, respectful, loyal, trustworthy, scrupulous, and honest so as to carry these out vigilantly, then this can be called the greatest filial piety. A proverb states, "Follow the Dao, not your lord. Follow yi, not your father." This expresses my meaning. And so, to face hard labor and physical exhaustion without losing one's respectfulness, to face calamities and difficulties without losing one's regard for yi, so that even in the unfortunate case of unsmooth relations and being hated [by one's parents] one still does not lose one's love for one's parents—none but the person of benevolence (ren) can do this. The Odes says, "Those filial sons will be untiring." This expresses my meaning.

...

《韩非子》/ Hanfeizi

十過第十
Chapter 10　　Ten Faults

昔者齊桓公九合諸候，一匡天下，爲五伯長，管仲佐之。管仲老，不能用事，休居於家。桓公從而問之曰："仲父家居有病，即不幸而不起此病，政安遷之？"管仲曰："臣老矣，不可問也。雖然，臣聞之，知臣莫若君，知子莫若父。君其試以心決之。"……公曰："衛公子開方何如？"管仲曰："不可。齊、衛之間不過十日之行，開方爲事君，欲適君之故，十五年不歸見其父母，此非人情也。其父母之不親也，又能親君乎？"公曰："然則易牙何？"管仲曰："不可。夫易牙爲君主味。君之所未嘗食唯人肉耳，易牙蒸其子首而進之，君所知也。人之情莫不愛其子，今蒸其子以爲膳於君，其子弗愛，又安能愛君乎？"

In bygone days, Duke Huan of Qi called the feudal lords to meet nine times, brought All-under-Heaven under one rule, and became the first of the Five Hegemonic Rulers. And Guan Zhong assisted him. When Guan Zhong became aged and unable to attend to his duties, he retired to live at his home. One day Duke Huan went to call on him and asked, "Uncle Zhong is ill at home. If by any unlucky chance you should not be up and helping me again, whom should I appoint as the prime minister?" In reply Guan Zhong said, "I am old and hardly worth consulting. Nevertheless, I have heard, 'Nobody knows the ministers better than the ruler does, just as nobody knows the sons better than the father does.' Why not tell me who Your Highness would like to select?"... "Then how about Prince Kai-fang of Wei?" asked the Duke. "No," replied Guan Zhong. "The distance between Qi and Wei is not more than ten days' walk. Yet in order to serve Your Highness, Kai-fang never went home for fifteen years to see his parents. Such is against human nature. Since he does not love his parents, how would he love Your Highness?" "Well, then, how about Yiya?" asked the Duke. "No," replied Guan Zhong. "Yiya was the chef for Your Highness. Finding that what Your Highness had never tasted was human flesh only, he cooked the head of his own son and presented it to Your Highness. Your Highness knows that. Now everybody loves his own son: this is human nature. However, Yiya cooked his own son to make food for Your Highness. Since he does not even love his own son, how would he love Your Highness?"

奸劫弑臣第十四
Chapter 14 Ministers Apt to Betray, Molest, or Murder the Ruler

楚莊王之弟春申君，有愛妾曰余，春申君之正妻子曰甲。余欲君之棄其妻也，因自傷其身以視君而泣，曰："得爲君之妾，甚幸。雖然，適夫人非所以事君也，適君非所以事夫人也。身故不肖，力不足以適二主，其勢不俱適，與其死夫人所者，不若賜死君前。妾以賜死，若復幸於左右，願君必察之，無爲人笑。"君因信妾余之詐，爲棄正妻。

Lord Chun-shen, younger brother of King Zhuang of Chu, had a beloved concubine named Yü. The son born by his legal wife was named Jia. Yü first wanted the lord to desert his legal wife. So she injured herself. Showing the injuries to the lord, she shed tears and said, "To be able to become Your Excellency's concubine is very fortunate indeed. However, to please Madame is not the way to serve Your Excellency; to please Your Excellency is not the way to serve Madame. Being unworthy myself and not able to please both Your Excellency and Madame, I will eventually displease both. Therefore, instead of dying at the Madame's place, I prefer to be allowed to kill myself in front of Your Excellency. After I die, if Your Excellency favors anybody else among the maids, I hope Your Excellency will be more careful than now, and never become a laughingstock of people." The lord believed the cunning words of Yü, and deserted his legal wife.

余又欲殺甲而以其子爲後，因自裂其親身衣之里，以示君而泣，曰："余之得幸君之日久矣，甲非弗知也，今乃欲强戲余。余與爭之，至裂余之衣，而此子之不孝，莫大於此矣！"君怒，而殺甲也。故妻以妾余之詐棄，而子以之死。

Yü next wanted to kill Jia and make her own son the heir apparent instead. So she tore the lining of her own petticoat. Showing the torn clothes to the lord, she shed tears and said, "I have enjoyed Your Excellency's favor for a long time, which Jia has known of course. However, just a while ago, he took liberties with me by force. I struggled with him, and he tore my clothes. No other filially impious act committed by a son could be worse than this!" Enraged thereby, the lord killed Jia. Thus, the wife was deserted because of the low cunning of the concubine Yü and the son was killed for the same reason.

從是觀之，父子愛子也，猶可以毀而害也；君臣之相與也，非有父子之親也，而群臣之毀言，非特一妾之口也，何怪夫賢聖之戮死哉！此商君之所以車裂於秦，而吳起之所以枝解於楚者也。

From this I can see that even the father's love of the son can be demolished and damaged. Now that the relationship between ruler and minister is not as close as that between father and son, and the slanderous words of the officials are not so simple as those coming out from the mouth of a concubine, no wonder worthies and sages were slaughtered and executed! This was the very reason why Lord Shang was torn to pieces by chariots in Qin, and why Wu Qi was dismembered in Chu.

凡人臣者，有罪固不欲誅，無功者皆欲尊顯。而聖人之治國也，賞不加於無功，而誅必行於有罪者也。然則有術數者之爲人也，固左右奸臣之所害，非明主弗能聽也。

In general, the government officials, when guilty of crimes, never want to be censured, but, when of no merit, all want to be honored and celebrated. But the sage, when governing the state, never bestows rewards on men of no merit but definitely inflicts censures on culprits. However, those who know the way to govern the state will be slandered or banished by the wicked government officials. Only an enlightened sovereign will listen to them.

內儲說上七術第三十
Chapter 30　Inner Congeries of Sayings, The Upper Series: Seven Tacts

成驩謂齊王曰："王太仁，太不忍人。"王曰："太仁，太不忍人，非善名邪？"對曰："此人臣之善也，非人主之所行也。夫人臣必仁而後可與謀，不忍人而後可近也；不仁則不可與謀，忍人則不可近也。"王曰："然則寡人安所太仁，安不忍人？"對曰："王太仁於薛公，而太不忍於諸田。太仁薛公，則大臣無重；太不忍諸田，則父兄犯法。大臣無重，則兵弱於外；父兄犯法，則政亂於內。兵弱於外，政亂於內，此亡國之本也。"

Cheng Huan said to the King of Qi, "Your Majesty is too benevolent and even too lenient with people." "Isn't it a good name to be too benevolent and too lenient?" asked the King. In reply Cheng Huan said, "It is a good name for ministers, but that is not what the lord of men ought to do. Indeed, ministers must be benevolent in order to be trustworthy, and must be lenient with people in order to be accessible. If not benevolent, he is not trustworthy; if not lenient, he is not accessible." "If so, to whom am I too benevolent? And with whom am I too lenient?" asked the King. In reply Cheng Huan said, "Your Majesty is too benevolent to the Duke of Xue and too lenient with your family, the various Tians. If Your Majesty remains too benevolent to the Duke of Xue, then the ministers will be not serious [in dealing with the state affairs]. If Your Majesty remains too lenient with your family, then your uncles and brothers will violate the law. If your ministers are not serious, the army will become weak abroad. If your uncles and brothers violate the law, then at home the government will fall into disorder. To have the army weakened abroad and the government disordered at home is to ruin the state."

外儲説左上第三十二
Chapter 32 Outer Congeries of Sayings, The Upper Left Series

人爲嬰兒也，父母養之簡，子長而怨。子盛壯成人，其供養薄，父母怒而誚之。子父至親也，而或譙或怨者，皆挾相爲而不周於爲己也。

If one received no good care in his childhood from his parents, he shows resentment at them when he grows up. If an adult is big and strong, but his provisions for his parents are rather scanty, then his parents become angry and reprimand him. Now, father and son are the closest relatives. Yet they either reprimand or show resentment at each other simply because one expects the other to benefit one, but·the other fails to live up to one's expectations.

夫賣庸而播耕者，主人費家而美食，調布而求易錢者，非愛庸客也，曰：“如是，耕者且深，耨者熟耘也。”庸客致力而疾耘耕者，盡巧而正畦陌畦時者，非愛主人也，曰：“如是，羹且美，錢布且易云也。”此其養功力，有父子之澤矣，而心調於用者，皆挾自爲心也。故人行事施予，以利之爲心，則越人易和；以害之爲心，則父子離且怨。

When a man sells his services as a farm hand, the landowner will give him good food and pay him money and cloth. This is not because the lardowner loves the farm hand, but he says, "In this way, the farm hand's ploughing of the ground will go deeper and his sowing of seeds will be more active." The farm hand, on the other hand, exerts his strength and works busily at tilling and weeding. He exerts all his skills cultivating the fields. This is not because he loves the lardowner, but he says, "In this way I shall have good soup, and money and cloth will come easily." Thus he expends his strength as if between them there were a bond of love such as that of father and son. The reason why they are willing to benefit each other is that they both harbor the idea of serving themselves. Therefore in the conduct of human affairs, if one has a mind to benefit others, it will be easy to remain harmonious with them, even with a native of Yue. But if one has a mind to do harm to others, even father and son will become estranged and feel hostile toward each other.

六反第四十六
Chapter 46　Six Contrarieties

今上下之接，無子父之澤，而欲以行義禁下，則交必有郄矣。且父母之於子也，產男則相賀，產女則殺之。此俱出父母之懷衽，然男子受賀，女子殺之者，慮其後便，計之長利也。故父母之於子也，猶用計算之心以相待也，而況無父子之澤乎？

Now the relationship between the superior and the inferior is far from being as close as the bond between the parents and the child. So if the superior wishes to control the inferior by relying on moral principles, then the relationship between the two will certainly have cracks. Further, when a son is born, the parents think it is worth celebrating; when a daughter was born, the parents think of killing her. The son and the daughter are both biological offspring of the parents, yet the parents celebrate the birth of the son, but think of killing the daughter as soon she is born. This is because the son will benefit the parents much more than the girl in the long run. Since the parents are calculating in treating their children, what can you expect from the relationship far from being as close as the bond between parents and children?

忠孝第五十一
Chapter 51　Loyalty and Filial Piety: A Memorial

天下皆以孝悌忠順之道爲是也，而莫知察孝悌忠順之道而審行之，是以天下亂。皆以堯舜之道爲是而法之，是以有弒君，有曲於父。堯、舜、湯、武或反君臣之義，亂後世之教者也。堯爲人君而君其臣，舜爲人臣而臣其君，湯、武爲人臣而弒其主、刑其尸，而天下譽之，此天下所以至今不治者也。夫所謂明君者，能畜其臣者也；所謂賢臣者，能明法辟，治官職，以戴其君者也。今堯自以爲明而不能以畜舜，舜自以爲賢而不能以戴堯，湯、武自以爲義而弒其君長，此明君且常與，而賢臣且常取也。故至今爲人子者有取其父之家，爲人臣者有取其君之國者矣。父而讓子，君而讓臣，此非所以定位一教之道也。

All-Under-Heaven approve the Dao of filial piety, fraternal respect, loyalty, and obedience, but never carefully investigate the Dao of filial piety, fraternal respect, loyalty, and obedience, nor do they act intelligently upon these; wherefore All-Under-Heaven is in disorder. As everybody approves the Dao of Yao and Shun and conforms to it, there are murderers of rulers and rebels against fathers. Yao, Shun, Tang, and Wu, each in his turn, acted contrary to the right relationship of ruler and minister, and the moral of the subsequent generations has consequently been upset. Yao, being the ruler of men, made a minister (i.e. Shun) his ruler.① Shun, while ministering to a ruler (i.e. Yao), made the ruler a minister. Tang and Wu, while ministering to rulers, murdered the sovereigns and dismembered their bodies. Yet All-Under-Heaven have honored them. This is the reason why All-Under-Heaven have hitherto not attained political order. Indeed, the intelligent ruler is one who is able to keep his ministers in his service; the worthy minister is one who is able to make laws clear and attend to his official duties so as to support his master. Now, Yao, assuming himself to be enlightened, could not keep Shun in his service; Shun, assuming himself to be worthy, could not continue supporting Yao; and Tang and Wu, assuming themselves to be righteous, murdered their masters and superiors. That was the way "enlightened"

---

① A minister was supposed to be a servant of the ruler. And the ruler was supposed to be the master of all ministers. Han Fei thinks that the master should not make a servant his master, nor should a servant make his master a servant.

rulers would give and "worthy" ministers would take. In consequence, hitherto there have been sons robbing their fathers' houses and ministers robbing their masters' states. Thus, fathers give way to sons and rulers give way to ministers. Such is not the right way to determine the distinction of rank between ruler and minister and unify the system of morale between father and son.

臣之所聞曰:"臣事君,子事父,妻事夫。三者順則天下治,三者逆則天下亂。此天下之常道也。"明王賢臣而弗易也,則人主雖不肖,臣不敢侵也。今夫上賢任智無常,逆道也,而天下常以爲治。是故田氏奪呂氏於齊,戴氏奪子氏於宋。此皆賢且智也,豈愚且不肖乎? 是廢常上賢則亂,舍法任智則危。故曰:上法而不上賢。

The servant has heard, "Minister serving ruler, son serving father, and wife serving husband, if these three relationships run in harmony, All-Under-Heaven will have order; if these three relationships run in discord, All-Under-Heaven will have disorder." If this is an immutable principle of the world, which neither the intelligent king nor the worthy minister dares to depart from, then even though the lord of men might be unworthy, no minister would dare to infringe his prerogative. In these days, however, the exaltation of the worthy (i.e. the able or skilled), the appointment of the clever, and the lack of a constant principle, all follow the wrong way; but All-Under-Heaven always regard it as the royal road to order. For this reason, the Tian Family usurped the throne of the Lü Family in Qi, and the Dai Family usurped the throne of the Zi Family in Song. Both Tian and Zi were worthy and clever: were they stupid and worthless? Thus, when the immutable principle is abolished and worthies are exalted, there will be disorder; when the law is discarded and clever men are taken into service, danger arises. Hence the saying, "Exalt law but never exalt worthiness."

記曰:"舜見瞽瞍,其容造焉。孔子曰:'當是時也,危哉! 天下岌岌! 有道者,父固不得而子,君固不得而臣也。'"臣曰:孔子本未知孝悌忠順之道也。然則有道者,進不爲主臣,退不爲父子耶?父之所以欲有賢子者,家貧則富之,父苦則樂之;君之所以欲有賢臣者,國亂則治之,主卑則尊之。今有賢子而不爲父,則父之處家也苦;有賢臣而不爲君,則君之處位也危。然則父有賢子,君有賢臣,適足以爲害耳,豈得利焉哉?所謂忠臣,不危其君;孝子,不非其親。今舜以賢取君之國,而湯、武以義放弒其君,此皆以賢而危主者也,而天下賢之。

The ancient records say, "Shun, when he saw his father, Gusou, looked uneasy." On this Confucius remarked, "How critical the age was! For All-Under-Heaven were then hanging by a hair. If anybody was a follower of the true path, even his father could not treat him as a son, and, even his ruler could not treat him as a servant." However, the servant would say, "Confucius in the first place did not understand the Dao of filial piety, fraternal respect, loyalty, and obedience." By that remark did he mean that a follower of the true path, when in the court, could not be a servant to the sovereign, and, when at home, could not be a son of the father? The reason why fathers want to have worthy sons is that the family, if poor, will be enriched by them, and the fathers, when unhappy, will be gladdened by them. The reason why the ruler wants to have worthy servants or ministers is that the state, if in chaos, will be put into order by them, and the sovereign, when humbled, will be elevated by them. Now supposing there were a son never doing his father any good, then the father in managing the domestic affairs would suffer. Again, supposing there were a worthy servant or minister never doing the ruler any good, then the ruler while safeguarding his throne would be jeopardized. If so, to have a worthy son and to have a worthy servant or minister will constitute a harm to the father and the ruler respectively. How can they get any benefit at all? They say the loyal servant or minister never endangers his ruler and the dutiful son never disowns his parents. Now, Shun, in virtue of his worthiness, took the ruler's state; Tang and Wu, in virtue of his righteousness, dethroned and murdered their rulers. Though all these people endangered their sovereigns in virtue of their worthiness, yet All-Under-Heaven have praised them highly.

古之烈士，進不臣君，退不爲家，是進則非其君，退則非其親者也。且夫進不臣君，退不爲家，亂世絕嗣之道也。是故賢堯、舜、湯、武而是烈士，天下之亂術也。瞽瞍爲舜父，而舜放之；象爲舜弟而殺之。放父殺弟，不可謂仁；妻帝二女而取天下，不可謂義。仁義無有，不可謂明。《詩》云："普天之下，莫非王土；率土之濱，莫非王臣。"信若《詩》之言也，是舜出則臣其君，入則臣其父，妾其母，妻其主女也。故烈士內不爲家，亂世絕嗣，而外矯於君。朽骨爛肉，施於土地，流於川谷，不避蹈水火，使天下從而效之，是天下徧死而願夭也。此皆釋世而不治是也。

The heroes of antiquity, when in public, would never serve any ruler, and, when in private, would never serve their families. By so doing, they disowned their rulers in public and their parents in private. Moreover, to serve no ruler when active in public and no family when retired in private is the road to world-disorder and family-extinction. Therefore, to regard Yao, Shun, Tang, and Wu as worthy, and to approve the so-called heroes, are to throw All-Under-Heaven into chaos. Gusou was Shun's father but Shun exiled him; Xiang was Shun's brother but Shun killed him. Who exiled his father and killed his brother could not be called benevolent. Nor could one who married the emperor's two daughters and took the rule over All-Under-Heaven be called righteous. Who was neither benevolent nor righteous, could not be called enlightened. It is said in *The Book of Odes*,

> Under the whole Heaven,
> Every spot is the sovereign's ground;
> To the borders of the land,
> Every individual is the sovereign's subject.

Against the principle expressed by this poem, Shun in public made his ruler a servant, and in private made his father a servant, his step-mother a concubine, and his ruler's daughters wives. Thus, the hero in private did nothing for his family, destroyed the order of the world, and left no offspring; and in public he attempts to oppose the ruler in every way. Even though his decaying bones and spoilt flesh would eventually lie unburied on the open ground or flow on the mountain-stream, he never avoided going through water and fire in order to make All-Under-Heaven take him as model, whereby he would make everybody in the world be willing to die and end his life young without regret. This type of man would always desert the world and never care about political order.

世之所爲烈士者，離衆獨行，取異於人，爲恬淡之學而理恍惚之言。臣以爲恬淡，無用之教也；恍惚，無法之言也。言出於無法，教出於無用者，天下謂之察。臣以爲人生必事君養親，事君養親不可以恬淡；治人必以言論忠信法術，言論忠信法術不可以恍惚。恍惚之言，恬淡之學，天下之惑術也。孝子之事父也，非競取父之家也；忠臣之事君也，非競取君之國也。夫爲人子而常譽他人之親曰："某子之親，夜寢早起，強力生財以養子孫臣妾。"是誹謗其親者也。爲人臣常譽先王之德厚而願之，是誹謗其君者也。非其親者知謂之不孝，而非其君者天下皆賢之，此所以亂也。故人臣毋稱堯、舜之賢，毋譽湯、武之伐，毋言烈士之高，盡力守法，專心於事主者爲忠臣。

Similarly, the so-call heroes in this age behave in a way different from most people, prefer things different from others, study the philosophy of tranquility, and are interested in elusive words. The servant, however, thinks the philosophy of tranquility is useless, and that elusive words are lawless. He whose words are lawless and whose philosophy is useless is regarded by the world as wise. The servant, however, maintains the following: Everybody during his lifetime should serve the ruler and take care of the parents, but this requirement is not compatible with the philosophy of tranquility; again, everybody during his lifetime should live up to his words, practice loyalty and sincerity, and obey the law, but this requirement cannot be fulfilled if elusive words prevail; wherefore the philosophy of tranquility and elusive words are nothing but bewildering crafts in the world. A dutiful son, in serving his father, never fights with his brothers for the father's household; a loyal minister, in serving the ruler, never struggles with other ministers for the ruler's state. Indeed, if a son always praises other people's parents, saying, for instance, "The parents of Mr. So and So go to bed late at night and get up early in the morning and work hard to make money and thereby support their children and grandchildren and keep so many men and women servants," he is a defamer of his parents. Similarly, if a minister always praises the early kings for the greatness of their virtues and longs after them, he is a defamer of his ruler. Now, one who defames his parents is called unfilial; whereas one who defames his ruler, the world considers worthy. This is the reason why there is chaos. Therefore, the minister, who neither extols the worthiness of Yao and Shun, nor admires the achievement of Tang and Wu, nor speaks well of the nobleness of the so-called heroes, but applies all his strength to observing the law and devotes his whole heart to serving the sovereign, is a loyal minister indeed.

二、義利 / Part II Righteousness

　　殺死一個無辜的人是不義的。但是，假設你是一個國家的君王，你可以通過搶奪和殺戮另一個國家的無辜居民，使本國更加強大，人民過上更好的生活，那麼你的搶奪和殺戮不符合道義嗎？一般來說，某個行爲符合何種標準，才是義行？如果可以通過做不道義的事情獲得我們想要的東西（比如財富和權力），那麼我們爲什麼還要遵守道義？是不是在有些情況下，唯有自殺才符合道義？如果是道義高於生命，說到底，生命的價值是什麼？

　　在這一部分，我們將看到儒、墨這兩個主要的哲學學派是如何討論這些問題的。閱讀選文時，可以試著找出這兩個學派之間的差別，並思考兩派的回答是否有道理。

　　It seems unrighteous to kill an innocent person. But suppose you are a king, and you can help your people live a better life and make your country more powerful by robbing and killing innocent people in another country. Would it be righteousness if you did so? In general, what makes an act righteous? If we can get what we desire (e.g. wealth and power) by doing an unrighteous thing, why should we be righteous? Is it true that sometimes the only righteous thing to do is to kill oneself? If so, why should we give priority to righteousness over our life? What makes a life worth living after all?

　　In this part, we will see how the two major philosophical schools, Confucianism and Mohism, address these questions. As you read the selections, try to figure out the differences between the two schools. Ask yourself how plausible their answers are.

《論語》/ The Analects

4.5 子曰："富與貴，是人之所欲也；不以其道得之，不處也。貧與賤，是人之惡也；不以其道得之，不去也。君子去仁，惡乎成名。君子無終食之間違仁，造次必於是，顛沛必於是。"

4.5 The Master said, "Wealth and social eminence are things that all people desire, and yet unless they are acquired in the proper way I will not accept them. Poverty and disgrace are things that all people hate, and yet unless they are avoided in the proper way I will not despise them. If the gentleman abandons benevolence, how can he fulfill the requirements of that name? The gentleman does not go against benevolence even for the amount of time required to finish a meal. Even in times of urgency or distress, he necessarily accords with it."

4.8 子曰："朝聞道，夕死可矣！"

4.8 The Master said, "If a man in the morning hears the Dao, he may die in the evening without regret."

4.9 子曰："士志於道，而恥惡衣惡食者，未足与議也！"

4.9 The Master said, "Aspiring to the Way, but ashamed of bad clothes and bad food: such a person knows nothing worth discussing."

4.10 子曰："君子之於天下也，無適也，無莫也，義之與比。"

4.10 The Master said, "With regard to the world, the gentleman has no predispositions for or against any person. He merely follows what is righteous."

4.16　子曰:"君子喻於義,小人喻於利。"

4.16　The Master said, "The gentleman is motivated by rightness, whereas the petty person is motivated by profit."

7.12　子曰:"富而可求也,雖執鞭之士,吾亦爲之。如不可求,從吾所好。"

7.12　The Master said, "If there were an honorable way to get rich, I'd do it, even if it meant being a stooge standing around with a whip. But if there isn't an honorable way, I just do what I like."

7.16　子曰:"飯疏食飲水,曲肱而枕之,樂亦在其中矣。不義而富且貴,於我如浮雲。"

7.16　The Master said, "Eating plain food and drinking water, having only your bent arm as a pillow—certainly there is joy to be found in this! Wealth and eminence attained improperly concern me no more than the floating clouds."

8.13　子曰:"篤信好學,守死善道。危邦不入,亂邦不居,天下有道則見,無道則隱。邦有道,貧且賤焉,恥也,邦無道,富且貴焉,恥也。"

8.13　The Master said, "Be sincerely trustworthy and love learning, and hold fast to the good Way until death. Do not enter a state that is endangered, and do not reside in a state that is disordered. If the Dao is being realized in the world, then show yourself; if it is not, then go into reclusion. In a state that has the Dao, if you are poor and of low status, you should feel shamed; in a state that is without the Dao, if you are wealthy and honored, you should also feel ashamed."

《孟子》/ Mencius

1A.1　孟子見梁惠王。王曰："叟！不遠千里而來，亦將有以利吾國乎？"

孟子對曰："王！何必曰利？亦有仁義而已矣。王曰：'何以利吾國？'大夫曰：'何以利吾家？'士庶人曰：'何以利吾身？'上下交徵利而國危矣。萬乘之國，弒其君者，必千乘之家；千乘之國，弒其君者，必百乘之家。萬取千焉，千取百焉，不爲不多矣。苟爲後義而先利，不奪不饜。未有仁而遺其親者也，未有義而後其君者也。王亦曰仁義而已矣，何必曰利？"

1A．1　Mencius went to see King Hui of Liang. The king said, "Venerable sir, since you have not counted it far to come here, a distance of a thousand li, may I presume that you are provided with counsels to profit my kingdom?"

Mencius replied, "Why must your Majesty use that word 'profit'? What I am provided with, are counsels to benevolence and righteousness, and these are my only topics. If your Majesty say, 'What is to be done to profit my kingdom?' The great officers will say, 'What is to be done to profit our families?' and the inferior officers and the common people will say, 'What is to be done to profit our persons?' From superiors to inferiors all will try to snatch this profit, and the kingdom will be endangered. In the kingdom of ten thousand chariots, the murderer of his sovereign shall be the chief of a family of a thousand chariots. In the kingdom of a thousand chariots, the murderer of his prince shall be the chief of a family of a hundred chariots. To have a thousand in ten thousand, and a hundred in a thousand, cannot be said not to be a large allotment, but if righteousness be put last, and profit be put first, they will not be satisfied without snatching all. There never has been a benevolent man who neglected his parents. There never has been a righteous man who made his sovereign an after consideration. Let Your Majesty also say benevolence and righteousness, and let these be your only themes. Why must you use that word—'profit'?"

1A.7 齊宣王問曰:"齊桓、晉文之事可得聞乎?"

孟子對曰:"仲尼之徒,無道桓、文之事者,是以後世無傳焉;臣未之聞也。無以,則王乎?"

曰:"德何如則可以王矣?"

曰:"保民而王,莫之能禦也。"

曰:"若寡人者,可以保民乎哉?"

曰:"可。"

曰:"何由知吾可也?"

曰:"臣聞之胡齕曰,王坐於堂上,有牽牛而過堂下者,王見之,曰:'牛何之?'對曰:'將以釁鐘。'王曰:'捨之!吾不忍其觳觫,若無罪而就死地。'對曰:'然則廢釁鐘與?'曰:'何可廢也?以羊易之!'不識有諸?"

曰:"有之。"

曰:"是心足以王矣。百姓皆以王爲愛也。臣固知王之不忍也。"

王曰:"然。誠有百姓者。齊國雖褊小,吾何愛一牛?即不忍其觳觫,若無罪而就死地,故以羊易之也。"

曰:"王無異於百姓之以王爲愛也。以小易大,彼惡知之?王若隱其無罪而就死地,則牛羊何擇焉?"

王笑曰:"是誠何心哉?我非愛其財而易之以羊也。宜乎百姓之謂我愛也。"

曰:"無傷也,是乃仁術也,見牛未見羊也。君子之於禽獸也,見其生,不忍見其死;聞其聲,不忍食其肉。是以君子遠庖廚也。"

王說曰:"《詩》云:'他人有心,予忖度之。'夫子之謂也。夫我乃行之,反而求之,不得吾心。夫子言之,於我心有戚戚焉。此心之所以合於王者,何也?"

曰:"有復於王者曰:'吾力足以舉百鈞,而不足以舉一羽;明足以察秋毫之末,而不見輿薪。'則王許之乎?"

曰:"否。"

"今恩足以及禽獸,而功不至於百姓者,獨何與?然則一羽之不舉,爲不用力焉;輿薪之不見,爲不用明焉;百姓之不見保,爲不用恩焉。故王之不王,不爲也,非不能也。"

曰:"不爲者與不能者之形何以異?"

曰:"挾太山以超北海,語人曰:'我不能。'是誠不能也。爲長者折枝,語人曰:'我不能。'是不爲也,非不能也。故王之不王,非挾太山以超北海之類也;王之不王,是折枝之類也。老吾老,以及人之老;幼吾幼,以及人之幼,天下可運於掌。

《詩》云：'刑於寡妻，至於兄弟，以御於家邦。'言舉斯心加諸彼而已。故推恩足以保四海，不推恩無以保妻子。古之人所以大過人者，無他焉，善推其所爲而已矣。今恩足以及禽獸，而功不至於百姓者，獨何與？權，然後知輕重；度，然後知長短。物皆然，心爲甚。王請度之！抑王興甲兵，危士臣，構怨於諸侯，然後快於心與？"

王曰："否！吾何快於是？將以求吾所大欲也。"

曰："王之所大欲，可得聞與？"

王笑而不言。

曰："爲肥甘不足於口與，輕暖不足於體與？抑爲采色不足視於目與？聲音不足聽於耳與？便嬖不足使令於前與？王之諸臣，皆足以供之，而王豈爲是哉？"

曰："否！吾不爲是也。"

曰："然則王之所大欲可知已，欲辟土地，朝秦楚，莅中國而撫四夷也。以若所爲，求若所欲，猶緣木而求魚也。"

王曰："若是其甚與？"

曰："殆有甚焉。緣木求魚，雖不得魚，無後災；以若所爲，求若所欲，盡心力而爲之，後必有災。"

曰："可得聞與？"

曰："鄒人與楚人戰，則王以爲孰勝？"

曰："楚人勝。"

曰："然則小固不可以敵大，寡固不可以敵衆，弱固不可以敵強。海內之地方千里者九，齊集有其一。以一服八，何以異於鄒敵楚哉？蓋亦反其本矣。今王發政施仁，使天下仕者皆欲立於王之朝，耕者皆欲耕於王之野，商賈皆欲藏於王之市，行旅皆欲出於王之途，天下之欲疾其君者皆欲赴愬於王。其若是，孰能御之？"

王曰："吾惛，不能進於是矣。願夫子輔吾志，明以教我。我雖不敏，請嘗試之。"

曰："無恆產而有恆心者，惟士爲能。若民，則無恆產，因無恆心。苟無恆心，放辟邪侈無不爲已。及陷於罪，然後從而刑之，是罔民也。焉有仁人在位罔民而可爲也？是故明君制民之產，必使仰足以事父母，俯足以畜妻子，樂歲終身飽，凶年免於死亡；然後驅而之善，故民之從之也輕。

"今之制民之產，仰不足以事父母，俯不足以畜妻子；樂歲終身苦，凶年不免於死亡。此惟救死而恐不贍，奚暇治禮義哉？

"王欲行之，則盍反其本矣：五畝之宅，樹之以桑，五十者可以衣帛矣。雞豚狗彘之畜，無失其時，七十者可以食肉矣。百畝之田，勿奪其時，八口之家可以無饑矣。謹庠序之教,申之以孝悌之義,頒白者不負戴於道路矣。老者衣帛食肉,黎民不饑不寒,然而不王者,未之有也。"

1A.7 King Xuan of Qi asked, saying, "May I be informed by you of the transactions of Huan of Qi and Wen of Jin?"

Mencius replied, "There were none of the disciples of Zhong Ni who spoke about the affairs of Huan and Wen, and therefore they have not been transmitted to these after-ages—your servant has not heard them. If you will have me speak, let it be about royal government."

The king said, "What virtue must there be in order to attain royal sway?"

Mencius answered, "The love and protection of the people; with this there is no power which can prevent a ruler from attaining to it."

The king asked again, "Is such a person as I competent to love and protect the people?"

Mencius said, "Yes."

"How do you know that I am competent for that?"

"I heard the following incident from Hu He: 'The king,' said he, 'was sitting aloft in the hall, when a man appeared, leading an ox past the lower part of it. The king saw him, and asked, "Where is the ox going?" The man replied, "We are going to consecrate a bell with its blood." The king said, "Let it go. I cannot bear its frightened appearance, as if it were an innocent person going to the place of death." The man answered, "Shall we then omit the consecration of the bell?" The king said, "How can that be omitted? Change it for a sheep."' I do not know whether this incident really occurred."

The king replied, "It did."

Mencius said, "The heart seen in this is sufficient to carry you to the royal sway. The people all supposed that Your Majesty grudged the animal, but your servant knows surely, that it was Your Majesty's not being able to bear the sight, which made you do as you did."

The king said, "You are right. And yet there really was an appearance of what the people condemned. But though Qi be a small and narrow state, how should I grudge one ox? Indeed it was because I could not bear its frightened appearance, as if it were an innocent person going to the place of death, that therefore I changed it for a sheep."

Mencius pursued, "Let not Your Majesty deem it strange that the people should think you were grudging the animal. When you chang a large one for a small, how should they know the true reason? If you felt pained by its being led without guilt to the place of death, what was there to choose between an ox and a sheep?"

The king laughed and said, "What really was my mind in the matter? I did not grudge the expense of it, and change it for a sheep! There was reason in the people's saying that I grudged it."

"There is no harm in their saying so," said Mencius. "Your conduct was an artifice of benevolence. You saw the ox, and had not seen the sheep. So is the superior man affected towards animals, that, having seen them alive, he cannot bear to see them die; having heard their dying cries, he cannot bear to eat their flesh. Therefore, he keeps away from his slaughter house and cook room."

The king was pleased, and said, "It is said in *The Book of Odes*, 'The minds of others, I am able by reflection to measure,'—this is verified, my Master, in your discovery of my motive. I indeed did the thing, but when I turned my thoughts inward, and examined into it, I could not discover my own mind. When you, Master, spoke those words, the movements of compassion began to work in my mind. How is it that this heart has in it what is equal to the royal sway?"

Mencius replied, "Suppose a man were to make this statement to Your Majesty—'My strength is sufficient to lift three thousand catties, but it is not sufficient to lift one feather; my eyesight is sharp enough to examine the point of an autumn hair, but I do not see a waggon-load of faggots,' would Your Majesty allow what he said?"

"No," was the answer, on which Mencius proceeded, "Now here is kindness sufficient to reach animals, and no benefits are extended from it to the people. How is this? Is an exception to be made here? The truth is, the feather is not lifted, because strength is not used; the waggon-load of firewood is not seen, because the eyesight is not used; and the people are not loved and protected, because kindness is not employed. Therefore, Your Majesty's not exercising the royal sway, is because you do not do it, not because you are not able to do it."

The king asked, "How may the difference between not doing a thing and not being able to do it be represented?"

Mencius replied, "In such a thing as taking the Tai Mountain under your arm, and leaping over the North Sea with it, if you say to people 'I am not able to do it,' that is a real case of not being able. In such a matter as breaking off a branch from a tree at the order of a superior, if you say to people 'I am not able to do it,' that is a case of not doing it; it is not a case of not being able to do it. Therefore Your Majesty's not exercising the royal sway, is not such a case as that of taking the Tai Mountain under your arm, and leaping over the North Sea with it. Your Majesty's not exercising the royal sway is a case like that of breaking off a branch from a tree. Treat with the reverence due to age the elders in your own family, so that the elders in the families of others shall be similarly treated; treat with the kindness due to youth the young in your own family, so that the young in the families of others shall be similarly treated—do this, and the kingdom may be made to go round in your palm. It is said in *The Book of Odes*, 'His example affected his wife. It reached his brothers, and his family of the state was governed by it.' The language shows how King Wen simply took his kindly heart, and exercised it towards those parties. Therefore the carrying out his kindness of heart by a prince will suffice for the love and protection of all within the four seas, and if he does not carry it out, he will not be able to protect his wife and children. The way in which the ancients came greatly to surpass other men, was no other but this—simply that they knew well how to carry out, so as to affect others, what they themselves did. Now your kindness is sufficient to reach animals, and no benefits are extended from it to reach the people. How is this? Is an exception to be made here? By weighing, we know what things are light, and what heavy. By measuring, we know what things are long, and what short. The relations of all things may be thus determined, and it is of the greatest importance to estimate the motions of the mind. I beg Your Majesty to measure it. You collect your equipments of war, endanger your soldiers and officers, and excite the resentment of the other princes—do these things cause you pleasure in your mind?"

The king replied, "No. How should I derive pleasure from these things? My object in them is to seek for what I greatly desire."

Mencius said, "May I hear from you what it is that you greatly desire?" The king laughed and did not speak.

Mencius resumed, "Are you led to desire it, because you have not enough of rich and sweet food for your mouth? Or because you have not enough of light and warm clothing for your body? Or because you have not enough of beautifully colored objects to delight your eyes? Or because you have not voices and tones enough to please your ears? Or because you have not enough of attendants and favorites to stand before you and receive your orders? Your Majesty's various officers are sufficient to supply you with those things. How can Your Majesty be led to entertain such a desire on account of them?"

"No," said the king, "my desire is not on account of them."

Mencius added, "Then, what Your Majesty greatly desires may be known. You wish to enlarge your territories, to have Qin and Chu wait at your court, to rule the Middle Kingdom, and to attract to you the barbarous tribes that surround it. But doing what you do to seek for what you desire is like climbing a tree to seek for fish."

The king said, "Is it so bad as that?"

"It is even worse," was the reply. "If you climb a tree to seek for fish, although you do not get the fish, you will not suffer any subsequent calamity. But doing what you do to seek for what you desire, doing it moreover with all your heart, you will assuredly afterwards meet with calamities."

The king asked, "May I hear from you the proof of that?"

Mencius said, "If the people of Zou should fight with the people of Chu, which of them does Your Majesty think would conquer?"

"The people of Chu would conquer."

"Yes and so it is certain that a small country cannot contend with a great, that few cannot contend with many, and that the weak cannot contend with the strong. The territory within the four seas embraces nine divisions, each of a thousand li square. All Qi together is but one of them. If with one part you try to subdue the other eight, what is the difference between that and Zou's contending with Chu? For, with such a desire, you must turn back to the proper course for its attainment. Now if Your Majesty will institute a government whose action shall be benevolent, this will cause all the officers in the kingdom to wish to stand in Your Majesty's court, all the farmers to wish to plough in Your Majesty's fields, all the merchants, both travelling and stationary, to wish to store their goods in Your Majesty's market places, all travelling strangers to wish to make their tours on your Majesty's roads, and all throughout the kingdom who feel aggrieved by their rulers to wish to come and complain to Your Majesty. And when they are so bent, who will be able to keep them back?"

The king said, "I am stupid, and not able to advance to this. I wish you, my Master, to assist my intentions. Teach me clearly; although I am deficient in intelligence and vigor, I will essay and try to carry your instructions into effect."

Mencius replied, "They are only men of education, who, without a certain livelihood, are able to maintain a fixed heart. As to the people, if they have not a certain livelihood, it follows that they will not have a fixed heart. And if they have not a fixed heart, there is nothing that they will not do, in the way of self-abandonment, of moral deflection, of depravity, and of wild license. When they thus have been involved in crime, to follow them up and punish them—this is to entrap the people. How can such a thing as entrapping the people be done under the rule of a benevolent man? Therefore an intelligent ruler will regulate the livelihood of the people, so as to make sure that, for those above them, they shall have sufficient wherewith to serve their parents, and, for those below them, they shall have sufficient wherewith to support their wives and children; that in good years they shall always be abundantly satisfied, and that in bad years they shall escape the danger of perishing. After this he may urge them, and they will proceed to what is good, for in this case the people will follow after it with ease. Now, the livelihood of the people is so regulated, that, above, they have not sufficient wherewith to serve their parents, and, below, they have not sufficient wherewith to support their wives and children. Notwithstanding good years, their lives are continually embittered, and, in bad years, they do not escape perishing. In such circumstances they only try to save themselves from death, and are afraid they will not succeed. What leisure have they to cultivate propriety and righteousness? If Your Majesty wishes to effect this regulation of the livelihood of the people, why not turn to that which is the essential step to it? Let mulberry trees be planted about the homesteads with their five mu, and persons of fifty years may be clothed with silk. In keeping fowls, pigs, dogs, and swine, let not their times of breeding be neglected, and persons of seventy years may eat flesh. Let there not be taken away the time that is proper for the cultivation of the farm with its hundred mu, and the family of eight mouths that is supported by it shall not suffer from hunger. Let careful attention be paid to education in schools, especially the inculcation of the filial and fraternal duties, and grey-haired men will not be seen upon the roads, carrying burdens on their backs or on their heads. It never has been that the ruler of a state where such results were seen, the old wearing silk and eating flesh, and the black-haired people suffering neither from hunger nor cold, did not attain to the royal dignity."

6B.4 宋牼將之楚，孟子遇於石丘，曰："先生將何之？"曰："吾聞秦楚構兵，我將見楚王說而罷之。楚王不悅，我將見秦王說而罷之。二王我將有所遇焉。"曰："軻也請無問其詳，願聞其指。說之將何如？"曰："我將言其不利也。"曰："先生之志則大矣，先生之號則不可。先生以利說秦楚之王，秦楚之王悅於利，以罷三軍之師,是三軍之士樂罷而悦於利也。爲人臣者懷利以事其君,爲人子者懷利以事其父,爲人弟者懷利以事其兄,是君臣、父子、兄弟終去仁義,懷利以相接,然而不亡者,未之有也。先生以仁義説秦楚之王,秦楚之王悦於仁義,而罷三軍之師,是三軍之士樂罷而悦於仁義也。爲人臣者懷仁義以事其君,爲人子者懷仁義以事其父,爲人弟者懷仁義以事其兄,是君臣、父子、兄弟去利,懷仁義以相接也,然而不王者,未之有也。何必曰利?」

6B.4 Song Keng being about to go to Chu, Mencius met him in Shi Qiu. "Master, where are you going?" asked Mencius.

Keng replied, "I have heard that Qin and Chu are fighting together, and I am going to see the king of Chu and persuade him to cease hostilities. If he shall not be pleased with my advice, I shall go to see the king of Qin, and persuade him in the same way. Of the two kings I shall surely find that I can succeed with one of them."

Mencius said, "I will not venture to ask about the particulars, but I should like to hear the scope of your plan. What course will you take to try to persuade them?"

Keng answered, "I will tell them how unprofitable their course is to them."

"Master," said Mencius, "your aim is great, but your argument is not good. If you, starting from the point of profit, offer your persuasive counsels to the kings of Qin and Chu, and if those kings are pleased with the consideration of profit so as to stop the movements of their armies, then all belonging to those armies will rejoice in the cessation of war, and find their pleasure in the pursuit of profit. Ministers will serve their sovereign for the profit of which they cherish the thought; sons will serve their fathers, and younger brothers will serve their elder brothers, for the same consideration—and the issue will be that, abandoning benevolence and righteousness, sovereign and minister, father and son, elder and younger brothers, will carry on all their intercourse with this thought of profit cherished in their breasts. But never has there been such a state of society, without ruin being the result of it. If you, starting from the ground of benevolence and righteousness, offer your counsels to the kings of Qin and Chu, and if those kings are pleased with the consideration of benevolence and righteousness so as to stop the operations of their armies, then all belonging to those armies will rejoice in the stopping from war, and find their pleasure in benevolence and righteousness. Ministers will serve their sovereign, cherishing the principles of benevolence and righteousness; sons will serve their fathers, and younger brothers will serve their elder brothers, in the same way and so, sovereign and minister, father and son, elder and younger brothers, abandoning the thought of profit, will cherish the principles of benevolence and righteousness, and carry on all their intercourse upon them. But never has there been such a state of society, without rising to the royal sway. Why must you use that word 'profit'?"

7A.25　孟子曰："雞鳴而起，孳孳為善者，舜之徒也；雞鳴而起，孳孳為利者，蹠之徒也。欲知舜與蹠之分，無他，利與善之間也。"

7A.25　Mencius said, "He who rises at cock-crowing and addresses himself earnestly to the practice of virtue, is a disciple of Shun. He who rises at cock-crowing, and addresses himself earnestly to the pursuit of gain, is a disciple of Zhi. If you want to know what separates Shun from Zhi, it is simply this: the interval between the thought of gain and the thought of virtue."

7A.26　孟子曰："楊子取為我，拔一毛而利天下，不為也。墨子兼愛，摩頂放踵利天下，為之。子莫執中。執中為近之。執中無權，猶執一也。所惡執一者，為其賊道也，舉一而廢百也。"

7A.26　Mencius said, "The principle of the philosopher Yang was 'Each one for himself'. Though he might have benefited the whole kingdom by plucking out a single hair, he would not have done it. The philosopher Mo loves all equally. If by rubbing smooth his whole body from the crown to the heel, he could have benefited the kingdom, he would have done it. Zi

Mo holds a medium between these. By holding that medium, he is nearer the right. But by holding it without leaving room for the exigency of circumstances, it becomes like their holding their one point. The reason why I hate that holding to one point is the injury it does to the way of right principle. It takes up one point and disregards a hundred others."

《墨子》/ Mozi

尚賢下第十
Chapter 10　Exaltation of the Virtuous Ⅲ

……

是故古之聖王之治天下也，其所富，其所貴，未必王公大人骨肉之親、無故富貴、面目美好者也。是故昔者舜耕於歷山，陶於河瀕，漁於雷澤，灰於常陽，堯得之服澤之陽，立爲天子，使接天下之政，而治天下之民。昔伊尹爲莘氏女師僕，使爲庖人，湯得而舉之，立爲三公，使接天下之政，治天下之民。昔者傅説居北海之洲，圜土之上，衣褐帶索，庸築於傅岩之城，武丁得而舉之，立爲三公，使之接天下之政，而治天下之民。是故昔者堯之舉舜也，湯之舉伊尹也，武丁之舉傅説也，豈以爲骨肉之親、無故富貴、面目美好者哉？惟法其言，用其謀，行其道，上可而利天，中可而利鬼，下可而利人，是故推而上之。

…

To the contrary, in governing the empire the sage-kings of old enriched and honored those who were not necessarily their relatives, the rich without merit, or the good-looking. At one time Shun cultivated land at Mt. Li, made pottery by the river, engaged in fishing in Lake Lei, and went peddling in Changyang. Yao discovered him at Fuze, made him emperor, and handed him the government of the empire and the rule over the people. Yi Yin once took part in the bridal party of the daughter of the Prince of Xin, and then was employed as a cook. Tang discovered him and exalted him to be High Duke, handing him the government of the empire and the rule over the people. Once Fu Yue lived in the District of Beihai and built the prison walls. His clothing was of coarse cloth and tied with ropes. Wu Ding discovered him and exalted him to be High Duke, handing him the government of the empire and the rule over the people. Now, when Yao exalted Shun, Tang exalted Yi Yin, and Wu Ding exalted Fu Yue, was it because they were their relatives, the rich without merit, or the good-looking? It was only because by adopting their views, carrying out their plans, and following their ways, Heaven on high would be blessed, the spirits in the middle would be blessed, and the people below would be blessed. Therefore they were promoted and exalted.

……先王之治天下也，必選擇賢者以爲其群屬輔佐。曰：今也天下之士君子，皆欲富貴而惡貧賤。曰：然女何爲而得富貴而辟貧賤？莫若爲賢。爲賢之道將奈何？曰有力者疾以助人，有財者勉以分人，有道者勸以教人。若此則飢者得食，寒者得衣，亂者得治。若飢則得食，寒則得衣，亂則得治，此安生生。

... when the ancient kings reigned over the empire they invariably selected the virtuous and made them officials and aids. The gentlemen in the world like riches and honor, and dislike poverty and humility. Now how can you obtain the former and avoid the latter? There is no better way than to practice virtue. What then is the way to practice virtue? Let him who has strength be alert to help others, let him who has wealth endeavor to share it with others, and let him who possesses the Dao teach others persuasively. With this, the hungry will be fed, the cold will be clothed, the disturbed will have order. When the hungry are fed, the cold are clothed, and the disturbed have order, this is procuring abundant life.

今王公大人其所富，其所貴，皆王公大人骨肉之親、無故富貴、面目美好者也。今王公大人骨肉之親、無故富貴、面目美好者，爲故必知哉！若不知，使治其國家，則其國家之亂可得而知也。今天下之士君子皆欲富貴而惡貧賤。然女何爲而得富貴，而辟貧賤哉？曰莫若爲王公大人骨肉之親、無故富貴、面目美好者。王公大人骨肉之親、無故富貴、面目美好者，此非可學能者也。使不知辯，德行之厚若禹、湯、文、武不加得也，王公大人骨肉之親，躄、瘖、聾、暴爲桀、紂，不加失也。是故以賞不當賢,罰不當暴,其所賞者已無故矣,其所罰者亦無罪。是以使百姓皆攸心解體,沮以爲善,垂其股肱之力而不相勞來也;腐臭余財,而不相分資也,隱慝良道,而不相教誨也。若此,則飢者不得食,寒者不得衣,亂者不得治。

But those whom the rulers now are enriching and honoring are all their relatives, the rich without merit, and the good-looking. What can there be that guarantees these to be wise? When the unwise are charged with the government of the country, disorder in the country can be predicted. Now the gentlemen of the world like riches and honor, and dislike poverty and humility. But how can you obtain the former and avoid the latter? There seems to be no other way than to be the rulers' relatives, the rich without merit, and the good-looking. Evidently one cannot become these by learning. So, when the art of judging is not understood, although some virtuous people may even compare with Yu, Tang, Wen, and Wu, there will be no commendation. And, although a relative of the ruler may be lame and dumb, deaf and blind, and evil like Jie and Zhou, there will be no condemnation. Therefore reward does not fall on the virtuous or punishment on the evil. As those rewarded are without merit, those punished are naturally without guilt. And so, people all became disintegrated in heart and dissipated in body, and despairing of doing good. With all their strength unused, they would not help one another; with all unused supplies rotting and fermenting, they would not share with one another; hiding the excellent Dao they would not show it to others. As a result of this, the hungry are not fed, the cold are not clothed, and the disturbed are not given order.

兼愛中第十五
Chapter 15　Universal Love Ⅱ

见"孝悌"部分《墨子》选读。

For the English translation of this chapter, see Part I of this book.

天志中第二十七
Chapter 27　Will of Heaven Ⅱ

子墨子言曰：今天下之君子之欲爲仁義者，則不可不察義之所從出。既曰不可以不察義之所欲出，然則義何從出？子墨子曰：義不從愚且賤者出，必自貴且知者出。何以知義之不從愚且賤者出，而必自貴且知者出也？曰：義者，善政也。何以知義之爲言政也？曰：天下有義則治，無義則亂，是以知義之爲善政也。夫愚且賤者，不得爲政乎貴且知者，然後得爲政乎愚且賤者，此吾所以知義之不從愚且賤者出，而必自貴且知者出也。然則孰爲貴？孰爲知？曰：天爲貴、天爲知而已矣。然則義果自天出矣。

Mozi said: Those gentlemen in the world who want to practice magnanimity and righteousness cannot but examine the origin of righteousness. Since we want to examine the origin of righteousness, then where does it originate? Mozi said: Righteousness does not originate with the stupid and humble but with the honorable and wise. How do we know it does not originate with the dull and humble but with the honorable and wise? For, righteousness is the standard. How do we know righteousness is the standard? For, with righteousness the world will be orderly and without it the world will be disorderly. Therefore righteousness is known to be the standard. As the dull and the humble cannot make the standard, and only the wise and honorable can, therefore I know righteousness does not come from the stupid and humble but from the honorable and wise. Now who is honorable and who is wise? Heaven is honorable; Heaven is wise. So, then, righteousness must originate with Heaven.

今天下之人曰：當若天子之貴諸侯，諸侯之貴大夫，高明知之。然吾未知天之貴且知於天子也。子墨子曰：吾所以知天之貴且知於天子者，有矣。曰：天子爲善，天能賞之。天子爲暴，天能罰之。天子有疾病禍祟，必齋戒沐浴，潔爲酒醴粢盛，以祭祀天鬼，則天能除去之。然吾未知天之祈福於天子也，此吾所以知天之貴且知於天子者。不止此而已矣，又以先王之書馴天明不解之道也知之。曰：明哲維天,臨君下土。則此語天之貴且知於天子。不知亦有貴知夫天者乎？曰：天爲貴、天爲知而已矣。然則義果自天出矣。

People in the world would say, "That the emperor is more honorable than the feudal lords and that the feudal lords are more honorable than the ministers, we clearly see. But that Heaven is more honorable and wise than the emperor, we do not see." Mozi said: I know Heaven is more honorable and wise than the emperor for a reason: when the emperor practices virtue Heaven rewards, when the emperor does evil Heaven punishes. When there are diseases and calamities the emperor will purify and bathe himself and prepare clean cakes and wine to do sacrifice and libation to Heaven and the spirits. Heaven then removes them. But I have not yet heard of Heaven invoking the emperor for blessing. So I know Heaven is more honorable and wise than the emperor. And, this is not all. We also learn of this from the book of the ancient kings which instructs us the vast and ineffable Dao of Heaven. It says: Brilliant and perspicacious Heaven on High, who enlightens and watches over the earth below! This shows Heaven is more honorable and wise than the emperor. But is there yet anyone more honorable and wise than Heaven? Heaven is really the most honorable and wise. Therefore, righteousness surely comes from Heaven.

是故子墨子曰：今天下之君子,中實將欲遵道利民,本察仁義之本,天之意不可不慎也。既以天之意以爲不可不慎已,然則天之將何欲何憎？子墨子曰：天之意,不欲大國之攻小國也,大家之亂小家也,強之暴寡,詐之謀愚,貴之傲賤,此天之所不欲也。不止此而已,欲人之有力相營,有道相教,有財相分也。又欲上之強聽治也,下之強從事也。上強聽治,則國家治矣。下強從事,則財用足矣。若國家治,財用足,則內有以潔爲酒醴粢盛,以祭祀天鬼；外有以爲環璧珠玉,以聘撓四鄰。諸侯之冤不興矣,邊境兵甲不作矣。內有以食饑息勞,持養其萬民,則君臣上下惠忠,父子弟兄慈孝。故唯毋明乎順天之意,奉而光施之天下,則刑政治,萬民和、國家富,財用足,百姓皆得暖衣飽食,便寧無憂。是故子墨子曰：今天下之君子,中實將欲遵道利民,本察仁義之本,天之意不可不慎也。

And hence Mozi said: If the gentlemen of the world really desire to follow the way and benefit the people, they must not disobey the will of Heaven, the origin of magnanimity and righteousness. Now that we must obey the will of Heaven, what does the will of Heaven desire and what does it abominate? Mozi said: The will of Heaven abominates the large state which attacks small states, the large house which molests small houses, the strong who plunder the weak, the clever who deceive the stupid, and the honored who disdain the humble—these are what the will of Heaven abominates. On the other hand, it desires people having energy to work for each other, those knowing the way to teach each other, and those possessing wealth to share with each other. And it desires the superior diligently to attend to government and the subordinate diligently to attend to their work. When the superior attends to the government diligently, the country will be orderly. When the subordinate attend to work diligently, wealth will be abundant. When the country is orderly and wealth is abundant, within the state there will be wherewith to prepare clean cakes and wine to sacrifice to God and the spirits, and in relation to outside countries there will be wherewith to furnish rings, stones, pearls, and jades by which to befriend surrounding neighbors. With the grudges of the feudal lords inactive and fighting on the borders suspended, and the people within provided with food and rest, the emperor and the ministers and the superiors and subordinates will be gracious and loyal respectively, and father and son and elder and younger brothers will be affectionate and filial respectively. Therefore when the principle of obeying the will of Heaven is understood and widely practiced in the world, then justice and government will be orderly, the multitudes will be harmonious, the country will be wealthy, the supplies will be plenteous, and the people will be warmly clothed and sufficiently fed, peaceful and without worry. Therefore Mozi said: If the gentlemen of the world really desire to follow the Dao and benefit the people they must carefully investigate the principle that the will of Heaven is the origin of magnanimity and righteousness.

且夫天子之有天下也，辟之無以異乎國君諸侯之有四境之内也。今國君諸侯之有四境之内也，夫豈欲其臣國萬民之相爲不利哉！今若處大國則攻小國，處大家則亂小家，欲以此求賞譽，終不可得，誅罰必至矣。夫天之有天下也，將無已異此。今若處大國則攻小國，處大都則伐小都，欲以此求福祿於天，福祿終不得，而禍祟必至矣。

The rule of Heaven over the world is not unlike the rule of the feudal lord over the state. In ruling the state does the feudal lord desire his ministers and people to work for mutual disadvantage? If leading a large state one attacks small states, if leading a large house one molests small houses and if by doing this one seeks reward and commendation [from the feudal lord], he cannot obtain it. On the contrary, punishment will visit him. Now, the rule of Heaven over the world is not unlike this. If leading a large state one attacks small states, if leading a large house one molests small houses and if by doing this one seeks reward and commendation [from Heaven], he cannot obtain it. On the contrary, punishment will visit him.

然有所不爲天之所欲，而爲天之所不欲，則夫天亦且不爲人之所欲，而爲人之所不欲矣。人之所不欲者何也？曰：病疾禍祟也。若己不爲天之所欲，而爲天之所不欲，是率天下之萬民以從事乎禍祟之中也。故古者聖王，明知天鬼之所福，而辟天鬼之所憎，以求興天下之利，而除天下之害。是以天之爲寒熱也節，四時調，陰陽雨露也時，五穀孰，六畜遂，疾菑戾疫凶饑則不至。是故子墨子曰：今天下之君子，中實將欲遵道利民，本察仁義之本，天意不可不慎也。

When [man] does not do what Heaven desires, but does what Heaven abominates, Heaven will also not do what man desires but do what he abominates. What man abominates are disease and calamities. Therefore not to do what Heaven desires but do what it abominates is to lead the multitudes in the world to calamity. Therefore the ancient sage-kings studied what Heaven and the spirits would bless and avoided what they would curse in order to procure benefits for the world and avoid calamities.

Thereupon, Heaven made heat and cold temperate, the four seasons harmonious, the Yin and Yang and rain and dew timely. The five grains were enabled to ripen and the six animals to mature. And disease, pestilence, and famine did not happen. Therefore Mozi said: If the gentlemen of the world really desire to follow the Dao and benefit the people they must be mindful of the principle that the will of Heaven is the origin of magnanimity and righteousness.

且夫天下蓋有不仁不祥者，曰：當若子之不事父，弟之不事兄，臣之不事君也。故天下之君子與謂之不祥者。今夫天，兼天下而愛之，撽遂萬物以利之，若豪之末，非天之所爲也，而民得而利之，則可謂否矣。然獨無報夫天，而不知其爲不仁不祥也。此吾所謂君子明細而不明大也。

In the world those who lack benevolence are unfortunate. If a son does not serve his father, a younger brother does not serve his elder brother, or a subordinate does not serve his superior, then all the gentlemen of the world will call him unfortunate. Now Heaven loves the whole world universally. Everything is prepared for the good of man. Even the tip of a hair is the work of Heaven. Substantial may be said of the benefits that are enjoyed by man. Yet there is no service in return. And they do not even know this to be unmagnanimous and unfortunate. This is why I say the gentlemen understand only trifles and not things of importance.

且吾所以知天之愛民之厚者，有矣。曰：以磨爲日月星辰，以昭道之。制爲四時春秋冬夏，以紀綱之。雷降雪霜雨露，以長遂五穀麻絲，使民得而財利之。列爲山川溪谷，播賦百事，以臨司民之善否。爲王公侯伯，使之賞賢而罰暴，賊金木鳥獸，從事乎五穀麻絲，以爲民衣食之財。自古及今，未嘗不有此也。今有人於此，歡若愛其子，竭力單務以利之。其子長，而無報子求父，故天下之君子與謂之不仁不祥。今夫天，兼天下而愛之，撽遂萬物以利之，若豪之末，非天之所爲，而民得而利之，則可謂否矣。然獨無報夫天，而不知其爲不仁不祥也，此吾所謂君子明細而不明大也。

Moreover I know Heaven loves men dearly not without reason. Heaven ordered the sun, the moon, and the stars to enlighten and guide them. Heaven ordained the four seasons, Spring, Autumn, Winter, and Summer, to regulate them. Heaven sent down snow, frost, rain, and dew to grow the five grains and flax and silk so that the people could use and enjoy them. Heaven established the hills and rivers, ravines and valleys, and arranged many things to minister to man's good or bring him evil. He appointed the dukes and lords to reward the virtuous and punish the wicked, and to gather metal and wood, birds and beasts, and to engage in cultivating the five grains and flax and silk to provide for the people's food and clothing. This has been taking from antiquity to the present. Suppose there is a man who is deeply fond of his son and has used his energy to the limit to work for his benefit. But when the son grows up he returns no love to the father. The gentlemen of the world will all call him unmagnanimous and miserable. Now Heaven loves the whole world universally. Everything is prepared for the good of man. The work of Heaven extends to even the smallest things that are enjoyed by man. Such benefits may indeed be said to be substantial, yet there is no service in return. And they do not even know this to be unmagnanimous. This is why I say the gentlemen of the world understand only trifles but not things of importance.

且吾所以知天愛民之厚者，不止此而足矣。曰：殺不辜者，天予不祥。殺不辜者誰也？曰：人也。予之不祥者誰也？曰：天也。若天不愛民之厚，夫胡說人殺不辜而天予之不祥哉？此吾所以知天之愛民之厚也。

Yet this does not exhaust my reasons whereby I know Heaven loves man dearly. It is said the murder of an innocent individual will call down a calamity. Who is the innocent? Man is. From whom is the visitation? From Heaven. If Heaven does not love the people dearly, why should Heaven send down a visitation upon the man who murders the innocent? Thus I know Heaven loves man dearly.

且吾所以知天之愛民之厚者，不止此而已矣。曰：愛人利人，順天之意，得天之賞者，有矣。憎人賊人，反天之意，得天之罰者，亦有矣。

This is still not all by which I know Heaven loves man dearly. There are those who love the people and benefit the people and obey the will of Heaven and obtain reward from Heaven. There are also those who hate the people and oppress the people and oppose the will of Heaven and incur punishment from Heaven.

夫愛人利人，順天之意，得天之賞者，誰也？曰：若昔三代聖王，堯、舜、禹、湯、文、武者是也。堯、舜、禹、湯、文、武焉所從事？曰：從事兼，不從事別。兼者，處大國不攻小國，處大家不亂小家，強不劫弱，衆不暴寡，詐不謀愚，貴不傲賤。觀其事，上利乎天，中利乎鬼，下利乎人。三利無所不利，是謂天德。聚斂天下之美名而加之焉，曰：此仁也，義也。愛人利人，順天之意，得天之賞者也。不止此而已，書於竹帛，鏤之金石，琢之槃盂，傳遺後世子孫，曰：將何以爲？將以識夫愛人利人，順天之意，得天之賞者也。《皇矣》道之曰："帝謂文王，予懷明德，不大聲以色，不長夏以革，不識不知，順帝之則。"帝善其順法則也，故舉殷以賞之，使貴爲天子，富有天下，名譽至今不息。故夫愛人利人，順天之意，得天之賞者，既可得留而已。夫憎人賊人，反天之意，得天之罰者，誰也？曰：若昔者三代暴王桀、紂、幽、厲者是也。桀、紂、幽、厲焉所從事？曰：從事別，不從事兼。別者，處大國則攻小國，處大家則亂小家，強劫弱，衆暴寡，詐謀愚，貴傲賤。觀其事，上不利乎天，中不利乎鬼，下不利乎人，三不利無所利，是謂天賊。聚斂天下之醜名而加之焉，曰：此非仁也，非義也。憎人賊人，反天之意，得天之罰者也。不止此而已，又書其事於竹帛，鏤之金石，琢之槃盂，傳遺後世子孫，曰：將何以爲？將以識夫憎人賊人，反天之意，得天之罰者也。《大誓》之道之，曰："紂越厥夷居，不肯事上帝，棄厥先神祇不祀，乃曰：'吾有命。'毋僇其務。"天亦縱棄紂而不葆。察天以縱棄紂而不葆者，反天之意也。故夫憎人賊人，反天之意，得天之罰者，既可得而知也。

Who are those that love the people and benefit the people, obey the will of Heaven and obtain reward from Heaven? They are the ancient sage-kings of the Three Dynasties, Yao, Shun, Yu, Tang, Wen, and Wu. What did Yao, Shun, Yu, Tang, Wen, and Wu do? They engaged themselves in universality and not partiality [in love]. Loving universally, they did not attack the small states with their large states, and they did not molest the small houses with their large houses. The strong did not plunder the weak, the many did not oppress the few, the clever did not deceive the stupid, and the honored did not disdain the humble. Such a regime was agreeable to Heaven above, to the spirits in the middle sphere, and to the people below. Being helpful to these three, it was helpful to all. And this was Heavenly virtue. The most excellent names in the world were gathered and attributed to them, and they were called magnanimous, righteous, beloved of man and beneficial to the people, obedient to the will of Heaven and rewarded by Heaven. Besides this, it is also recorded on the bamboos and silk, cut in metals and stones, and engraved on the dishes and cups to be handed down to posterity. What is this for? It is to mark out those who loved the people and benefited them, obeyed the will of Heaven and obtained reward from Heaven. Thus "The Ode of Huang Yi" says: "God said to King Wen, 'I cherish your intelligent virtue. It was not proclaimed with much noise or gesture. It was not modified after the possession of the empire. How instructively and naturally submissive to the scheme of Heaven!'" Because he was obedient to God's scheme, He rewarded him with Yin and honored him to be emperor and enriched him with the empire. And his fame is not forgotten even unto this day. Hence we are enabled to know who are those that loved the people and benefited them, obeyed the will of Heaven and obtained reward from Heaven. Now, who are those that hated the people and oppressed them, opposed the will of Heaven and incurred punishment from Heaven? They are the ancient wicked kings of the Three Dynasties, Jie, Zhou, You, and Li. What did they do? They were selfish and ungenerous. Being selfish they attacked the small states with their large states, and they molested the small houses with their large houses. The strong plundered the weak, the many oppressed the few, the clever deceived the ignorant, and the honored disdained the humble. Such a regime was not helpful to Heaven above, to the spirits in the middle sphere, or to the people below. Since it was not helpful to these three, it was helpful to none. And they were called the enemies of Heaven. The most evil names in the world were gathered and attributed to them, and they were called unmagnanimous, unrighteous, haters of man and oppressors of the people, disobedient to the will of Heaven and punished by Heaven. Besides this, it is also recorded on the bamboos and silk, cut in the metals and stones, and engraved on the plates and cups to be handed down to posterity. What is this for? It is to mark out those that hated the people and oppressed them, opposed the will of Heaven and incurred punishment from Heaven. Thus relates "The Great Declaration": "Zhou went beyond the proper limits and became insolent. He would not worship God and pushed away the ancestors and spirits without offering them sacrifices. And he said 'Fortune is with me,' and neglected and betrayed his duty. Heaven thereupon deserted him and withdrew its protection." Heaven deserted Zhou and withdrew its support because Zhou opposed the will of Heaven. Hence we are enabled to know who are those that hated the people and oppressed them, that opposed the will of Heaven and incurred punishment from Heaven.

是故子墨子之有天之，辟人無以異乎輪人之有規，匠人之有矩也。今夫輪人操其規，將以量度天下之圜與不圜也，曰："中吾規者謂之圜，不中吾規者謂之不圜。"是以圜與不圜，皆可得而知也。此其故何？則圜法明也。匠人亦操其矩，將以量度天下之方與不方也，曰："中吾矩者謂之方，不中吾矩者謂之不方。"是以方與不方皆可得而知之。此其故何？則方法明也。故子墨子之有天之意也，上將以度天下之王公大人爲刑政也，下將以量天下之萬民爲文學、出言談也。觀其行，順天之意，謂之善意行。反天之意，謂之不善意行。觀其言談，順天之意，謂之善言談。反天之意，謂之不善言談。觀其刑政，順天之意，謂之善刑政。反天之意，謂之不善刑政。故置此以爲法，立此以爲儀，將以量度天下之王公大人卿大夫之仁與不仁，譬之猶分黑白也。是故子墨子曰：今天下之王公大人士君子，中實將欲遵道利民，本察仁義之本，天之意不可不順也。順天之意者，義之法也。

Therefore the will of Heaven is like the compasses to the wheelwright and the square to the carpenter. The wheelwright tests the circularity of every object in the world with his compasses, saying: "That which satisfies my compasses is circular; that which does not is not circular." Therefore whether an object is circular or not is all known, because the standard of circularity is all established. The carpenter also tests the squareness of every object in the world with his square, saying: "That which satisfies my square is square; that which does not is not square." Therefore whether any object is square or not is all known. Why so? Because the standard of squareness is established. Similarly, with the will of Heaven Mozi will measure the jurisdiction and government of the lords in the empire on the one hand, and the doctrines and teachings of the multitudes in the empire on the other. If some conduct is observed to be in accordance with the will of Heaven, it is called good conduct; if it is in opposition to the will of Heaven it is called bad conduct. If a teaching is observed to be in accordance with the will of Heaven it is called good teaching; if it is in opposition to the will of Heaven it is called bad teaching. And if a government is observed to be in accordance with the will of Heaven it is called good government; if it is in opposition to the will of Heaven it is called bad government. With this as the model and with this as the standard, whether the lords and the ministers are magnanimous or not can be measured as [easily as] to distinguish black and white. Therefore Mozi said: If the rulers and the gentlemen of the world really desire to follow the Dao and benefit the people they have only to obey the will of Heaven, the origin of magnanimity and righteousness. Obedience to the will of Heaven is the standard of righteousness.

非命上第三十五
Chapter 35　Anti-Fatalism Ⅰ

子墨子言曰：古者王公大人爲政國家者，皆欲國家之富，人民之衆，刑政之治。然而不得富而得貧，不得衆而得寡，不得治而得亂，則是本失其所欲，得其所惡，是故何也？子墨子言曰：執有命者以雜於民間者衆。執有命者之言曰："命富則富，命貧則貧，命衆則衆，命寡則寡，命治則治，命亂則亂，命壽則壽，命夭則夭。命雖強勁，何益哉？"上以說王公大人，下以駔百姓之從事。故執有命者不仁，故當執有命者之言，不可不明辨。

Mozi said: At present, in governing the states the rulers all desire to have their countries wealthy, their population large, and their administration orderly. But instead of wealth they obtain poverty, instead of an increase they obtain a decrease in population, and instead of order they obtain chaos; i.e. they lose what they like but obtain what they dislike. What is the reason for this? Mozi said: It is due to the large number of fatalists among the people. The fatalists say: "When fate decrees that a man shall be wealthy he will be wealthy; when it decrees poverty, he will be poor; when it decrees a large population, it will be large; and when it decrees a small population it will be small; if order is decreed, there will be order; if chaos, there will be chaos. If fate decrees old age, there will be old age; if untimely death, there will be untimely death. Even if a man sets himself against his fate, what is the use?" With this doctrine the rulers are urged above and the people are kept away from their work below. Hence the fatalists are unmagnanimous. And their doctrines must be clearly examined.

然則明辨此之說，將奈何哉？子墨子言曰：言必立儀。言而毋儀，譬猶運鈞之上而立朝夕者也，是非利害之辨，不可得而明知也。故言必有三表。何謂三表？子墨子言曰：有本之者，有原之者，有用之者。於何本之？上本之於古者聖王之事。於何原之？下原察百姓耳目之實。於何用之？廢以為刑政，觀其中國家百姓人民之利。此所謂言有三表也。

Now, how is this doctrine to be examined? Mozi said: Some standard of judgment must be established. To expound a doctrine without regard to the standard is similar to determining the directions of sunrise and sunset on a revolving potter's wheel. By this means the distinction of right and wrong, benefit and harm, cannot be known. Therefore there must be three tests. What are the three tests? Mozi said: Its basis, its verifiability, and its applicability. How is it to be based? It should be based on the deeds of the ancient sage-kings. How is it to be verified? It is to be verified by the senses of hearing and the sight of the common people. How is it to be applied? It is to be applied by adopting it in government and observing its benefits to the country and the people. This is what is meant by the three tests of every doctrine.

經說上第四十二
Chapter 42 Exposition of Canon Ⅰ

利,得是而喜,則是利也。其害也,非是也。害。得是而惡,則是害也。其利也,非是也。

If you are pleased to get this one, this is the beneficial one (*li*), and the harmful one is not this one. If you dislike getting this one, this is the harmful one (*hai*), and the one which is beneficial is not this one.

三、治亂 / Part Ⅲ　Governance

　　假設，政府對你提出以下要求：每天晚上十點鐘準時睡覺，三十歲前必須結婚，必須繼承父親的職業，唯一能讀的書只有儒家經典，不可公開批評政府的首領，等等。想必你不會認爲這是一個好的政府。好的政府治理是有所爲有所不爲的。政府過分作爲或過多干涉，會讓人民生活過得很痛苦。那麼，什麼事情是政府應該做或者可以做的呢？政府應該確保每個孩子都獲得教育嗎？政府可以向富人徵稅來救濟窮人嗎？政府可以公開支持那些向精英人才傾斜的政策嗎？這些問題引起了許多中國古代哲學家的興趣。

　　閱讀選文時，試著找出道家、儒家和法家對以下問題看法的不同之處：政府應該得到何種程度的限制？

　　Suppose the government requires that you sleep at 10:00 every night, that you get married before 30, that you do what your father does, that you only read the Confucian Classics, that you never publically criticize the head of government, etc. You would not think it is a good government. Good governance consists of not doing certain things. A government that overdoes things or interferes too much will make the people live a miserable life. But what should/can a government do? Should the government ensure that every child gets education? Can the government tax the rich more to help the poor? Can the government endorse the policies that favor the talented people? These are the questions that interested most ancient Chinese philosophers.

As you read the selections, try to figure out the differences between Daoism, Confucianism, and Legalism. To what extent should a government be limited?

《老子》/ Laozi or *Dao De Jing*

1. 道可道，非常道。名可名，非常名。無名天地之始；有名萬物之母。故常無欲，以觀其妙；常有欲，以觀其徼。此兩者，同出而異名，同謂之玄。玄之又玄，眾妙之門。

1. The Dao or the Way that can be trodden is not the enduring and unchanging Dao or Way.
The name that names is not the enduring and unchanging name.
The nameless is the origin of Heaven and Earth;
The named is the Mother of all things.
Thus, without desire one can see Dao's subtleties;
with desire, one can only observe its external attributes.
Under these two aspects, it is really the same;
but as development takes place, it receives the different names.
Together we call them the Mystery.
Where the Mystery is the deepest
is the gateway to all subtleties.

2. 天下皆知美之為美，斯惡已。皆知善之為善，斯不善已。故有無相生，難易相成，長短相較，高下相傾，音聲相和，前後相隨。是以聖人處無為之事，行不言之教；萬物作焉而不辭，生而不有。為而不恃，功成而弗居。夫唯弗居，是以不去。

2. All beneath Heaven knows beauty is beauty
only because there's ugliness,
and knows good is good
only because there's evil.

Thus Being and Absence give birth to one another,
difficult and easy complete one another;
long and short measure one another;
high and low fill one another;
music and noise harmonize one another;
before and after follow one another:

Therefore, the sage manages affairs without doing anything,
and conveys his instructions without the use of speech.
He works with the myriad creatures and turns none away.
He produces without possessing.
He acts with no expectation of reward.
When his work is done, he does not take credits for it.
And, by not taking credits, he will never be removed.

3. 不尚賢,使民不爭;不貴難得之貨,使民不爲盜;不見可欲,使民心不亂。是以聖人之治,虛其心,實其腹,弱其志,強其骨。常使民無知無欲。使夫智者不敢爲也。爲無爲,則無不治。

3. Not to value and employ men of superior ability
is the way to keep the people from rivalry among themselves.
Not to prize articles which are difficult to procure
is the way to keep the people from becoming thieves.
Not to show the people what is likely to excite their desires
is the way to keep their minds from confusion.

Therefore the sage governs a country
by emptying the people's minds,
filling their bellies,
weakening their wills,
and strengthening their bones.
He makes sure that the people are without knowledge or desires,

and that those with knowledge do not dare to act.

If you do nothing, everything will become well ordered.

5. 天地不仁，以萬物爲芻狗；聖人不仁，以百姓爲芻狗。天地之間，其猶橐籥乎？虛而不屈，動而愈出。多聞數窮，不如守中。

5. Heaven and Earth are not benevolent;
they treat the myriad creatures as straw dogs.
Sages are not benevolent;
they treat the people as straw dogs.

May not the space between heaven and earth be compared to a bellows?

It is empty, yet it is inexhaustible.
It moves, and sends forth air the more.
An excess of speech will lead to exhaustion.
It is better to hold on to the mean.

10. 載營魄抱一，能無離乎？專氣致柔，能嬰兒乎？滌除玄覽，能無疵乎？愛民治國，能無爲乎？天門開闔，能爲雌乎？明白四達，能無知乎？生之、畜之，生而不有，爲而不恃，長而不宰。是謂玄德。

10. Can you let your spirit embrace primal unity without drifting away?
Can you focus *qi* into such softness that you're a newborn again?
Can you polish the dark-enigma mirror to a clarity beyond stain?
Can you care for the people and govern the country without doing anything?
Can you open and close the gate of Heaven as a female?
Can you understand everything within the four directions without knowing anything?

[The Dao] produces [all things] and nourishes them;
it produces them and does not claim them as its own;
it does all, and yet does not boast of it;
it presides over all, and yet does not control them.
This is what I call "The mysterious Quality" [of the Dao].

13. 寵辱若驚,貴大患若身。何謂寵辱若驚? 寵爲下,得之若驚,失之若驚,是謂寵辱若驚。何謂貴大患若身? 吾所以有大患者,爲吾有身,及吾無身,吾有何患? 故貴以身爲天下者,若可寄天下;愛以身爲天下者,若可託天下。

13. [The saint] feels alarm over honor similar to that over insult.
He takes priority on national disaster like it is happening to his body.

Why does he feel alarm over honor similar to that over insult?
To receive honor is to be in the position of a subordinate.
When a person receives honor, he should feel alarm [because the honor comes with expectation and burden to keep that honor].
When he loses the honor, he should feel alarm [because he will be punished].

Why does [the saint] take priority on national disaster like it is happening to his body?
I can suffer disaster only because I have a body.
When I no longer have a body, what disaster can possibly affect me?

Therefore, if you value the world as your body, the world will be entrusted on you.
If you love the world as your body, the world will be given to you.①

---

① This is an obscure passage. Some scholars think that a few words are missing.

17. 太上,不知有之;其次,親而譽之;其次,畏之;其次,侮之。信不足焉,有不信焉。悠兮,其貴言。功成事遂,百姓皆謂:"我自然"。

17. The greatest of rulers is the one whose existence remains imperceptible;
Next is the ruler who the people love and praise;
Next is the one who the people fear;
Next is the one who the people despise.
He who does not trust enough,
will not be trusted.
Quiet! Take great care over words.
When one does things well,
people will say it happened on its own.

18. 大道廢,有仁義;智慧出,有大偽;六親不和,有孝慈;國家昏亂,有忠臣。

18. When the great Way is abandoned, benevolence and righteousness are invented.
When intelligence comes forth, great hypocrisy appears.
When familial harmony ends, filial piety and parental love are advocated;
When the state falls into disorder, loyal ministers show up.

19. 絕聖棄智,民利百倍;絕仁棄義,民復孝慈;絕巧棄利,盜賊無有。此三者以爲文,不足。故令有所屬,見素抱樸,少私寡欲。

19. If we could renounce our sageness and discard our wisdom,
it would be better for the people a hundredfold.
If we could renounce our benevolence and discard our righteousness,
the people would again become filial and kindly.
If we could renounce our artful contrivances and discard our [scheming for] gain,

there would be no thieves nor robbers.

But these three are mere refinements, nowhere near enough.

They depend on something more:

> observe origin's weave,
>
> embrace uncarved simplicity,
>
> self nearly forgotten, desires rare.

22. "曲則全，枉則直，窪則盈，敝則新，少則得，多則惑。"是以聖人抱一爲天下式。不自見，故明；不自是，故彰；不自伐，故有功；不自矜，故長。夫唯不爭，故天下莫能與之爭。古之所謂"曲則全"者，豈虛言哉！誠全而歸之。

22. "If you want to become whole,

first let yourself become broken.

If you want to become straight,

first let yourself become twisted.

If you want to become full,

first let yourself become empty.

If you want to become new,

first let yourself become worn."

Those who desire little are satisfied;

those who desire much go astray.

This is why sages embrace the One as the measure of all beneath Heaven.

They do not make a display of themselves and so are illustrious.

They do not affirm their own views and so are well known.

They do not brag about themselves and so are accorded merit.

They do not boast about themselves and so are heard of for a long time.

Because they do not contend, no one in the world can contend with them.

When the ancient masters said,

"If you want to become whole,

then first let yourself be broken,"

they weren't using empty words.

All who do this will be made complete.

29. 將欲取天下而爲之，吾見其不得已。天下神器，不可爲也，不可執也。爲者敗之，執者失之。夫物或行或隨；或噓或吹；或强或羸；或載或隳。是以聖人去甚，去奢，去泰。

29. If anyone should wish to rule the world and improve it,
I see that he will not succeed.
The world is a spirit-like thing.
It cannot be improved.
He who tries to improve it destroys it;
he who tries to hold it in his grasp loses it.
Things sometimes lead and sometimes follow;
sometimes breathe gently and sometimes breathe hard;
sometimes strong and sometimes weak;
sometimes inherit and sometimes overturn.
This is why the sage casts off whatever is extreme, extravagant, or excessive.

31. 夫佳兵者，不祥之器，物或惡之，故有道者不處。君子居則貴左，用兵則貴右。兵者不祥之器，非君子之器，不得已而用之，恬淡爲上。勝而不美，而美之者，是樂殺人。夫樂殺人者，則不可以得志於天下矣。吉事尚左，凶事尚右。偏將軍居左，上將軍居右，言以喪禮處之。殺人之衆，以哀悲泣之，戰勝以喪禮處之。

31. Fine weapons are the tools of misfortune;
all creatures find them repulsive.
And so a master of the Way stays clear of them.
At home, the gentleman gives precedence to the left;
at war, the gentleman gives precedence to the right.
Weapons are the tools of misfortune, not the tools of the gentleman;
only when it is unavoidable he uses them.
Peace and quietude he holds high.

A military victory is not a thing of beauty.
To beautify victory is to delight in the slaughter of human beings.
One who delights in the slaughter of human beings will never achieve his goal beneath Heaven.
We honor the left in celebrations and honor the right in lamentations.
A lieutenant takes his honored place on the left;
a general takes his honored place on the right,
which is said, in order to observe rituals of mourning.
When a great number of people have been killed,
one weeps for them in grief and sorrow.
Military victory should be conducted like a funeral.

36. 將欲歙之，必故張之；將欲弱之，必故強之；將欲廢之，必故興之；將欲取之，必故與之。是謂微明。柔弱勝剛強。魚不可脫於淵，國之利器不可以示人。

36. What you intend to shrink, you first must stretch.
What you intend to weaken, you first must strengthen.
What you intend to abandon, you first must make flourish.
What you intend to steal from, you first must provide for.
This is called "Hiding the light [of your procedure]".
The soft overcomes the hard, and the weak the strong.
Fish should not be taken out of the deep pools.
A nation's honed instruments of power should be kept well-hidden from the people.

37. 道常無爲而無不爲。侯王若能守之，萬物將自化。化而欲作，吾將鎭之以無名之樸。鎭之以無名之樸。無名之樸，夫亦將無欲。不欲以靜，天下將自正。

37. The Way does nothing yet nothing is left undone.
If princes and kings were able to maintain it,
the myriad creatures will transform themselves.
After they are transformed, should some still desire to act,

I shall press them down with the uncarved nameless simplicity.

The uncarved nameless simplicity is the perfect absence of desire.

Without desire and remaining still, the world will settle itself.

38. 上德不德,是以有德;下德不失德,是以無德。上德無爲而無以爲;下德無爲而有以爲。上仁爲之而無以爲;上義爲之而有以爲。上禮爲之而莫之應,則攘臂而扔之。故失道而後德,失德而後仁,失仁而後義,失義而後禮。夫禮者,忠信之薄,而亂之首。前識者,道之華,而愚之始。是以大丈夫處其厚,不居其薄;處其實,不居其華。故去彼取此。

38. Those of highest virtue do not strive for it and so they have it.

Those of lowest virtue stick with it and so they do not have higher virtues.

Those of highest virtue do nothing and have no motives.

Those of lowest virtue does something and have sure motives.

Those of highest benevolence do something, but without any motives.

Those of highest righteousness do something, and with sure motives.

Those who are ritually correct do something, but if others do not respond, they roll up their sleeves and resort to force [rather than ritual].

And so,

when the Way was lost there was virtue;

when virtue was lost there was benevolence;

when benevolence was lost there was righteousness;

when righteousness was lost there was ritual.

The ritual marks the waning of loyalty and trust, and the beginning of chaos.

The ability to predict what is to come is an embellishment of the Way, and the beginning of ignorance.

This is why the most accomplished reside in what is solid, not in what is flimsy.

They reside in what is most substantial, not in mere embellishment.

And so they cast off the one and take up the other.

39. 昔之得一者：天得一以清；地得一以寧；神得一以靈；谷得一以盈；萬物得一以生；侯王得一以爲天下貞。其致之也，謂天無以清，將恐裂；地無以寧，將恐廢；神無以靈，將恐歇；谷無以盈，將恐竭；萬物無以生，將恐滅；侯王無以正，將恐蹶。故貴以賤爲本，高以下爲基。是以侯王自稱孤、寡、不穀。此非以賤爲本邪？非乎？故致數譽無譽。是故不欲琭琭如玉，珞珞如石。

39. In the past, among those who attained the One were these:

Heaven attained the One and became clear;

Earth attained the One and became settled;

Gods attained the One and became numinous;

the valley attained the One and so came to have flowing water;

the myriad creatures attained the One and so came to being;

princes and kings attained the One and so came to be able to rectify all beneath Heaven.

All of this came about through the One.

Without what made it clear, Heaven would rend.

Without what made it settled, Earth would crumble.

Without what made them numinous, gods would cease their activity.

Without what made it have flowing water, the valley would run dry.

Without what made them come to being, the myriad creatures would disappear.

Without what made them able to rectify all beneath Heaven, princes and kings would fall.

And so what is honored has its root in what is base;

What is lofty has its foundation in what is lowly.

This is why princes and kings refer to themselves as, "The Orphan", "The Desolate", or "The Forlorn".

Is this not a case where what is base serves as the foundation? Is it not?

Thus too much praise is no praise.

Thus the sage does not desire to glitter like a jewel.

He prefers to be as plain as a small stone.

40. 反者道之動；弱者道之用。天下萬物生於有，有生於無。

40. Turning back is how the Dao moves.
Weakness is how the Dao operates.
All things under Heaven arise from what is there;
what is there arises from what is not there.

42. 道生一，一生二，二生三，三生萬物。萬物負陰而抱陽，沖氣以爲和。人之所惡，唯孤、寡、不穀，而王公以爲稱。故物或損之而益，或益之而損。人之所教，我亦教之。强梁者不得其死，吾將以爲教父。

The Dao produced One;
One produced Two;
Two produced Three;
Three produced All things.
All things leave behind them the Darkness or the Yin [out of which they have come],
and go forward to embrace the Brightness or the Yang [into which they have emerged],
while they are harmonized by the Breath of Vacancy.

What men dislike is to be orphaned, desolate or forlorn;
and yet these are the designations which kings and princes use for themselves.
And so sometimes diminishing a thing adds to it;
sometimes adding to a thing diminishes it.

I only teach what the people teach.
The violent and strong do not die their natural death.
I will make this the basis of my teaching.

49. 聖人常無心，以百姓心爲心。善者，吾善之；不善者，吾亦善之；德善。信者，吾信之；不信者，吾亦信之；德信。聖人在天下，歙歙焉，爲天下渾其心，百姓皆注其耳目，聖人皆孩之。

49. The sage's mind is never his own:
he makes the hundredfold people's mind his mind:
I am good to those who are good;
I am also good to those who are not good;
and thus [all] get to be good.
I am also sincere to those who are sincere;
I am also sincere to those who are not sincere;
and thus [all] get to be sincere.
The sage has in the world an appearance of indecision,
and keeps his mind in a state of indifference to all.
The people all keep their eyes and ears directed to him,
and he deals with them all as his children.

57. 以正治國，以奇用兵，以無事取天下。吾何以知其然哉？以此：天下多忌諱，而民彌貧；民多利器，國家滋昏；人多伎巧，奇物滋起；法令滋彰，盜賊多有。故聖人云："我無爲，而民自化；我好靜，而民自正；我無事，而民自富；我無慾，而民自樸。"

57. Use justice to govern a country.
Use surprise to wage war.
Use non-action to win all beneath Heaven.
How do I know that things are this way?
Through the following:
    The more restrictions and prohibitions there are,
    the poorer the people will be.
    The more sharp weapons people have in a country,
    the bigger the disorder will be.
    The more clever and cunning people are,

the stranger the events will be.
The more laws and commands there are,
the more thieves and robbers there will be.
And so the sage says,
"I do nothing and the people transform themselves;
I prefer stillness and the people correct and regulate themselves;
I engage in no activity and the people prosper on their own;
I am without desires and the people simplify their own lives."

58. 其政悶悶，其民淳淳；其政察察，其民缺缺。禍兮福之所倚，福兮禍之所伏。孰知其極？其無正。正復爲奇，善復爲妖。人之迷，其日固久。是以聖人方而不割，廉而不劌，直而不肆，光而不燿。

58. When government is pensive and withdrawn
people are honest and simple.
When government is confident and effective
people are cunning and secretive.
Good fortune rests upon disaster;
disaster lies hidden within good fortune.
Who knows what either will come to in the end?
Perhaps there is nothing that is truly correct and regular!
What is correct and regular turns strange and perverse;
what is good turns monstrous.
People have been confused for such a long long time
Therefore the sage is like a square which cuts no one [with its angles];
like a corner which injures no one [with its sharpness].
He is straightforward, but never provokes;
he is bright, but does not dazzle.

59. 治人事天，莫若嗇。夫爲嗇，是謂早服；早服謂之重積德；重積德則無不克；無不克則莫知其極；莫知其極，可以有國；有國之母，可以長久；是謂深根固柢，長生久視之道。

59. To govern people and serve heaven, nothing is as good as frugality.
To be frugal is called submitting early on.
Submitting early on is known as deeply accumulating virtue.
If you deeply accumulate virtue, nothing can stand in your way.
If nothing can stand in your way, no one will know your limits.
If no one knows your limits, you can rule a state.
If you rule the state like a mother, you can be the ruler for a long time.
This is known as deep roots and strong stems.
This is the Way of long life and enduring insight.

60. 治大國,若烹小鮮。以道蒞天下,其鬼不神,非其鬼不神;其神不傷人,非其神不傷人。聖人亦不傷人。夫兩不相傷,故德交歸焉。

60. Governing a great state is like cooking small fish.
When one manages the world through the Way,
ghosts lose their numinous qualities.
It's not that ghosts really lose their numinous qualities,
but that their numinous qualities lose the ability to harm human beings.
Just as ghosts can lose their ability to harm,
the sage shuns the use of violence.
If neither of these two injures human beings,
then virtue will return by itself.

61. 大國者下流,天下之交,天下之牝。牝常以靜勝牡,以靜爲下。故大國以下小國,則取小國;小國以下大國,則取大國。故或下以取,或下而取。大國不過欲兼畜人,小國不過欲入事人。夫兩者各得其所欲,大者宜爲下。

61. A great state is like the delta of a mighty river;
it is where the whole world gathers;
it is the female of the whole world.
The female always gets the better of the male through stillness.

Through stillness, she places herself below the male.

And so, a great state, by placing itself below a small state, can take the small state.

A small state, by placing itself below a great state, can win the support of the great state.

And so, one places itself below in order to take;

the other places itself below in order to win support.

A great nation wanting nothing more than to unite and nurture the people

and a small nation wanting nothing more than to join and serve the people:

Each can succeed in what they want [by placing itself in the lower position].

But the great state must learn to place itself in the lower position.

62. 道者萬物之奧，善人之寶，不善人之所保。美言可以市，尊行可以加人。人之不善，何棄之有？故立天子，置三公，雖有拱璧以先駟馬，不如坐進此道。古之所以貴此道者何？不曰：以求得，有罪以免耶？故爲天下貴。

62. The Dao is the source of all things,
the treasure of the good man,
and the refuge of the bad.
One can pay people to praise him,
and use great deeds to promote him.
Therefore, when a man falls, do not abandon him.
And so, on the day the Son of Heaven is enthroned and the three dukes installed,
do not offer up precious jades and a carriage drawn by a team of four horses,
but remain still and offer the Dao.
Why was this Dao so honored in ancient times?
Was it not because [through the Dao]

"One could get what one seeks and escape punishment for one's crimes?"

This is why it is honored by the whole world.

63. 爲無爲，事無事，味無味。大小多少，報怨以德。圖難於其易，爲大於其細；天下難事，必作於易，天下大事，必作於細。是以聖人終不爲大，故能成其大。夫輕諾必寡信，多易必多難。是以聖人猶難之，故終無難矣。

63. [It is the way of the Dao] to govern without interfering;
to serve without making trouble,
to taste without discerning any flavor,
to enlargethe small,
to enrich the scarce,
and to treat those who hate you with kindness.
Plan for what is difficult while it is easy.
Work at what is great while it is small.
The difficult undertakings in the world all start with what is easy.
The great undertakings in the world all begin with what is small.
Therefore the sage, while he never does what is great,
is able on that account to accomplish the greatest things.
He who lightly promises is sure to keep but little faith;
he who is continually thinking things easy is sure to find them difficult.
Therefore the sage sees difficulty even in what seems easy,
and so he ends up without difficulties.

64. 其安易持，其未兆易謀。其脆易泮，其微易散。爲之於未有，治之於未亂。合抱之木，生於毫末；九層之臺，起於累土；千里之行，始於足下。爲者敗之，執者失之。是以聖人無爲故無敗；無執故無失。民之從事，常於幾成而敗之。慎終如始，則無敗事。是以聖人欲不欲，不貴難得之貨；學不學，復衆人之所過，以輔萬物之自然，而不敢爲。

64. That which is at rest is easily restrained;

that which has not yet appeared is easily prevented;
that which is brittle is easily broken;
that which is very small is easily dispersed.
Work at things before they come to be;
regulate things before they become disordered.
A tree you can barely reach around grows from the tiniest rootlet;
a nine-tiered tower starts as a basket of dirt;
a thousand-mile journey begins with a single step.
Work at things and you ruin them;
cling to things and you lose them.
That's why the sage does nothing and so ruins nothing,
clings to nothing and so loses nothing.
People often ruin things just when they are on the verge of success.
Be as careful at the end as you are at the beginning and you will not ruin things.
This is why the sage desires what other men do not desire,
and shows no regard for precious goods.
He learns what other men do not learn,
and turns back to what the multitude of men have passed by.
Thus he helps the natural development of all things,
and does not dare to act [with a purpose of his own].

65. 古之善爲道者，非以明民，將以愚之。民之難治，以其智多。故以智治國，國之賊；不以智治國，國之福。知此兩者亦稽式。常知稽式，是謂"玄德"。玄德深矣，遠矣，與物反矣，然後乃至大順。

65. In ancient times, those who master the Dao
did not use it to enlighten the people,
but rather to keep them in the dark.
The people are hard to govern because they know too much.
And so to govern a state with knowledge is to be a detriment to the state.

Not to govern a state through knowledge is to be a blessing to the state.
He who knows the difference between these two knows the standard.
The ability to know the standard is called Enigmatic Virtue.
How profound and far-reaching is Enigmatic Virtue!
It turns back with things;
And only then is there the Great Compliance.

66. 江海之所以能爲百谷王者，以其善下之，故能爲百谷王。是以聖人欲上民，必以言下之；欲先民，必以身後之。是以聖人處上而民不重，處前而民不害。是以天下樂推而不厭。以其不爭，故天下莫能與之爭。

66. The Yangtze River and the Sea are able
to receive the homage and tribute of all the valley streams,
because they are good at placing themselves in the lower position.
Similarly, when the sage wants to be above the people
he always proclaims that he is below them.
When he wants to lead the people, he always puts himself behind them.
This is how he is able to reside above the people without being considered a burden,
and how he is able to be out in front of the people without being regarded as a harm.
Hence the whole world always delights in supporting him.
Because he does not contend, no one in the world can contend with him.

67. 天下皆謂我道大，似不肖。夫唯大，故似不肖。若肖，久矣其細也夫！我有三寶，持而保之。一曰慈，二曰儉，三曰不敢爲天下先。慈故能勇；儉故能廣；不敢爲天下先，故能成器長。今捨慈且勇；捨儉且廣；捨後且先；死矣！夫慈以戰則勝，以守則固。天將救之，以慈衛之。

67. All people say that my Dao is great. But it appears unworthy.
It is only because it is great that it appears to be unworthy.
If it had appeared worthy, it would have become small long ago.

There are three treasures that I hold on to and preserve:
　　The first I call loving kindness;
　　The second I call frugality;
　　The third I call never daring to put oneself first in the world.
With loving kindness I can be courageous;
With frugality I can be generous;
since I never dare to put myself first in the world,
I can become the leader of the various officials.
Nowadays they are courageous without loving kindness,
generous without frugality,
putting themselves first without putting themselves behind others.
These will lead to death.
If one has loving kindness, in attack one will be victorious,
and in defense one will be secure.
For Heaven will save you and protect you with loving kindness.

74. 民不畏死,奈何以死懼之？若使民常畏死,而爲奇者,吾得執而殺之,孰敢？常有司殺者殺。夫代司殺者殺,是謂代大匠斲。夫代大匠斲者,希有不傷其手矣。

74. The people do not fear death;
why threaten them with death?
Suppose the people always fear death,
and I could always seize and put to death
those who act in strange or perverse ways.
Then who would dare to act in strange or perverse ways?
That nature always does the job of the executioner, it's true.
But to undertake the killing yourself—
that's like trying to carve lumber for a master carpenter.
Try to carve lumber for a master carpenter
and you'll soon have blood on your hands.

75. 民之饑，以其上食稅之多，是以饑。民之難治，以其上之有爲，是以難治。民之輕死，以其上求生之厚，是以輕死。夫唯無以生爲者，是賢於貴生。

The people suffer from famine
because the taxes are too high.
The people are difficult to govern
because the rulers are too active.
The people make light of death
because those above demand too much of life.
Those who have no concern for life are wiser than those who cherish life.

77. 天之道，其猶張弓歟？高者抑之，下者舉之；有餘者損之，不足者補之。天之道，損有餘而補不足。人之道，則不然，損不足以奉有餘。孰能有餘以奉天下，唯有道者。是以聖人爲而不恃，功成而不處，其不欲見賢。

77. The Dao or Way of Heaven is like the bending of a bow.
The high is lowered, and the low is raised.
If the string is too long, it is shortened;
if there is not enough, it is made longer.
The Dao of Heaven is to take from those who have too much
and give to those who do not have enough.
The Way of human beings is not like this.
It takes from those who do not have enough
and gives to those who already have too much.
Who is able to offer what they have in excess to the world?
Only the man of Dao.
Thus the sage acts without presumption.
When his work is done, he does not claim credit.
He does not desire to make a display of his worthiness.

78. 天下莫柔弱於水，而攻堅強者莫之能勝，以其無以易之。弱之勝強，柔之勝剛，天下莫不知，莫能行。是以聖人云："受國之垢，是謂社稷主；受國不祥，是爲天下王。"正言若反。

78. There is nothing in the world softer and weaker than water,
and yet for attacking things that are firm and strong,
nothing succeeds like water,
and so nothing can take its place.
Everyone in the world knows that the soft overcomes the hard, and the weak the strong,
but no one is able to carry it out in practice.
Therefore the sage said,
"Whoever assumes a nation's disgrace
is called the sacred leader of a country,
and whoever assumes a nation's misfortune
is called the emperor of all beneath Heaven."
Words that are strictly true seem to be paradoxical.

79. 和大怨，必有餘怨，安可以爲善？是以聖人執左契，而不責於人。有德司契，無德司徹。天道無親，常與善人。

79. When a reconciliation is effected [between two parties] after a great animosity,
there is sure to be a grudge remaining.
How can the reconciliation be regarded as good?
Thus the sage holds the creditor's half of contracts
and yet asks nothing of others.
A man of virtue performs his part,
but a man without virtue requires others to fulfill his obligations.
In the Way of Heaven, there is no partiality of love;
it is always on the side of the good.

80. 小國寡民。使有什伯之器而不用；使民重死而不遠徙。雖有舟輿，無所乘之,雖有甲兵,無所陳之。使民復結繩而用之。甘其食,美其服,安其居,樂其俗。
鄰國相望,雞犬之聲相聞,民至老死,不相往來。

> Let nations grow smaller and smaller
> and people fewer and fewer;
> let weapons become rare and superfluous;
> let people feel death's gravity again
> and never wander far from home.
> Then the boat and carriage will sit unused
> and the shield and sword lie unnoticed.
> Let people knot ropes for notation again
> and never need anything more.
> Let them find pleasure in their food
> beauty in their clothes,
> peace in their homes
> and joy in their ancestral ways.
> Then even though neighboring states are within sight of each other,
> even though they can hear the sounds of each other's dogs and chickens,
> their people will grow old and die without ever having visited one another.

81. 信言不美,美言不信。善者不辯,辯者不善。知者不博,博者不知。聖人不積,既以爲人,己愈有,既以與人,己愈多。天之道,利而不害;聖人之道,爲而不爭。

> 81. Words worthy of trust are not refined;
> refined words are not worthy of trust.
> Those who are skilled [in the Dao] do not dispute [about it];
> the disputatious are not skilled in it.
> Those who know [the Dao] are not extensively learned;
> the extensively learned do not know it.
> The sage does not accumulate [for himself].

The more he expends for others, the more he possesses of his own;

The more he gives to others, the more he has himself.

The Way of Heaven is to benefit and not harm.

The Way of the sage is to act [in accordance with the Dao] but not contend.

《莊子》/ Zhuangzi

應帝王第七
Chapter 7　The Normal Course for Rulers and Kings①

齧缺問于王倪，四問而四不知。齧缺因躍而大喜，行以告蒲衣子。蒲衣子曰："而乃今知之乎？有虞氏不及泰氏。有虞氏，其猶藏仁以要人；亦得人矣，而未始出于非人。泰氏，其臥徐徐，其覺于于；一以己爲馬，一以己爲牛；其知情信，其德甚真，而未始入于非人。"

Gap Tooth (Nie-que) put four questions to Horizon Imperial (Wang-ni), not one of which did Horizon Imperial know [how to answer]. In great delight, Gap Tooth leaped up, and ran to tell Master Grass Coat (Puyizi). "You mean you're only now realizing that there are no answers?" said Master Grass. "Shun may be a sage emperor, but he's no match for Emperor Inception. Shun never stops treasuring benevolence (ren) and using it to lead people. He's mastered the human but never been able to detach him from the nonhuman. Inception, on the other hand, slept in peaceful contentment and woke wide-eyed and blank. He might have been a horse one minute and an ox the next. His understanding was faithful and precise, his Integrity utterly true. He was never influenced by the nonhuman or the human either."

---

① The English translation of this chapter draws heavily on David Hinton's beautiful rendering of Zhuangzi.

肩吾見狂接輿。狂接輿曰："日中始何以語女？"肩吾曰："告我君人者以己出經式義度，人孰敢不聽而化諸！"狂接輿曰："是欺德也；其于治天下也，猶涉海鑿河而使蚉負山也。夫聖人之治也，治外乎？正而後行，確乎能其事者而已矣。且鳥高飛以避矰弋之害，鼷鼠深穴乎神丘之下以避熏鑿之患，而曾二蟲之無知！"

Bearing-Me-Up (Jianwu) went to see Convergence Crazy-Cart (Jieyu). Crazy-Cart said to him, "What did Noon Start tell you?" The reply was, "He told me that rulers should serve as examples, establishing canons and standards, precepts and regulations, and then the people will follow and be transformed." Crazy-Cart said, "That is the Integrity of oppression. Using it to govern all beneath Heaven is like it trying to wade through the sea and dig through the river, or employing a mosquito to carry a mountain on its back. And when sages govern, do you think they worry about mere appearance? First they set the terms themselves aright and then they just let it all happen. In that way things can simply do what they were meant to do. Think of the bird which flies high, to avoid being hurt by the dart on the string of the archer, and the little mouse which makes its hole deep under sacred mounds to avoid the danger of being smoked or dug out; are rulers less knowing than these two little creatures?"

天根遊于殷陽，至蓼水之上，適遭無名人而問焉，曰："請問爲天下。"無名人曰："去！汝鄙人也！何問之不豫也？予方將與造物者爲人，厭，則又乘夫莽眇之鳥，以出六極之外，而遊無何有之鄉，以處壙埌之野。汝又何帠以治天下感予之心爲？"又復問。無名人曰："汝遊心于淡，合氣于漠，順物自然而無容私焉，而天下治矣。"

Heaven-Root (Tian-gen) was wandering at the Bright-Abundance Mountain. There, along the banks of the Vacant River, he met Nameless (Wu-ming-ren) and said: "Might I ask about bringing order to all beneath Heaven?" "Get lost!" shouted Nameless. "What a slob. How could you ask such annoying questions? I wander with the Maker-of-Things and just now stumbled into this human form. When I get tired of this, I'll mount the Subtle-Confusion Bird and soar out beyond the six horizons. I'll wander in a village where there's nothing at all, dwell in a land where emptiness stretches away forever. So why are you cluttering my mind with your talk about governing all beneath Heaven?" Heaven-Root asked again. "Let your mind wander the pure and simple," replied Nameless. "Blend yourself with qi in idle indifference, allow all things to take their natural course, and don't let selfhood get in the way. Then all beneath Heaven will be governed well."

陽子居見老聃，曰："有人于此，向疾強梁，物徹疏明，學道不倦。如是者，可比明王乎？"老聃曰："是于聖人也，胥易技系，勞形怵心者也。且也虎豹之文來田，猿狙之便、執斄之狗來藉。如是者，可比明王乎？"陽子居蹴然曰："敢問明王之治。"老聃曰："明王之治：功蓋天下而似不自己，化貸萬物而民弗恃；有莫舉名，使物自喜；立乎不測，而遊于無有者也。"

Adept Light-Dweller (Yang-zi-ju) went to see Laozi and said, "Here is a man, alert and vigorous in responding to all matters, clear-sighted and widely intelligent, and an unwearied student of the Dao. Can he be compared to the enlightened kings of ancient times?" "Compared to those ancient sages," replied Laozi, "such a person is a scribbling clerk, a craftsman who toils his body and distresses his mind with his various contrivances. The beautiful fur of tigers and leopards makes men hunt them, and the agility of the monkey and the sagacity of the dog that catches the yak make men put them on a leash. So how can a person like that be compared to the enlightened kings of ancient times?" Light-Dweller looked discomposed and said, "I venture to ask you what the government of the enlightened kings is." Laozi replied, "When he governs, the sage emperor fills all beneath Heaven with bounty, and yet he's nowhere to be found. He transforms the ten thousand things, and yet no one thinks to rely on him: people never even mention his name, for he lets things find their own joy. He stands firm in the immeasurable and wanders free in realms where there's nothing at all."

鄭有神巫曰季咸,知人之死生存亡,禍福壽夭,期以歲月旬日,若神。鄭人見之,皆棄而走。列子見之而心醉,歸,以告壺子,曰:"始吾以夫子之道爲至矣,則又有至焉者矣。"壺子曰:"吾與汝既其文,未既其實,而固得道與?衆雌而無雄,而又奚卵焉?而以道與世亢,必信,夫故使人得而相汝。嘗試與來,以予示之。"

明日,列子與之見壺子。出而謂列子曰:"嘻!子之先生死矣!弗活矣!不以旬數矣!吾見怪焉!見濕灰焉。"列子入,泣涕沾襟以告壺子。壺子曰:"鄉吾示之以地文,萌乎不震不正。是殆見吾杜德機也。嘗又與來。"

明日,又與之見壺子。出而謂列子曰:"幸矣子之先生遇我也!有瘳矣,全然有生矣!吾見其杜權矣!"列子入,以告壺子。壺子曰:"鄉吾示之以天壤,名實不入,而機發于踵。是殆見吾善者機也。嘗又與來。"

明日,又與之見壺子。出而謂列子曰:"子之先生不齊,吾無得而相焉。試齊,且複相之。"列子入,以告壺子。壺子曰:"吾鄉示之以太冲莫勝,是殆見吾衡氣機也。鯢桓之審爲淵,止水之審爲淵,流水之審爲淵。淵有九名,此處三焉。嘗又與來。"

明日,又與之見壺子。立未定,自失而走。壺子曰:"追之。"列子追之不及。反,以報壺子曰:"已滅矣,已失矣,吾弗及已。"壺子曰:"鄉吾示之以未始出吾宗。吾與之虛而委蛇,不知其誰何,因以爲弟靡,因以爲波流,故逃也。"

然後列子自以爲未始學而歸。三年不出,爲其妻爨,食豕如食人。於事無與親。雕琢復樸,塊然獨以其形立。紛而封哉,一以是終。

In Zheng there was a mysterious wizard called Seasons-Alike (Ji-xian). He knew all about the deaths and births of men, their preservation and ruin, their misery and happiness, and whether their lives would be long or short. He could predict it all like some god, right down to the year, month, week, and day. When the people of Zheng saw him, they all ran out of his way. Liezi went to see him, and was fascinated by him. Returning, he told Master Winepot (Huzi), "I considered your doctrine, my master, to be perfect, but I have found another which is superior to it." Master Winepot replied, "I've shown you the surface, but I've never shown you the reality. Did you really think you'd mastered the Way of mine? If you have a bunch of hens and no rooster, what kind of eggs will you get? When you confront the world with your doctrine, you are sure to show in your face all that is in your mind. It's no wonder such people can know you through and through just by looking at your face. Bring him along next time, and we'll let him take a look at me."

The next day Liezi brought Seasons-Alike to see Master Winepot. When they went out, the wizard said, "Alas! Your master is a dead man. He will not live, not for ten days more! I saw something strange about him. I saw the ashes of his life all slaked with water!" When Liezi returned to Master Winepot, he wept, his robes soaked with tears. He told Master Winepot what the wizard had said. Master Winepot said, "This time I let him see the earth's veined surface just before spring breaks out: nothing moving, nothing still. But I guess all he saw was the wellspring of my Integrity blocked up. Bring him along next time."

The next day, accordingly, Liezi brought the wizard to see Master Winepot again. When they went out, the wizard said, "It is a fortunate thing for your master that he met with me. He will get better; he has all the signs of living! I can see that his blockage was only temporary." Liezi went in, and reported these words to his master. "This time," replied Master Winepot, "I let him see the fertile ground of Heaven before appearance and reality emerged, where the very wellsprings themselves arise. But I guess all he saw was the wellspring of my vitality. Bring him back for another look sometime."

The next day Liezi came with the wizard again. When they went out, the wizard said, "Your master is never the same. I studied his face but couldn't divine anything about him. If he'll try to steady himself, I'll come back and take another look." Liezi went in and reported this to Master Winepot, who said, "This time I let him see the Mighty Void where nothing wins out. But I guess all he saw was the wellspring of my qi in balance. Where the water wheels due to the movements of a dugong, there is an abyss; where still water gathers, there is an abyss. Where flowing water gathers, there is an abyss. The abyss has nine names. Here I have revealed three of them. Bring him back for another look somtime."

The next day Liezi came with the wizard again. They entered, but before he'd even greeted Master Winepot, the wizard went mad and fled wildly. "Catch him!" shouted Master Winepot. Liezi chased after him but couldn't catch him. "He's disappeared," reported Liezi when he returned, "Totally vanished. I couldn't catch him." Master Winepot said, "Just now I appeared to him as Not Yet Emerged from My Source. I came at him empty, wriggling and turning, not knowing anything about 'who' or 'what,' now dipping and bending, now flowing in waves—that's why he ran away."

After this, Liezi considered that he had not yet begun to learn his master's doctrine. He returned to his house, and for three years did not go out. He did the cooking for his wife. He fed the pigs as if he were feeding men. He took no part or interest in occurring affairs. He whittled and polished himself back to utter simplicity: a body standing alone like a clump of earth. Amid all distractions he was silent and shut up in himself. And in this way he continued to the end of his life.

無爲名尸,無爲謀府;無爲事任,無爲知主。體盡無窮,而遊無朕;盡其所受乎天,而無見得,亦虛而已。至人之用心若鏡,不將不迎,應而不藏,故能勝物而不傷。

Don't be a carcass of names or treasure-house of schemes; don't be a servant of pursuits or proprietor of fine wisdom. Make the inexhaustible your body and wander beyond origins. Fulfill all that you have received from Heaven, and do not think that you have anything. Live empty, perfectly empty. The perfect man always employs his mind like a pure mirror: welcome nothing, refuse nothing, reflect everything, and hold nothing. Thus he is able to deal successfully with all things, and injures none.

南海之帝爲儵,北海之帝爲忽,中央之帝爲渾沌。儵與忽時相與遇於渾沌之地,渾沌待之甚善。儵與忽謀報渾沌之德,曰:"人皆有七竅以視聽食息,此獨無有,嘗試鑿之。"日鑿一竅,七日而渾沌死。

At the origin of things there was Thunder, ruler of the Southern Ocean, and Bolt, ruler of the Northern Ocean. And in the Middle Realm, Primal-Dark ruled. Thunder and Bolt often met together in the lands of Primal-Dark, and Primal-Dark was always a most gracious host. Eventually, Thunder and Bolt tried to think of a way to repay Primal-Dark's kindness. They said: "People all have seven holes so they can see and hear, eat and breathe. Only Primal-Dark is without them. Why don't we try cutting some for him?" So they began cutting holes, one each day. On the seventh day, Primal-Dark died.

《論語》/ The Analects

2.3　子曰:"道之以政,齊之以刑,民免而无耻;道之以德,齊之以禮,有耻且格。"

2.3　The Master said, "If you try to guide the common people with coercive regulations (zheng) and keep them in line by means of punishments, the common people will become evasive and will have no sense of shame. If, however, you guide them with virtue, and keep them in line by means of ritual, the people will have a sense of shame and will rectify themselves."

12.11　齊景公問政於孔子。孔子對曰:"君,君;臣,臣;父,父;子,子。"公曰:"善哉! 信如君不君,臣不臣,父不父,子不子,雖有粟,吾得而食諸?"

12.11　Duke Jing of Qi asked Confucius about governing. Confucius responded, "Let the sovereign be a true sovereign, the ministers true ministers, the fathers true fathers, and the sons true sons." The Duke replied, "Well put! Certainly if the sovereign is not a true sovereign, the ministers not true ministers, the fathers not true fathers, and the sons not true sons, even if there is sufficient grain, will I ever get to eat it?"

12.19　季康子問政於孔子曰："如殺無道，以就有道，何如？"孔子對曰："子爲政，焉用殺？子欲善，而民善矣！君子之德風；小人之德草；草上之風必偃。"

12.19　Ji Kang asked Confucius about government, saying, "What do you say to killing the unprincipled for the good of the principled?" Confucius replied, "Sir, in carrying on your government, why should you use killing at all? Let your evinced desires be for what is good, and the people will be good. The relation between superiors and inferiors is like that between the wind and the grass. The grass must bend, when the wind blows across it."

13.2　仲弓爲季氏宰，問政。子曰："先有司，赦小過，舉賢才。"曰："焉知賢才而舉之？"曰："舉爾所知。爾所不知，人其舍諸？"

13.2　Zhonggong, serving as the chief of staff for the Ji Family, asked Confucius about governing. The Master said, "Depend on the lesser officials. Forgive their minor offenses and raise up worthy talents." "How can I recognize those who are worthy and talented so that I can promote them?" "Just promote the ones you know. As for those you do not know, will others allow them to be passed over?"

13.3　子路曰："衛君待子而爲政，子將奚先？"子曰："必也正名乎！"子路曰："有是哉？子之迂也！奚其正？"子曰："野哉，由也！君子於其所不知，蓋闕如也。名不正，則言不順；言不順，則事不成；事不成，則禮樂不興；禮樂不興，則刑罰不中；刑罰不中，則民無所措手足。故君子名之必可言也，言之必可行也。君子於其言，無所苟而已矣！"

13.3　Zilu asked, "If the Duke of Wei were to employ you to serve in the government of his state, what would be your first priority?" The Master answered, "It would, of course, be the rectification of names (zhengming)." Zilu said, "Could you, Master, really be so far off the mark? Why worry about rectifying names?" The Master replied, "How boorish you are, Zilu!

When it comes to matters that he does not understand, the gentleman should remain silent. If names are not rectified, speech will not accord with reality; when speech does not accord with reality, things will not be successfully accomplished. When things are not successfully accomplished, ritual and music will fail to flourish; when ritual and music fail to flourish, punishments and penalties will not be properly awarded. And when punishments and penalties are not properly awarded, then people can't put their hands and feet anywhere without fear of losing them. This is why the gentleman only applies names that can be properly spoken and assures that what he says can be properly put into action. The gentleman simply guards against arbitrariness in his speech. That is all there is to it."

13.4 樊遲請學稼,子曰:"吾不如老農。"請學為圃,曰:"吾不如老圃。"樊遲出,子曰:"小人哉,樊須也!上好禮,則民莫敢不敬;上好義,則民莫敢不服;上好信,則民莫敢不用情。夫如是,則四方之民,襁負其子而至矣;焉用稼!"

13.4 Fan Chi asked to learn about plowing and growing grain [from Confucius]. The Master said, "When it comes to that, any old farmer would be a better teacher than me." He asked to learn about growing fruits and vegetables. The Master said, "When it comes to that, any old gardener would be a better teacher than me." Fan Chi then left. The Master remarked, "What a petty man (xiaoren) that Fan Chi is! When a ruler loves propriety, then none among his people will dare to be disrespectful. When a ruler loves righteousness, then none among his people will dare not to obey. When a ruler loves trustworthiness, then none of his people will dare not to be honest. To such a country, people would flock from everywhere with their babies strapped to their backs. Of what use, then, is the study of agriculture?"

13.6 子曰:"其身正,不令而行;其身不正,雖令不從。"

13.6 The Master said, "When the ruler's personal conduct is correct, his government is effective without the issuing of orders. If his personal conduct is not correct, he may issue orders, but they will not be followed."

13.9　子適衛,冉有僕。子曰:"庶矣哉!"冉有曰:"既庶矣,又何加焉?"曰:"富之。"曰:"既富矣,又何加焉?"曰:"教之。"

13.9　The Master traveled to Wei, with Ran Qiu as his carriage driver. [Upon arriving,] the Master remarked, "How numerous the people of this state are!" Ran Qiu asked, "Being already numerous, what can be done to further improve them?" The Master replied, "Make them wealthy." "Once they are wealthy, what else can be done to improve them?" "Educate them."

13.11　子曰:"'善人爲邦百年,亦可以勝殘去殺矣。'誠哉是言也!"

13.11　The Master said, "'If good men were to govern a country in succession for a hundred years, they would be able to transform the violently bad, and dispense with capital punishments.' True indeed is this saying!"

13.12　子曰:"如有王者,必世而後仁。"

13.12　The Master said, "If a true king were to arise, though, we would certainly see a return to benevolence after a single generation."

13.13　子曰:"苟正其身矣,於從政乎何有? 不能正其身,如正人何?"

13.13　The Master said: "Once you've rectified yourself, you can serve in government without difficulty. But if you haven't rectified yourself, how can you rectify the people?"

13.15　定公問:"一言而可以興邦,有諸?"孔子對曰:"言不可以若是其幾也! 人之言曰:'爲君難,爲臣不易。'如知爲君之難也,不幾乎一言而興邦乎?"曰:"一言而喪邦,有諸?"孔子對曰:"言不可以若是其幾也! 人之言曰:'予無樂乎爲君,唯其言而莫予違也。'如其善而莫之違也,不亦善乎? 如不善而莫之違也,不幾乎一言而喪邦乎?"

13.15　Duke Ding asked whether there was a single sentence which could make a country prosperous. Confucius replied, "Such an effect cannot be expected from one sentence. There is a saying, however, 'To be a sovereign is difficult; to be a minister is not easy.' If a ruler knows this—the difficulty of being a sovereign—may there not be expected from this one sentence the prosperity of his country?" The duke then said, "Is there a single sentence which can ruin a country?" Confucius replied, "Such an effect as that cannot be expected from one sentence. There is, however, the saying which people have—'In ruling, there is but one joy: no one dares defy me.' If a ruler is good and no one dares defy him, isn't that good? But if a ruler is evil and no one dares defy him, may there not be expected from this one sentence the ruin of his country?"

13.16　葉公問政。子曰:"近者説,遠者來。"

13.16　The Duke of She asked about government. The Master said, "Good government obtains, when those who are near are made happy, and those who are far off are attracted."

13.17　子夏爲莒父宰,問政。子曰:"無欲速;無見小利。欲速則不達;見小利則大事不成。"

13.17　Zixia, serving as chief of staff of Jufu, asked about governing. The Master said, "Do not be desirous to have things done quickly; do not think about small advantages. Desiring to have things done quickly prevents their being done thoroughly. Thinking about small advantages prevents great affairs from being accomplished."

16.1　季氏將伐顓臾。冉有、季路見於孔子曰："季氏將有事於顓臾。"孔子曰："求！無乃爾是過與？夫顓臾，昔者先王以爲東蒙主，且在邦域之中矣，是社稷之臣也。何以伐爲？"冉有曰："夫子欲之，吾二臣者皆不欲也。"孔子曰："求！周任有言曰：'陳力就列，不能者止。'危而不持，顛而不扶，則將焉用彼相矣？且爾言過矣。虎兕出於柙，龜玉毀於櫝中，是誰之過與？"冉有曰："今夫顓臾，固而近於費。今不取，後世必爲子孫憂。"孔子曰："求！君子疾夫舍曰欲之，而必爲之辭。丘也聞有國有家者，不患寡而患不均，不患貧而患不安。蓋均無貧，和無寡，安無傾。夫如是，故遠人不服，則修文德以來之。既來之，則安之。今由與求也，相夫子，遠人不服而不能來也；邦分崩離析而不能守也。而謀動干戈於邦內。吾恐季孫之憂，不在顓臾，而在蕭牆之內也。"

16.1　The Ji Family was about to attack Zhuanyu. Ran Qiu and Zilu came to see Confucius and told him, "The Ji Family is about to settle things with Zhuanyu." Confucius replied, "Ran Qiu! Is this not, after all, your fault? Long ago, our former king appointed the ruler of Zhuanyu to preside over the sacrifices to Mount Dongmeng. Moreover, Zhuanyu lies within the boundaries of the state of Lu, and its ruler serves these same gods of earth and grain. What possible reason could there be to attack Zhuanyu?" Ran Qiu replied, "Our Master desires it. We two ministers are against it." Confucius replied, "Ran Qiu! Zhou Ren had a saying, 'When he can put forth his ability, he takes his place in the ranks of office; when he finds himself unable to do so, he retires from it.' If you are a guide to a blind man but does not support him when he is tottering, nor raise him up when he is falling, what good are you? Furthermore, what you have just said is incorrect. Isn't someone to blame if tigers and wild bulls escape from their cages, or jewelry of tortoiseshell and jade is crushed in its box?" Ran Qiu said, "Well, Zhuanyu is strong and close to the Ji Family stronghold of Fei. If it is not taken now, it will certainly be a source of anxiety for the Ji Family descendants for ages to come." Confucius replied, "Ran Qiu! The gentleman despises those declining to say 'I want such and such a thing', and framing explanations for their conduct. I have heard that those who possess a state or noble house are not concerned about whether their people are scarce, but rather about whether their people are content; they are not concerned about poverty, but rather concerned that whether their wealth is fairly distributed.① If wealth is fairly distributed, there should be no poverty; if your state or house is in harmony, there should be no scarcity; and if your people are content, there should be no instability. This being the case, if those who are distant will not submit, simply refine your culture and virtue in order to attract them. Once they come to you, you should make them content. Now, you two, Ran Qiu and Zilu, are supposed to be assisting your masters. Yet those who are far away will not submit, and you are unable to attract them; the country is falling apart, and you can do nothing to preserve it; and now you are planning to move with spears and shields against your own countrymen. I am afraid that the source of the Ji Family's troubles lies not in Zhuanyu, but rather within their own chambers."

20.2 子張問於孔子曰:"何如,斯可以從政矣?"子曰:"尊五美,屏四惡,斯可以從政矣。"子張曰:"何謂五美?"子曰:"君子惠而不費;勞而不怨;欲而不貪;泰而不驕;威而不猛。"子張曰:"何謂惠而不費?"子曰:"因民之所利而利之,斯不亦惠而不費乎？擇可勞而勞之,又誰怨！欲仁而得仁,又焉貪！君子無眾寡,無小大,無敢慢,斯不亦泰而不驕乎！君子正其衣冠,尊其瞻視,儼然,人望而畏之,斯不亦威而不猛乎！"子張曰:"何謂四惡?"子曰:"不教而殺謂之虐;不戒視成謂之暴;慢令致期謂之賊;猶之與人也,出納之吝,謂之有司。"

20.2 Zizhang asked Confucius, "What must a person be like before he can be employed in government service?" The Master replied, "He must respect the five virtues, and get rid of the four vices. Then he can be employed in government service." Zizhang asked, "What are the five virtues?" The Master replied, "That the gentleman is beneficent without great expenditure, imposes labor upon the people without incurring their

---

① As commentators and other translators have noted, and as can be discerned from the context, "寡" and "貧" have obviously been transposed here.

resentment, and pursues what he desires without being covetous, is grand without being arrogant, and is awe-inspiring without being severe." Zizhang asked, "What does it mean to be beneficent without great expenditure?" The Master replied, "Benefiting the people based on an understanding of what is truly beneficial to them—is this not 'beneficent without great expenditure'? Imposing labor upon the people only at the right time and on the right projects—who will resent it? Desiring benevolence and attaining it—what is there left to covet? Whether he is dealing with many people or few, or with things great or small, the gentleman does not dare to be conceited—is this not 'grand without being arrogant'? The gentleman is exacting in his dress and exalted in his gaze, and is so dignified in appearance that people look upon him with awe—is this not 'awe-inspiring without being severe'?" Zizhang asked, "What are the four vices?" The Master replied, "Executing the people without having instructed them—this is cruelty. Expecting perfection without having warned people when they are about to make a mistake—this is oppressive. Being late in giving orders yet demanding punctuality—this is to be a pest. Being consistently stingy when it comes to disbursing funds and rewarding people—this is officious."

《大学》/ Great Learning

大學之道,在明明德,在親民,在止於至善。知止而后有定,定而后能靜,靜而后能安,安而后能慮,慮而后能得。物有本末,事有終始,知所先後,則近道矣。

What the Great Learning teaches, is to illustrate illustrious virtue, to renovate the people, and to stop in the highest excellence. When you know where to stop, you have stability. When you have stability, you can be tranquil. When you are tranquil, you can be at ease. When you are at ease, you can deliberate. When you can deliberate you can attain your aims. Things have their root and their branches. Affairs have their end and their beginning. To know what is first and what is last will lead near to what is taught in the Great Learning.[①]

古之欲明明德於天下者，先治其國；欲治其國者，先齊其家；欲齊其家者，先脩其身；欲脩其身者，先正其心；欲正其心者，先誠其意；欲誠其意者，先致其知，致知在格物。物格而后知至，知至而后意誠，意誠而后心正，心正而后身脩，身脩而后家齊，家齊而后國治，國治而后天下平。自天子以至於庶人，壹是皆以脩身爲本。其本亂而末治者否矣，其所厚者薄，而其所薄者厚，未之有也！此謂知本，此謂知之至也。

The ancients, who wished to illustrate illustrious virtue throughout the kingdom, first ordered well their own states. Wishing to order well their states, they first regulated their families. Wishing to regulate their families, they first cultivated virtues in themselves. Wishing to cultivate virtues in themselves, they first rectified their minds. Wishing to rectify their minds, they first sought to be sincere in their thoughts. Wishing to be sincere in their thoughts, they first extended to the utmost their knowledge. Such extension of knowledge lay in the investigation of things. Things being investigated, knowledge became complete. Their knowledge being complete, their thoughts were sincere. Their thoughts being sincere, their minds were then rectified. Their minds being rectified, their virtues were cultivated. Their virtues being cultivated, their families were regulated. Their families being regulated, their states were rightly governed. Their states being rightly governed, All-Under-Heaven will have peace. From the Son of Heaven down to the mass of the people, all must consider virtue cultivation the root of everything besides. It cannot be, when the root is neglected, that what should spring from it will be well ordered. It never has been the case that what was of great importance has been slightly cared for, and, at the same time, that what was of slight importance has been greatly cared for. This is called, "Knowing the root." This is called, "The extension of

---

① The English translation here draws on both James Legge's and A. Charles Muller's translations.

knowledge."

所謂誠其意者,毋自欺也,如惡惡臭,如好好色,此之謂自謙,故君子必慎其獨也!小人閒居爲不善,無所不至,見君子而后厭然,揜其不善,而著其善。人之視己,如見其肺肝然,則何益矣!此謂誠於中,形於外,故君子必慎其獨也。曾子曰:"十目所視,十手所指,其嚴乎!"富潤屋,德潤身,心廣體胖,故君子必誠其意。

"Making the thoughts sincere" means no self-deception. Like when we allow ourselves to be disgusted by a bad smell or become infatuated with an attractive appearance. This is called self-enjoyment. Therefore, the gentleman must be watchful over himself when he is alone. When the inferior man is at leisure, there is no limit to the extent of his evil. But when he sees the gentleman, he instantly tries to disguise himself, concealing his evil, and displaying what is good. When people observe him, they see right to his core. Of what use is his disguise? This is an instance of the saying "What truly is within will be manifested without." Therefore, the gentleman must be watchful over himself when he is alone. Zengzi said, "What ten eyes see, what ten fingers indicate, is this not to be taken seriously?" Riches adorn a house, and virtues adorn a person. When the mind is expanded, the body is at ease. Therefore, the gentleman must make his thoughts sincere.

《詩》云:"瞻彼淇澳,菉竹猗猗。有斐君子,如切如磋,如琢如磨。瑟兮僴兮,赫兮喧兮。有斐君子,終不可諠兮。""如切如磋"者,道學也;"如琢如磨"者,自修也;"瑟兮僴兮"者,恂慄也;"赫兮喧兮"者,威儀也;"有斐君子,終不可諠兮"者,道盛德至善,民之不能忘也。《詩》云:"於戲前王不忘。"君子賢其賢而親其親,小人樂其樂而利其利,此以沒世不忘也。

The Book of Odes also says, Look at the bend in the Qi River, and how green and luxuriant the bamboo trees are there! Here is our refined prince, who is like a gem cut and filed, carved and polished! How dignified he is, and how awesome! How majestic and distinguished! Our illustrious prince will never be forgotten. "Like a gem cut and filed" refers to the way of study. "Like a gem carved and polished" refers to self-cultivation. "How dignified and awesome" refers to a cautious respect. "How majestic and distinguished" refers to his awe-inspiring way of handling himself. "Our illustrious prince will never be forgotten" means that the Dao flourishes in him and his virtue reaches excellence, hence, the people will be unable to forget him.

The Book of Odes also says, "Aah, the ancient kings are not forgotten!" The gentleman treats the worthy as worthy and loves his family. The inferior man enjoys his enjoyment and grabs profit whenever he has a chance. It is in this way that they are not forgotten after their death.

《康誥》曰:"克明德。"《太甲》曰:"顧諟天之明命。"《帝典》曰:"克明峻德。"皆自明也。

In "The Announcement of Kang" it is said, "He was able to manifest his virtue." "Taijia" says, "He contemplated Heaven's unveiled mandate." "The Canon of Yao" says, "He was able to manifest his lofty virtue." These passages all show how those sovereigns made themselves illustrious.

湯之《盤銘》曰:"苟日新,日日新,又日新。"《康誥》曰:"作新民。"《詩》曰:"周雖舊邦,其命惟新。"是故君子無所不用其極。

On the bathing tub of King Tang, the following words were engraved, "If you renew yourself for one day, you can renew yourself daily, and continue to do so." In "The Announcement of Kang" it says, "Carry out the renewal of the people." The Book of Odes says, "Even though Zhou was an ancient state, its mandate was sustained anew." Therefore there is nothing in which the gentleman does not fully exert himself.

《詩》云:"邦畿千里,惟民所止。"《詩》云:"緡蠻黃鳥,止于丘隅。"子曰:"於止,知其所止,可以人而不如鳥乎?"《詩》云:"穆穆文王,於緝熙敬止!"爲人君,止於仁；爲人臣，止於敬；爲人子，止於孝；爲人父，止於慈；與國人交，止於信。

The *Book of Odes* says, "The people only stay [comfortably] in a state where there is security." The *Book of Odes* also says, "The chirping bird only rests in the wooded part of the hill." The Master said, "When it rests, it knows where to rest. Can a person possibly be less knowing than a bird?" The *Book of Odes* also says, "How sublime was King Wen! He rested in clear, shining reverence." As a sovereign, he rested in benevolence. As a minister, he rested in reverence. As a son, he rested in filial piety. As a father, he rested in kindness. In communication with his subjects, he rested in trustworthiness.

子曰："聽訟，吾猶人也，必也使無訟乎！"無情者不得盡其辭，大畏民志。此謂知本。

Confucius said, "In hearing legal cases I am just like anyone else. What we really need is to not have legal cases." Those who lack sincerity should not be allowed to speak on and on. They should also have a great awe for the will of the people. This is called knowing the root.

所謂脩身在正其心者，身有所忿懥，則不得其正；有所恐懼，則不得其正；有所好樂，則不得其正；有所憂患，則不得其正。心不在焉，視而不見，聽而不聞，食而不知其味。此謂脩身在正其心。

"The cultivation of virtues lies in the correction of the mind." When you are angry, you cannot be correct; when you are frightened, you cannot be correct; when there is something you desire, you cannot be correct; when there is something you are anxious about, you cannot be correct. When the mind is not present, we look, but do not see; we listen, but do not hear; we eat, but don't taste our food. This is the meaning of "the cultivation of the virtues lies in the correction of the mind".

所謂齊其家在脩其身者，人之其所親愛而辟焉，之其所賤惡而辟焉，之其所畏敬而辟焉，之其所哀矜而辟焉，之其所敖惰而辟焉。故好而知其惡，惡而知其美者，天下鮮矣！故諺有之曰："人莫知其子之惡，莫知其苗之碩。"此謂身不脩不可以齊其家。

"The regulation of the family lies in the cultivation of virtues." When there is someone you love, you are biased. When there is something you hate, you are biased. When there is something you are in awe of, you are biased. When there is someone you pity, you are biased. When you are lazy, you are biased. Those who love someone and yet know their shortcomings, or who hate someone and yet know their merits, are few and far between. Hence there is the proverb, "A man does not know of his own son's shortcomings, or the richness of his own corn." This shows that if you do not cultivate virtues, you cannot regulate your family.

所謂治國必先齊其家者，其家不可教而能教人者，無之。故君子不出家而成教於國：孝者，所以事君也；弟者，所以事長也；慈者，所以使衆也。《康誥》曰："如保赤子"，心誠求之，雖不中不遠矣。未有學養子而后嫁者也！一家仁，一國興仁；一家讓，一國興讓；一人貪戾，一國作亂。其機如此。此謂一言僨事，一人定國。堯、舜率天下以仁，而民從之；桀、紂率天下以暴，而民從之。其所令反其所好，而民不從。是故君子有諸己而后求諸人，無諸己而后非諸人。所藏乎身不恕，而能喻諸人者，未之有也。故治國在齊其家。《詩》云："桃之夭夭，其葉蓁蓁；之子于歸，宜其家人。"宜其家人，而后可以教國人。《詩》云："宜兄宜弟。"宜兄宜弟，而后可以教國人。《詩》云："其儀不忒，正是四國。"其爲父子兄弟足法，而后民法之也。此謂治國在齊其家。

"Before governing the country, you must first regulate your family" means the following thing. There has never been a case where a man could not educate his own family, and yet could educate others. The gentleman, without going beyond his family, completes the lessons for the state: filial piety is the means by which you serve your ruler; fraternal submission is the means by which you serve your elders; kindness is the means by which you deal with everyone. "The Announcement of Kang" says, "It is like a mother completely giving herself to the care of her baby." She may not be perfect, but she won't be far off, even though she never took a course on child-rearing before having the baby. When one family becomes benevolent, the whole country will become benevolent. When one family becomes easy to get along with, all the people in the country become easy to get along with. If one man greedily upsets things, the whole country can be plunged into chaos. Such is the nature of the influence. This verifies the saying, "One word can win the whole affair; one man can settle the whole kingdom." Yao and Shun led All-Under-Heaven by benevolence and the people submitted to them. Jie and Zhou led All-Under-Heaven with aggression, and the people submitted to them, but did not go along with laws that they didn't like. The gentleman looks for merits in others only after possessing them in himself. He negates the shortcomings in others only after ridding them from himself. There has never been a case where a person was able to teach others the things he had learned, if he lacked a sense of reciprocity or empathy (shu). Therefore, the governing of the country lies in the regulation of the family. The Book of Odes says, "The peach tree so ripe, its leaves so luxuriant. The girl is going to her husband's house, and she will harmonize the household." Once the household is harmonized, the people of the country can be taught. The Book of Odes says, "He treated his elder brothers right; he treated his younger brothers right." If you can treat your brothers right, then you can teach your countrymen. The Book of Odes says, "His manner unchanging, he rectifies his whole state." Only when the ruler, as a father, a son, and a brother, is a model, will the people imitate him. Thus, it is said, "The ability to govern the country lies in regulating the family."

所謂平天下在治其國者，上老老而民興孝，上長長而民興弟，上恤孤而民不倍，是以君子有絜矩之道也。所惡於上，毋以使下；所惡於下，毋以事上；所惡於前，毋以先後；所惡於後，毋以從前；所惡於右，毋以交於左；所惡於左，毋以交於右。此之謂絜矩之道。《詩》云："樂只君子，民之父母。"民之所好好之，民之所惡惡之，此之謂民之父母。《詩》云："節彼南山，維石巖巖。赫赫師尹，民具爾瞻。"有國者不可以不慎,辟則爲天下僇矣。

"Bringing peace to the realm lies in the ability to govern the country" means the following thing. If you respect the aged, the people will be encouraged to be filial. If you respect your elders, the people will be stimulated to respect their elders. If you pity the weak and defenseless, the people won't hurt them. Therefore the gentleman has the Dao of Correcting. What he hates in his superiors, he does not give to his inferiors; what he hates in those below him, he does not pass up to those above him. What he hates in those who are in front, he does not pass on to those behind; what he hates in those behind, he does not pass on to those in front. What he hates on the right, he doesn't transfer to the left; what he hates on the left, he doesn't transfer to the right. This is the Dao of Correcting. *The Book of Odes* says, "How wonderful is the prince! The parent of the people." What the people like, he likes. What the people hate, he hates. Thus he is called "the parent of the people". *The Book of Odes* says, "Lofty is that southern hill, with its rugged masses of rocks! Greatly distinguished are you, O grand-teacher Yin, the people all look up to you." He who possesses the country must be prudent. If he errs, he will be insulted by All-Under-Heaven.

《詩》云:"殷之未喪師,克配上帝。儀監于殷,峻命不易。"道得衆則得國,失衆則失國。是故君子先愼乎德。有德此有人,有人此有土,有土此有財,有財此有用。德者本也,財者末也,外本內末,爭民施奪。是故財聚則民散,財散則民聚。是故言悖而出者,亦悖而入;貨悖而入者,亦悖而出。《康誥》曰:"惟命不于常!"道善則得之,不善則失之矣。《楚書》曰:"楚國無以爲寶,惟善以爲寶。"舅犯曰:"亡人無以爲寶,仁親以爲寶。"

The Book of Odes says, "Before the sovereigns of the Yin Dynasty had lost the hearts of the people, they could appeal directly to the Lord on High. Learn from the Yin: The lofty mandate is not easy to maintain." This shows that, by gaining the people, the kingdom is gained, and, by losing the people, the kingdom is lost. Therefore the ruler must be concerned about his own virtue first. If he has virtue, he will have the people. If he has the people, he will have the land. If he has the land, he will have wealth. If he has wealth, he will be able to function. Thus, virtue is the "root" and wealth is the "branches". If you put the roots outside and the branches inside, you will struggle against your people, and make them grab for anything they can. If you gather the wealth, you will scatter the people. If you scatter the wealth, you will gather the people. Just like that the wrong words going out will result in the wrong words coming back in, wealth taken wrongly will also leave wrongly. "The Announcement of Kang" says, "The decree indeed may not always rest on us." When our ways are good we obtain it. When our ways are not good we lose it. The Chu Record says, "The state of Chu has no treasure. It treasures its good men." Uncle Fan (maternal uncle to a prince in exile) said, "Our exiled prince has no treasure. To be good to his parents is his only treasure."

《秦誓》曰："若有一介臣,斷斷兮無他技,其心休休焉,其如有容焉。人之有技,若己有之;人之彥聖,其心好之,不啻若自其口出。實能容之,以能保我子孫黎民,尚亦有利哉！人之有技,媢嫉以惡之;人之彥聖,而違之俾不通。實不能容,以不能保我子孫黎民,亦曰殆哉！"唯仁人放流之,迸諸四夷,不與同中國,此謂唯仁人爲能愛人,能惡人。見賢而不能舉,舉而不能先,命也;見不善而不能退,退而不能遠,過也。好人之所惡,惡人之所好,是謂拂人之性,菑必逮夫身。是故君子有大道,必忠信以得之,驕泰以失之。

"The Oath of the King of Qin" says, "I would like to have just one decisive man, without all kinds of specific abilities, whose mind was broad and easy, so that he could utilize the talents of others as if they were his own. Finding sages, he would sincerely love them with his heart, and not just give them lip-service. By being able to accept and utilize everyone in this way, he would be ensuring safety for me, my sons, grandsons and all the people. Wouldn't the benefits be great? But what can you do when you have a man who gets jealous of the abilities of others and hates them? When he hates the sage, he creates disturbances for them and keeps them from advancing. Since he cannot protect me, my son, grandsons or the common people, isn't he quite dangerous?" Only a man of benevolence can banish such a minister and send him out to live with the barbarian tribes away from the middle kingdoms. Thus the saying, "Only the benevolent man can love people and hate people." To see a worthy and be incapable of promoting him; to promote him, but not to the top—this is avoiding responsibility. To see someone evil and not remove him; or to remove him, but not completely get rid of him—this is a fatal error. To love that which the people hate, and hate that which the people love—this is to ignore human nature, and you are sure to bring great harm to yourself. Therefore the ruler attains the Great Dao through loyalty and trust, and loses it with arrogance and extravagance.

生財有大道。生之者眾，食之者寡，爲之者疾，用之者舒，則財恒足矣。仁者以財發身，不仁者以身發財。未有上好仁而下不好義者也，未有好義其事不終者也，未有府庫財非其財者也。

There is also a Great Dao for becoming wealthy. If producers are many and consumers are few, and production is rapid and use is slow, then there will always be enough. The benevolent ruler, by means of his wealth, makes himself more distinguished. The vicious ruler accumulates wealth, at the expense of his life. There is no such case where those in power love benevolence and those below dislike Justice (yi). And there is no case where a man loves Justice and is not thorough in his work. In this situation, there are no treasure houses in the state which do not belong to the ruler.

孟獻子曰：「畜馬乘，不察於雞豚；伐冰之家，不畜牛羊；百乘之家，不畜聚斂之臣。與其有聚斂之臣，寧有盜臣。」此謂國不以利爲利，以義爲利也。長國家而務財用者，必自小人矣。彼爲善之，小人之使爲國家，菑害並至。雖有善者，亦無如之何矣！此謂國不以利爲利，以義爲利也。

Meng Xianzi said, "The man who keeps horses and chariots does not look after chickens and pigs. The family that stores ice does not raise cattle and sheep. A hundred-chariot clan does not keep a tax-collector. If they are going to have a tax-collector, they might just as well have a thug." Thus the saying, "A state does not benefit by profiteering; it benefits by its Justice (yi)." One who rules a state or a clan and is fond of wealth must be under the influence of an inferior man. He may regard him as good, but if this man handles the affairs of the state or clan, calamities from Heaven and harm from men will be visited upon him. Even if a good man is finally found, what can he do? Thus the saying, "A state does not benefit from profiteering; it benefits from Justice."

《荀子》/ Xunzi

王制篇第九
Chapter 9　The Rule of a True King

請問爲政？曰：賢能不待次而舉，罷不能不待須而廢，元惡不待教而誅，中庸不待政而化。分未定也，則有昭繆。雖王公士大夫之子孫也，不能屬於禮義，則歸之庶人。雖庶人之子孫也，積文學，正身行，能屬於禮義，則歸之卿相士大夫。故姦言，姦說，姦事，姦能，遁逃反側之民，職而教之，須而待之，勉之以慶賞，懲之以刑罰。安職則畜，不安職則棄。五疾，上收而養之，材而事之，官施而衣食之，兼覆無遺。才行反時者死無赦。夫是之謂天德，是王者之政也。

Let us inquire into how to conduct the government. I say: In the case of worthy and able men, promote them without waiting for their turn to come up. In the case of inferior and incompetent men, dismiss them without hesitation. In the case of incorrigibly evil men, punish them without trying to reform them. In the case of people of average capacity, teach them what is right without attempting to force them into goodness. Thus, even where rank has not yet been fixed, the distinction between good and bad will be as clear as that between the left and right ancestors in the mortuary temple. Although a man may be the descendant of kings, dukes, or high court ministers, if he cannot adhere to ritual principles, he should be ranked among the commoners. Although a man may be the descendant of commoners, if he has acquired learning, is upright in conduct, and can adhere to ritual principles, he should be promoted to the post of prime minister or high court official. When it comes to men of perverse words and theories, perverse undertakings and talents, or to people who are slippery or vagrant, they should be given tasks to do, taught what is right, and allowed a period of trial. Encourage them with rewards, discipline them with punishments, and if they settle down to their work, then look after them as subjects; but if not, cast them out. In the case of those who belong to the five incapacitated groups, the government should gather them together, look after them, and give them whatever work they are able to do. Employ them, provide them with food and clothing, and take care to see that none are left out. If anyone is found acting or using his talents to work against the good of the time, condemn him to death without mercy. This is what is called the virtue of Heaven and the government of a true king.

聽政之大分：以善至者待之以禮，以不善至者待之以刑。兩者分別，則賢不肖不雜，是非不亂。賢不肖不雜，則英傑至，是非不亂，則國家治。若是，名聲日聞，天下願，令行禁止，王者之事畢矣。

These are the essential points to remember when listening to proposals in government. If you use ritual to treat those who come bearing goodness, and use punishment to treat those who come bearing badness, then the worthy and unworthy will not be jumbled up, and what is right and what is wrong will not be confused. If the worthy and unworthy are not jumbled up, then heroes and outstanding men will come. If what is right and what is wrong are not confused, then the state and family will be well ordered. If things are like this, then your fame will increase each day, all people under Heaven will esteem you, what you order will be carried out, what you prohibit will come to a stop, and the work of a true king will be complete.

凡聽：威嚴猛厲，而不好假道人，則下畏恐而不親，周閉而不竭。若是，則大事殆乎弛，小事殆乎遂。和解調通，好假道人，而無所凝止之，則姦言並至，嘗試之說鋒起。若是，則聽大事煩，是又傷之也。故法而不議，則法之所不至者必廢。職而不通，則職之所不及者必隊。故法而議，職而通，無隱謀，無遺善，而百事無過，非君子莫能。故公平者，聽之衡也；中和者，聽之繩也。其有法者以法行，無法者以類舉，聽之盡也。偏黨而無經，聽之辟也。故有良法而亂者，有之矣，有君子而亂者，自古及今，未嘗聞也。傳曰："治生乎君子，亂生乎小人。"此之謂也。

In listening to reports and proposals, if you are too stern and severe and have no patience in guiding and drawing others out, then your subordinates will be fearful and distant and will withdraw into themselves and be unwilling to speak. In such a case important matters are likely to be left unattended to and minor matters to be botched. If, however, you are too sympathetic and understanding, too fond of leading and drawing others out, and have no sense of where to stop, then men will come with all sorts of perverse suggestions and you will be flooded with dubious proposals. In such a case you will find yourself with too much to listen to and too much to do, and this also will be inimical to good government.

If there are laws, but in actual practice they do not prove to be of general applicability, then points not specifically covered by the laws are bound to be left undecided. If men are appointed to posts but they have no overall understanding of their duties, then matters which do not specifically fall within their jurisdiction are bound to be neglected. Therefore there must be laws that prove applicable in practice and men in office who have an overall understanding of their duties. There must be no hidden counsels or overlooked ability on the lower levels and all matters must proceed without error. Only a gentleman is capable of such government. Fair-mindedness is the balance in which to weigh proposals; upright harmoniousness is the line by which to measure them. Where laws exist, to carry them out; where they do not exist, to act in the spirit of precedent and analogy—this is the best way to hear proposals. To show favoritism and partisan feeling and be without any constant principles—this is the worst you can do. It is possible to have good laws and still have disorder in the state. But to have a gentleman acting as ruler and disorder in the state—from ancient times to the present I have never heard of such a thing. This is what the old text means when it says, "Order is born from the gentleman, disorder from the petty man."

分均則不偏,埶齊則不壹,眾齊則不使。有天有地,而上下有差;明王始立,而處國有制。夫兩貴之不能相事,兩賤之不能相使,是天數也。埶位齊,而欲惡同,物不能澹則必爭;爭則必亂,亂則窮矣。先王惡其亂也,故制禮義以分之,使有貧富貴賤之等,足以相兼臨者,是養天下之本也。《書》曰:"維齊非齊。"此之謂也。

"Where divisions of goods are all even, there will not be enough goods to go around; where power is equally distributed, there will be a lack of unity; where there is equality among the masses, it will be impossible to employ them. The very existence of Heaven and Earth exemplifies the principle of higher and lower, but only when an enlightened king appears on the throne can the nation be governed according to regulation. Two men of equal eminence cannot govern each other; two men of equally humble station cannot employ each other. This is the rule of Heaven. If men are of equal power and station and have the same likes and dislikes, then there will not be enough goods to supply their wants and they will inevitably quarrel. Quarreling must lead to disorder, and disorder to exhaustion. The former kings abhorred such disorder and therefore they regulated the principles of ritual in order to set up ranks. They established the distinctions between the rich and the poor, the eminent and the humble, making it possible for those above to join together and watch over those below. This is the basis upon which the people of the world are nourished. This is what The Book of Documents means when it says, "Complete equality is not order."

馬駭輿,則君子不安輿;庶人駭政,則君子不安位。馬駭輿,則莫若靜之;庶人駭政,則莫若惠之。選賢良,舉篤敬,興孝弟,收孤寡,補貧窮。如是,則庶人安政矣。庶人安政，然後君子安位。傳曰："君者，舟也；庶人者，水也。水則載舟，水則覆舟。"此之謂也。故君人者，欲安，則莫若平政愛民矣；欲榮，則莫若隆禮敬士矣；欲立功名，則莫若尚賢使能矣。是君人者之大節也。三節者當，則其餘莫不當矣。三節者不當，則其餘雖曲當，猶將無益也。孔子曰："大節是也，小節是也，上君也；大節是也，小節一出焉，一入焉，中君也；大節非也，小節雖是也，吾無觀其餘矣。"

If the horses are uneasy with the chariot, then the gentleman will not feel secure in riding the chariot. If the common people are uneasy with the government, then the gentleman will not feel secure in holding his position. When the horses are uneasy with the chariot, then nothing works better than calming them. When the common people are uneasy with the government, then nothing works better than treating them generously. Pick out those who are worthy and good. Raise high those who are dedicated and respectful. Promote those who are filial and act as good younger brothers. Take in those who are orphaned or widowed. Assist those who are poor and in dire straits. If you do this, then the common people will feel at ease with the government. When the common people feel at ease with the government, only then will the gentleman feel at ease in holding his position. There is a saying, "The lord is the boat. The common people are the water. The water can support the boat. The water can also overturn the boat." This expresses my meaning. Thus, if the lord of men wishes to be secure, then nothing works better than governing evenhandedly and showing concern for the people. If he wishes to have glory, then nothing works better than exalting ritual and respecting well-bred men. If he wishes to have accomplishments, then nothing works better than elevating the worthy and employing the capable. These are the great regulations in being the lord of men. If you abide by these three regulations, then the rest of your acts will all happen fittingly. If you do not abide by these three regulations, then even if the rest of your acts all happen fittingly, it will be of no benefit. Confucius says, "He who is right on the great regulations and right on the lesser regulations is a superior lord. He who is right on the great regulations, but who departs from the lesser regulations in some things while clinging to them in others, is a middling lord. For him who is wrong on the great regulations, even if he is right on the lesser regulations, I do not think he is competent."

成侯、嗣公聚斂計數之君也，未及取民也。子產取民者也，未及爲政也。管仲爲政者也，未及修禮也。故修禮者王，爲政者彊，取民者安，聚斂者亡。故王者富民，霸者富士，僅存之國富大夫，亡國富筐篋，實府庫。筐篋已富，府庫已實，而百姓貧，夫是之謂上溢而下漏。入不可以守，出不可以戰，則傾覆滅亡可立而待也。故我聚之以亡，敵得之以彊。聚斂者，召寇、肥敵、亡國、危身之道也，故明君不蹈也。

Marquis Cheng and Lord Si were rulers who knew how to collect taxes and keep accounts, but they did not succeed in winning the support of people. Zichan was a person who won over the people, but he never went as far as making government work. Guan Zhong was a person who made government work, but he never went as far as cultivating ritual. Thus:

He who cultivates ritual becomes a true king.

He who makes government work becomes strong.

He who wins over the people will be secure.

He who pays attention only to the collection of taxes will not last long.

Thus, a king enriches his people, a hegemon enriches his soldiers, a state that is barely managing to survive enriches its high officers, and a doomed state enriches only its coffers and stuffs its storehouses. When the coffers are rich and the treasuries are full, but the common people are destitute, this is called "overflowing at the top but leaking at the bottom". At home one cannot protect oneself, and abroad one cannot fight against enemies, and its downfall and destruction can be looked for at any moment. Hence,

If I collect excessive taxes then I cannot last long.

My enemy uses this chance to grow strong.

Too much attention to tax collecting invites bandits and fattens one's enemies. It is the path which leads to the destruction of the state and the peril of its lord, and for that reason the enlightened ruler does not follow it.

王奪之人,霸奪之與,彊奪之地。奪之人者臣諸侯,奪之與者友諸侯,奪之地者敵諸侯。臣諸侯者王,友諸侯者霸,敵諸侯者危。

He who seeks to become a true king seizes upon the right people. He who seeks to become a hegemon seizes upon good relations. He who seeks to rule by brute force seizes upon territory. He who seizes upon the right people will make the feudal lords his ministers. He who seizes upon good relations will make the feudal lords his friends. He who seizes upon territory will make the feudal lords his enemies. He who can make the feudal lords his ministers is a true king. He who can make the feudal lords his friends is a hegemon. He who makes the feudal lords his enemies is endangering himself.

用彊者:人之城守,人之出戰,而我以力勝之也,則傷人之民必甚矣;傷人之民甚,則人之民必惡我甚矣;人之民惡我甚,則日欲與我鬬。人之城守,人之出戰,而我以力勝之,則傷吾民必甚矣;傷吾民甚,則吾民之惡我必甚矣;吾民之惡我甚,則日不欲爲我鬬。人之民日欲與我鬬,吾民日不欲爲我鬬,是彊者之所以反弱也。地來而民去,累多而功少,雖守者益,所以守者損,是以大者之所以反削也。

He who lives by brute force must use his might to conquer the cities that other men guard and to defeat the soldiers that other men send forth to battle, and in doing so he inevitably inflicts great injury upon the people of other states. If he inflicts great injury upon them, they will inevitably hate him fiercely and will day by day grow more eager to fight against him. Moreover, he who uses his might to conquer the cities that other men guard and to defeat the soldiers that other men send forth to battle must inevitably inflict great injury upon his own people as well. If he inflicts great injury upon his own people, they will inevitably hate him fiercely and will day by day grow less eager to fight his battles. With the people of other states growing daily more eager to fight against him, and his own people growing daily less eager to fight in his defense, the ruler who relies upon strength will on the contrary be reduced to weakness. He acquires territory but loses the support of his people; his worries increase while his accomplishments dwindle. He finds himself with more and more cities to guard and less and less of the means to guard them with; thus in time the great state will on the contrary be stripped down in this way to insignificance.

諸侯莫不懷交接怨,而不忘其敵,伺彊大之間,承彊大之敝,此彊大之殆時也。知彊大者不務彊也,慮以王命,全其力,凝其德。力全則諸侯不能弱也,德凝則諸侯不能削也,天下無王霸主,則常勝矣,是知彊道者也。

The other feudal lords never cease to eye him with hatred and to dream of revenge; never do they forget their enmity. They spy out his weak points and take advantage of his defects, so that he lives in constant peril. He who truly understands how to use force does not work at being strong. He deliberates with a view to obtaining the kingly mandate. He keeps his strength undivided and solidifies his virtue. Since he keeps his strength undivided, then the feudal lords cannot weaken him. Since he solidifies his virtue, the feudal lords cannot diminish him. Thus, if he happens to live in a time when there is no true king or dictator in the world, he will always be victorious. This is the way of one who truly understands how to use force.

彼霸者則不然:辟田野,實倉廩,便備用,案謹募選閱材伎之士,然後漸慶賞以先之,嚴刑罰以糾之。存亡繼絕,衛弱禁暴,而無兼并之心,則諸侯親之矣。修友敵之道,以敬接諸侯,則諸侯說之矣。所以親之者,以不并也;并之見,則諸侯疏矣。所以說之者,以友敵也;臣之見,則諸侯離矣。故明其不并之行,信其友敵之道,天下無王霸主,則常勝矣。是知霸道者也。閔王毀於五國,桓公劫於魯莊,無它故焉,非其道而慮之以王也。

The hegemon is not so. He opens up lands for cultivation, fills the granaries, and sees that the people are provided with the goods they need. He is careful in selecting his officials and employs men of talent, leading them on with rewards and correcting them with punishments. He restores states that have perished, protects ruling lines that are in danger of dying out, guards the weak, and restrains the violent. If he shows no intention of annexing the territories of his neighbors, then the other feudal lords will draw close to him. If he treats them as friends and equals and is respectful in his dealings with them, he will win their favor. He can win their intimacy by not attempting to annex them, but if he shows any inclination to annex their lands, they will turn away from him. He can win their favor by treating them as friends and equals, but if he shows any inclination to treat them as subjects, they will reject him. Therefore he makes it clear from his actions that he does not wish to annex their territory, and inspires faith in them that he will always treat them as friends and equals. Thus, if he happens to live in a time when there is no true king in the world, he will always be victorious. This is the way of one who truly understands how to be a hegemon. The reason that King Min of Qi was defeated by the armies of the five states, and that Duke Huan of Qi was threatened by Duke Zhuang of Lu was none other than this: they did not follow the way appropriate to their own positions, but tried to act in the manner of a true king.

彼王者不然：仁眇天下，義眇天下，威眇天下。仁眇天下，故天下莫不親也；義眇天下，故天下莫不貴也；威眇天下，故天下莫敢敵也。以不敵之威，輔服人之道，故不戰而勝，不攻而得，甲兵不勞而天下服，是知王道者也。知此三具者，欲王而王，欲霸而霸，欲彊而彊矣。

The true king is not so: His ren (benevolence) towers over the world. His yi (righteousness) towers over the world. His awe-inspiring authority towers over the world. His ren towers over the world, and so no one in the world fails to have affection for him. His yi towers over the world, and so no one in the world fails to honor him. His awe-inspiring authority towers over the world, and so no one in the world dares to oppose him. He uses the awe-inspiring authority that cannot be opposed to assist his way of making people submit, and so he is victorious without engaging in battle, and makes gains without attacking people. Without labors of weapons and armor, the whole world submits to him. Such is one who understands the Dao of a true king. For one who understands these three means (i.e. ren, yi, and awe-inspiring authority), if he wishes to become a true king, then he becomes a true king. If he wishes to become a hegemon, then he becomes a hegemon. If he wishes to be strong, then he is strong.

王者之人：飾動以禮義，聽斷以類，明振毫末，舉措應變而不窮，夫是之謂有原。是王者之人也。

The character of a true king is that he ornaments his every move with ritual and yi. He hears and decides cases in accordance with their proper kinds. He has a clear view of all small things. His policies adapt to changes endlessly. This is called having a proper source [of action]. Such is the character of a true king.

王者之制：道不過三代，法不二後王；道過三代謂之蕩，法二後王謂之不雅。衣服有制，宮室有度，人徒有數，喪祭械用皆有等宜。聲則非雅聲者舉廢，色則凡非舊文者舉息，械用則凡非舊器者舉毀，夫是之謂復古，是王者之制也。

The rule of a true king is such that his ways do not go back beyond the Three Dynasties, and his models do not deviate from the later kings. If a person's way goes back beyond the Three Dynasties, he calls it reckless. If a person's model deviates from the later kings, he calls it unrefined. His clothing and garments are properly regulated. His palaces and homes have their proper measure. His followers have their proper order. In funerals and sacrifices, the implements all accord with rank and proper position. As for music, everything that is not of classical elegance is discarded. As for sights, everything that is not the patterns of old is discontinued. As for implements, everything that is not the equipment of old is destroyed. This is called recovering the ancient ways. Such is the rule of a true king.

王者之論：無德不貴，無能不官，無功不賞，無罪不罰。朝無幸位，民無幸生。尚賢使能，而等位不遺；析愿禁悍，而刑罰不過。百姓曉然皆知夫爲善於家，而取賞於朝也；爲不善於幽，而蒙刑於顯也。夫是之謂定論。是王者之論也。

The judgments of a true king are such that those without virtue are not honored, those without ability are not given office, those without meritorious accomplishment are not rewarded, and those without criminal trespass are not punished. In the court, no one obtains their position through luck. Among the people, no one obtains a livelihood through luck. He elevates the worthy and employs the capable, and no ranks and positions are left unattended. He cuts off false shows of virtue and prohibits brutality, but his punishments and penalties are not excessive. The common people then all clearly understand that if they do good deeds among their family they will receive rewards in the court, and if they do bad deeds in secret they will suffer punishment in the open. This is called having conclusive judgments. Such are the judgments of a true king.

王者之法：等賦、政事、財萬物，所以養萬民也。田野什一，關市幾而不征，山林澤梁，以時禁發而不稅。相地而衰政。理道之遠近而致貢。通流財物粟米，無有滯留，使相歸移也，四海之內若一家。故近者不隱其能，遠者不疾其勞，無幽閒隱僻之國，莫不趨使而安樂之。夫是之爲人師。是王者之法也。

On the model (fa) of a true king: He employs graduated taxation, governmental actions, and the myriad things to nourish the people. He only takes one-tenth of the produce from the fields. The mountain passes and markets are overseen but no fees are collected. The exploitation of mountain forests and dammed marshes is not taxed, but is prohibited in certain seasons. He measures up the quality of the land and adjusts his government policies accordingly. He reckons upon the distance of the route and requires contributions accordingly. He causes resources, goods, and grain to circulate without delays and causes each to move to its appropriate place, so that the entire region within the four seas becomes like a single family. Thus, those nearby do not hide their abilities, and those far away are not troubled by the required labor. Among the isolated and remote states, all quickly send envoys and take comfort and delight in him. This is called being the teacher of the people. Such is the model of a true king.

......

以類行雜,以一行萬。始則終,終則始,若環之無端也,舍是而天下以衰矣。天地者,生之始也;禮義者,治之始也;君子者,禮義之始也;爲之,貫之,積重之,致好之者,君子之始也。故天地生君子,君子理天地;君子者,天地之參也,萬物之摠也,民之父母也。無君子,則天地不理,禮義無統,上無君師,下無父子,夫是之謂至亂。君臣、父子、兄弟、夫婦,始則終,終則始,與天地同理,與萬世同久,夫是之謂大本。故喪祭、朝聘、師旅一也;貴賤、殺生、與奪一也;君君、臣臣、父父、子子、兄兄、弟弟一也;農農、士士、工工、商商一也。

...

One starts with general categories and moves to particular ones; one starts with unity and moves to plurality. What begins must end; what ends must begin again; and so the cycle repeats itself without interruption. If you abandon these things, then the whole world will consequently fall into decline. Heaven and Earth are the beginning of life. Ritual and yi are the beginning of order. The gentleman is the beginning of ritual and yi. Practicing them, habituating oneself in them, accumulating great regard for them, making oneself fond of them—these are the beginning of becoming a gentleman. Thus, Heaven and Earth give birth to the gentleman, and the gentleman brings order to Heaven and Earth. The gentleman is a third partner to Heaven and Earth, a supervisor for the myriad things, and a parent to the people. If there were no gentleman, then Heaven and Earth would not be properly ordered, and ritual and yi would be without a unifying guide. Above, there would be no lords or teachers, and below, there would be no fathers or sons. Such a state is called Utmost Chaos. The principles that apply to lord and minister, father and son, older brother and younger brother, husband and wife, from the beginning to the end and from the end to the beginning, are the same as the principles of Heaven and Earth, and these principles will never change—this is called the great root. And so, funerals, sacrifices, court appearances, royal greetings, and military matters all proceed by this one standard. Ennobling and degrading, killing and giving birth, and bestowing and taking all proceed by this one standard. To treat the lord as lord, the minister as minister, the father as father, the son as son, the elder brother as elder brother, and the younger brother as younger brother, all proceed by this one standard. To treat the farmer as farmer, the officer as officer, the craftsman as craftsman, and the merchant as merchant, all proceed by this one standard.

水火有氣而無生，草木有生而無知，禽獸有知而無義，人有氣、有生、有知，亦且有義，故最爲天下貴也。力不若牛，走不若馬，而牛馬爲用，何也？曰：人能群，彼不能群也。人何以能群？曰：分。分何以能行？曰：義。故義以分則和，和則一，一則多力，多力則彊，彊則勝物；故宮室可得而居也。故序四時，裁萬物，兼利天下，無它故焉，得之分義也。故人生不能無群，群而無分則爭，爭則亂，亂則離，離則弱，弱則不能勝物；故宮室不可得而居也，不可少頃舍禮義之謂也。

Water and fire have qi but are without life. Grasses and trees have life but are without awareness. Birds and beasts have awareness but are without yi. Humans have qi, life and awareness, and moreover they have yi. So they are the most precious things under Heaven. They are not as strong as oxen or as fast as horses, but oxen and horses are used by them. How is this so? I say it is because humans are able to form communities while the animals cannot. Why are humans able to form communities? I say it is because of social divisions. How can social divisions be put into practice? I say it is because of yi. And so if they use yi in order to make social divisions, then they will be harmonized. If they are harmonized, then they will be unified. If they are unified, then they will have more force. If they have more force, then they will be strong. If they are strong, then they will be able to overcome the animals. And so they can get to live in homes and palaces. Thus, the reason why humans can arrange things in accordance with the change of seasons, govern the myriad things, and bring benefit to all under Heaven is none other than that they are able to get these social divisions and yi. And so human life cannot be without community. If humans form communities but are without social divisions, then they will struggle. If they struggle, then there will be chaos. If there is chaos then they will disband. If they disband then they will be weak. If they are weak then they cannot overcome the animals. And so they will not get to live in homes and palaces. This is the meaning of saying that "one must not let go of ritual and yi for even a moment".

能以事親謂之孝,能以事兄謂之弟,能以事上謂之順,能以使下謂之君。君者,善群也。群道當,則萬物皆得其宜,六畜皆得其長,群生皆得其命。故養長時,則六畜育;殺生時,則草木殖;政令時,則百姓一,賢良服。

One who can use these to serve his parents is called filial. One who can use these to serve his elder brother is called a proper younger brother. One who can use these to serve his superiors is called properly compliant. One who can use these to employ his subordinates is called a proper lord. The true lord is one who is good at forming community. When the way of forming community is properly practiced, then the myriad things will each obtain what is appropriate for them, the six domestic animals will each obtain their proper growth, and all the various living things will obtain their proper life spans. And so, when nurturing accords with the proper times, then the six domestic animals will multiply. When reaping accords with the proper times, then the grasses and trees will flourish. If government commands accord with the proper times, then the common people will be united, and good and worthy men will submit and obey.

聖王之制也:草木榮華滋碩之時,則斧斤不入山林,不夭其生,不絕其長也。黿鼉魚鱉鰍鱣孕別之時,罔罟毒藥不入澤,不夭其生,不絕其長也。春耕、夏耘、秋收、冬藏,四者不失時,故五穀不絕,而百姓有餘食也。汙池淵沼川澤,謹其時禁,故魚鱉優多,而百姓有餘用也。斬伐養長不失其時,故山林不童,而百姓有餘材也。

These are the regulations of a sage king. When the grasses and trees are flowering and abundant, then axes and hatchets are not allowed to enter the mountains and forests, so as not to cut short their life, and not to break off their growth. When the turtles and crocodiles, fish and eels are pregnant and giving birth, then nets and poisons are not allowed to enter the marshes, so as not to cut short their life, and not to break off their growth. Plow in the spring, weed in the summer, harvest in the fall, and store in the winter. These four activities are not to miss their proper times, and then the five grains will not be depleted, and the common people will have a surplus to eat. Be vigilant in the seasonal prohibitions concerning ponds, rivers, and marshes, and then turtles and fish will be fine and plentiful, and the common people will have a surplus to use. Cutting and nurturing are not to miss their proper times, and then the mountains and forests will not be barren, and the common people will have surplus materials.

聖王之用也：上察於天，下錯於地，塞備天地之間，加施萬物之上，微而明，短而長，狹而廣，神明博大以至約。故曰：一與一是爲人者，謂之聖人。
......

This is the way a sage king operates. He observes Heaven above, and applies this knowledge on Earth below. He arranges completely everything between Heaven and Earth and spreads beneficence over the myriad things.

His actions are subtle, yet they are shining.

Though they are brief, their results are long-lasting.

Their scope is narrow, their impact wide-ranging.

He has spirit-like powers of intelligence that are broad and vast, yet works by the utmost restraint. Thus it is said: the person who by even the slightest movements always does what is right is called a sage.

...

《韓非子》/ Hanfeizi

主道第五
Chapter 5　The Dao of the Ruler

道者，萬物之始，是非之紀也。是以明君守始以知萬物之源，治紀以知善敗之端。故虛靜以待令，令名自命也，令事自定也。虛則知實之情，靜則知動者正。有言者自爲名，有事者自爲形，形名參同，君乃無事焉，歸之其情。

The Dao is the beginning of the myriad things and the standard of right and wrong. That being so, the intelligent ruler, by holding to the beginning, knows the source of everything, and, by keeping to the standard, knows the origin of good and evil. Therefore, he waits, empty and still, for the course of nature to enforce itself so that all names will be defined of themselves and all affairs will be settled of themselves. Empty, he knows the essence of fullness; still, he can correct the mover. Those whose duty is to speak will come forward to name themselves; those whose duty is to act will produce results. When names and results match, the ruler needs to do nothing more and the true aspect of all things will be revealed.

故曰：君無見其所欲，君見其所欲，臣自將雕琢；君無見其意，君見其意，臣將自表異。故曰：去好去惡，臣乃見素；去舊去智，臣乃自備。故有智而不以慮，使萬物知其處；有賢而不以行，觀臣下之所因；有勇而不以怒，使群臣盡其武。是故去智而有明，去賢而有功，去勇而有強。群臣守職，百官有常，因能而使之，是謂習常。

Hence the saying, "The ruler must not reveal his desires. For, if he reveals his desires, the ministers will polish their manners accordingly. The ruler must not reveal his views. For, if he reveals his views, the ministers will display their hues differently." Hence another saying, "If the like and hate of the ruler be concealed, the true hearts of the ministers will be revealed. If the experience and wisdom of the ruler be discarded, the ministers will take precautions." Accordingly, the ruler, wise as he is, should not bother but let everything find its proper place; worthy as he is, should not be self-assumed but observe closely the motives of his ministers; and, courageous as he is, should not flaunt his bravery in shows of indignation. So, leave the ruler's wisdom, then you will find the ministers' intelligence; leave the ruler's worthiness, then you will find the ministers' merits; and leave the ruler's courage, then you will find the ministers' strength. In such cases, ministers will attend to their duties, magistrates will have definite work routine, and everybody will be employed according to his special ability. Such a course of government is called "constant and immutable".

故曰：寂乎其無位而處，漻乎莫得其所。明君無爲於上，群臣竦懼乎下。明君之道，使智者盡其慮，而君因以斷事，故君不窮於智；賢者勑其材，君因而任之，故君不窮於能；有功則君有其賢，有過則臣任其罪，故君不窮於名。是故不賢而爲賢者師，不智而爲智者正。臣有其勞，君有其成功，此之謂賢主之經也。

Hence the saying, "So quiet, he seems to dwell nowhere at all; so vacant, he cannot be located." Thus, the intelligent ruler does nothing, but his ministers tremble all the more. This is the Dao of the intelligent ruler: he makes the wise men exhaust their mental energy and makes his decisions accordingly; hence his own wisdom is never exhausted. He makes the worthy men exert their talents and appoints them to office accordingly; hence his own worth never comes to an end. Where there are accomplishments, the ruler takes credit for their worth; where there are errors, the ministers are held responsible for the blame; hence the ruler's reputation never dies. Therefore, the ruler, even though not worthy, becomes the master of the worthies, and, even though not wise, becomes the corrector of the wise men. It is the ministers who do the toil; it is the ruler who enjoys the success. This is the everlasting principle of the worthy sovereign.

道在不可見，用在不可知。虛靜無事，以闇見疵。見而不見，聞而不聞，知而不知。知其言以往，勿變勿更，以參合閱焉。官有一人，勿令通言，則萬物皆盡。函掩其跡，匿其端，下不能原。去其智，絕其能，下不能意。保吾所以往而稽同之，謹執其柄而固握之。絕其能望，破其意，毋使人欲之。

The Dao lies in what cannot be seen, its function in what cannot be known. Be empty, still, and idle, and from your place of darkness observe the defects of others. See but do not appear to see; listen but do not seem to listen; know but do not let others known that you know. When you perceive the trend of a man's word, do not change them, do not correct them, but examine them and compare them with results. Assign one man to each office and do not let men talk to each other, and then all will do their utmost. Hide your tracks, conceal your sources, so that your subordinates cannot trace the springs of your action. Discard wisdom, and forswear ability, so that your subordinates cannot guess what you are about. Stick to your objectives and examine the results to see how they match; take hold of the handles of government carefully and grip them tightly. Destroy all hope, smash all intention of wresting the handles from you; allow no man to covet them.

不謹其閉，不固其門，虎乃將存。不慎其事，不掩其情，賊乃將生。弒其主，代其所，人莫不與，故謂之虎。處其主之側，爲姦臣，聞其主之忒，故謂之賊。散其黨，收其餘，閉其門，奪其輔，國乃無虎。大不可量，深不可測，同合刑名，審驗法式，擅爲者誅，國乃無賊。

If you do not guard the door, if you do not strengthen the gate, then tigers will lurk there. If you are not cautious in your undertakings, if you do not hide their true aspect, then traitors will arise. They murder their sovereign and usurp his place, and all men in fear make common cause with them. Hence they are called tigers. They sit by the ruler's side and, in the service of cunning ministers, spy into his secrets. Hence they are called traitors. Smash their cliques, arrest their backers, shut the gate, deprive them of all hope of support, and the nation will be free of tigers. Be immeasurably great, be unfathomably deep, make certain that names and results tally, examine laws and customs, punish those who act willfully, and the state will be without traitors.

是故人主有五壅：臣閉其主曰壅，臣制財利曰壅，臣擅行令曰壅，臣得行義曰壅，臣得樹人曰壅。臣閉其主則主失位，臣制財利則主失德，臣擅行令則主失制，臣得行義則主失明，臣得樹人則主失黨。此人主之所以獨擅也，非人臣之所以得操也。

The ruler of men stands in danger of being blocked in five ways. When the ministers shut out their ruler, this is one kind of block. When they get control of the wealth and resources of the state, this is a second kind of block. When they are free to issue orders as they please, this is a third kind. When they are able to do righteous deeds in their own name, this is a fourth kind. When they are able to build up their own cliques, this is a fifth kind. If the ministers shut out the ruler, then the ruler loses the effectiveness of his position. If they control wealth and resources, he loses the means of dispensing bounty to others. If they issue orders as they please, he loses the means of command. If they are able to carry out righteous deeds in their own name, he loses his claim to wisdom. And if they can build up cliques of their own, he loses his supporters. All these are rights that should be exercised by the ruler alone; they should never pass into the hands of his ministers.

人主之道，靜退以為寶。不自操事而知拙與巧，不自計慮而知福與咎。是以不言而善應，不約而善增。言已應則執其契，事已增則操其符。符契之所合，賞罰之所生也。故群臣陳其言，君以其言授其事，事以責其功。功當其事，事當其言則賞；功不當其事，事不當其言則誅。明君之道，臣不得陳言而不當。

The way of the ruler of men is to treasure stillness and reclusion. Without handling affairs himself, he can recognize clumsiness or skill in others; without laying plans of his own, he knows what will bring fortune or misfortune. Hence he does not need to speak any words, but good answers will be given to him; he does not need to exact any promises, but good works will increase. When proposals have been brought before him, he takes careful note of their content; when undertakings are well on their way, he takes careful note of the result; and from the degree to which proposals and results tally, rewards and punishments are born. Thus the ruler assigns undertakings to his various ministers on the basis of the words they speak, and assesses their accomplishments according to the way they have carried out the undertaking. When accomplishments match the undertaking, and the undertaking matches what was said about it, then he rewards the man; when these things do not match, he punishes the man. It is the way of the enlightened ruler never to allow his ministers to speak words that cannot be matched by results.

是故明君之行賞也，曖乎如時雨，百姓利其澤；其行罰也，畏乎如雷霆，神聖不能解也。故明君無偷賞，無赦罰。賞偷則功臣墮其業，赦罰則姦臣易為非。是故誠有功，則雖疏賤必賞；誠有過，則雖近愛必誅。疏賤必賞，近愛必誅，則疏賤者不怠，而近愛者不驕也。
……

For this reason, the wise ruler, in bestowing rewards, is as benign as the seasonable rain that profits all people; in inflicting punishments, he is so terrible like the loud thunder that even divines and sages cannot assuage him. Thus the wise ruler is never overliberal in his rewards, never overlenient in his punishments. If his rewards are too liberal, then ministers who have won merit in the past will grow lax in their duties; and if his punishments are too lenient, then cunning ministers will find it easy to do wrong. Thus if a man has truly won merit, no matter how humble and far removed he may be, he must be rewarded; and if he has truly committed error, no matter how close and dear to the ruler he may be, he must be punished. If those who are humble and far removed can be sure of reward, and those close and dear to the ruler can be sure of punishment, then the former will not become lazy and the latter will not grow proud.①

二柄第七
Chapter 7　The Two Handles

明主之所導制其臣者，二柄而已矣。二柄者，刑德也。何謂刑德？曰：殺戮之謂刑，慶賞之謂德。爲人臣者畏誅罰而利慶賞，故人主自用其刑德，則群臣畏其威而歸其利矣。故世之姦臣則不然，所惡則能得之其主而罪之，所愛則能得之其主而賞之。今人主非使賞罰之威利出於己也，聽其臣而行其賞罰，則一國之人皆畏其臣而易其君，歸其臣而去其君矣。此人主失刑德之患也。

The means whereby the wise ruler controls his ministers are two handles only. The two handles are punishment and reward. What do punishment and reward mean? To inflict death or torture upon culprits is called punishment; to bestow honor or wealth on men of merit is called reward. Ministers are afraid of punishment but fond of reward. Therefore, if the ruler uses the handles of punishment and reward, all ministers will fear his awesomeness and flock to receive his benefits. The villainous ministers of the age are different. They persuade the ruler to let them inflict punishment themselves on men they hate and bestow favors on men they like. Now suppose the ruler does not insist upon reserving to himself the authority to dispense profit in the form of rewards and show his awesome power in punishments, but instead allows his ministers to hand these out. Then the people of the state will all fear the ministers and treat the ruler with disrespect; they will flock to the ministers and desert the ruler. This is the danger that arises when the ruler loses control of punishments and rewards.

---

　　① In this part, I often pick Burton Watson's translation instead of W. K. Liao's, because the former is more reliable than the latter. When I find Watson's translation inaccurate, I offer my own translation.

夫虎之所以能服狗者,爪牙也。使虎釋其爪牙而使狗用之,則虎反服於狗矣。人主者,以刑德制臣者也,今君人者釋其刑德而使臣用之,則君反制於臣矣。故田常上請爵祿而行之群臣,下大斗斛而施於百姓,此簡公失德而田常用之也,故簡公見弒。子罕謂宋君曰:"夫慶賞賜予者,民之所喜也,君自行之;殺戮刑罰者,民之所惡也,臣請當之。"於是宋君失刑而子罕用之,故宋君見劫。田常徒用德而簡公弒,子罕徒用刑而宋君劫。故今世爲人臣者兼刑、德而用之,則是世主之危甚於簡公、宋君也。故劫殺擁蔽之主,兼失刑、德而使臣用之而不危亡者,則未嘗有也。

The tiger is able to overpower the dog because of his claws and teeth, but if he discards his claws and teeth and lets the dog use them, then he will be overpowered by the dog. The ruler of men uses punishments and rewards to control his ministers, but if he discards his punishments and rewards and lets his ministers dispense them, then he will fall under the control of his ministers. Tian Chang petitioned the ruler for various offices and stipends which he then dispensed to the lesser ministers, and he used oversize measures when he doled out grain to the common people. In this way the ruler, Duke Jian of Qi, lost the exclusive right to dispense favors, and it passed into Tian Chang's hands. Thus it was that Duke Jian came to be assassinated. Zihan said to the King of Song, "Since the people all delight in honor and wealth, you should bestow them yourself; but since they hate torture and death sentences, allow me to dispense these for you." Thereupon the King of Song gave up control over penalties and it passed into the hands of Zihan. Thus it was that the King of Song came under the power of others. Tian Chang got hold of the power to reward and Duke Jian was assassinated; Zihan got hold of the power to punish and the King of Song fell under his power. Ministers today are permitted to gain control over both punishment and reward; their rulers put themselves in greater peril than Duke Jian and the King of Song. When rulers are coerced, assassinated, obstructed, or subject to deception, it is invariably because they lost control over punishment and reward to their ministers, and thus brought about their own peril and downfall.

人主將欲禁姦,則審合刑名;刑名者,言與事也。爲人臣者陳而言,君以其言授之事,專以其事責其功。功當其事,事當其言則賞;功不當其事,事不當其言則罰。故群臣其言大而功小者則罰,非罰小功也,罰功不當名也。群臣其言小而功大者亦罰,非不說於大功也,以爲不當名之害甚於有大功,故罰。

If the ruler of men wishes to put an end to evil-doing, then he must be careful to match up names and results, that is to say, words and deeds. The ministers come forward to present their proposals; the ruler assigns them tasks on the basis of their words, and then concentrates on demanding the accomplishment of the task. If the accomplishment fits the task, and the task fits the words, then he bestows reward; if they do not match, he doles out punishment. Hence, if one of the ministers comes forward with big words but produces only small accomplishments, the ruler punishes him, not because the accomplishments are small, but because they do not match the name that was given to the undertaking. Likewise, if one of the ministers comes forward with small words but produces great accomplishments, he too is punished, not because the ruler is displeased at great accomplishments, but because he considers the discrepancy in the name given to the undertaking to be a fault too serious to be outweighed by great accomplishments.

昔者韓昭侯醉而寢,典冠者見君之寒也,故加衣於君之上,覺寢而説,問左右曰:"誰加衣者?"左右對曰:"典冠。"君因兼罪典衣與典冠。其罪典衣,以爲失其事也;其罪典冠,以爲越其職也。非不惡寒也,以爲侵官之害甚於寒。故明主之畜臣,臣不得越官而有功,不得陳言而不當。越官則死,不當則罪,守業其官,所言者貞也,則群臣不得朋黨相爲矣。

Once in the past, Marquis Zhao of Han got drunk and fell asleep. The keeper of the royal hat, seeing that the marquis was cold, laid a robe over him. When the marquis awoke, he was pleased and asked his attendants,

"Who covered me with a robe?" "The keeper of the hat," they replied. The marquis thereupon punished both the keeper of the royal hat and the keeper of the royal robe. He punished the keeper of the robe for failing to do his duty, and the keeper of the hat for overstepping his office. It was not that he liked catching a cold, but he considered the trespass of one official upon the duties of another to be a greater danger than catching a cold. Hence a wise ruler, in handling his ministers, does not permit them to gain merit by overstepping their offices, or to speak words that do not tally with their actions. Those who overstep their offices are condemned to die; those whose words and actions do not tally are punished. If the ministers are made to stick to their proper duties and speak only what they can deliver, then they will be unable to band together in cliques to work for each other's benefit.

人主有二患：任賢，則臣將乘於賢以劫其君；妄舉，則事沮不勝。故人主好賢，則群臣飾行以要君欲，則是群臣之情不效；群臣之情不效，則人主無以異其臣矣。故越王好勇而民多輕死；楚靈王好細腰而國中多餓人；齊桓公妒而好內，故豎刁自宮以治內；桓公好味，易牙蒸其子首而進之；燕子噲好賢，故子之明不受國。

The ruler has two difficulties to face: if he appoints only worthy men to office, his ministers will use the appeal to worthiness as a means to intimidate him; if he makes arbitrary promotions of officials, then state affairs will be bungled and will never reach a successful conclusion. Hence, if the ruler shows a fondness for worth, his ministers will all strive to put a pleasing facade on their actions in order to satisfy his desires. In such a case, they will never show their true colors, and if they never show their true colors, then the ruler will have no way to distinguish the able from the worthless. For instance, because the King of Yue admired bravery, many of his subjects defied death; because King Ling of Chu liked slim waists, his state was full of half-starved people on diets. Because Duke Huan of Qi was jealous and loved women, Shu Diao castrated himself in order to be put in charge of the harem; because the duke was fond of unusual food, Yiya steamed his sons head and offered it to the duke. Because Zikuai of Yan admired worthy men, Zizhi pretended that he would not accept the throne even if it were offered to him.

故君見惡，則群臣匿端；君見好，則群臣誣能。人主欲見，則群臣之情態得其資矣。故子之託於賢以奪其君者也，豎刁、易牙因君之欲以侵其君者也。其卒子噲以亂死，桓公蟲流出戶而不葬。此其故何也？人君以情借臣之患也。人臣之情非必能愛其君也，爲重利之故也。今人主不掩其情，不匿其端，而使人臣有緣以侵其主，則群臣爲子之、田常不難矣。故曰："去好去惡，群臣見素。"群臣見素，則大君不蔽矣。

Thus, if the ruler reveals what he dislikes, his ministers will be careful to disguise their motives; if he shows what he likes, his ministers will feign abilities they do not have. In short, if he lets his desires be known, he gives his ministers a clue as to what attitude they had best assume. Hence, by playing the part of a worthy, Zizhi was able to snatch power from his sovereign; Shu Diao and Yiya, by catering to the rulers' desires, were able to invade their authority. As a result, Zikuai died in the chaos that ensued, and Duke Huan was left unburied for so long that maggots came crawling out the door of his death chamber. What caused this? It is an example of the calamity that comes when the ruler reveals his feelings to his ministers. Every minister in his heart of hearts does not necessarily love the ruler. If he does, it is for the sake of his own great advantage. Now if the ruler does not hide his feelings and conceal his motives, but instead gives his ministers a foothold by which they may invade his authority, then they will have no difficulty in doing what Zizhi and Tian Chang did. Hence it is said, "Do away with likes, do away with hates, and the ministers will show their true colors. And when the ministers have shown their true colors, the ruler will never be deceived."

大體第二十九
Chapter 29　Fundamental Principles

　　古之全大體者：望天地，觀江海，因山谷，日月所照，四時所行，雲布風動；不以智累心，不以私累己；寄治亂於法術，托是非於賞罰，屬輕重於權衡；不逆天理，不傷情性；不吹毛而求小疵，不洗垢而察難知；不引繩之外，不推繩之內；不急法之外，不緩法之內；守成理，因自然；禍福生乎道法，而不出乎愛惡；榮辱之責在乎己，而不在乎人。

　　The ancients who understood the whole and the fundamental principles observed Heaven and Earth, surveyed rivers and oceans, and followed mountains and ravines; wherefore they ruled as the sun and the moon shine, worked as the four seasons rotate, and benefited the world in the way clouds spread and winds move. They never burdened their mind with schemes, nor did they ever burden themselves with selfish gain. Instead, they employed law and tact to maintain social order and avoid chaos, depended upon reward and punishment for praising the right and blaming the wrong, and assigned all measures of lightness and heaviness to yard and weight. They never acted contrary to the course of Heaven, never went against human nature, never blew at the hair to look for a mote, never washed off any dirt to investigate anything hard to know, never drew the inked string off the line and never pushed the inked string inside the line, and was neither severe beyond the boundary of law nor lenient within the boundary of law; but observed acknowledged principles and followed the laws of nature. Whether you acquire good things or suffer depends on whether you follow the Dao and the law, not on whether you love or hate something; whether you obtain honor or disgrace depends on yourself rather than others.

　　故至安之世，法如朝露，純樸不散，心無結怨，口無煩言。故車馬不疲弊於遠路，旌旗不亂乎大澤，萬民不失命於寇戎，雄駿不創壽於旗幢；豪傑不著名於圖書，不錄功於盤盂，記年之牒空虛。故曰：利莫長乎簡，福莫久于安。

In the perfectly peaceful society, the law is like the morning dew, pure and simple but not yet dispersed. There is no resentment in the mind nor is there any quarrelsome word from the mouth. Carriages and horses, accordingly, are never worn out on the road; flags and banners are never confused on the big swamps; the myriad people never get killed by bandits and enemies; courageous warriors never die under the flags of the state; heroes are not reputed in pictures and books nor are their merits recorded on plates and vases; and documents of annals are left empty. Hence the saying: "Only simplicity can bring about the utmost benefits; only peace can bring about the lasting happiness."

使匠石以千歲之壽，操鉤，視規矩，舉繩墨，而正太山；使賁、育帶干將而齊萬民；雖盡力于巧，極盛于壽，太山不正，民不能齊。故曰：古之牧天下者，不使匠石極巧以敗太山之體，不使賁、育盡威以傷萬民之性。

Suppose the stonemason can live one thousand years and try to use his hook, compasses, set square, and inked string to rectify Mountain Tai. No matter however long the stonemason tries, Mountain Tai cannot be thereby corrected. Suppose strong and brave men like Ben and Yu try to use the Ganjiang Sword to unify the myriad people. No matter however skillful and strong these men are, the people cannot be thereby unified. Hence the saying, "The ancient ruler of the world did not employ a skillful stonemason for he can only destroy Mountain Tai, nor did they employ strong people like Ben and Yu for they can only harm the human nature of the myriad people."

因道全法，君子樂而大奸止。澹然閒靜，因天命，持大體。故使人無離法之罪，魚無失水之禍。如此，故天下少不可。

Following the Dao and completely understanding the law, the

gentleman is happy. There are no masters of cunning. Placid, serene, and leisurely, the wise ruler simply follows the decree of Heaven and applies the fundamental principles to deal with public affairs. Therefore, he makes the people commit no crime of going astray from law and the fish suffer no disaster like losing water. Consequently, few things in the world do not go well.

上不天則下不遍覆,心不地則物不畢載。太山不立好惡,故能成其高;江海不擇小助,故能成其富。故大人寄形於天地而萬物備,曆心於山海而國家富。上無忿怒之毒,下無伏怨之患,上下交順,以道爲舍。故長利積,大功立,名成於前,德垂於後,治之至也。

If the ruler's position is not as high as Heaven, he never will be able to protect all creatures; if his mind is not as firm as Earth, he never will be able to support all creatures. Mountain Tai, seeing no difference between desirable and undesirable stones, can maintain its height; the Yangtze and the oceans, making no discrimination against small streams, can accomplish their abundance. If the superior follows the way of Heaven and Earth, he will have everything; if he follows the way of Mountain Tai, the Yangtze, and the oceans, the state will be rich. The superior does not punish anybody out of anger, and the inferior does not want to rebel against the superior out of resentment. Instead, the superior and the inferior are on friendly terms and both follow the Dao. Consequently, long-term interests will be obtained, great projects will be accomplished, great reputation will be enjoyed during the lifetime, and great virtue will be admired by the future generations. This is the perfect government.

五蠹第四十九

Chapter 49 Five Vermin: A Pathological Analysis of Politics

上古之世,人民少而禽獸衆,人民不勝禽獸蟲蛇。有聖人作,搆木爲巢以避羣害,而民悅之,使王天下,號之曰有巢氏。民食果、蓏、蚌、蛤,腥、臊、惡、臭,而傷害腹胃,民多疾病。有聖人作,鑽燧取火,以化腥臊,而民說之,使王天下,號之曰燧人氏。中古之世,天下大水,而鯀、禹決瀆。近古之世,桀、紂暴亂,而湯、武征伐。今有構木鑽燧於夏后氏之世者,必爲鯀、禹笑矣;有決瀆於殷、周之世者,必爲湯、武笑矣。然則今有美堯、舜、禹、湯、武之道於當今之世者,必爲新聖笑矣。是以聖人不期循古,不法常行,論世之事,因爲之備。

In the age of remote antiquity, human beings were few while birds and beasts were numerous. Human beings were unable to overcome birds, beasts, insects, and serpents. There appeared a sage who made nests by putting pieces of wood together to shelter people from harm. The people were so delighted that they made him ruler of All-Under-Heaven and called him the Nest-Builder. In those days the people lived on the fruits of trees and seeds of grass as well as mussels and clams, which smelt rank and fetid and hurt the digestive organs. As many of them were affected with diseases, there appeared a sage who twisted a drill to make fire which changed the fetid and musty smell. The people were so delighted that they made him ruler of All-Under-Heaven and called him the Drill Man.

In the age of middle antiquity, there was a great deluge in All-Under-Heaven, wherefore Gun and Yu opened channels for the water. In the age of recent antiquity, Jie and Zhou were violent and turbulent, wherefore Tang and Wu overthrew them.

Now if anyone had built wooden nests or drilled for fire in the time of the Xia Dynasty, Gun and Yu would have laughed at him, and if anyone had tried to open channels for the water during the Yin or Zhou Dynasties, Tang and Wu would have laughed at him.

That is the reason why the sage neither seeks to follow the ways of the ancients nor establishes any fixed standard for all times but examines the things of his age and then prepares to deal with them.

宋人有耕田者,田中有株,兔走觸株,折頸而死。因釋其耒而守株,冀復得兔,兔不可復得,而身爲宋國笑。今欲以先王之政,治當世之民,皆守株之類也。

There was in Song a man, who tilled a field in which there stood the trunk of a tree. Once a hare, while running fast, rushed against the trunk, broke its neck, and died. Thereupon the man cast his plough aside and watched that tree, hoping that he would get another hare in the same way. Yet he never caught another hare and was himself ridiculed by the people of Song. Now if somebody wanted to govern the people of the present age with the policies of the early kings, he would be doing exactly the same thing as that man who watched the tree.

古者丈夫不耕，草木之實足食也；婦人不織，禽獸之皮足衣也。不事力而養足，人民少而財有餘，故民不爭。是以厚賞不行，重罰不用，而民自治。今人有五子不爲多，子又有五子，大父未死而有二十五孫。是以人民衆而貨財寡，事力勞而供養薄，故民爭，雖倍賞累罰而不免於亂。

In olden times, men did not need to till, for the seeds of grass and the fruits of trees were sufficient to feed them; nor did women have to weave, for the skins of birds and beasts were sufficient to clothe them. Thus, without working hard, they had an abundance of supply. As the people were few, their possessions were more than sufficient. Therefore the people never quarreled. As a result, neither large rewards were bestowed nor were heavy punishments employed, but the people governed themselves. Nowadays, however, people do not regard five children as many. Each child may in his or her turn beget five offspring, so that before the death of the grandfather there may be twenty-five grand-children. As a result, people have become numerous and supplies scanty; toil has become hard and provisions meager. Therefore people quarrel so much that, though rewards are doubled and punishments repeated, disorder is inevitable.

堯之王天下也，茅茨不翦，采椽不斲，糲粢之食，藜藿之羹；冬日麑裘，夏日葛衣，雖監門之服養，不虧於此矣。禹之王天下也，身執耒臿，以爲民先，股無胈，脛不生毛，雖臣虜之勞，不苦於此矣。以是言之，夫古之讓天子者，是去監門之養，而離臣虜之勞也，古傳天下而不足多也。今之縣令，一日身死，子孫累世絜駕，故人重之。是以人之於讓也,輕辭古之天子,難去今之縣令者,薄厚之實異也。

When Yao ruled the world, he left the thatch of his roof untrimmed, and his speckled beams were not planed. He ate coarse millet and a soup of greens, wore deer skin in winter days and rough fiber robes in summer. Even a lowly gatekeeper was no worse clothed and provided for than Yao. When Yu ruled the world, he took plow and spade in hand to lead his people, working until there was no more down on his thighs or hair on his shins. Even the toil of a slave taken prisoner in the wars was no bitterer than his. Therefore those men in ancient times who abdicated and relinquished the rule of the world were, in a manner of speaking, merely forsaking the life of a gatekeeper and escaping from the toil of a slave. Therefore they thought little of handing over the rule of the world to someone else. Nowadays, however, the magistrate of a district dies and his sons and grandsons are able to go riding about in carriages for generations after. Therefore people prize such offices. In the matter of relinquishing things, people thought nothing of stepping down from the position of the Son of Heaven in ancient times, yet they are very reluctant to give up the post of district magistrate today; this is because of the difference in the actual benefits received.

夫山居而谷汲者,膢臘而相遺以水;澤居苦水者,買庸而決竇。故饑歲之春,幼弟不饟;穰歲之秋,疏客必食。非疏骨肉愛過客也,多少之實異也。是以古之易財,非仁也,財多也;今之爭奪,非鄙也,財寡也。輕辭天子,非高也,勢薄也;重爭士橐,非下也,權重也。故聖人議多少,論薄厚爲之政。故罰薄不爲慈,誅嚴不爲戾,稱俗而行也。故事因於世,而備適於事。

Those who live in the mountains and must descend to the valley to fetch their water give each other gifts of water at festival time. Those who live in the swamps and are troubled by dampness actually hire laborers to dig ditches to drain off the water. In the spring following a famine year even the little boys of the family get no food; in the fall of a year of plenty even casual visitors are feasted. It is not that men are indifferent to their own flesh and blood and generous to passing visitors; it is because of the difference in the amount of food to be had. Hence, when men of ancient times made light of material goods, it was not because they were benevolent, but because there was a surplus of goods; and when men quarrel and snatch today, it is not because they are vicious, but because goods have grown scarce. When men lightly relinquish the position of the Son of Heaven, it is not because they are high-minded, but because the advantages of the post are slight; when men strive for sinecures in the government, it is not because they are base, but because the power they will acquire is great. When the sage rules, he takes into consideration the quantity of things and deliberates on scarcity and plenty. Though his punishments may be light, this is not due to his compassion; though his penalties may be severe, this is not because he is cruel; he simply follows the custom appropriate to the time. Circumstances change according to the age, and ways of dealing with them change with the circumstances.

　　古者，文王處豐、鎬之間，地方百里，行仁義而懷西戎，遂王天下。徐偃王處漢東，地方五百里，行仁義，割地而朝者三十有六國。荊文王恐其害己也，舉兵伐徐，遂滅之。故文王行仁義而王天下，偃王行仁義而喪其國，是仁義用於古而不用於今也。故曰："世異則事異。"當舜之時，有苗不服，禹將伐之。舜曰："不可。上德不厚而行武，非道也。"乃修教三年，執干戚舞，有苗乃服。共工之戰，鐵銛距者及乎敵，鎧甲不堅者傷乎體。是干戚用於古不用於今也。故曰："事異則備變。"

In ancient times, King Wen of Zhou lived in the area between Feng and Hao, his domain no more than a hundred li square, but he practiced benevolence and righteousness, won over the Western Barbarians, and eventually became ruler of the world. King Yan of Xu lived east of the Han River in a territory five hundred li square. He practiced benevolence and righteousness, and thirty-six states came with gifts of territory to pay him tribute, until King Wen of Jing, fearing for his own safety, called out his troops, attacked Xu, and wiped it out. Thus King Wen of Zhou practiced benevolence and righteousness and became ruler of the world, but King Yan of Xu practiced benevolence and righteousness and destroyed his state. This is because benevolence and righteousness served for ancient times, but no longer serve today. So I say that circumstances differ with the age. In the time of Shun, the Miao tribes were unsubmissive, and Yu proposed to attack them. But Shun said, "That will not do! To take up arms while the virtue of the ruler is not yet perfected would be a violation of the Dao." Shun cultivated virtue for the following three years, and then took up shield and battle-ax and performed the war dance, and the Miao submitted. But in the war with the Gonggong, men used iron lances with steel heads that reached the enemy, so that unless one was protected by a stout helmet and armor he was likely to be wounded. Hence shields and battle-axes served for ancient times, but no longer serve today. So I say that as circumstances change the ways of dealing with them alter too.

上古競於道德,中世逐於智謀,當今爭於氣力。齊將攻魯,魯使子貢說之。齊人曰:"子言非不辯也,吾所欲者土地也,非斯言所謂也。"遂舉兵伐魯,去門十里以爲界。故偃王仁義而徐亡,子貢辯智而魯削。以是言之,夫仁義、辯智,非所以持國也。去偃王之仁,息子貢之智,循徐、魯之力,使敵萬乘,則齊、荊之欲不得行於二國矣。

Men of high antiquity strove for moral virtue; men of middle times sought out clever schemes; men of today vie to be known for strength and spirit. Qi was once planning an attack on Lu. Lu dispatched Zigong to dissuade the men of Qi, but they replied, "Your words are eloquent enough. But what we want is territory, and that is the one thing you have not mentioned." So in the end Qi called out its troops, attacked Lu, and fixed its boundary line only ten li away from the Lu capital gate. King Yan practiced benevolence and righteousness and the state of Xu was wiped out; Zigong employed eloquence and cleverness and Lu lost territory. So it is obvious that benevolence, righteousness, eloquence, and cleverness are not the means by which to maintain the state. Discard the benevolence of King

Yan and put an end to Zigong's cleverness; build up the might of Xu and Lu until they can stand face to face with a state of ten thousand war chariots—then Qi and Jing will no longer be able to do with them as they please!

　　夫古今異俗，新故異備。如欲以寬緩之政，治急世之民，猶無轡策而御駻馬，此不知之患也。今儒、墨皆稱先王兼愛天下，則視民如父母。何以明其然也？曰："司寇行刑，君爲之不舉樂；聞死刑之報，君爲流涕。"此所舉先王也。夫以君臣爲如父子則必治，推是言之，是無亂父子也。人之情性，莫先於父母，皆見愛而未必治也，雖厚愛矣，奚遽不亂？今先王之愛民，不過父母之愛子，子未必不亂也，則民奚遽治哉？且夫以法行刑，而君爲之流涕，此以效仁，非以爲治也。夫垂泣不欲刑者，仁也；然而不可不刑者，法也。先王勝其法，不聽其泣，則仁之不可以爲治，亦明矣。

　　Past and present have different customs; new and old adopt different measures. To try to use the ways of a generous and lenient government to rule the people of a critical age is like trying to drive a runaway horse without using reins or whip. This is the misfortune that ignorance invites. Now the Confucians and Mohists all praise the ancient kings for their universal love of the world, claiming that these ancient kings looked after the people as parents look after a beloved child. And how do they prove this claim? They say, "Whenever the minister of justice administered some punishment, the ruler would purposely cancel all musical performances; and whenever the ruler learned that the death sentence had been passed on someone, he would shed tears." For this reason they praise the ancient kings.

　　Now if ruler and subject must become like father and son before there can be order, then we must suppose that there is no such a thing as an unruly father or son. Among human affections none takes priority over the love of parents for their children. But though all parents may show love for their children, the children do not always well behave. And though the parents may love them even more, will this prevent the children from becoming unruly? Now the love of the ancient kings for their people was no greater than the love of parents for their children. And if such love cannot prevent children from becoming unruly, then how can it bring the people to order?

As for the ruler's shedding tears when punishments are carried out in accordance with the law—this is a fine display of benevolence but contributes nothing to the achievement of order. Benevolence may make one shed tears and be reluctant to apply penalties, but law makes it clear that such penalties must be applied. The ancient kings allowed law to be supreme and did not give in to their tearful longings. Hence it is obvious that benevolence cannot be used to achieve order in the state.

且民者，固服於勢，寡能懷於義。仲尼，天下聖人也，修行明道以遊海内，海内說其仁，美其義，而爲服役者七十人。蓋貴仁者寡，能義者難也。故以天下之大，而爲服役者七十人，而仁義者一人。魯哀公，下主也，南面君國，境内之民莫敢不臣。民者固服於勢，勢誠易以服人，故仲尼反爲臣而哀公顧爲君。仲尼非懷其義，服其勢也。故以義，則仲尼不服於哀公；乘勢，則哀公臣仲尼。今學者之説人主也，不乘必勝之勢，而曰"務行仁義，則可以王"，是求人主之必及仲尼，而以世之凡民皆如列徒，此必不得之數也。

Moreover, the people will bow naturally to authority, but few of them can be moved by righteousness. Confucius was one of the greatest sages of the world. He perfected his conduct, made clear the Dao, and traveled throughout the area within the four seas, but in all that area those who rejoiced in his benevolence, admired his righteousness, and were willing to become his disciples numbered only seventy. For to honor benevolence is a rare thing, and to adhere to righteousness is hard. Therefore within the vast area of the world only seventy men became his disciples, and only one man—he himself— was truly benevolent and righteous.

Duke Ai of Lu was a mediocre ruler, yet when he ascended the throne and faced south as sovereign of the state, there was no one within its boundaries who did not acknowledge allegiance to him. The people will bow naturally to authority, and he who wields authority may easily command men to submit. Therefore Confucius remained a subject and Duke Ai continued to be his ruler. It was not that Confucius was won by the duke's righteousness; he simply bowed before his authority. On the basis of righteousness alone, Confucius would never have bowed before Duke Ai; but because the duke wielded authority, he was able to make Confucius acknowledge his sovereignty.

Nowadays, when scholars counsel a ruler, they do not urge him to wield authority, which is the certain way to success, but instead insist that he must practice benevolence and righteousness before he can become a true king. This is, in effect, to demand that the ruler rise to the level of Confucius and that all the ordinary people of the time be like Confucius' disciples. Such a policy is bound to fail.

今有不才之子，父母怒之弗爲改，鄉人譙之弗爲動，師長教之弗爲變。夫以父母之愛，鄉人之行，師長之智，三美加焉，而終不動其脛毛，不改。州部之吏，操官兵，推公法，而求索姦人，然後恐懼，變其節，易其行矣。故父母之愛不足以教子，必待州部之嚴刑者，民固驕於愛，聽於威矣。

Now here is a young man of bad character. His parents rail at him but he does not reform; the neighbors scold him but he is unmoved; his teachers instruct him but he refuses to change his ways. Thus, although three fine influences are brought to bear on him—the love of his parents, the efforts of the neighbors, the wisdom of his teachers—yet he remains unmoved and refuses to change so much as a hair on his shin. But let the local magistrate send out the government soldiers to enforce the law and search for evildoers, and then he is filled with terror, reforms his conduct, and changes his ways. Thus the love of parents is not enough to make children learn what is right, but must be backed up by the strict penalties of the local officials; it is because people are naturally spoiled by love and obedient to authority.

故十仞之城，樓季弗能踰者，峭也；千仞之山，跛牂易牧者，夷也。故明主峭其法而嚴其刑也。布帛尋常，庸人不釋；鑠金百溢，盜跖不掇。不必害，則不釋尋常；

必害手,則不掇百溢。故明主必其誅也。是以賞莫如厚而信,使民利之;罰莫如重而必,使民畏之;法莫如一而固,使民知之。故主施賞不遷,行誅無赦,譽輔其賞,毀隨其罰,則賢、不肖俱盡其力矣。

Even the nimble Louji could not climb a city wall ten spans high, because it is too precipitous; but lame sheep may easily graze up and down a mountain a hundred times as high, because the slope is gradual. Therefore the enlightened ruler makes his laws precipitous and his punishments severe. Ordinary people are unwilling to discard a few feet of cloth, but even Robber Zhi would not pick up a hundred tales of molten gold. As long as there is no harm involved, people will not discard a few feet of cloth, but because they are certain to hurt their hands they refuse to pick up a hundred tales of molten gold. Therefore the enlightened ruler makes his punishments certain.

The best rewards are those that are generous and predictable, so that the people may profit by them. The best penalties are those that are severe and inescapable, so that the people will fear them. The best laws are those that are uniform and inflexible, so that the people can understand them. Therefore, the ruler should never delay in handing out rewards, nor be merciful in administering punishments. If praise accomplishes the reward, and disgrace follows on the heels of punishment, then worthy and unworthy men alike will put forth their best efforts.

今則不然。以其有功也爵之,而卑其士官也;以其耕作也賞之,而少其家業也;以其不收也外之,而高其輕世也;以其犯禁也罪之,而多其有勇也。毀譽、賞罰之所加者,相與悖繆也,故法禁壞,而民愈亂。今兄弟被侵,必攻者,廉也;知友被辱,隨仇者,貞也。廉貞之行成,而君上之法犯矣。人主尊貞廉之行,而忘犯禁之罪,故民程於勇,而吏不能勝也。不事力而衣食,則謂之能;不戰功而尊,則謂之賢。賢能之行成,而兵弱而地荒矣。人主說賢能之行,而忘兵弱地荒之禍,則私行立而公利滅矣。

But this is not the way things are done at present. The rulers hand out official titles to men who have achieved merit but treat government officials with contempt. They give rewards to the farmers but in practice actually reduce their means of livelihood. They dissociate themselves from those who spurn official position but at the same time praise their contempt for the world. They punish those who violate the prohibitions but at the same time admire their bravery. Thus the things which they condemn or praise are completely at odds with those which they reward or punish. No wonder laws and interdicts are ruined and the people are becoming more and more violent.

Nowadays, he who makes certain to avenge any wrong done to his brother is called an upright man, and he who joins his friend in attacking the perpetrator of an insult is called a man of honor. Yet once these deeds of uprightness and purity are done, the law of the ruler is violated. But the ruler, lost in admiration for such upright and honorable deeds, forgets to punish the violation of his laws, and hence the people outdo each other in shows of valor and the magistrates can no longer control them. Likewise, he who manages to get clothing and food without working hard is called an able man, and he who wins esteem without having achieved any merit in battle is called a worthy man. But the deeds of such able and worthy men actually weaken the army and bring waste to the land. If the ruler rejoices in the deeds of such men, and forgets the harm they do by weakening the army and bringing waste to the land, then private interests will prevail and public profit will come to naught.

儒以文亂法，俠以武犯禁，而人主兼禮之，此所以亂也。夫離法者罪，而諸先生以文學取；犯禁者誅，而羣俠以私劍養。故法之所非，君之所取；吏之所誅，上之所養也。法、取、上、下，四相反也，而無所定，雖有十黃帝，不能治也。故行仁義者非所譽，譽之則害功；工文學者非所用，用之則亂法。

The Confucians with their learning bring confusion to the law; the swordsmen with their martial prowess violate the prohibitions. Yet the ruler treats both groups with respect, and so we have disorder. People who deviate from the law should be treated as criminals, and yet the Confucian scholars actually attain posts in the government because of their literary accomplishments. People who violate the prohibitions ought to be punished, and yet the swordsmen are able to make a living by wielding their swords in a private cause. Hence, those whom the law condemns, the ruler accepts, and those whom the magistrates seek to punish, the higher officials patronize. Thus law and practice, high official and lowly magistrate, are all set at odds, and there is no fixed standard. Under such circumstances even ten Yellow Emperors could not bring the state to order. Those who practice benevolence and righteousness should not he praised, for to praise them is to cast aspersion on military achievements; men of literary accomplishment should not he employed in the government, for to employ them is to bring confusion to the law.

楚之有直躬，其父竊羊而謁之吏。令尹曰："殺之！"以爲直於君而曲於父，報而罪之。以是觀之，夫君之直臣，父之暴子也。魯人從君戰，三戰三北。仲尼問其故，對曰："吾有老父，身死莫之養也。"仲尼以爲孝，舉而上之。以是觀之，夫父之孝子，君之背臣也。故令尹誅而楚姦不上聞，仲尼賞而魯民易降北。上下之利若是其異也，而人主兼舉匹夫之行，而求致社稷之福，必不幾矣。

In the state of Chu there was a man named Zhigong (Upright Gong). When his father stole a sheep, he reported the theft to the authorities. But the local magistrate, considering that the man was honest in the service of his sovereign but a villain to his own father, replied, "Put him to death!" and the man was accordingly sentenced and executed. Thus we see that a man who is an honest subject of the sovereign may be an unfilial son to his father.

There was a man of Lu who followed the ruler to war. Three times he went into battle, and three times he ran away. When Confucius asked him the reason, he replied, "I have an aged father and, if I should die, there would be no one to take care of him." Confucius, considering the man filial, recommended him and had him promoted to a post in the government. Thus we see that a man who is a filial son to his father may be a traitorous subject of the ruler.

Because the magistrate of Chu executed Zhigong, crimes were never reported to the authorities. Because Confucius rewarded the man who ran away, the people of Lu easily surrendered or ran away in battle. The interests of the superior and the inferior are as disparate as all this, thus it is hopeless for the ruler to praise the actions of the private individual and at the same time try to insure blessing to the state's altars of the soil and grain.

古者，蒼頡之作書也，自環者謂之私，背私謂之公。公私之相背也，乃蒼頡固以知之矣。今以爲同利者，不察之患也。然則爲匹夫計者，莫如脩仁義而習文學。仁義脩則見信，見信則受事；文學習則爲明師，爲明師則顯榮；此匹夫之美也。然則無功而受事，無爵而顯榮，爲政如此，則國必亂，主必危矣。

In ancient times when Cang Jie created the system of writing, he used the character for "private" to express the idea of self-centeredness, and combined the elements for "private" and "opposed to" to form the character for "public." The fact that public and private are mutually opposed was already well understood at the time of Cang Jie. To regard the two as being identical in interest is a disaster which comes from lack of consideration.

If I were to give advice from the point of view of the private individual, I would say the best thing is to practice benevolence and righteousness and cultivate the literary arts. By practicing benevolence and righteousness, you become trusted, and when you have become trusted you may receive official appointment. Similarly, by cultivating the literary arts you may become an eminent teacher, and when you have become an eminent teacher you will win honor and fame. This is the highest goal of the private individual. But when this happens, then, from the point of view of the state, someone who has performed no meritorious service to the nation is receiving official appointment, and someone who holds no government title is enjoying honor and fame. If the government is conducted in this fashion, then the state will face certain disorder and the ruler will surely be in peril.

故不相容之事，不兩立也。斬敵者受賞，而高慈惠之行；拔城者受爵禄，而信兼愛之説；堅甲厲兵以備難，而美薦紳之飾；富國以農，距敵恃卒，而貴文學之士；廢敬上畏法之民，而養遊俠私劍之屬。舉行如此，治强不可得也。國平養儒俠，難至用介士，所利非所用，所用非所利。是故服事者簡其業，而游學者日衆，是世之所以亂也。

Incompatible things cannot prevail at the same time. For instance, to reward those who cut off the heads of the enemy and yet to admire acts of mercy and compassion; to hand out titles and stipends to those who capture the enemy's cities and yet to give ear to doctrines of universal love; to strengthen one's armor and sharpen one's weapons in preparation for the time of trouble, and yet to praise the elegant attire of the civil gentry; to hope to enrich the nation through agriculture and ward off the enemy with trained soldiers, and yet to pay honor to men of literary accomplishment; to spurn those people who respect their rulers and fear the law, and instead to patronize the bands of wandering swordsmen—to indulge in contradictory acts like these is to insure that the state will never be well ordered. The nation at peace benefits Confucian scholars and swordsmen. But when it is in danger it calls upon fighting men. Thus those who the nation benefits are not those it needs [in danger], and those who the nation needs [in danger] are not those it benefits. As a result, those who attend to public affairs become careless in their jobs and wandering scholars increase in number day by day. This is the reason why the age is full of chaos.

且世之所謂賢者，貞信之行也。所謂智者，微妙之言也。微妙之言，上智之所難知也。今爲衆人法，而以上智之所難知，則民無從識之矣。故糟糠不飽者，不務粱肉。短褐不完者，不待文繡。夫治世之事，急者不得，緩者非所務也。今所治之政，民間之事，夫婦所明知者不用，而慕上智之論，則其於治反矣。故微妙之言，非民務也。

The world calls worthy those whose conduct is marked by integrity and trustworthiness, and wise those whose words are subtle and mysterious. But even the wisest man has difficulty understanding words that are subtle and mysterious. Now if you want to set up laws for the masses and you try to base the laws on doctrines that even the wisest men have difficulty in understanding, how can the common people comprehend them? A man who cannot even get his fill of the coarsest grain does not insist on meat and fine millet; a man with a short coat all in rags does not insist on waiting for embroidered robes. It is the same in government affairs; if you cannot find the solution to critical problems, you have no business worrying about unimportant ones. Now in administering public affairs and dealing with the people, if you do not speak in terms that any man and woman can plainly understand, but long to apply the doctrines of the wise men, then you will defeat your own efforts at rule. Subtle and mysterious words are no business of the people.

若夫賢貞信之行者，必將貴不欺之士。貴不欺之士者，亦無不可欺之術也。布衣相與交，無富厚以相利，無威勢以相懼也，故求不欺之士。今人主處制人之勢，有一國之厚，重賞嚴誅，得操其柄，以修明術之所燭，雖有田常、子罕之臣，不敢欺也，奚待於不欺之士？今貞信之士不盈於十，而境內之官以百數，必任貞信之士，則人不足官。人不足官，則治者寡而亂者眾矣。故明主之道，一法而不求智，固術而不慕信，故法不敗，而羣官無姦詐矣。

If people regard those who act with integrity and trustworthiness as worthy, it must be because they value men who have no deceit, and they value men of no deceit because they themselves have no means to protect themselves from deceit. The common people in selecting their friends, for example, have no wealth by which to win others over, and no authority by which to intimidate others. For that reason, they seek for men who are without deceit to be their friends. But the ruler occupies a position whereby he may impose his will upon others, and he has the whole wealth of the nation at his disposal; he may dispense lavish rewards and severe penalties and, by wielding these two handles, may improve things with the illumination of his wise policies. In that case, even traitorous ministers like Tian Chang and Zihan would not dare to deceive him. Why should he have to wait for men who are by nature not deceitful?

Hardly ten men of true integrity and trustworthiness can be found today, and yet the offices of the state number in the hundreds. If they must be filled by men of integrity and trustworthiness, then there will never be enough men to go around; and if the offices are left unfilled, then very few cities can maintain order while most of the cities would be in chaos. Therefore the Dao of the wise ruler is to solely rely on the laws instead of seeking for wise men, to lay down firm policies instead of longing for men of trustworthiness. Hence his laws never fail him, and there is no felony or deceit among his officials.

今人主之於言也，説其辯，而不求其當焉；其用於行也，美其聲，而不責其功焉。是以天下之衆，其言談者，務爲辯而不周於用，故舉先王言仁義者盈廷，而政不免於亂。行身者，競於爲高而不合於功，故智士退處巖穴，歸禄不受，而兵不免於弱。兵不免於弱，政不免於亂，此其故何也？民之所譽，上之所禮，亂國之術也。

These days, when the ruler listens to men's words, he delights in their eloquence and does not bother to inquire if these words can help bring good results, and when he observes men's acts, he admires those that win fame but does not strictly check over their accomplishments. For this reason, the people of the world, when they come to make a speech, strive for eloquence and disregard the question of whether their words are practical. Hence the court is filled with men quoting the former kings and discussing benevolence and righteousness, and the government cannot escape disorder. Likewise, in the matter of personal conduct, men try to outdo each other in high-minded deeds, regardless of whether they produce any useful results. Hence, intelligent people retire from government service and go off to live in caves, refusing the stipends that are offered them, and as a result the armies grow weaker and the government cannot escape disorder. What is the cause of all this? The fact that what the people praise and the ruler honors are actually policies that lead to the ruin of the state.

今境內之民皆言治，藏商、管之法者家有之，而國愈貧，言耕者眾，執耒者寡也。境內皆言兵，藏孫、吳之書者家有之，而兵愈弱，言戰者多，被甲者少也。故明主用其力，不聽其言；賞其功，必禁無用。故民盡死力以從其上。

Now the people of the state all discuss good government, and everyone has a copy of the works on law by Shang Yang and Guan Zhong in his house, and yet the state gets poorer and poorer, for though many people talk about farming, very few put their hands to a plow. The people of the state all discuss military affairs, and everyone has a copy of the works of Sun Wu and Wu Qi in his house, and yet the armies grow weaker and weaker, for though many people talk about war, very few buckle on armor. Therefore, a wise ruler will make use of men's strength but will not heed their words, will reward their accomplishments but will prohibit useless activities. Then the people will be willing to exert themselves to the point of death in the service of their sovereign.

夫耕之用力也勞，而民為之者，曰：可得以富也。戰之為事也危，而民為之者，曰：可得以貴也。今修文學，習言談，則無耕之勞而有富之實，無戰之危而有貴之尊，則人孰不為也？是以百人事智而一人用力，事智者眾則法敗，用力者寡則國貧，此世之所以亂也。

Farming requires a lot of hard work but people will do it because, as they say, "This way we can get rich." War is a dangerous undertaking but people will take part in it because, as they say, "This way we can become eminent." Now if men who devote themselves to literature or study the art of persuasive speaking are able to get the fruits of wealth without the hard work of the farmer, and can gain the advantages of eminence without the danger of battle, then who will not take up such pursuits? So for every man who works with his hands there will be a hundred devoting themselves to the pursuit of cleverness. If those who pursue cleverness are numerous, the laws will be defeated, and if those who labor with their hands are few, the state will grow poor. That is the reason why the world is in chaos.

故明主之國，無書簡之文，以法爲教；無先生之語，以吏爲師；無私劍之捍，以斬首爲勇。是境内之民，其言談者必軌於法，動作者歸之於功，爲勇者盡之於軍。是故無事則國富，有事則兵強，此之謂王資。既畜王資而承敵國之釁，超五帝，侔三王者，必此法也。

Therefore, in the state of the enlightened sovereign there is no literature written on bamboo slips, but the law is the only teaching; there are no quoted sayings of the early kings, but the magistrates are the only instructors; there is no fierce swordsmen who are only loyal to their patrons, but slaughter of the enemy of the state is the only courageous deed. Hence, when the people of such a state make a speech, they say nothing that is in contradiction to the law; when they act, it is in some way that will bring useful results; and when they do brave deeds, they do them in the army. Therefore, in times of peace the state is rich, and in times of trouble its armies are strong. These are what are called the resources of the ruler. The ruler must store them up, and then wait for an opening to strike at his enemy. He who would surpass the Five Emperors of antiquity and rival the Three Kings must proceed by this method.

今則不然，士民縱恣於内，言談者爲勢於外，外内稱惡，以待強敵，不亦殆乎！故群臣之言外事者，非有分於從衡之黨，則有仇讎之忠，而借力於國也。從者，合衆弱以攻一強也；而衡者，事一強以攻衆弱也；皆非所以持國也。

But this is not the way things are now. Within the state the people behave as they please, while the speechmakers work to spread their influence abroad. If both foreign and home affairs alike are bad, is it not dangerous for the ruler to confront strong enemies? When the ministers speak on foreign affairs, they are either acting as spokesmen for the Horizontal or Vertical Alliances or trying to enlist the aid of the state to avenge some personal wrong. But neither the Vertical Alliance, in which one joins with a number of weak states in hopes of attacking a strong one, nor the Horizontal Alliance, in which one serves a strong state for the purpose of attacking a number of weak ones, can insure the survival of one's own state.

今人臣之言衡者,皆曰:"不事大,則遇敵受禍矣。"事大未必有實,則舉圖而委,效璽而請兵矣。獻圖則地削,效璽則名卑,地削則國弱,名卑則政亂矣。事大爲衡,未見其利也,而亡地亂政矣。人臣之言從者,皆曰:"不救小而伐大,則失天下,失天下則國危,國危而主卑。"救小未必有實,則起兵而敵大矣。救小未必能存,敵大未必不有疏,有疏則爲強國制矣。出兵則軍敗,退守則城拔。救小爲從,未見其利,而亡地敗軍矣。是故事強,則以外權士官於內;救小,則以內重求利於外。國利未立,封土厚祿至矣;主上雖卑,人臣尊矣;國地雖削,私家富矣。事成,則以權長重;事敗,則以富退處。

Those ministers who urge the Horizontal Alliance all say, "If we do not enter the service of a powerful state, we will be attacked by enemies and will face disaster!" Now when you enter the service of a powerful state, you cannot yet be certain of the practical advantages, and yet you must hand over all the maps of your territory and put your state seal in pawn for military aid. Once the maps have been presented, you will be stripped of territory, and once your state seal has been put into the hands of another, your prestige will vanish. If your territory is stripped away, the state will be weakened, and if your prestige vanishes, the government will fall into disorder. So you gain no benefit by entering the Horizontal Alliance in the service of a powerful state, but merely lose territory and undermine the government.

Those ministers who urge the Vertical Alliance all say, "If we do not rescue the smaller states and attack the powerful one, we will lose the support of the people. If we lose the support of the people, our own state will be in peril and our ruler will face contempt!" Now you are not yet certain that you can actually save the smaller states, and yet you must call out your troops and face a powerful enemy. When you try to save the smaller states, you cannot always be sure of preserving them from destruction, and when you face a powerful enemy, you cannot always be sure that your allies will remain loyal. And if your allies break with you, you will be at the mercy of the powerful state. Then if you send out troops to battle, your armies will be defeated, and if you withdraw and try to protect your own realm, your cities will fall. So you gain no benefit by entering the Vertical Alliance in an attempt to save the smaller states, but lose your own lands and destroy your own army.

Hence, if you enter the service of a powerful state, it will dispatch its own men of authority to take over the offices in your government; and if you work to rescue the smaller states, your own important ministers will take advantage of the situation to further their interests abroad. No benefit will come to the state as a whole, but only fiefs and rich rewards for its ministers. They will enjoy all the honor, while the ruler is despised; their families will grow rich, while the state is stripped of its lands. If their schemes succeed, they will use their power to prolong their eminence; if their schemes fail, they will retire with all their wealth intact.

人主之聽說於其臣，事未成，則爵祿已尊矣。事敗而弗誅，則游說之士，孰不為用矰繳之說而徼倖其後？故破國亡主，以聽言談者之浮說。此其故，何也？是人君不明乎公私之利，不察當否之言，而誅罰不必其後也。皆曰："外事，大可以王，小可以安。"夫王者，能攻人者也；而安，則不可攻也。強者，能攻人者也；而治，則不可攻也。治強不可責於外，內政之有也。今不行法術於內，而事智於外，則不至於治強矣。

But if the ruler, when listening to the proposals of his ministers, honors and rewards them with titles and stipends before their advice has produced successful results, and fails to punish them when it has proved unsuccessful, then who among the wandering theorists will not come forward with some hit-or-miss scheme in hopes of benefiting by a stroke of luck? Why do the rulers listen to the wild theories of the lobbyists, and bring destruction to the state and ruin to themselves? Because they never distinguish clearly between public and private interests, never scrutinizes whether the ideas are true or false, and never definitely enforces censure and punishment.

Each ruler says, "By attending to foreign affairs I can perhaps become a king, and if not I will at least ensure security for myself." Now a king is one who is able to attack others, and a secure state is one that cannot be attacked. Only a powerful state can attack others, and only a well ordered state cannot be attacked. Neither power nor order, however, depends on foreign affairs—they are wholly a matter of internal government. Now if the ruler does not apply the proper laws and procedures within his state, but stakes all on the wisdom of his foreign policy, his state will never become powerful and well ordered.

鄙諺曰："長袖善舞，多財善賈。"此言多資之易爲工也。故治強易爲謀，弱亂難爲計。故用於秦者，十變而謀希失；用於燕者，一變而計希得。非用於秦者必智，用於燕者必愚也，蓋治亂之資異也。故周去秦爲從，期年而舉；衛離魏爲衡，半歲而亡。是周滅於從，衛亡於衡也。使周、衛緩其從衡之計，而嚴其境內之治，明其法禁，必其賞罰，盡其地力，以多其積，致其民死，以堅其城守，天下得其地則其利少，攻其國則其傷大，萬乘之國，莫敢自頓於堅城之下，而使強敵裁其弊也。此必不亡之術也。舍必不亡之術而道必滅之事，治國者之過也。智困於外而政亂於內，則亡不可振也。

The proverb says, "If you have long sleeves, you'll be good at dancing; if you have lots of money, you'll be good at business." This means that it is easy to become skillful when you have ample resources. Hence, it is easy to scheme for a state that is powerful and orderly but difficult to make any plan for one that is weak and chaotic. Those who scheme for the state of Qin can make ten changes and still their plans will seldom fail; but those who plan for the state of Yan can scarcely make one change and still hope for success. It is not that those who plan for Qin are necessarily wise and those who plan for Yan are stupid— it is simply that the resources they have to work with—

order in one case, disorder in the other—are different.

Zhou deserted the side of Qin and joined the Vertical Alliance, and within a year it had lost everything. Wey (衛) turned its back on Wei (魏) to join the Horizontal Alliance, and in half a year it was ruined. Thus Zhou was ruined by the Vertical Alliance and Wey was destroyed by the Horizontal Alliance. Instead of being so hasty in their plans to join an alliance, they should have worked to strengthen the order within their domains, to make their laws clear and their rewards and punishments certain, to utilize the full resources of the land in building up stores of provisions, and to train their people to defend the cities to the point of death, thus ensuring that any other ruler would gain little profit by trying to seize their lands, but on the contrary would suffer great injury if he attempted to attack their states. In that case, even the ruler of a state of ten thousand war chariots would not have dared to wear out his armies before their strong walls and invite the attack of powerful enemies. This would have been the way to escape destruction. To abandon a way which assures escape from destruction, and follow instead a path that leads to certain downfall, is the greatest error one can make in governing a state. Once the wisdom of its foreign policy is exhausted and its internal government has fallen into disorder, no state can be saved from ruin.

民之故計,皆就安利如辟危窮。今爲之攻戰,進則死於敵,退則死於誅,則危矣。棄私家之事而必汗馬之勞,家困而上弗論,則窮矣。窮危之所在也,民安得勿避? 故事私門而完解舍,解舍完則遠戰,遠戰則安。行貨賂而襲當塗者則求得,求得則利。安利之所在,安得勿就? 是以公民少而私人衆矣。

The people, in planning for their welfare, are most concerned in finding security and profit and avoiding danger and poverty. But if they must go off to fight foreign wars for the state, they face death at the hands of the enemy should they advance and death from official punishment should they retreat—hence they are in danger. If they must abandon their domestic affairs and go off to endure the sweat and hardship of battle, their families will grow poor and the ruler is likely never to reward them for their services—hence they face poverty. If such poverty and danger lie before them, how can you expect the people not to try to escape them? So they flock to the gates of influential men seeking a guarantee of exemption from military service, for with such a guarantee they may stay far from the scene of battle and live in safety.

Likewise, they slip bribes to the men in office in order to get some appointment, for with such an appointment they can acquire profit. Wherever lie security and profit, how can the people do other than crowd? Hence men who are concerned with public welfare grow fewer, and those who think only of private interests increase in number.

夫明王治國之政，使其商工游食之民少而名卑，以趣本務而外末作。今世近習之請行，則官爵可買，官爵可買，則商工不卑也矣。姦財貨賈得用於市，則商人不少矣。聚斂倍農，而致尊過耕戰之士，則耿介之士寡，而商賈之民多矣。

A wise ruler will administer his state in such a way as to decrease the number of merchants, artisans, and other men who make their living by wandering from place to place, and will see to it that such men are looked down upon. In this way he lessens the number of people who abandon primary pursuits (i. e. agriculture) to take up secondary occupations. Nowadays, however, if a man can enlist the private pleading of someone at court, he can buy offices and titles. When offices and titles can be bought, you may be sure that merchants and artisans will not remain despised for long; and when wealth and money, no matter how dishonestly gotten, can buy what is in the market, you may be sure that the number of merchants will not remain small for long. When a man who sits back and collects taxes makes twice as much as the farmer and enjoys greater honor than the plowman or the soldier, then public-spirited men will grow few and merchants and tradesmen will increase in number.

是故亂國之俗，其學者則稱先王之道，以籍仁義，盛容服而飾辯說，以疑當世之法，而貳人主之心。其言談者，爲設詐稱，借於外力，以成其私，而遺社稷之利。其帶劍者，聚徒屬，立節操，以顯其名，而犯五官之禁。其患御者，積於私門，盡貨賂，而用重人之謁，退汗馬之勞。其商工之民，修治苦窳之器，聚弗靡之財，蓄積待時，而侔農夫之利。此五者，邦之蠹也。人主不除此五蠹之民，不養耿介之士，則海內雖有破亡之國，削滅之朝，亦勿怪矣。

Here are the customs of a disordered state. Its scholars praise the ways of the former kings and imitate their benevolence and righteousness, put on a fair appearance and speak in elegant phrases, thus casting doubt upon the laws of the time and causing the ruler to be of two minds. Its speech-makers propound false schemes and borrow influence from abroad, furthering their private interests and forgetting the welfare of the state's altars of the soil and grain. Its swordsmen gather pupils and dependents and set up standards of self-discipline and fidelity with a view to cultivate their fame but thereby violate the prohibitions of the five government bureaus. Those of its people who are worried about military service flock to the gates of private individuals and pour out their wealth in bribes to influential men who will plead for them, in this way escaping the hardship of battle. Its merchants and artisans spend their time making articles of no practical use and gathering stores of luxury goods, accumulating riches, waiting for the best time to sell, and exploiting the farmers. These five groups are the vermin of the state. If the rulers do not wipe out such vermin, and do not encourage men of integrity and public spirit, then they should not be surprised, when they look about the area within the four seas, to see states perish and ruling houses wane and die.

顯學第五十

Chapter 50　Learned Celebrities: A Critical Estimate of Confucians and Mohists

世之顯學，儒、墨也。儒之所至，孔丘也。墨之所至，墨翟也。……孔、墨之後，儒分爲八，墨離爲三，取舍相反、不同，而皆自謂真孔、墨，孔、墨不可復生，將誰使定世之學乎？孔子、墨子俱道堯、舜，而取舍不同，皆自謂真堯、舜，堯、舜不復生,將誰使定儒、墨之誠乎？殷、周七百餘歲,虞、夏二千餘歲,而不能定儒、墨之真,今乃欲審堯、舜之道於三千歲之前,意者其不可必乎！無參驗而必之者,愚也,弗能必而據之者,誣也。故明據先王,必定堯、舜者,非愚則誣也。愚誣之學,雜反之行,明主弗受也。

In the present age, the Confucians and Mohists are well known for their learning. The Confucians pay the highest honor to Confucius, the Mohists to Mo Di. ... Since the death of its founder, the Confucian school has split into eight factions, and the Mohist School into three. Their doctrines and practices are different or even contradictory, and yet each claims to represent the true teaching of Confucius and Mo Di. But since we cannot call Confucius and Mo Di back to life, who is to decide which of the present versions of the doctrine is the right one? Confucius and Mo Di both talked about the Dao of Yao and Shun, and though their practices differed, each claimed to be following the genuine Dao of Yao and Shun. But since we cannot call Yao and Shun back to life, who is to decide whether it is the Confucians or the Mohists who are telling the truth? Now over seven hundred years have passed since Yin and early Zhou times, and over two thousand years since Yu and early Xia times. If we cannot even decide which present versions of Confucian and Mohist doctrines are genuine ones, how can we hope to scrutinize the Dao of Yao and Shun, who lived three thousand years ago? Obviously we can be sure of nothing! He who claims to be sure of something for which there is no evidence is a fool, and he who acts on the basis of what cannot be proved is an imposter. Hence it is clear that those who claim to follow the ancient kings and to be able to describe with certainty the Dao of Yao and Shun must be either fools or imposters. The learning of fools and impostors, doctrines that are motley and contradictory—such things as these the wise ruler will never accept.

故敵國之君王雖說吾義,吾弗入貢而臣；關內之侯雖非吾行,吾必使執禽而朝。是故力多則人朝,力寡則朝於人。故明君務力。夫嚴家無悍虜,而慈母有敗子。吾以此知威勢之可以禁暴,而德厚之不足以止亂也。

Although the ruler of a state whose power is equal to yours may admire your righteousness, you cannot force him to come with tribute and acknowledge your sovereignty; but although one of the marquises within your borders may disapprove of your actions, you can make him bring the customary gifts and attend your court. Thus he who has great power at his disposal may force others to pay him court, but he whose power is weak must pay court to others. For this reason, the wise ruler works to build up power. In a strict household there are no unruly slaves, but the children of a kindly mother often turn out bad. From this I know that power and authority can prevent violence, but kindness and generosity are insufficient to put an end to disorder.

夫聖人之治國，不恃人之爲吾善也，而用其不得爲非也。恃人之爲吾善也，境內不什數；用人不得爲非，一國可使齊。爲治者用衆而舍寡，故不務德而務法。

When a sage rules the state, he does not depend on people's doing good of themselves; he sees to it that they are not allowed to do what is bad. If he depends on people's doing good of themselves, then within his borders he can count less than ten instances of success. But if he sees to it that they are not allowed to do what is bad, then the whole state can be brought to a uniform level of order. Those who rule must employ measures that will be effective with the majority and discard those that will be effective with only a few. Therefore they devote themselves not to virtue but to law.

夫必恃自直之箭，百世無矢；恃自圜之木，千世無輪矣。自直之箭，自圜之木，百世無有一，然而世皆乘車射禽者，何也？隱栝之道用也。雖有不恃隱栝，而有自直之箭，自圜之木，良工弗貴也。何則？乘者非一人，射者非一發也。不恃賞罰而恃自善之民，明主弗貴也。何則？國法不可失，而所治非一人也。故有術之君，不隨適然之善，而行必然之道。

If you depend on arrow shafts' becoming straight of themselves, you will never produce one arrow in a hundred generations. If you depend on pieces of wood's becoming round of themselves, you will never get a cartwheel in a thousand years. If in a hundred generations you never find such a thing as an arrow shaft that makes itself straight or a piece of wood that makes itself round, then how is it that people all manage to ride around in carriages and shoot down birds? Because the tools of straightening and bending are used. And even if, without the application of such tools, there were an arrow shaft that made itself straight or a piece of wood that made itself round, a good craftsman would not prize it. Why? Because it is not only one man who wants to ride, and not just one shot that the archer wants to make. And similarly, even if, without depending upon rewards and punishments, there were a man who became good of himself, the wise ruler would not prize him. Why? Because the laws of the state must not be ignored, and it is more than one man who must be governed. Therefore a ruler who understands policy does not pursue fortuitous goodness, but follows the way of certain success.

今或謂人曰："使子必智而壽。"則世必以爲狂。夫智,性也;壽,命也。性命者,非所學於人也,而以人之所不能爲說人,此世之所以謂之爲狂也。謂之不能然,則是諭也。夫以仁義教人,是以智與壽說人也,有度之主弗受也。故善毛嗇、西施之美,無益吾面;用脂澤粉黛,則倍其初。言先王之仁義,無益於治;明吾法度,必吾賞罰者,亦國之脂澤粉黛也。故明主急其功而緩其頌,故不道仁義。

……

If someone were to go around telling people, "I can give you talent and long life!" then the world would regard him as an impostor. Talent is a matter of man's nature, and long life is a matter of fate, and neither human nature nor fate can be got from others. Because the man tells people he can do what is impossible, the world naturally considers him an impostor. To say you can do something which you cannot do is simply to make an empty assertion, and an empty assertion cannot affect human nature. Likewise, to try to teach people to be benevolent and righteous is the same as saying you can make them talented and long-lived. A ruler who has proper standards will not listen to such an idea. You may admire the beauty of a lovely woman like Maoqiang or Xishi all you like, but it will not improve your own looks. If you apply rouge, powder, and paint, however, you may make yourself twice as attractive as you were to begin with. You may talk about the benevolence and righteousness of the former kings all you like, but it will not make your own state any better ordered. But if you make your laws and regulations clear and your rewards and punishments certain, it is like applying rouge, powder, and paint to the state. The wise ruler pays close attention to such aids to rule, and has little time for extolling the ancients. Therefore he does not talk about benevolence and righteousness.

...

今不知治者必曰："得民之心。"得民之心而可以爲治，則是伊尹、管仲無所用也，將聽民而已矣。民智之不可用，猶嬰兒之心也。夫嬰兒不剔首則復痛，不副痤則寖益。剔首、副痤必一人抱之，慈母治之，然猶啼呼不止，嬰兒不知犯其所小苦，致其所大利也。今上急耕田墾草，以厚民産也，而以上爲酷；脩刑重罰，以爲禁邪也，而以上爲嚴；徵賦錢粟，以實倉庫，且以救飢饉、備軍旅也，而以上爲貪；境内必知介而無私解，并力疾鬭，所以禽虜也，而以上爲暴。此四者，所以治安也，而民不知悅也。夫求聖通之士者，爲民知之不足師用。昔禹決江濬河，而民聚瓦石；子産開畝樹桑，鄭人謗訾。禹利天下，子産存鄭，皆以受謗，夫民智之不足用亦明矣。故舉士而求賢智，爲政而期適民，皆亂之端，未可與爲治也。

Nowadays, those who do not understand how to govern invariably say, "You must win the hearts of the people!" If you could assure good government merely by winning the hearts of the people, then there would be no need for men like Yi Yin and Guan Zhong—you could simply listen to what the people say. The reason you cannot rely upon the wisdom of the people is that they have the minds of little children. If the child's head is not shaved, his sores will spread; and if his boil is not lanced, he will become sicker than ever. But when he is having his head shaved or his boil lanced, someone must hold him while the loving mother performs the operation, and he yells and screams incessantly, for he does not understand that the little pain he suffers now will bring great benefit later. Now the ruler presses the people to till the land and to open up new pastures so as to increase their means of livelihood, and yet the people consider him harsh; he draws up a penal code and makes the punishments more severe in order to put a stop to evil, and yet the people consider him stern. He levies taxes in cash and grain in order to fill the coffers and granaries so that there will be food for the starving and funds for the army, and yet the people consider him avaricious. He makes certain that everyone within his borders understands warfare and sees to it that there are no private exemptions from military service; he unites the strength of the state and fights fiercely in order to take its enemies captive, and yet the people consider him violent. These four types of undertaking all ensure order and safety to the state, and yet the people do not have sense enough to rejoice in them.

The ruler seeks for men of superior understanding and ability precisely because he knows that the wisdom of the people is not sufficient to be of any use. In ancient times Yu opened up channels for the rivers and deepened the waterways, and yet the people gathered tiles and stones to throw at him; Zichan opened up the fields and planted mulberry trees, and yet the people of Zheng spoke ill of him. Yu profited the whole world, Zichan preserved the state of Zheng, and yet both men suffered slander—it is evident from this, then, that the wisdom of the people is not sufficient to be of use. In appointing men, to seek among the people for those who are worthy and wise; in governing, to try to please the people—methods such as these are the source of disorder. They are of no help in ensuring good government.

四、心性 / Part IV Human Nature

人們會做許多不道德的事情，並且至今仍然在做，如詐欺、偷盜、強姦、搶掠、毆打、謀殺、戰爭，等等。此外，我們常常說，沒有一個人在道德上是完美的。這是否意味著人性在道德上就是惡的？如果人性本惡，那麼又該如何解釋這些事情：我們有時會不計個人得失地幫助他人，有時會替他人感到由衷的難過，有時也會真心地希望他人獲得成功，等等。這些事實是否又反而表明人性本善？

在這一部分，我們將會看到孟子和荀子這兩位儒家學者對這些問題的論述。閱讀選文時，試著找出二人回答之間的差別，並思考何者的論述更具說服力。

Humans committed and are committing a lot of moral evils: fraud, theft, rape, robbery, battery, murder, war, etc. It is said that no one is morally perfect. Does this suggest that human nature is morally evil? If human nature is evil, how can we explain the fact that we do sometimes help others without calculation, that we truly feel sorry for others, that we sincerely wish others success, etc. Do these facts instead suggest that human nature is morally good?

In this part, we will see how the two Confucian philosophers, Mencius and Xunzi, address these questions. As you read the selections, try to figure out the differences between them. Ask yourself which of their theories is more convincing.

《孟子》/ Mencius

11.1 告子曰:"性,猶杞柳也;義,猶桮棬也。以人性爲仁義,猶以杞柳爲桮棬。"孟子曰:"子能順杞柳之性而以爲桮棬乎?將戕賊杞柳而後以爲桮棬也?如將戕賊杞柳而以爲桮,則亦將戕賊人以爲仁義與?率天下之人而禍仁義者,必子之言夫!"

11.1 The philosopher Gao said, "Man's nature is like the qi-willow, and righteousness is like a cup or a bowl. Fashioning benevolence and righteousness out of man's nature is like making cups and bowls from the qi-willow."

Mencius replied, "Can you, leaving untouched the nature of the willow, make with it cups and bowls? You must do violence and injury to the willow, before you can make cups and bowls with it. If you must do violence and injury to the willow in order to make cups and bowls with it, on your principles you must in the same way do violence and injury to humanity in order to fashion from it benevolence and righteousness! Your words will cause everyone in the world to think of benevolence and righteousness as misfortunes!"

11.2 告子曰:"性,猶湍水也,決諸東方則東流,決諸西方則西流。人性之無分於善不善也,猶水之無分於東西也。"孟子曰:"水信無分於東西,無分於上下乎?人性之善也,猶水之就下也。人無有不善,水無有不下。今夫水搏而躍之,可使過顙,激而行之,可使在山,是豈水之性哉?其勢則然也。人之可使爲不善,其性亦猶是也。"

11.2 The philosopher Gao said, "Human's nature is like water whirling round in a corner. Open a passage for it to the east, and it will flow to the east; open a passage for it to the west, and it will flow to the west. Human's nature is indifferent to good and evil, just as the water is indifferent to the east and west."

Mencius replied, "Water indeed will flow indifferently to the east or west, but will it flow indifferently up or down? The tendency of human's nature to good is like the tendency of water to flow downwards. Everyone has this tendency to good, just as all water always flows downwards. Now by striking water and causing it to leap up, you may make it go over your forehead, and, by damming and leading it you may force it up a hill, but are such movements according to the nature of water? It is the force that makes them happen. While people can be made to do what is not good, what happens to their nature is like this."

11.3 告子曰:"生之謂性。"孟子曰:"生之謂性也,猶白之謂白與?"曰:"然。""白羽之白也,猶白雪之白,白雪之白,猶白玉之白歟?"曰:"然。""然則犬之性猶牛之性,牛之性猶人之性歟?"

11.3 The philosopher Gao said, "Life is what we call nature!" Mencius said, "When you say that 'life is what we call nature', is this like saying that 'white is what we call white'?" "Yes." "Is the whiteness of a white feather like the whiteness of snow, and the whiteness of snow like the whiteness of white jade?" "Yes." "Then is the nature of a dog like the nature of an ox, and the nature of an ox like the nature of a human being?"

11.4 告子曰:"食色,性也。仁,內也,非外也。義,外也,非內也。"孟子曰:"何以謂仁內義外也?"曰:"彼長而我長之,非有長於我也。猶彼白而我白之,從其白於外也,故謂之外也。"曰:"異於白馬之白也,無以異於白人之白也!不識長馬之長也,無以異於長人之長歟?且謂長者義乎?長之者義乎?"曰:"吾弟則愛之,秦人之弟則不愛也,是以我爲悅者也,故謂之內。長楚人之長,亦長吾之長,是以長爲悅者也,故謂之外也。"曰:"嗜秦人之炙,無以異於嗜吾炙。夫物則亦有然者也。然則嗜炙亦有外歟?"

11.4 The philosopher Gao said, "The appetites for food and sex are human nature. Benevolence is internal rather than external; righteousness is external rather than internal." Mencius said, "Why do you say that benevolence is internal while righteousness is external?" He replied, "One who is older than I, I treat as an elder. It is not because there is in me some sense of respect due to elders. It is like something being white and my recognizing it as white; I am responding to the whiteness, which is external. Therefore I call rightness external." Mencius said, "There is no difference between the whiteness of a white horse and the whiteness of a white man. But is there no difference between the age of an old horse and the age of an old man? What is it which is called righteousness—the man's being old or my regarding him with the respect due to one who is old?"

Gao said, "There is my younger brother; I love him. But the younger brother of a man of Qin I do not love: that is, the feeling is determined by myself, and therefore I say that benevolence is internal. On the other hand, I show respect to an old man of Chu, and I also show respect to an old man of my own people: that is, the feeling is determined by the age, and therefore I say that righteousness is external."

Mencius answered him, "Our enjoyment of meat roasted by a man of Qin does not differ from our enjoyment of meat roasted by ourselves. Thus, what you insist on takes place also in the case of such things, and will you say likewise that our enjoyment of a roast is external?"

11.5　孟季子問公都子曰："何以謂義內也？"曰："行吾敬,故謂之內也。""鄉人長於伯兄壹歲,則誰敬？"曰："敬兄。""酌則誰先？"曰："先酌鄉人。""所敬在此,所長在彼,果在外,非由內也。"公都子不能答,以告孟子。

孟子曰："敬叔父乎？敬弟乎？彼將曰：'敬叔父。'曰：'弟爲尸,則誰敬？'彼將曰：'敬弟。'子曰：'惡在其敬叔父也？'彼將曰：'在位故也。'子亦曰：'在位故也。庸敬在兄,斯須之敬在鄉人。'"季子聞之,曰："敬叔父則敬,敬弟則敬,果在外,非由內也。"公都子曰："冬日則飲湯,夏日則飲水,然則飲食亦在外也？"

11.5　The disciple Meng Ji asked Gong Du, saying, "Why do you say that righteousness is internal？" Gong Du replied, "We therein act out our feeling of respect, and therefore it is said to be internal."

"Suppose there were a villager who was one year older than your older brother—whom would you respect?"

"I would respect my older brother."

"For whom would you pour wine first when serving at a feast?"

"I would pour it first for the villager."

"You respect the one, but treat the other as older. So in the end, righteousness is external and not internal."

Gong Du was unable to reply, and told the conversation to Mencius. Mencius said, "Ask him, whom he respects more, his uncle or his younger brother. He will say that he respects his uncle. You then ask him, if his younger brother were impersonating the deceased at a sacrifice, whom he would respect more. He will say that he would respect his younger brother. Then ask, where is the respect due to his uncle. He will say that it is because of his younger brother's position that he shows him greater respect. Then you may also say that it is because of the position of the villager that you show him respect. While ordinarily the respect belongs to your brother, on occasion the respect belongs to the villager."

Meng Ji heard this and observed, "When respect is due to my uncle, I respect him, and when respect is due to my younger brother, I respect him; the thing is certainly determined by what is external, and does not proceed from within."

Gong Du replied, "In winter we drink things hot, in summer we drink things cold. Does this mean that drinking and eating too are externally determined?"

11.6　公都子曰:"告子曰:'性無善無不善也。'或曰:'性可以爲善,可以爲不善,是故文武興則民好善,幽厲興則民好暴。'或曰:'有性善,有性不善,是故以堯爲君而有象,以瞽瞍爲父而有舜,以紂爲兄之子且以爲君,而有微子啟、王子比干。'今曰'性善',然則彼皆非歟?"孟子曰:"乃若其情則可以爲善矣,乃所謂善也。若夫爲不善,非才之罪也。惻隱之心,人皆有之;羞惡之心,人皆有之;恭敬之心,人皆有之;是非之心,人皆有之。惻隱之心,仁也;羞惡之心,義也;恭敬之心,禮也;是非之心,智也。仁義禮智,非由外鑠我也,我固有之也,弗思耳矣。故曰:求則得之,舍則失之。或相倍蓰而無算者,不能盡其才者也。《詩》曰:'天生蒸民,有物有則。民之秉彝,好是懿德。'孔子曰:'爲此詩者,其知道乎! 故有物必有則,民之秉彝也,故好是懿德。'"

11.6 The disciple Gong Du said, "The philosopher Gao says, 'Human nature is neither good nor bad.' Some say, 'Human nature may be made to practice good, and it may be made to practice evil, and accordingly, during the reigns of Kings Wen and Wu, the people were inclined to goodness, whereas under the reigns of You and Li, the people were inclined to violence.' Some say, 'The natures of some are good and the natures of others are not good, which is why, when Yao was the ruler, there could be Xiang, while, with a father like Gusou, there could be Shun, and with Zhou as the son of their older brother as well as their ruler, there could be Qi, the Viscount of Wei, and Prince Bigan.' And now you say, 'The nature is good.' Then are all those wrong?"

Mencius said, "One's natural tendencies enable one to do good; this is what I mean by human nature being good. When one does what is not good, it is not the fault of one's native capacities. The mind of pity and commiseration is possessed by all human beings; the mind of shame and dislike is possessed by all human beings; the mind of respectfulness and reverence is possessed by all human beings; and the mind that knows right and wrong is possessed by all human beings. The mind of pity and commiseration is benevolence; the mind of shame and dislike is righteousness; the mind of respectfulness and reverence is propriety; and the mind that knows right and wrong is wisdom. Benevolence, righteousness, propriety, and wisdom are not infused into us from without. We are certainly furnished with them. It is just that we do not think about it, that is all. Therefore it is said, 'Seek and you will get it; let go and you will lose it.' That some differ from others by as much as twice, or five times, or an incalculable order of magnitude is because there are those who are unable fully to develop their natural capacities. The Odes says, 'Heaven gave birth to humankind, and whatever it is has its own laws: cleaving to what makes us human, people delight in stately Integrity.' Of this,

Confucius said, 'Whoever wrote this song knew the Dao well. So whatever it is must have its own laws, and whenever they cleave to what makes us human, the people must delight in stately Integrity.'"

11.7 孟子曰:"富歲,子弟多賴;兇歲,子弟多暴。非天之降才爾殊也,其所以陷溺其心者然也。今夫麰麥,播種而耰之,其地同,樹之時又同,浡然而生,至於日至之時,皆熟矣。雖有不同,則地有肥磽,雨露之養、人事之不齊也。故凡同類者,舉相似也,何獨至於人而疑之?聖人與我同類者。故龍子曰:'不知足而爲屨,我知其不爲蕢也。'屨之相似,天下之足同也。口之於味,有同嗜也,易牙先得我口之所嗜者也。如使口之於味也,其性與人殊,若犬馬之與我不同類也,則天下何嗜皆從易牙之於味也?至於味,天下期於易牙,是天下之口相似也。惟耳亦然,至於聲,天下期於師曠,是天下之耳相似也。惟目亦然,至於子都,天下莫不知其姣也;不知子都之姣者,無目者也。故曰:口之於味也,有同嗜焉;耳之於聲也,有同聽焉;目之於色也,有同美焉。至於心,獨無所同然乎?心之所同然者,何也?謂理也,義也。聖人先得我心之所同然耳。故理義之悅我心,猶芻豢之悅我口。"

11.7 Mencius said, "In good years, young men are mostly fine. In bad years, they're mostly cruel and violent. It isn't that Heaven endows them with such different capacities, only that their minds are mired in such different situations. Think about barley: if you plant the seeds carefully at the same time and in the same place, they'll all sprout and grow ripe by summer solstice. If they don't grow the same—it's because of inequities in richness of soil, amounts of rainfall, or the care given to them by farmers. And so, all members belonging to a given species of thing are the same. Why should humans be the lone exception? The sage and I—surely we belong to the same species of thing. That's why Longzi said, 'Even if a cobbler makes a pair of sandals for feet he's never seen, he certainly won't make a pair of baskets.' Sandals are all alike because feet are the same throughout all beneath Heaven. And all tongues savor the same flavors. Yiya was just the first to discover what our tongues savor. If taste differes by nature from person to person, just like horses and dogs differ by species from us, then how is it people throughout all beneath Heaven savor the tastes Yiya savored? People throughout all beneath Heaven share Yiya's tastes, therefore people's tongues are alike throughout all beneath Heaven. It's true for the ear too: people throughout all beneath Heaven share Maestro Kuang's sense of music, therefore people's ears are alike thoughout all beneath Heaven. And it's no less true for the eye: no one throughout all beneath Heaven could fail to see the beauty of Zidu. If you can't see his beauty, you simply haven't eyes. Hence it is said, 'All tongues savor the same flavors, all ears hear the same music, and all eyes see the same beauty.' Why should the mind alone not be alike in us all? But what is it about our minds that is alike? Isn't it what we call reason and righteousness? The sage is just the first to discover what is common to our minds. Hence, reason and righteousness please our minds just like meat pleases our tongues."

11.8 孟子曰：＂牛山之木嘗美矣。以其郊於大國也，斧斤伐之，可以爲美乎？是其日夜之所息，雨露之所潤，非無萌蘖之生焉，牛羊又從而牧之，是以若彼濯濯也。人見其濯濯也，以爲未嘗有材焉，此豈山之性也哉？雖存乎人者，豈無仁義之心哉？其所以放其良心者，亦猶斧斤之於木也。旦旦而伐之，可以爲美乎？其日夜之所息，平旦之氣，其好惡與人相近也者幾希，則其旦晝之所爲，有梏亡之矣。梏之反覆，則其夜氣不足以存。夜氣不足以存，則其違禽獸不遠矣。人見其禽獸也，而以爲未嘗有才焉者，是豈人之情也哉？故苟得其養，無物不長；苟失其養，無物不消。孔子曰：＇操則存，舍則亡。出入無時，莫知其鄉。＇惟心之謂與！＂

11.8 Mencius said, "The trees of the Ox Mountain were once beautiful. But as they were near a great city, axes cleared them little by little. Now there's nothing left of their beauty. They rest day and night, rain and dew falling in plenty, and there's no lack of fresh sprouts. But people graze oxen and sheep there, so the mountain's stripped bare. When people see how bare it is, they think that's all the potential it has. But does that mean this is the nature of the Ox Mountain? Without the mind of benevolence and righteousness alive in us, how can we be human? When we abandon this noble mind, it's like cutting those trees: a few axe blows each day, and pretty soon there's nothing left. Then you can rest day and night, take in the clarity of morning's healing qi—but the values that make you human keep thinning away. All day long, you're tangled in your life. If these tangles keep up day after day, even the clarity of night's healing qi isn't enough to preserve you. And if the clarity of night's healing qi isn't enough to preserve you, you aren't much different from an animal. When people see you're like an animal, they think that's all the potential you have. But does that mean this is the human constitution? With proper sustenance, anything will grow; and without proper sustenance, anything will fade away. Confucius said, 'Embrace it and it endures. Forsake it and it dies. It comes and goes without warning, and no one knows its route.' He was speaking of the mind."

11.15 公都子問曰："鈞是人也，或爲大人，或爲小人，何也？"孟子曰："從其大體爲大人，從其小體爲小人。"曰："鈞是人也，或從其大體，或從其小體，何也？"曰："耳目之官不思，而蔽於物。物交物，則引之而已矣。心之官則思；思則得之，不思則不得也。此天之所與我者，先立乎其大者，則其小者不能奪也。此爲大人而已矣。"

11.15 The disciple Gong Du said, "If we're all equally human, but some are great, and some are small—how is this?"

"Great people abide by what is great in them;" replied Mencius, "small people abide by what is small in them."

"If we're all equally human, how is it that some abide by what is great in them and some abide by what is small in them?"

"The senses cannot think, and so ear and eye are easily deceived by things. And things interact together, which only makes it worse. It is the mind which thinks, and so understands. Without thought there is no understanding. Heaven has given us these two things: mind and senses. If you insist from the beginning on what is great in you, what is small cannot steal it away. This is what makes a person great without fail."

12.2 曹交問曰："人皆可以爲堯舜，有諸？"孟子曰："然。""交聞文王十尺，湯九尺；今交九尺四寸以長。食粟而已，如何則可？"曰："奚有於是？亦爲之而已矣。有人於此，力不能勝一匹雛，則爲無力人矣。今曰舉百鈞，則爲有力人矣。然則舉烏獲之任，是亦爲烏獲而已矣。夫人豈以不勝爲患哉？弗爲耳。徐行後長者，謂之弟；疾行先長者，謂之不弟。夫徐行者，豈人所不能哉？所不爲也。堯舜之道，孝弟而已矣。子服堯之服、誦堯之言、行堯之行，是堯而已矣。子服桀之服、誦桀之言、行桀之行，是桀而已矣。"曰："交得見於鄒君，可以假館，願留而受業於門。"曰："夫道若大路然，豈難知哉？人病不求耳。子歸而求之，有餘師。"

12.2 Jiao of Cao asked Mencius, saying, "It is true that all human beings are capable of becoming a Yao or a Shun?"

Mencius replied, "It is."

Jiao went on, "I have heard that King Wen was ten cubits high, and Tang nine. Now I am nine cubits four inches in height. But I can do nothing but eat my millet. What am I to became a Yao or a Shun?"

"Isn't it easy?" said Mencius. "Just act like Yao and Shun. If you can't lift a baby chicken, you are weak indeed. If you can lift three thousand pounds, you are strong indeed. And if you can lift as much as Wu Huo, you're a Wu Huo. Why do people agonize over what they cannot do? They simply aren't trying. If you follow your elders, walking with dignity and respect, you can be called a younger brother. If you hurry ahead of your elders, you cannot be called a younger brother. How can anyone say they haven't the capacity to walk slowly behind? They just aren't trying. The Dao of Yao and Shun is simple: act with the respect proper to a son and a younger brother. If you dress the way Yao dressed, speak the way Yao spoke, and act the way Yao acted—then you're a Yao. And if you dress the way Shun dressed, speak the way Shun spoke, and act the way Shun acted—then you're a Shun. It's that simple."

"The Zou Sovereign would listen to me and give me a place to live," said Jiao, "but I want to stay here, receiving your beautiful teachings with the other disciples."

"The Dao is like a great highway," replied Mencius. "It's easy to find. People just don't bother to look. Go back to your home. Look for it there, and you'll find teachers aplenty."

《荀子》/ Xunzi

禮論篇第十九
Chapter 19　Discourse on Ritual

……性者，本始材朴也；偽者，文理隆盛也。無性則偽之無所加，無偽則性不能自美。性偽合，然後成聖人之名一，天下之功於是就也。故曰：天地合而萬物生，陰陽接而變化起，性偽合而天下治。天能生物，不能辨物也；地能載人，不能治人也；宇中萬物生人之屬，待聖人然後分也。……

…Human nature is the original beginning and the raw material, and deliberate effort is what makes it patterned, ordered, and exalted. If there were no human nature, then there would be nothing for deliberate effort to be applied to. If there were no deliberate effort, then human nature would not be able to beautify itself. Human nature and deliberate effort must unite, and then the reputation of the sage and the work of unifying all under Heaven are thereupon brought to completion. And so I say, when Heaven and Earth unite, then the myriad creatures are born. When yin and yang interact, then changes and transformations arise. When human nature and deliberate effort unite, then all under Heaven becomes ordered. For Heaven can give birth to creatures, but it cannot distinguish among creatures. Earth can support people, but it cannot govern a state. In the world, all members of the myriad things and the human race must await the sage, and only then will they be appropriately divided up. …

性惡篇第二十三
Chapter 23　Human Nature Is Bad

人之性惡，其善者偽也。今人之性，生而有好利焉，順是，故爭奪生而辭讓亡焉；生而有疾惡焉，順是，故殘賊生而忠信亡焉；生而有耳目之欲，有好聲色焉，順是，故淫亂生而禮義文理亡焉。然則從人之性，順人之情，必出於爭奪，合於犯分亂理，而歸於暴。故必將有師法之化，禮義之道，然後出於辭讓，合於文理，而歸於治。用此觀之，然則人之性惡明矣，其善者偽也。

Human nature is bad. Their goodness is a matter of deliberate effort. Human nature is such that we are born with a fondness for profit. Hence, if people follow along with their nature, then struggle and contention will arise, and yielding and deference will perish therein. Human nature is such that we are born with feelings of jealousy and hatred. If people follow along with their nature, then cruelty and villainy will arise, and loyalty and trustworthiness will perish therein. They are born with desires of the eyes and ears: eyes desire beautiful sights and ears desire beautiful sounds. If they follow along with these, then lasciviousness and chaos will arise, and ritual and yi, proper form and order, will perish therein. Thus, if people follow along with their nature and indulge in their inborn dispositions, they are sure to come to struggle and contention, turn to disrupting social divisions and order, and end up becoming violent. So, it is necessary to await the transforming influence of teachers and models and the guidance of ritual and yi, and only then will people come to yielding and deference, turn to proper form and order, and end up becoming controlled. In view of this, it is clear that human nature is bad, and what is good is a result of deliberate effort.

故枸木必將待檃栝烝矯然後直，鈍金必將待礱厲然後利。今人之性惡，必將待師法然後正，得禮義然後治，今人無師法，則偏險而不正；無禮義，則悖亂而不治，古者聖王以人之性惡，以爲偏險而不正，悖亂而不治，是以爲之起禮義，制法度,以矯飾人之情性而正之,以擾化人之情性而導之也,始皆出於治,合於道者也。今之人化師法,積文學,道禮義者爲君子;縱性情,安恣睢,而違禮義者爲小人。用此觀之,然則人之性惡明矣,其善者僞也。

Crooked wood cannot become straight without being steamed and straightened on the shaping frame. Blunt metal cannot become sharp without being honed and grinded. Now since human nature is bad, people must await teachers and proper models, and only then do they become correct. They must have ritual and yi, and only then do they become well ordered. Now without teachers or proper models for people, they will be deviant, dangerous, and not correct. Without ritual and yi, they will be unruly, chaotic, and not well ordered. In ancient times, the sage-kings saw that because human nature is bad, ordinary people were deviant, dangerous, and not correct, unruly, chaotic, and not well ordered. Therefore, the sage-kings set up ritual and yi, and established proper models and measures. They did this in order to straighten out and beautify people's nature and dispositions and thereby correct them, and in order to train and transform people's nature and dispositions and thereby guide them, so that for the first time they all came to order and conformed to the Dao. Among people of today, those who are transformed by teachers and proper models, who accumulate culture and learning, and who make ritual and yi their path, become gentlemen. Those who give rein to their nature and inborn dispositions, who take comfort in being utterly unrestrained, and who violate ritual and yi, become petty men. In view of this, it is clear that human nature is bad, and what is good is a result of deliberate effort.

孟子曰:"人之學者,其性善。"曰:是不然,是不及知人之性,而不察乎人之性僞之分者也。凡性者,天之就也,不可學,不可事。禮義者,聖人之所生也,人之所學而能,所事而成者也。不可學,不可事,而在人者,謂之性;可學而能,可事而成之在人者,謂之僞,是性僞之分也。今人之性,目可以見,耳可以聽,夫可以見之明不離目,可以聽之聰不離耳,目明而耳聰,不可學,明矣。

Mencius says, when people engage in learning, this manifests the goodness of their nature. I say: This is not so. This is a case of not attaining knowledge of human nature and of not seeing clearly the division between people's nature and their deliberate efforts. In every case, the nature of a thing is the accomplishment of Heaven. It cannot be learned. It cannot be worked at. Ritual and yi are what the sage produces. They are things that people become capable of through learning, things that are achieved through working at them. Those things in people which cannot be learned and cannot be worked at are called their "nature". Those things in people which they become capable of through learning and which they achieve through working at them are called their "deliberate efforts". This is the division between nature and deliberate effort. Now people's nature is such that their eyes can see, and their ears can hear. The brightness by which they see does not depart from their eyes, and the acuity by which they hear does not depart from their ears. Their eyes are simply bright, and their ears are simply acute. Clearly, they do not learn to have these qualities.

孟子曰："今人之性善,將皆失喪其性故也。"曰:若是則過矣。今人之性,生而離其朴,離其資,必失而喪之。用此觀之,然則人之性惡明矣。所謂性善者,不離其朴而美之,不離其資而利之也。使夫資朴之於美,心意之於善,若夫可以見之明不離目,可以聽之聰不離耳。故曰:目明而耳聰也。今人之性,飢而欲飽,寒而欲煖,勞而欲休,此人之情性也。今人飢見長而不敢先食者,將有所讓也;勞而不敢求息者,將有所代也。夫子之讓乎父,弟之讓乎兄,子之代乎父,弟之代乎兄,此二行者,皆反於性而悖於情也。然而孝子之道,禮義之文理也。故順情性則不辭讓矣,辭讓則悖於情性矣。用此觀之,然則人之性惡明矣,其善者偽也。

Mencius says, human nature is good, but they all wind up losing their nature and original state. I say: Mencius is simply mistaken. Human nature is such that as soon as they are born, they will depart from their original simplicity and from their original material; this cannot be stopped. In view of this, it is clear that human nature is bad. The so-called goodness of human nature would mean for one not to depart from one's original simplicity and instead beautify it, not to depart from one's original material and instead make use of it. In this view, the beauty of one's original simplicity and original material, or the goodness of one's will, is just like the brightness that enables eyes to see, or the acuity that enables the ears to hear: brightness is an intrinsic property of [normally-functioning] eyes, and acuity is an intrinsic property of [normally-functioning] ears. Thus I have said, The eyes are simply bright and the ears are simply keen. Now people's nature is such that when hungry they desire satiety, when cold they desire warmth, and when tired they desire rest. This is people's inborn disposition and nature. Now if people are hungry and see food but do not dare to eat first, that is because they have to feed someone. If people are tired but do not dare to seek rest, that is because they have to work for someone. When a son gives food to his father, a younger brother gives food to his older brother, a son works for his father, or a younger brother works for his older brother, these two kinds of conduct both go against one's nature and are at odds with one's inborn dispositions. Nevertheless, they are in accordance with the way of a filial child, and the proper form and order contained in ritual and yi. Thus, if one follows along with one's inborn dispositions and nature, then one will not defer and give way. If one defers and gives way, then one is at odds with one's inborn dispositions and nature. In view of this, it is clear that human nature is bad, and what is good is a result of deliberate effort.

問者曰："人之性惡,則禮義惡生？"應之曰:凡禮義者,是生於聖人之偽,非故生於人之性也。故陶人埏埴而爲器,然則器生於陶人之偽,非故生於人之性也。故工人斲木而成器,然則器生於工人之偽,非故生於人之性也。聖人積思慮,習偽故,以生禮義而起法度,然則禮義法度者,是生於聖人之偽,非故生於人之性也。若夫目好色,耳好聲,口好味,心好利,骨體膚理好愉佚,是皆生於人之情性者也,感而自然,不待事而後生之者也。夫感而不能然,必且待事而後然者,謂之生於偽。是性偽之所生,其不同之徵也。

Someone might ask, if human nature is bad, then from what are ritual and yi produced? I respond that in every case, ritual and yi are produced from the deliberate effort of the sage; they are not produced from human nature. Thus, when the potter mixes up clay and makes vessels, the vessels are produced from the deliberate efforts of the craftsman; they are not produced from the nature of the craftsman. Similarly, when the carpenter carves wood and makes utensils, the utensils are produced from his deliberate efforts; they are not produced from his nature. The sage thinks carefully about human affairs in order to produce ritual and yi and in order to establish proper models and measures. So, ritual and yi and proper models and measures are produced from the deliberate efforts of the sage; they are not produced from human nature. As for the reason why the eyes like pretty colors, the ears like beautiful sounds, the mouth likes good flavors, the heart likes what is beneficial, and the bones and flesh like what is comfortable—all these are due to people's inborn dispositions and nature. These are things that come about of themselves in response to stimulation, things that do not need to await being worked at before being produced. Those things that are not immediate responses to stimulation, that must await being worked at before they are so, are said to be produced from deliberate effort. These are the things that nature and deliberate effort produce, and they have different characteristics.

故聖人化性而起偽，偽起而生禮義，禮義生而制法度。然則禮義法度者，是聖人之所生也。故聖人之所以同於衆，其不異於衆者，性也；所以異而過衆者，偽也。夫好利而欲得者，此人之情性也。假之人有弟兄資財而分者，且順情性，好利而欲得，若是，則兄弟相拂奪矣。且化禮義之文理，若是，則讓乎國人矣。故順情性則弟兄爭矣，化禮義則讓乎國人矣。

So, the sage transforms his [evil] nature and makes deliberate effort. In making deliberate effort, he produces ritual and yi. In producing ritual and yi he institutes proper models and measures. Thus, ritual and yi and proper models and measures are produced by the sage. Thus, that in which the sage is like the masses, that in which he is no different from the masses, is his nature. That in which he differs from and surpasses the masses is his deliberate efforts. Liking what is beneficial and desiring gain are people's inborn dispositions and nature. Suppose there were brothers who had some property to divide, and that they followed desire for benefit and gain in their inborn dispositions and nature. If they were to do so, then the brothers would conflict and contend with each other for it. However, if they are transformed by the proper form and order contained in ritual and yi, then they would even give the property over to their countrymen. Thus, following along with inborn dispositions and nature, even brothers will struggle with each other for the property. If transformed by ritual and yi, then they will even give it over to their countrymen.

凡人之欲爲善者,爲性惡也。夫薄願厚,惡願美,狹願廣,貧願富,賤願貴,苟無之中者,必求於外。故富而不願財,貴而不願埶,苟有之中者,必不及於外。用此觀之,人之欲爲善者,爲性惡也。今人之性,固無禮義,故彊學而求有之也;性不知禮義,故思慮而求知之也。然則生而已,則人無禮義,不知禮義。人無禮義則亂,不知禮義則悖。然則生而已,則悖亂在己。用此觀之,人之性惡明矣,其善者僞也。

In every case where people desire to become good, it is because their nature is bad. The person who has little desires to have much. The person of narrow experience desires to have broader experiences. The ugly person desires to be beautiful. The poor person desires to be rich. The base person desires to be noble. That which one does not have within oneself, one is sure to seek outside. Thus, when one is rich, one does not desire wealth. When one is noble, one does not desire power. That which one has within oneself, one is sure not to seek outside. In view of this, people desire to become good because their nature is bad. Now people's nature is originally without ritual and yi. Thus, they must force themselves to engage in learning and seek to possess them. Their nature does not know of ritual and yi, so they must think and reflect and seek to know them. So, going only by what they have from birth, people lack ritual and yi and do not know of ritual and yi. If people are not constrained by ritual and yi, then there will be chaos. If they do not understand ritual and yi, then they will be unruly. So, going only by what they have from birth, unruliness and disorder are within them. In view of this, it is clear that human nature is bad, and what is good is a result of deliberate effort.

孟子曰:"人之性善。"曰:是不然。凡古今天下之所謂善者,正理平治也;所謂惡者,偏險悖亂也,是善惡之分也矣。今誠以人之性固正理平治邪,則有惡用聖王,惡用禮義哉?雖有聖王禮義,將曷加於正理平治也哉?今不然,人之性惡,故古者聖人以人之性惡,以爲偏險而不正,悖亂而不治,故爲之立君上之埶以臨之,明禮義以化之,起法正以治之,重刑罰以禁之,使天下皆出於治,合於善也。是聖王之治,而禮義之化也。今當試去君上之埶,無禮義之化,去法正之治,無刑罰之禁,倚而觀天下民人之相與也。若是,則夫彊者害弱而奪之,衆者暴寡而譁之,天下之悖亂而相亡,不待頃矣。用此觀之,然則人之性惡明矣,其善者僞也。

Mencius says, human nature is good. I say, this is not so. In every case, both in ancient times and in the present, what everyone under Heaven calls good is being correct, ordered, peaceful, and controlled. What they call bad is being deviant, dangerous, unruly, and chaotic. This is the division between good and bad. Now does he really think that human nature is originally correct, ordered, peaceful, and controlled. Then what use would there be for sage-kings? What use for ritual and yi? Even though there are sage-kings and ritual and yi, whatever could these add to its correct, ordered, peaceful, and controlled state? Now that is not the case. Human nature is bad. In ancient times the sage-kings saw that because people's nature is bad, people were deviant, dangerous, and not correct, unruly, chaotic, and not well-ordered. Therefore, for the people's sake they made lords and superiors powerful in order to oversee the people. They made ritual and yi clear in order to transform people. They set up laws and standards in order to make people well ordered. They made punishments and fines harsh in order to restrain people. As a result, they caused all under Heaven to come to order and conform to goodness. Such are the ordering influence of the sage-kings and the transformative effects of ritual and yi.

Now suppose we do away with the power of lords and superiors, the transformation from ritual and yi, the order of laws and standards, and the restraint of punishments and fines. Then lean against the door and observe how all the people of the world treat each other. Here are what would happen: the strong would harm the weak and snatch what the weak have; the many would tyrannize the few and shout them down. One would not have to wait even a moment for all under Heaven to arrive at unruliness and chaos and perish. In view of this, it is clear that human nature is bad, and what is good is a result of deliberate effort.

故善言古者,必有節於今;善言天者,必有徵於人。凡論者貴其有辨合,有符驗。故坐而言之,起而可設,張而可施行。今孟子曰:"人之性善。"無辨合符驗,坐而言之,起而不可設,張而不可施行,豈不過甚矣哉! 故性善則去聖王,息禮義矣。性惡則與聖王,貴禮義矣。故檃栝之生,爲枸木也;繩墨之起,爲不直也;立君上,明禮義,爲性惡也。用此觀之,然則人之性惡明矣,其善者偽也。直木不待檃栝而直者,其性直也。枸木必將待檃栝烝矯然後直者,以其性不直也。今人之性惡,必將待聖王之治,禮義之化,然後始出於治,合於善也。用此觀之,然則人之性惡明矣,其善者偽也。

So, those who are good at speaking of ancient times are sure to test their doctrines against the present experience. Those who are good at speaking of Heaven are surely able to apply their doctrines to human affairs. A theory is valuable only if it is confirmed by experience and applicable to human affairs. For a good theory, not only one can sit and talk about it, but also one can implement it when one stands up, and one can put it into practice when one unfolds it. Now Mencius says, human nature is good. This theory can neither be confirmed by experience nor is it applicable to human affairs. He sits and talks about it, but when he stands up, he cannot implement it, and when he unfolds it, he cannot put it into practice. Is his error not great indeed! If human nature is good, then one may do away with the sage kings and put ritual and yi to rest. If human nature is bad, then one simply must side with the sage kings and honor ritual and yi.

Thus, the press frame originated because of crooked wood. The ink-line was invented because of things that are not straight. Lords and superiors were established and ritual and yi were made clear because of the fact that human nature is bad. In view of this, it is clear that human nature is bad, and what is good is a result of deliberate effort.

Straight wood does not await the press frame in order to become straight, because its nature is to be straight. Crooked wood must await the press frame, steaming and bending and only then will it be straight, because it is by nature not straight. Now people's nature is bad, and so they must certainly await the ordering influence of sage-kings and the transformative effects of ritual and yi and only then will they all come to order and conform to goodness. In view of this, it is clear that human nature is bad, and what is good is a result of deliberate effort.

問者曰："禮義積偽者，是人之性，故聖人能生之也。"應之曰：是不然。夫陶人埏埴而生瓦，然則瓦埴豈陶人之性也哉？工人斲木而生器，然則器木豈工人之性也哉？夫聖人之於禮義也，辟則陶埏而生之也。然則禮義積偽者，豈人之本性也哉！凡人之性者，堯舜之與桀跖，其性一也；君子之與小人，其性一也。今將以禮義積偽為人之性邪？然則有曷貴堯禹，曷貴君子矣哉。凡所貴堯禹君子者，能化性，能起偽，偽起而生禮義。然則聖人之於禮義積偽也，亦猶陶埏而生之也。用此觀之，然則禮義積偽者，豈人之性也哉！所賤於桀跖小人者，從其性，順其情，安恣睢，以出乎貪利爭奪。故人之性惡明矣，其善者偽也。天非私曾騫孝已而外眾人也，然而曾騫孝已獨厚於孝之實，而全於孝之名者，何也？以綦於禮義故也。天非私齊魯之民而外秦人也，然而於父子之義，夫婦之別，不如齊魯之孝共敬文者，何也？以秦人之從情性，安恣睢，慢於禮義故也，豈其性異矣哉！

Someone might say, it is human nature to establish ritual and yi by deliberate effort and that is why the sage is able to produce them. I answer, this is not so. The potter mixes clay and produces tiles. Yet, how could the clay of the tiles be the potter's nature? The carpenter carves wood and makes utensils. Yet, how could the wood of the utensils be the carpenter's nature?

The relationship of the sage to ritual and yi can be compared to mixing up clay and producing things. So, how could establishing ritual and yi by deliberate effort be people's original nature? In every aspect of human nature, the nature of Yao and Shun was one and the same as that of Jie and Robber Zhi. The nature of the gentleman is one and the same as that of the petty man. Now will you take ritual and yi and the accumulation of deliberate effort to be a matter of human nature? Then for what do you value Yao and Shun? For what do you value the gentleman? Everything that one values in Yao and Shun and the gentleman is due to the fact that they were able to transform their nature and to make deliberate effort. In making deliberate effort, they produced ritual and yi. Thus, the sage's establishing ritual and yi by deliberate effort is like producing a tile by mixing up clay. In view of this, then how could ritual and yi and the accumulation of deliberate effort be people's nature? What one finds base in Jie and Robber Zhi and the petty man is due to the fact that they follow along with their inborn dispositions and nature and take pleasure in utter lack of restraint, so that they are greedy and fight with each other. Thus, it is clear that human nature is bad, and that their goodness is a result of deliberate effort. Heaven did not favor Zengzi, Minzi Qian, and Xiao Yi and exclude the masses. Then why is it that only Zengzi, Minzi Qian, and Xiao Yi were good at practicing filial piety and were perfect in their reputation for filial piety? It is because they exerted themselves to the utmost in ritual and yi. Heaven does not favor people of Qi and Lu and exclude the people of Qin. Then why is it that with regard to the yi between father and son, and the distinction between husband and wife, the people of Qin are not as good at practicing filial piety and mutual respect as those of Qi and Lu? It is because the people of Qin follow along with their inborn dispositions and nature, take pleasure in utter lack of restraint, and are lax in regard to ritual and yi. How could it be because their nature is different?

塗之人可以爲禹，曷謂也？曰：凡禹之所以爲禹者，以其爲仁義法正也。然則仁義法正，有可知可能之理。然而塗之人也，皆有可以知仁義法正之質，皆有可以能仁義法正之具,然則其可以爲禹明矣。今以仁義法正爲固無可知可能之理邪?然則唯禹不知仁義法正,不能仁義法正也。將使塗之人固無可以知仁義法正之質,而固無可以能仁義法正之具邪?然則塗之人也,且內不可以知父子之義,外不可以知君臣之正。不然,今塗之人者,皆內可以知父子之義,外可以知君臣之正,然則其可以知之質,可以能之具,其在塗之人明矣。今使塗之人者,以其可以知之質,可以能之具,本夫仁義之可知之理,可能之具,然則其可以爲禹明矣。今使塗之人伏術爲學,專心一志,思索孰察,加日縣久,積善而不息,則通於神明,參於天地矣。故聖人者,人之所積而致矣。

Anyone on the streets could become a Yu. What do I mean by this? I say, the reason Yu was Yu was that he was benevolent (ren), righteous (yi), lawful, and correct. Now benevolence (ren), righteousness (yi), lawfulness, and correctness have patterns that can be known and can be practiced. However, people on the streets all have the material for knowing benevolence (ren), righteousness (yi), lawfulness, and correctness, and they all have the equipment for practicing them. Thus, it is clear that they could become a Yu. Now if benevolence (ren), righteousness (yi), lawfulness, and correctness originally had no patterns that could be known or practiced, then even Yu would not have known benevolence (ren), righteousness (yi), lawfulness, and correctness, nor would he have practiced them. Shall we suppose that people on the streets originally do not have the material to know benevolence (ren), righteousness (yi), lawfulness, and correctness, and that they originally do not have the equipment for practicing them? If so, then people on the streets could not know the yi of father and son within the family, and they could not know the proper relations of lord and minister outside the family. This is not so. Rather, it is the case that anyone on the streets can know the yi of father and son within the family, and can know the proper relations of lord and minister outside the family. Thus, it is clear that the material for understanding these things and the equipment for practicing them are present in people on the streets. Now if people on the streets use their material for understanding and the equipment for practicing to understand

and practice the aspects of benevolence (ren) and righteousness (yi) that can be understood and practiced, then it is clear that anyone on the streets could become a Yu. Now if people on the streets are convinced by the correct philosophy, submit themselves to learning, concentrate on one thing, think carefully, observe broadly, keep up the good work, make progress every day and never give up, they will acquire spirit-like powers and achieve great understanding, so that they will form a triad with Heaven and Earth. Thus, becoming a sage is something that people could achieve through accumulation.

曰："聖可積而致,然而皆不可積,何也?"曰:可以而不可使也。故小人可以爲君子,而不肯爲君子;君子可以爲小人,而不肯爲小人。小人君子者,未嘗不可以相爲也,然而不相爲者,可以而不可使也。故塗之人可以爲禹,則然;塗之人能爲禹,未必然也。雖不能爲禹,無害可以爲禹。足可以徧行天下,然而未嘗有能徧行天下者也。夫工匠農賈,未嘗不可以相爲事也,然而未嘗能相爲事也。用此觀之,然則可以爲,未必能也;雖不能,無害可以爲。然則能不能之與可不可,其不同遠矣,其不可以相爲明矣。

Someone says, sageliness is achieved through accumulation, but why is it that not all people can accumulate thus? I say, they can do it, but they cannot be made to do it. Thus, the petty man can become a gentleman, but he is not willing to become a gentleman. The gentleman can become a petty man, but he is not willing to become a petty man. It has never been that the petty man and the gentleman are incapable of becoming each other. However, the reason they do not become each other is that they can do so but cannot be made to do so. Thus, it is the case that anyone on the streets could become a Yu, but it is not necessarily the case that anyone on the streets will be able to become a Yu. Even if one is not able to become a Yu, this does not harm the fact that one could become a Yu. One's feet could walk everywhere under Heaven. Even so, there has not yet been anyone who has been able to walk everywhere under Heaven. It has never been that craftsmen, carpenters, farmers, and merchants could not do each other's business. However, none have ever been able to do each other's business. In view of this, then one is not always able to do what one could do. Even if one is not able to do it, this is no harm to the fact that one could do it. Thus, the difference between being able and unable, and could and could-not is big indeed. It is clear, then, that [the gentleman and the petty man] are unable to become one another.

堯問於舜曰："人情何如？"舜對曰："人情甚不美，又何問焉！妻子具而孝衰於親，嗜欲得而信衰於友，爵祿盈而忠衰於君。人之情乎！人之情乎！甚不美，又何問焉！唯賢者爲不然。"
......

Yao asked Shun, "What are people's inborn dispositions like?" Shun answered, "People's inborn dispositions are most unlovely! Why ask about them? When one has a wife and son, then one's filial piety to one's parents declines. When one's appetites and desires are fulfilled, then one's faithfulness to friends declines. When one's rank and salary are high, then one's loyalty to one's lord declines. People's inborn dispositions? People's inborn dispositions? They are most unlovely. Why ask about them? Only the worthy man is not like that."
...

五、名實 / Part Ⅴ　Lauguage

洛克說，語言是"維繫社會的重要紐帶"。如果沒有語言，我們很難彼此交流知識、情感、願望、等等。如果人們彼此之間不能有效地交流，紛爭就難以避免，社會秩序就會崩塌。因此，語言在我們的社會中扮演了重要的角色。然而，人們經常濫用語言，尤其是政治家，爲了能夠欺騙民衆和打擊反對者，常常濫用語言，遮蔽真相。喬治·奧威爾曾經說過，政治語言在他那個年代是"爲了使謊言聽起來真實，使謀殺看起來正當，把空話說得真有其事而設計的"。中國古代哲學家注意到他們所處的時代有同樣的問題。

我們應該如何處理語言的濫用問題？是否應該接受道家的建議——既然這是個沒有辦法解決的問題，那我們就盡可能地少說話、少寫文章？如果這行不通，那我們要怎樣才能確保人們正確使用詞語描述事物，以及確保事物與它們的名稱相符？要回答這個問題，我們需要明白一串符號爲什麼有意義？爲什麼某個名詞指代某物而非彼物？在這一部分，我們將會閱讀公孫龍子和荀子對這些問題的論述。

Language, as John Locke said, is "the great bond that holds society together". Without language we can barely communicate with each other our knowledge, feelings, hopes, and so on. If we cannot effectively communicate with each other, then conflicts would be prevalent and social order would be impossible. Hence, language plays a vital role in our society. However, people often misuse words. In particular, politicians often abuse language to darken the truth so that they can deceive the people and defeat their opponents. George Orwell said that the political language in his time was "designed to make lies sound truthful and murder respectable, and to give an appearance of solidity to pure wind." Ancient Chinese philosophers observed the same thing in their time.

How should we then address the problem of the corruption of language? Should we say/write as little as we can [since there is no cure], as Daoists suggest? If not, how can we make sure that people use the right words to describe things and that things live up to their names? To answer these questions, we need to understand what makes a string of symbols meaningful. In particular, what makes a name refer to a certain thing rather than some other thing? In this part, we will see how Gongsun Longzi and Xunzi address these questions.

《公孫龍子》/ Gongsun Longzi

白馬論第二
Chapter 2　　On White and Horse (*BAIMA LUN*)

"白馬非馬",可乎?
曰:可。
曰:何哉?
曰:馬者,所以命形也;白者,所以命色也。命色者非名形也。故曰:"白馬非馬。"

INT: Is "a white horse is not a horse" admissible?
GSL: It is admissible.
INT: How so?
GSL: "Horse" is what names form. "White" is what names color. What names color is not what names form. Therefore I say, "A white horse is not a horse."

曰:有白馬不可謂無馬也。不可謂無馬者,非馬也? 有白馬爲有馬,白之非馬,何也?

曰:求馬,黃、黑馬皆可致;求白馬,黃、黑馬不可致。使白馬乃馬也,是所求一也。所求一者，白者不異馬也，所求不異，如黃、黑馬有可有不可，何也？可與不可，其相非明。故黃、黑馬一也，而可以應有馬，而不可以應有白馬，是白馬之非馬，審矣！

INT: If there is a white horse, it is inadmissible to say there is not a horse. In the case of it being inadmissible to say there is not a horse, is there not a horse? There being a white horse is taken as there being a horse, so how is a white horse not a horse?

GSL: When a horse is sought, yellow and black horses may both be sent. When a white horse is sought, yellow and black horses may not be sent. If a white horse is, in fact, a horse, this is a case of what is sought being identical. If what is sought is identical, a white horse is not different from a horse. If what is sought is not different, how is there "may be" and "may not be" with respect to yellow and black horses? That "may be" and "may not be" are mutually exclusive is evident. Therefore yellow and black horses are the same in that they "may be" taken to correspond to there being a horse, while "may not be" taken to correspond to there being a white horse. This clearly shows "a white horse is not a horse".

曰：以馬之有色爲非馬，天下非有無色之馬。天下無馬可乎？

曰：馬固有色，故有白馬。使馬無色，如有馬已耳，安取白馬？故白者非馬也。白馬者，馬與白也。馬與白，馬也？故曰白馬非馬也。

INT: You take a horse that has color not to be a horse yet the world does not have horses without color. A world without horses—is that admissible?

GSL: Horses fundamentally have color; therefore there are white horses. If horses were not colored there would be horses and that is all—how would you choose a white horse? Therefore a white horse is not a horse. A white horse is horse combined with white. Horse combined with white is not horse. Therefore I say, "A white horse is not a horse."

曰：馬未與白爲馬，白未與馬爲白。合馬與白，復名白馬。是相與以不相與爲名,未可。故曰:"白馬非馬"未可。
曰:以"有白馬爲有馬",謂有白馬爲有黃馬,可乎?
曰:未可。

INT: Horse not combined with white is horse; white not combined with horse is white. Joining horse and white [forms] the double name, "white horse". This is to take "combined with" to be the name of what is "not combined with"—surely this is inadmissible. Therefore to say, "[a] white horse is not [a] horse" is inadmissible.

GSL: To take there being a white horse as there being a horse, and to say there being a white horse is for there to be a yellow horse—is this admissible?

INT: It is inadmissible.

曰:以"有馬爲異有黃馬",是異黃馬與馬也;異黃馬與馬,是以黃馬爲非馬。以黃馬爲非馬,而以白馬爲有馬,此飛者入池而棺槨異處,此天下之悖言亂辭也。

GSL: To take there being a horse as different from there being a yellow horse is to differentiate a yellow horse from a horse. To differentiate a yellow horse from a horse is to take a yellow horse as not being a horse. To take a yellow horse as not being a horse yet to take a white horse as being a horse—this is like a flying creature entering a pool or the inner and outer coffins being in different places. These are the world's perverse words and confusing statements.

曰:以"有白馬不可謂無馬"者,離白之謂也;是離者有白馬不可謂有馬也。故所以爲有馬者,獨以馬爲有馬耳,非以白馬爲有馬。故其爲有馬也,不可以謂"馬馬"也。

曰:"白者不定所白",忘之而可也。白馬者,言白定所白也,定所白者非白也。馬者,無去取於色,故黃、黑皆所以應;白馬者,有去取于色,黃、黑馬皆所以色去,故唯白馬獨可以應耳。無去者非有去也,故曰:"白馬非馬"。

INT: If it is inadmissible to say there is not a horse when there is a white horse, there is setting aside the saying of white. If there is not setting aside, it is inadmissible to say there is a horse when there is a white horse. Therefore what is taken as there being a horse is to take horse alone as there being a horse, and not there being a white horse as there being a horse. Therefore in the case of taking there to be a horse, it is inadmissible to take saying "horse is horse".

GSL: In the case of white, it is not fixed to that which is white; setting it aside is possible. In the case of white horse, this says white is fixed to that which is white. What is fixed to that which is white is not [identical with] white. In the case of horse, there is not rejecting or selecting in terms of color. Therefore yellow and black horses both meet the requirements [for a horse]. In the case of white horse, there is rejecting or selecting in terms of color, yellow and black horses all being rejected on the basis of color. Therefore only a white horse alone may meet the requirement. What does not involve rejection is not [identical with] what does involve rejection. Therefore I say, "A white horse is not a horse."

堅白論第五
Chapter 5 On Hard and White (*JIANBAI LUN*)

堅白石三,可乎?
曰:不可。
曰:二,可乎?
曰:可。
曰:何哉?
曰:無堅得白,其舉也二;無白得堅,其舉也二。

INT: Hard, white and stone are three—is that admissible?
GSL: It is not admissible.
INT: Is two admissible?
GSL: It is admissible.

INT: How so?

GSL: Without the hard one gets the white—two are raised. Without the white one gets the hard—two are raised.

曰：得其所白，不可謂無白；得其所堅，不可謂無堅：而之石也之於然也，非三也？

曰：視不得其所堅而得其所白者，無堅也。拊不得其所白而得其所堅，得其堅也，無白也。

INT: If you get its whiteness you cannot say there is not whiteness. If you get its hardness you cannot say there is not hardness. Yet it is the stone that is thus, so are there not three?

GSL: Seeing, you do not get its hardness but you do get its whiteness so there is not hardness. Touching, you do not get its whiteness but you do get its hardness so there is not whiteness.

曰：天下無白，不可以視石；天下無堅，不可以謂石。堅白石不相外，藏三可乎？

曰：有自藏也，非藏而藏也。

INT: In a world without whiteness it would not be possible to see the stone. In a world without hardness it would not be possible to feel the stone. Hard, white and stone do not exclude one another—is it possible to hide the third?

GSL: It hides itself. It is not that it is hidden and so concealed.

曰：其白也，其堅也，而石必得以相盛盈。其自藏奈何？

曰：得其白，得其堅，見與不見離。不見離，一一不相盈，故離。離也者，藏也。

INT: Its whiteness, its hardness, and the stone certainly achieve filling one another. How is there concealing itself?

GSL: Getting its whiteness, getting its hardness, the seen and the not seen, are separate. The one and the two do not fill each other and are therefore separate. Being separate is being concealed.

曰：石之白，石之堅，見與不見，二與三，若廣修而相盈也。其非舉乎？
曰：物白焉，不定其所白；物堅焉，不定其所堅。不定者兼，惡乎其石也？

INT: The stone's whiteness, the stone's hardness, the seen and the not seen, the two and the three, are like breadth and length and mutually fill one another. Is this a false raising?

GSL: A thing that is white does not limit (fix) its whiteness. A thing that is hard does not limit (fix) its hardness. What is not limited (fixed) is shared (general). How is it the stone's [specific attribute]?

曰：循石，非彼無石。非石，無所取乎白石。不相離者，固乎然其無已。
曰：於石一也，堅白二也，而在於石，故有知焉，有不知焉；有見焉，有不見焉。故知與不知相與離，見與不見相與藏。藏故，孰謂之不離？

INT: If you touch the stone and it is not hard, it is not a stone. If it is not a stone there is not that which "selects" white. Hard, white and stone not being separate from one another was originally the case and was never otherwise.

GSL: The stone is one, hard and white are two, and exist in the stone. There is, then, the known in it and there is the not known in it. There is the seen in it and there is the not seen in it. Therefore the known and the not known are separate from one another; the seen and the not seen are hidden from one another. Because of the concealment, who is to say there is not separation?

曰：目不能堅，手不能白。不可謂無堅，不可謂無白。其異任也，其無以代也。堅白域于石，惡乎離？
曰：堅未與石爲堅，而物兼未與爲堅。而堅必堅其不堅。石物而堅，天下未有若堅，而堅藏。白固不能自白，惡能白石物乎？若白者必白，則不白物而白焉。黃黑與之然。石其無有，惡取堅白石乎？故離也。離也者因是。力與知果，不若因是。且猶白以目、以火見。而火不見；則火與目不見，而神見。神不見，而見離。堅以手，而手以捶；是捶與手知而不知，而神與不知。神乎，是之謂"離"焉。離也者天下，故獨而正。

INT: The eye is not able [to perceive] hardness; the hand is not able [to perceive] whiteness. [Still], it cannot be said that there is not hardness and it cannot be said that there is not whiteness. They (the senses) differ in their duties; one does not substitute for the other. Hard and white are bounded in the stone—how are they separate?

GSL: Hardness not joined with stone is hardness and things share [it]. Not joined with things it is hardness, and hardness is essentially hardness. There is not a hard stone thing and hardness. The world does not have what is like hardness; hardness is concealed. If white is fundamentally not able to exist by itself, how is it able to make white stones and things? If white is essentially whiteness, how are there not white things and white? The same goes for yellow and black. If stones did not have [these], how could one select a hard white stone? Therefore there is separation. Separation is because of this. The results of sense perception and cognition are dissimilar due to this. Moreover it is like whiteness is seen by means of the eyes, and the eyes see by means of light, nevertheless light does not see. Then light and the eyes do not see yet the spirit sees. The spirit [itself] does not see, and seeing is separate. Hardness is known by means of the hand; the hand knows by means of striking. This is striking and the hand knowing but [striking] not knowing, and the spirit also not knowing. Ah, the spirit! This is to speak of separation. Separation is a consequence of the world so it is correct to take these things as independent.

《荀子》/ Xunzi

正名篇第二十二
Chapter 22　Correct Naming

……

故王者之制名，名定而實辨，道行而志通，則慎率民而一焉。故析辭擅作名，以亂正名，使民疑惑，人多辨訟，則謂之大姦。其罪猶爲符節度量之罪也。故其民莫敢託爲奇辭以亂正名，故其民愨；愨則易使，易使則公。其民莫敢託爲奇辭以亂正名，故壹於道法，而謹於循令矣。如是則其跡長矣。跡長功成，治之極也。是謹於守名約之功也。今聖王沒，名守慢，奇辭起，名實亂，是非之形不明，則雖守法之吏，誦數之儒，亦皆亂也。若有王者起，必將有循於舊名，有作於新名。然則所爲有名，與所緣以同異，與制名之樞要，不可不察也。

...

So when the kings established names, the names were fixed, and the corresponding objects were thus distinguished. This way was followed, and the kings' intentions were thus made understood. They then carefully led the people to adhere to these things single-mindedly. Thus, they called it great vileness to mince words and recklessly create names such as to disorder the correct names and thereby confuse the people and cause them to engage in much disputation and litigation. This wrongdoing was considered to be just like the crime of forging tallies and measures. Hence, none of their people dared to make up strange names so as to disorder the correct names, and so the people were honest. Since they were honest, they were easy to employ, and since they were easy to employ, tasks were accomplished. Because none of the people dared to make up strange names so as to disorder the correct names, they were unified in following the proper model of the Dao and were diligent in following commands. Because they were like this, the legacy of the kings was long-lasting. To have such a long-lasting legacy and to achieve such accomplishments is the height of good order. Such is what can be accomplished by diligently preserving the agreed names. Nowadays, the sage-kings have passed away, and the preservation of these names has become lax. Strange words have arisen, the names and their corresponding objects are disordered, and the forms of right and wrong are unclear. As a result, even officers who assiduously preserve the proper models and ru who assiduously recite the proper order are also all thrown into chaos. If there arose a true king, he would surely follow the old names in some cases and create new names in other cases. Thus, one must examine the reason for having names, the proper means for distinguishing the same and the different, and the essential points in establishing names.

異形離心交喻，異物名實玄紐，貴賤不明，同異不別；如是，則志必有不喻之患，而事必有困廢之禍。故知者爲之分別制名以指實，上以明貴賤，下以辨同異。貴賤明，同異別，如是則志無不喻之患，事無困廢之禍，此所爲有名也。

When different forms make contact with the mind, they were understood as different things.① If the names and their corresponding objects are tied together in a confused fashion, then the distinction between the noble and the base will not be clear, and the same and the different will not be differentiated. If this is so, then the problem of intentions not being understood will surely happen, and the disaster of affairs being thereby impeded and abandoned will surely occur. Thus, the wise person uses different names to refer to different objects. Most importantly, he makes clear the distinction between the noble and the base, and more generally, he distinguishes the same from the different. When the noble and the base are clearly distinguished, and the same and the different are differentiated, then the problem of intentions not being understood will not happen, and the disaster of affairs being thereby impeded and abandoned will not occur. This is the reason for having names.

---

① Scholars disagree on what "異形離心交喻" means. The translation of this sentence is based on Gongzhe Xiong's interpretation.

然則何緣而以同異？曰：緣天官。凡同類同情者，其天官之意物也同。故比方之疑似而通，是所以共其約名以相期也。形體、色理以目異；聲音清濁、調竽、奇聲以耳異；甘、苦、鹹、淡、辛、酸、奇味以口異；香、臭、芬、鬱、腥、臊、漏庮、奇臭以鼻異；疾、癢、凔、熱、滑、鈹、輕、重以形體異；説、故、喜、怒、哀、樂、愛、惡、欲以心異。

That being the case, then what does one follow and use to distinguish the same and the different? I say, one follows one's Heaven-given faculties. For all creatures belonging to the same category and having the same dispositions, their Heaven-given faculties cognize things in the same way. Thus, one compares similarities with another party and thereby has communication. This is the means by which one shares agreed-upon names so as to align people with one another. Form, color, and pattern are differentiated by the eyes. Notes, tones, high, low, tunings, pipes, and other strange sounds are differentiated by the ear. Sweet, bitter, salty, bland, piquant, sour, and other strange flavors are differentiated by the mouth. Fragrant, foul, flowery, rotten, putrid, sharp, sour, and other strange smells are differentiated by the nose. Pain, itch, cold, hot, slippery, sharp, light, and heavy are differentiated by the body. Persuasions, reasons, happiness, anger, sorrow, joy, love, hate, and desire are differentiated by the heart.

心有徵知。徵知，則緣耳而知聲可也，緣目而知形可也。然而徵知必將待天官之當簿其類，然後可也。五官簿之而不知，心徵知而無説，則人莫不然謂之不知。此所緣而以同異也。然後隨而命之，同則同之，異則異之。單足以喻則單，單不足以喻則兼；單與兼無所相避則共；雖共不爲害矣。知異實者之異名也。故使異實者莫不異名也，不可亂也，猶使同實者莫不同名也。

The mind has the power to judge its awareness. If one's mind judges its awareness, then by following along with the ears one can know a sound, and by following along with the eyes one can know a form. However, judging awareness must await the Heaven-given faculties to appropriately encounter their respective kinds and only then can it work. If the five faculties encounter them but have no awareness, or if the mind judges among them but has no persuasive explanations [for its judgments], then everyone will say that such a person does not know. These are what one follows and uses to distinguish the same and the different. Only after doing this does one then follow it up by naming things. One treats the same thing as the same, and one treats different things as different. When a single word is sufficient to make oneself understood, then one uses a single word. When a single word is not sufficient to make oneself understood, then one combines words. When the single and combined words in no way contradict each other, then one considers them a group, and even though one groups them together, this will do no harm, for one understands how different objects are named differently. Thus, one causes different objects all to have different names, and this is something that one must not throw into disorder. Moreover, one causes the same object to have the same name in all cases.

故萬物雖衆，有時而欲無舉之，故謂之物；物也者，大共名也。推而共之，共則有共，至於無共然後止。有時而欲偏舉之，故謂之鳥獸。鳥獸也者，大別名也。推而別之，別則有別，至於無別然後至。

Thus, even though the things are very numerous, sometimes one desires to refer to them all together, and so one calls them "things". "Things" is a case of large-scale group naming. By drawing analogies, one groups things together, grouping and grouping, until there is nothing more to group, and then one stops. Sometimes one wishes to refer to them partially, and so one calls them "birds" and "beasts". "Birds" and "beasts" are instances of large-scale differentiated naming. By drawing analogies, one differentiates things, differentiating and differentiating, until there is nothing more to differentiate, and then one stops.

名無固宜，約之以命，約定俗成謂之宜，異於約則謂之不宜。名無固實，約之以命實，約定俗成，謂之實名。名有固善，徑易而不拂，謂之善名。物有同狀而異所者，有異狀而同所者，可別也。狀同而爲異所者，雖可合，謂之二實。狀變而實無別而爲異者，謂之化。有化而無別，謂之一實。此事之所以稽實定數也。此制名之樞要也。後王之成名，不可不察也。

    Names have no predetermined appropriateness. People in the beginning make agreement that they shall use a certain name in a certain way. When all people agree and it becomes conventional, the usage of the name is called appropriate, and what differs from the agreed usage is called inappropriate. Names have no predetermined objects. People in the beginning make agreement that they shall use a certain name to refer to a certain thing. When all people agree and it becomes conventional, this name is called the name of that object. Names do have a predetermined goodness. If they are straightforward, simple, and do not conflict, then they are called good names. Some things look the same but belong to different classes, and others look differently but belong to the same class, and these two can be differentiated. For those which look the same but belong to different classes, even though they appear to be the same thing, they are called two separate objects. If the appearance changes but the object does not become different so as to belong to a different class, this is called a transformation. When there is transformation without such difference, it is still called one and the same object. These are what to rely upon in observing the objects and determining their numbers. This is the essential point in establishing names, and the names established by the later kings must not go unexamined.

六、知行 / Part VI Knowledge

　　我們經常不同意別人的觀點。如何才能知道誰的觀點正確呢？訴諸於第三方來裁判嗎？那如何才知道第三方的觀點就是正確的？訴諸於我們的感覺嗎？那如何才能知道我們的感覺是可靠的？如何才能排除我們的生活可能只是一場夢？如果我們的確能夠獲得知識，那麼哪些知識是值得獲取的呢？比如，知道孔子父親的生日有價值嗎？关于如何治理國家的知識是否比关于如何賺錢的知識更有價值？

　　在這一部分，我們將會讀到莊子和荀子對這些問題的論述。閱讀選文時，試著找出他們之間的差別，並思考二者理論的合理性。

　　We often disagree with each other. How do we know whose view is true? Appealing to a third party? How do we know that the third party holds the true view? Appealing to our senses? How do we know that our senses are reliable? How can we rule out the possibility that our life is just a dream? If we can know certain things, what knowledge is worth acquiring? Is it worth finding out, say, the date of birth of Confucius' father? Is the knowledge of how to govern a country more valuable than the knowledge of how to make money?

　　In this part, we will see how Zhuangzi and Xunzi address these questions. As you read the selections, try to figure out the differences between them. Ask yourself how plausible their theories are.

《莊子》/ Zhuangzi

逍遥遊第一
Chapter 1　Wandering Boundless and Free

　　北冥有魚，其名爲鯤。鯤之大，不知其幾千里也。化而爲鳥，其名爲鵬。鵬之背，不知其幾千里也；怒而飛，其翼若垂天之雲。是鳥也，海運則將徙於南冥。南冥者，天池也。齊諧者，志怪者也。諧之言曰："鵬之徙於南冥也，水擊三千里，摶扶搖而上者九萬里，去以六月息者也。"……
　　蜩與學鳩笑之曰："我決起而飛，槍榆、枋，時則不至而控於地而已矣，奚以之九萬里而南爲？"適莽蒼者三飡而反，腹猶果然；適百里者宿舂糧；適千里者三月聚糧。之二蟲又何知！小知不及大知，小年不及大年。

　　In the Northern Darkness there is a fish and its name is Kun. The Kun is so huge I don't know how many thousand li it measures. It changes into a bird with the name of Peng. I don't know how many thousand li the back of the Peng measures. When this bird rises up and flies, its wings are like clouds all round the sky. It churns up the sea and sets out on its migration to the Southern Darkness, which is the Lake of Heaven. There is a book called Qi Xie, a record of marvels. We have in it these words, "When the Peng journeys to the Southern Darkness, the waters are roiled for three thousand li. It beats the whirlwind and rises ninety thousand li. It flies on and on for six months, and then it rests."...
　　The cicada and the little dove laugh at this story, saying, "When we make an effort and fly up, we can get as far as the elm or the sapanwood tree, but sometimes we don't make it and just fall down on the ground. Now how is it possible for anyone to go ninety thousand li to the south!" If you go off to the green woods nearby, you can take along food for three meals and come back with your stomach as full as ever. But if you're going a hundred li, you need to hull enough grain to stay the night. And if you're going a thousand li, you'll have to gather enough grain to last three months. So

what do those two little creatures know? Little knowledge cannot come up to great knowledge; the short-lived cannot come up to the long-lived.

奚以知其然也？朝菌不知晦朔，蟪蛄不知春秋，此小年也。楚之南有冥靈者，以五百歲爲春，五百歲爲秋；上古有大椿者，以八千歲爲春，八千歲爲秋。而彭祖乃今以久特聞，衆人匹之，不亦悲乎！……

How do I know this is so? The morning mushroom knows nothing of twilight and dawn; the summer cicada knows nothing of spring and autumn. They are the short-lived. South of Chu there is a caterpillar that counts five hundred years as one spring and five hundred years as one autumn. Long long ago there was a great rose of Sharon that counted eight thousand years as one spring and eight thousand years as one autumn. They are the long-lived. Yet Pengzu alone is famous today for having lived a long time, and everybody tries to ape him.[①] Isn't it sad! ...

故夫知效一官，行比一鄉，德合一君而徵一國者，其自視也亦若此矣。而宋榮子猶然笑之。且舉世而譽之而不加勸，舉世而非之而不加沮，定乎內外之分，辯乎榮辱之境，斯已矣。彼其於世，未數數然也。雖然，猶有未樹也。夫列子御風而行，泠然善也，旬有五日而後反。彼於致福者，未數數然也。此雖免乎行，猶有所待者也。若夫乘天地之正，而御六氣之辯，以遊無窮者，彼且惡乎待哉！故曰：至人無己，神人無功，聖人無名。……

Men who have wisdom fine enough to take high office, conduct noble enough to inspire the villages, virtue deep enough to govern, and who are therefore called to rule the country, see themselves the way those little birds see themselves. Master Bright-Beauty (Song-Rong-Zi) just laughed at them. For even if the whole world praised him, he'd be no more heartened; and even if the whole world denounced him, he'd be no more downcast. He was clear about the difference between inner and outer, and he recognized the

---

[①] Pengzu is the Chinese Methuselah.

boundaries of true glory and disgrace. But that was all. As far as the world went, he didn't fret and worry, but there was still ground he left unturned.

Liezi could ride the wind and go soaring around with cool and breezy skill, but after fifteen days he came back to earth. As far as the search for good fortune went, he didn't fret and worry. He escaped the trouble of walking, but he still had to depend on something to get around. If he had only mounted on the truth of Heaven and Earth, ridden the changes of the six breaths, and thus wandered through the boundless, then what would he have had to depend on? Therefore I say, the Perfect Man has no self; the Holy Man has no merit; the sage has no name. ...

齊物論第二
Chapter 2　　The Adjustment of Controversies

南郭子綦隱机而坐，仰天而噓，荅焉似喪其耦。顏成子游立侍乎前，曰："何居乎？形固可使如槁木，而心固可使如死灰乎？今之隱机者，非昔之隱机者也？"子綦曰："偃，不亦善乎，而問之也！今者吾喪我，汝知之乎？女聞人籟而未聞地籟，女聞地籟而未聞天籟夫！"

子游曰："敢問其方。"子綦曰："夫大塊噫氣，其名爲風。是唯无作，作則萬竅怒呺。而獨不聞之翏翏乎？山林之畏佳，大木百圍之竅穴，似鼻，似口，似耳，似枅，似圈，似臼，似洼者，似污者；激者、謞者、叱者、吸者、叫者、譹者、宎者、咬者，前者唱于而隨者唱喁。泠風則小和，飄風則大和，厲風濟則衆竅爲虛。而獨不見之調調，之刁刁乎？"子游曰："地籟則衆竅是已，人籟則比竹是已，敢問天籟。"子綦曰："夫吹萬不同，而使其自已也，咸其自取，怒者其誰邪！"

Leaning on his desk, Ziqi of South Wall sat gazing into the sky, breath shallow and face blank, as if he were lost to himself. Yancheng Ziyou stood before him, waiting. Finally he said, "How is it possible? How can you make your body withered wood and your heart dead ash? The person leaning on your desk today isn't the person who was leaning on it yesterday." "That's a fine question, Ziyou," replied Ziqi. "Just then I'd lost myself completely. Do you understand such things? Perhaps you've heard the music of humans, but you haven't heard the music of earth. Or if you've heard the music of earth, you haven't heard the music of Heaven."

Ziyou said, "I venture to ask from you a description of all these." The reply was, "When the breath of the Great Mass comes strongly, it is called Wind. Sometimes it does not come so; but when it does, then the ten thousand holes cry and moan. Haven't you heard them wailing on and on? On the projecting cliff of a mountain forest, there are huge trees a hundred feet around, and they're full of wailing hollows and holes—like noses, like mouths, like ears, like jugs, like cups, like mortars, like rifts, like ruts. They roar like waves, whistle like arrows, screech, gasp, cry, wail, moan, and howl, those in the lead calling out 'yeee!' those behind answering 'yuuu!' Gentle winds produce a small response, violent winds a great one. When the fierce gusts have passed away, all the holes are empty—have you not seen this in the bending and quivering of the branches and leaves?"

"So the music of earth means all those holes singing together," said Ziyou, "and the music of humans means bamboo pipes singing. Could I ask you to explain the music of Heaven for me?" Ziqi replied, "Sounding the ten thousand things differently, so each becomes itself according to itself alone—who could make such music?"

大知閑閑,小知閒閒;大言炎炎,小言詹詹。

Great knowledge is wide and comprehensive; small knowledge is partial and restricted. Great words are bright and open; small words are chit and chat.

其寐也魂交,其覺也形開,與接爲搆,日以心鬭。縵者,窖者,密者。小恐惴惴,大恐縵縵。其發若機栝,其司是非之謂也;其留如詛盟,其守勝之謂也;其殺若秋冬,以言其日消也;其溺之所爲之,不可使復之也;其厭也如緘,以言其老洫也;近死之心,莫使復陽也。喜怒哀樂,慮嘆變慹,姚佚啟態;樂出虛,蒸成菌。日夜相代乎前,而莫知其所萌。已乎,已乎！旦暮得此,其所由以生乎！

When we sleep, our spirits roam. When we wake, our bodies hustle. Day after day, all that we touch entangles us, and we are scheming against each other: some speak slowly; some speak deceptively; some speak cautiously. Small fear is mean and trembly; great fear is stunned and overwhelming. We bound off like an arrow or a crossbow pellet, certain that we are the arbiters of right and wrong. We cling to their position as though we had sworn before the gods, sure that we are holding on to victory. We fade away day by day, dying like autumn into winter. But we're drowning, and nothing we do can bring any of it back. We grow old and close-minded, like being tied up with cords. A mind near death cannot recover that autumn blaze. Joy and anger, sorrow and delight, hope and regret, doubt and ardor, diffidence and abandon, candor and reserve: they're all music rising out of emptiness, mushrooms appearing out of mist. Day and night come and go, but who knows where it all begins? Enough! Enough! Morning and evening we obtain these, and this is how we live!

非彼无我，非我无所取。是亦近矣，而不知其所爲使。若有真宰，而特不得其眹。可行己信，而不見其形，有情而無形。百骸，九竅，六藏，賅而存焉，吾誰與爲親？汝皆説之乎？其有私焉，如是皆有爲臣妾乎？其臣妾不足以相治乎？其遞相爲君臣乎？其有真君存焉，如求得其情與不得，無益損乎其真。

No other and no self, no self and no distinctions—that's almost it. But I don't know what makes it this way. Something true seems to govern, but I can't find the least trace of it. It acts—nothing could be more apparent, but we never see its form. It has a nature, but no form.

Given the body, with its hundred parts, its nine openings, and its six internal organs, all complete in their places, which do I love the most? Do you love them all equally? Each of them is selfish and partial. So are they all mere servants? But if they all are servants, then how can they keep order among themselves? Or do they take turns being lord and servant? There seems to be something true that rules. If we go looking for its nature, there's nothing to find. But that doesn't make its truth any more perfect, or any more ruined.

一受其成形,不忘以待盡。與物相刃相靡,其行盡如馳,而莫之能止,不亦悲乎！終身役役而不見其成功,苶然疲役而不知其所歸,可不哀邪！人謂之不死,奚益！其形化,其心與之然,可不謂大哀乎？人之生也,固若是芒乎？其我獨芒,而人亦有不芒者乎？

Once we happen into the form of this body, we cannot forget it. And so it is that we wait out the end. Grappling and tangling with things, we rush headlong toward the end, and there's no stopping it. It's sad, isn't it? We slave our lives away and never get anywhere, work ourselves ragged and never find our way home. It's woeful, isn't it? Men may say, "But it is not death." But what good is that? When the body decays, the mind follows it. It is very deplorable, isn't it? Life is total confusion. Or is it that I'm the only one who's confused?

夫隨其成心而師之,誰獨且无師乎？奚必知代而心自取者有之？愚者與有焉。未成乎心而有是非,是今日適越而昔至也。是以无有爲有。无有爲有,雖有神禹,且不能知,吾獨且奈何哉！

If a man follows the mind given to him and makes it his teacher, then who can be without a teacher? You don't need to understand the realm of change; when mind turns to itself, you've found your teacher. Even an idiot has his teacher. Not to realize yourself in mind, and to insist on "yes this" and "no that", this is like saying that you set off for Yue today and got there yesterday. This is to claim that what doesn't exist exists. If you claim that what doesn't exist exists, then even the holy sage Yu couldn't understand you, much less a person like me!

夫言非吹也,言者有言。其所言者特未定也。果有言邪？其未嘗有言邪？其以爲異於鷇音,亦有辯乎？其無辯乎？道惡乎隱而有真僞？言惡乎隱而有是非？

道惡乎往而不存？言惡乎存而不可？道隱於小成，言隱於榮華。故有儒墨之是非，以是其所非而非其所是。欲是其所非而非其所是，則莫若以明。

Words are not just wind. Speakers have something to say. But if what they have to say is not constant, then do they really say something? Or do they say nothing? People think we are different from baby birds cheeping, but are we saying any more than they are?

How could the Dao be so hidden that there is a distinction between truth and falsity? How could words be so hidden that there is a debate on what is right and what is wrong? How could the Dao leave and exist no more? How could words exist and be inappropriate? These days, the Dao is hidden in small realizations and words hidden in florid extravagance, so we have the philosophies of Confucius and Mozi declaring "yes this" and "no that". They each affirm what the other denies, deny what the other affirms. If you want to affirm all that they deny and deny all that they affirm, you can't beat illumination.

物無非彼，物無非是。自彼則不見，自知則知之。故曰彼出於是，是亦因彼。彼是方生之說也，雖然，方生方死，方死方生；方可方不可，方不可方可；因是因非，因非因是。是以聖人不由，而照之於天，亦因是也。是亦彼也，彼亦是也。彼亦一是非，此亦一是非。果且有彼是乎哉？果且無彼是乎哉？彼是莫得其偶，謂之道樞。樞始得其環中，以應无窮。是亦一無窮，非亦一無窮也。故曰莫若以明。

Everything has its "that", and everything has its "this". From the point of view of "that", you cannot see it; but through understanding, you can know it. So I say, "that" comes out of "this", and "this" depends on "that"—which is to say that "this" and "that" give birth to each other. But where there is birth, there must be death; where there is death, there must be birth. Where there is acceptability, there must be unacceptability; where there is unacceptability, there must be acceptability. Where there is recognition of right, there must be recognition of wrong; where there is recognition of wrong, there must be recognition of right. Therefore the sage does not proceed in such a way but illuminates all in the light of Heaven. He, too, recognizes a "this" that is also "that", a "that" that is also "this." His "that" has both a right and a wrong in it; his "this", too, has both a right and a wrong in it. So, in fact, does he still have a "this" and "that"? Or does he, in fact, no longer have a "this" or "that"? A state in which "this" and "that" no longer find their opposites is called the hinge of the Way. Keep that hinge at the center of things, and your movements are inexhaustible. Then "yes this" is whole and inexhaustible, and "no that" is whole and inexhaustible. And so the saying: You can't beat illumination.

以指喻指之非指,不若以非指喻指之非指也;以馬喻馬之非馬,不若以非馬喻馬之非馬也。天地一指也,萬物一馬也。

Instead of using a finger to demonstrate how a finger is no-finger, use no-finger to demonstrate how a finger is no-finger. Instead of using a horse to demonstrate how a horse is no-horse, use no-horse to show how a horse is no-horse. All Heaven and Earth is one finger, and the ten thousand things are all one horse.[①]

可乎可,不可乎不可。道行之而成,物謂之而然。惡乎然? 然於然。惡乎不然? 不然於不然。物固有所然,物固有所可。無物不然,無物不可。故爲是舉莛與楹,厲與西施,恢憰譎怪,道通爲一。其分也,成也;其成也,毀也。凡物無成與毀,復通爲一。唯達者知通爲一,爲是不用而寓諸庸。庸也者,用也;用也者,通也;通也者,得也;適得而幾矣。因是已,已而不知其然,謂之道。

What is acceptable we call acceptable; what is unacceptable we call unacceptable. A road is made by people walking on it; things are so because they are called so. What makes them so? Making them so makes them so. What makes them not so? Making them not so makes them not so. Things all

---

① This passage by itself is obscure. But scholars widely agree that it refers to the statements of the logician Gongsun Longzi.

must have that which makes them so; things all must have that which makes them acceptable. There is nothing that is not so, nothing that is not acceptable.

For this reason, whether you point to a little stalk or a great pillar, a leper or the beautiful Xishi, things ribald and shady, or things grotesque and strange, they are one and the same in light of the Dao. When things are differentiated, each comes into existence; if a thing comes into existence, it will be destroyed. But in light of the Dao, there is no distinction between coming into existence and being destroyed. All things are one and the same. Only one who has seen through things understands they are one and the same. So he has no use [for distinctions] but relegates all to the constant. The constant is the useful; the useful is the passable; the passable is the successful; and with success, all is accomplished. He relies on this alone, relies on it and does not know how. This is called the Dao.

勞神明爲一而不知其同也，謂之朝三。何謂朝三？狙公賦芧，曰："朝三而暮四"，衆狙皆怒。曰："然則朝四而暮三"，衆狙皆悅。名實未虧而喜怒爲用，亦因是也。是以聖人和之以是非而休乎天鈞，是之謂兩行。

But to wear out your brain trying to make things into one without realizing that they are all the same—this is called "three in the morning". What do I mean by "three in the morning"? When the monkey trainer was handing out acorns, he said, "You get three in the morning and four at night." This made all the monkeys furious. "Well, then," he said, "you get four in the morning and three at night." The monkeys all were delighted. There was no change in the reality behind the words, and yet the monkeys responded with joy and anger. Let them, if they want to. This is why the sage brings "yes this" and "no that" together and rests in Heaven the Equalizer. This is called taking two paths at once.

古之人，其知有所至矣。惡乎至？有以爲未始有物者，至矣，盡矣，不可以加矣。其次以爲有物矣，而未始有封也。其次以爲有封焉，而未始有是非也。是非之彰也，道之所以虧也。道之所以虧，愛之所以成。果且有成與虧乎哉？果且无成與虧乎？有成與虧，故昭氏之鼓琴也；無成與虧，故昭氏之不鼓琴也。昭文之鼓琴也，師曠之枝策也，惠子之據梧也，三子之知幾乎，皆其盛者也，故載之末年。惟其好之也，以異於彼，其好之也，欲以明之。彼非所明而明之，故以堅白之昧終。而其子又以文之綸終，終身无成。若是而可謂成乎？雖我亦成也。若是而不可謂成乎？物與我無成也。是故滑疑之耀，聖人之所圖也。爲是不用而寓諸庸，此之謂以明。

Among the men of old their knowledge reached the extreme point. What was that extreme point? Some held that in the beginning there was not anything. This is the extreme point, the utmost point to which nothing can be added. Those at the next stage thought that things exist but recognized no boundaries among them. Those at the next stage thought there were boundaries but recognized no right and wrong. Because right and wrong appeared, the Dao waned, and when the Dao waned, personal preference waxed.

But do waning and waxing really exist, or do they not? There is such a thing as waning and waxing—Mr. Zhao playing the Qin is an example. There is such a thing as no waning and waxing—Mr. Zhao not playing the Qin is an example. Zhao Wen played the Qin; Master Kuang waved his baton; Huizi debated with others under the phoenix tree. The knowledge of these three was close to perfection. All were masters, and therefore their names have been handed down to later ages. Only in their likes were they different from the true sage. What they liked, they tried to make clear. What they were not clear about, they tried to make clear, and so they ended up in the darkness of arcane distinctions and foolish quibbling. Zhao Wen had a son who carried on his practice, but his son failed to reached any completion.

Can these men be said to have attained completion? If so, then so have all the rest of us. Or can they not be said to have attained completion? If so, then neither we nor anything else has ever attained it. The torch of chaos and doubt—this is what the sage steers by. So he does not use things but relegates all to the constant. This is called illumination.①

今且有言於此，不知其與是類乎？其與是不類乎？類與不類，相與爲類，則與彼無以異矣。雖然，請嘗言之。有始也者，有未始有始也者，有未始有夫未始有始也者。有有也者，有無也者，有未始有無也者，有未始有夫未始有無也者。俄而有無矣，而未知有無之果孰有孰无也。今我則已有謂矣，而未知吾所謂之其果有謂乎，其果無謂乎？

Now I am going to make a statement here. I don't know whether or not it fits into the category of other people's statements. But whether it fits into their category or whether it doesn't, it obviously fits into some category. So in that respect, it is no different from their statements. However, let me try making my statement. There was a beginning. There was a not-yet-beginning before that beginning. There was a not-yet-beginning previous to that not-yet-beginning before there was the beginning. There was existence; there had been non-existence. There was a beginning before the beginning of that non-existence. There was beginning previous to the beginning before the beginning of that non-existence. If suddenly there was nonexistence, we do not know whether it was really anything existing, or really not existing. Now I have said what I have said, but I do not know whether what I have said be really anything to the point or not.

天下莫大於秋豪之末，而大山爲小；莫壽於殤子，而彭祖爲夭。天地與我並存，而萬物與我爲一。既已爲一矣，且得有言乎？既已謂之一矣，且得無言乎？一與言爲二，二與一爲三。自此以往，巧曆不能得，而況其凡乎！故自无適有以至於三，而況自有適有乎！无適焉，因是已！

Under Heaven there is nothing greater than the tip of a hair of a bird in the autumn, and the Tai Mountain is small. There is no one more long-lived than a child who dies prematurely, and Pengzu did not live out his time.

---

① This passage is notoriously obscure.

Heaven and Earth were born at the same time I was, and the ten thousand things are one with me. Since they are one, can there be speech about them? But since they are spoken of as one, must there not be room for speech? One and Speech are two; two and one are three. Going on from this [in our enumeration], the most skillful reckoner cannot reach [the end of the necessary numbers], and how much less can ordinary people do so! If by moving from nonbeing to being, we get to three, how far will we get if we move from being to being? Better not to move but to let things be!

夫道未始有封，言未始有常，爲是而有畛也，請言其畛：有左，有右，有倫，有義，有分，有辯，有競，有爭，此之謂八德。六合之外，聖人存而不論；六合之內，聖人論而不議。春秋經世先王之志，聖人議而不辯。故分也者，有不分也；辯也者，有不辯也。曰：何也？聖人懷之，眾人辯之以相示也。故曰辯也者有不見也。

The Way has never known boundaries; speech has no constancy. But because of [the recognition of a] "this", there came to be demarcation. Let me tell you about demarcation. There's left and there's right. There's relationship and there's Duty. There's difference and there's division. There's strife and there's struggle. Call them anything—how about the eight virtues? Outside the limits of the world of men, the sage admits it exists but does not talk about it; inside those limits he talks about it but does not judge. In *The Spring and Autumn Annals*, which records the history of the former kings, the sage indicates his judgments, but does not argue [in vindication of them]. Thus it is that he differentiates things without appearing to do so, and argues without the form of argument. How does he do so? The sage grasps the Dao silently, while men generally debate about the Dao, trying to show others they have grasped it. Hence we have the saying, "Those who argue fail to see."

夫大道不稱，大辯不言，大仁不仁，大廉不嗛，大勇不忮。道昭而不道，言辯而不及，仁常而不成，廉清而不信，勇忮而不成。五者园而幾向方矣，故知止其所不知，至矣。孰知不言之辯，不道之道？若有能知，此之謂天府。注焉而不滿，酌焉而不竭，而不知其所由來，此之謂葆光。故昔者堯問於舜曰："我欲伐宗、膾、胥敖，南面而不釋然。其故何也？"舜曰："夫三子者，猶存乎蓬艾之閒。若不釋然，何哉？昔者十日並出，萬物皆照，而況德之進乎日者乎！"

The Great Way is not named; Great Discriminations are not spoken; Great Benevolence is not benevolent; Great Honesty is not humble; Great Courage does not attack. The Dao that is displayed is not the Dao. Words that are argumentative do not reach the point. The benevolence that has a constant object cannot be universal. The honesty that is fastidious cannot be trusted. The courage that attacks cannot be effectual. These five all are round, but they tend toward the square.

Therefore the knowledge that stops at what it does not know is the greatest. Who knows the argument that needs no words, and the Way that is not to be trodden? If he can know this, he may be called the Reservoir of Heaven. Pour into it, and it never fills up. Pour from it, and it never empties out, and yet it does not know where the supply comes from. This is called the Inward Radiance.

So it is that long ago Yao said to Shun, "I want to attack the rulers of Zong, Kuai, and Xu'ao. Even as I sit on my throne, this thought nags at me. Why is this?" Shun replied, "These three rulers are only little dwellers in the weeds and brush. Why this nagging desire? Long ago, ten suns came out all at once, and the ten thousand things were all lighted up. And how much greater is virtue than these suns!"

齧缺問乎王倪曰："子知物之所同是乎？"曰："吾惡乎知之！""子知子之所不知邪？"曰："吾惡乎知之！""然則物无知邪？"曰："吾惡乎知之！雖然，嘗試言之。庸詎知吾所謂知之非不知邪？庸詎知吾所謂不知之非知邪？且吾嘗試問乎女：民溼寢則腰疾偏死，鰌然乎哉？木處則惴慄恂懼，猨猴然乎哉？三者孰知正處？民食芻豢，麋鹿食薦，蝍且甘帶，鴟鴉耆鼠，四者孰知正味？猨猵狙以爲雌，麋與鹿交，鰌與魚游。毛嬙麗姬，人之所美也；魚見之深入，鳥見之高飛，麋鹿見之決驟，四者孰知天下之正色哉？自我觀之，仁義之端，是非之塗，樊然殽亂，吾惡能知其辯！"齧缺曰："子不知利害，則至人固不知利害乎？"王倪曰："至人神矣！大澤焚而不能熱,河漢冱而不能寒,疾雷破山飄風振海而不能驚。若然者,乘雲氣,騎日月,而遊乎四海之外,死生无變於己,而況利害之端乎!"

Gap-Tooth asked Horizon-Imperial, "Do you know how it is that all things are one and the same?" "How would I know that?" replied Horizon-Imperial. "Do you know that you do not know?" "How would I know that?" "So then, no creatures know anything?" "And how would I know that?" replied Horizon-Imperial. "But still, there may be something I can tell you. How do I know that what I call knowledge is knowledge? And how do I know that what I call ignorance is not knowledge?"

"Now maybe there's something I can ask you," he continued. "If a man sleeps in a damp place, he will have a pain in his back, and half of his body will be as if it were dead; but will it be so with an eel? If he lives in a tree, he will be frightened and all in a tremble; but will it be so with a monkey? So of these three, which knows the truth about dwelling? Humans eat meat. Deer eat grass. Centipedes relish snakes. Owls crave mice. So of these four, which knows the truth about flavors? Gibbons mate with gibbons. Deer mingle with deer. Fish play around with fish. Men consider Maoqiang and Lady Li the most beautiful of women. But if fish saw them, they would dive to the bottom of the stream; if birds saw them, they would fly away; and if deer saw them, they would break into a run. So of these four, which knows the truth about beauty for all beneath Heaven? The way I see it, the rules of benevolence and righteousness and the paths of right and wrong all are hopelessly snarled and jumbled. How could I know anything about such discriminations?

"If you don't know what is profitable or harmful," asked Gap-Tooth, "then does the Perfect Man likewise know nothing of such things?" "The Perfect Man is godlike," replied Horizon-Imperial. "Ponds and lakes could burn, but he'd feel no heat. Streams and rivers could freeze, but he'd feel no cold. Fierce lightning could shatter mountains and gale storms churn up the sea, but he'd feel no fright. Mounting cloud and sky to ride the sun and the moon, the Perfect Man wanders beyond the four seas. Even life and death have no effect on him, much less the rules of profit and loss!"

瞿鵲子問乎長梧子曰:"吾聞諸夫子,聖人不從事於務,不就利,不違害,不喜求,不緣道;無謂有謂,有謂無謂,而遊乎塵垢之外。夫子以爲孟浪之言,而我以爲妙道之行也。吾子以爲奚若?"

長梧子曰:"是黃帝之所聽熒也,而丘也何足以知之!且女亦大早計,見卵而求時夜,見彈而求鴞炙。予嘗爲女妄言之,女以妄聽之。奚旁日月,挾宇宙?爲其脗合,置其滑涽,以隸相尊。衆人役役,聖人愚芚,參萬歲而一成純。萬物盡然,而以是相蘊。

"予惡乎知説生之非惑邪!予惡乎知惡死之非弱喪而不知歸者邪!麗之姬,艾封人之子也。晉國之始得之也,涕泣沾襟;及其至於王所,與王同筐牀,食芻豢,而後悔其泣也。予惡乎知夫死者不悔其始之蘄生乎?

"夢飲酒者,旦而哭泣;夢哭泣者,旦而田獵。方其夢也,不知其夢也。夢之中又占其夢焉,覺而後知其夢也。且有大覺而後知此其大夢也,而愚者自以爲覺,竊竊然知之。君乎,牧乎,固哉丘也!與女皆夢也。予謂女夢,亦夢也。是其言也,其名爲弔詭。萬世之後而一遇大聖,知其解者,是旦暮遇之也。

"既使我與若辯矣,若勝我,我不若勝,若果是也,我果非也邪?我勝若,若不吾勝,我果是也,而果非也邪?其或是也,其或非也邪?其俱是也,其俱非也邪?我與若不能相知也。則人固受其黮闇,吾誰使正之?使同乎若者正之?既與若同矣,惡能正之!使同乎我者正之?既同乎我矣,惡能正之!使異乎我與若者正之?既異乎我與若矣,惡能正之!使同乎我與若者正之?既同乎我與若矣,惡能正之!然則我與若與人俱不能相知也,而待彼也邪?

"化聲之相待、若其不相待。和之以天倪,因之以曼衍,所以窮年也。何謂和之以天倪?曰:是不是,然不然。是若果是也,則是之異乎不是也亦無辯;然若果然也,則然之異乎不然也亦無辯。忘年忘義,振於无竟,故寓諸无竟。"

Master Timid-Magpie inquired of Master Noble-Tree, "I have heard from Confucius of the following talk: a sage pays no attention to the concerns of this world, doesn't chase after profit and doesn't avoid harm, doesn't search for happiness and doesn't follow Way, says something when saying nothing, says nothing when saying something, wanders in realms beyond the tawdry dust of this world. Confucius considers such talk as nonsense, but I believe it describes the working of the mysterious Way. What do you think of it, master?"

"Even the Yellow Emperor would be perplexed at hearing such things," began Master Noble-Tree, "so how could Confucius understand? As for you, you're always jumping ahead to grand conclusions. Seeing an egg, you look for a rooster crowing. Seeing a crossbow, you look for an dove roasting over the fire. Listen, I'll try out a few careless and doubtful words, and you listen carelessly and doubtfully. Okay?

"How could anyone stand by the side of the sun and moon, and hold under his arm all space and all time? [Such language only means that] the sage keeps his mouth shut, leaves the confusion and muddle as it is, and looks on slaves no different from the exalted. Ordinary people strain and struggle. But the sage, being stupid and thoughtless, bundles ten thousand years into a single purity, letting the ten thousand things be what they are, gathering themselves together in that pure whole.

"How do I know that the love of life is not a delusion and that the dislike of death is not like a young person's losing his way, and not knowing that he is really going home? Li Ji was a daughter of the border Warden of Ai. When the ruler of the state of Jin first got possession of her, she wept till the tears wetted all the front of her dress. But then she came to the palace of the king, sharing his fine bed and savoring imperial food. And pretty soon she regretted that she had wept. How do I know that the dead do not repent of their former craving for life?

"Those who dream of (the pleasures of) drinking may in the morning wail and weep; those who dream of wailing and weeping may in the morning be going out to hunt. Moreover, when they were dreaming they did not know it was a dream; in their dream they may even have tried to interpret it; but when they awoke they knew that it was a dream. And there is the great awaking, after which we shall know that this life is a great dream. Meanwhile, fools everywhere think they're wide awake. They steal around as if they understood things, calling this a king and that a cowherd. Bigoted was that Qiu! He and you are both dreaming. When I say that you are dreaming, I am dreaming myself. These words seem paradoxical. But ten thousand generations from now, we'll meet a great sage who understands these things. We will meet him as if the morning meets the evening.①

"Suppose you and I have an argument. Suppose you win and I lose. Does that mean you're really right and I'm wrong? Suppose I win and you lose. Does that mean I'm really right and you're wrong? Is one of us right and the other wrong? Are we both right and both wrong? If we can't figure it out ourselves, others must be totally in the dark, so who could we get to settle it? We could get someone who agrees with you, but if they agree with you how could they decide who's right and wrong? We could get someone who agrees with me, but if they agree with me how could they decide? We could get someone who disagrees with either of us, but if they disagree with either of us how could they decide? We could get someone who agrees with both of us, but if they agree with both of us how could they decide? Not I nor you nor anyone else can know who is right and who wrong. So what do we do? Shall we wait for still another person?

"But waiting for one shifting voice [to pass judgment on] another is the same as waiting for none of them. Harmonize them all with the Heavenly Equality, leave them to their endless changes, and so live out your years. What do I mean by harmonizing them with the Heavenly Equality? Right is not right; so is not so. If right were really right, it would differ so clearly from not right that there would be no need for argument. If so were really so, it would differ so clearly from not so that there would be no need for argument. Forget the years; forget morality. Leap into the boundless and make it your home!"②

罔兩問景曰："曩子行,今子止；曩子坐,今子起。何其无特操與?"景曰："吾有待而然者邪? 吾所待又有待而然者邪? 吾待蛇蚹蜩翼邪? 惡識所以然！惡識所以不然！"

---

① Scholars widely disagree on what "旦暮遇之" means.
② There are different versions of this passage.

The Penumbra asked the Shadow, saying, "Formerly you were walking on, and now you have stopped; formerly you were sitting, and now you have risen up. How is it that you are so without stability?" The Shadow replied, "I wait for the movements of something else to do what I do, and whatever I wait for waits for something else again to make it do as it does. What am I waiting for, snake skins and cicada wings? How do I know why it is so? How do I know why it isn't so?"

昔者莊周夢爲胡蝶，栩栩然胡蝶也。自喻適志與！不知周也。俄然覺，則蘧蘧然周也。不知周之夢爲胡蝶與，胡蝶之夢爲周與？周與胡蝶，則必有分矣。此之謂物化。

Long ago, a certain Zhuang Zhou dreamt he was a butterfly—a butterfly fluttering here and there on a whim, happy and carefree, knowing nothing of Zhuang Zhou. Then all of a sudden he woke to find that he was, to his joyful surprise, Zhuang Zhou. Who knows if it was Zhuang Zhou dreaming of a butterfly, or a butterfly dreaming of Zhuang Zhou? This is not to deny that there's a difference between Zhuang Zhou and butterfly. Instead, it is called Indifferent-to-the-Differences-between-Things (Wuhua).

大宗師第六

Chapter 6 The Great and Most Honored Master

知天之所爲，知人之所爲者，至矣。知天之所爲者，天而生也；知人之所爲者，以其知之所知以養其知之所不知，終其天年而不中道夭者，是知之盛也。雖然，有患。夫知有所待而後當，其所待者特未定也。庸詎知吾所謂天之非人乎？所謂人之非天乎？且有真人而後有真知。何謂真人？古之真人，不逆寡，不雄成，不謨士。若然者，過而弗悔，當而不自得也。若然者，登高不慄，入水不濡，入火不熱。是知之能登假於道者也若此。

He who knows what it is that Heaven does, and knows what it is that man does, has reached the peak. Knowing what it is that Heaven does, he lives with Heaven. Knowing what it is that man does, he uses the knowledge of what he knows to help out the knowledge of what he doesn't know and lives out the years that Heaven gave him without being cut off midway—this is the perfection of knowledge.

Even so, problems remain. Knowledge depends on something else for its accuracy. And what it depends on never stays fixed and constant. So how can we know that what we call Heaven is not human and what we call human is not Heaven? There must first be a True Man before there can be true knowledge.

What do I mean by a True Man? The True Man of ancient times did not avoid want, did not grow proud in plenty, and did not plan his affairs. A man like this could commit an error and not regret it, could meet with success and not make a show. A man like this could climb the high places and not be frightened, could enter the water and not get wet, could enter the fire and not get burned. By his knowledge he was able to climb all the way up to the Dao.

古之真人，其寢不夢，其覺无憂，其食不甘，其息深深。真人之息以踵，衆人之息以喉。屈服者，其嗌言若哇；其耆欲深者，其天機淺。古之真人，不知説生，不知惡死；其出不訢，其入不距；翛然而往，翛然而來而已矣。不忘其所始，不求其所終；受而喜之，忘而復之，是之謂不以心捐道，不以人助天。是之謂真人。若然者，其心志，其容寂，其顙頯；淒然似秋，煖然似春，喜怒通四時，與物有宜而莫知其極。

……

The True men of old did not dream when they slept, had no anxiety when they awoke, and did not care that their food should be pleasant. Their breathing came deep and silently. The breathing of the true man comes from his heels, while men generally breathe from their throats. When men are defeated in argument, their words come from their gullets as if they were vomiting. When men's desires run deep, the impulse of Heaven runs shallow in them.

The True men of old never loved life and never hated death. Entrance into life occasioned them no joy; the exit from it awakened no resistance. Composedly they went and came. They did not forget what their beginning had been, and they did not inquire into what their end would be. They accepted whatever happened to them and rejoiced in it; they forgot life and death and returned to the original state. This is what I call not using the mind to repel the Dao, not using the human to help out Heaven. Whoever lives this way is called a True Man. Being such, their minds were free from all thought; their faces are calm; their foreheads beamed simplicity. They are chilly like autumn, balmy like spring, and their joys and angers are as natural as the change of seasons. They are in accord with all things, and no one knows their limits.

...

南伯子葵問乎女偊曰："子之年長矣，而色若孺子，何也？"曰："吾聞道矣。"南伯子葵曰："道可得學邪？"曰："惡！惡可！子非其人也。夫卜梁倚有聖人之才而无聖人之道，我有聖人之道而无聖人之才，吾欲以教之，庶幾其果爲聖人乎！不然，以聖人之道告聖人才，亦易矣。吾猶守而告之，參日而後能外天下；已外天下矣，吾又守之，七日而後能外物；已外物矣，吾又守之，九日，而後能外生；已外生矣，而後能朝徹；朝徹，而後能見獨；見獨，而後能无古今；无古今，而後能入於不死不生。殺生者不死，生生者不生。其爲物，無不將也，無不迎也；無不毀也，無不成也。其名爲攖寧。攖寧也者，攖而後成者也。"……

Adept Sunflower (Nan-bo Zi-kui) asked Dame Crookback (Nu Yu), saying, "You are old, Sir, while your complexion is like that of a child; how is it so?" The reply was, "I have become acquainted with the Dao." The other said, "Can I learn the Dao?" Dame Crookback said, "No. How can you? You, Sir, are not the man to do so. Oracle Bridgeworks (Bu-liang Yi) had the talent of a sagely man, but not the Dao, while I had the Dao, but not the talent. So I decided to teach him, thinking he could become a real sage. If nothing else, it should be easy to explain the Dao of a sage to someone with the talent of a sage. Still, I had to instruct and guide him carefully.

After three days he was able to banish from his mind the worldly power. But even though he was able to banish from his mind the worldly power, I still had to guide him carefully. After seven days he was able to banish from his mind the material things. But even though he was able to banish from his mind the material things, I still had to guide him carefully. After nine days he was able to banish from his mind the love of life. And once he was able to banish from his mind the love of life, his insight had the clarity of dawn light. Once his insight had the clarity of dawn light, he could see the singular. Once he saw the singular, he could extinguish past and present. And once he'd extinguished past and present, he could enter a place deathless and lifeless. That which kills life does not die; that which gives life to life does not live. This is the kind of thing it is: there's nothing it doesn't send off, nothing it doesn't welcome, nothing it doesn't destroy, nothing it doesn't complete. Its name is Peace-in-Strife. After the strife, it attains completion." ...

意而子見許由，許由曰："堯何以資汝？"意而子曰："堯謂我：'汝必躬服仁義而明言是非。'"許由曰："而奚來為軹？夫堯既已黥汝以仁義，而劓汝以是非矣，汝將何以遊夫遙蕩恣睢轉徙之塗乎？"意而子曰："雖然，吾願遊於其藩。"許由曰："不然。夫盲者无以與乎眉目顏色之好，瞽者无以與乎青黃黼黻之觀。"意而子曰："夫无莊之失其美，據梁之失其力，黃帝之亡其知，皆在鑪捶之間耳。庸詎知夫造物者之不息我黥而補我劓，使我乘成以隨先生邪？"許由曰："噫！未可知也。我為汝言其大略，吾師乎！吾師乎！整萬物而不為義，澤及萬世而不為仁，長於上古而不為老，覆載天地刻彫衆形而不為巧。此所遊已。"

When Master Deliberation (Yierzi) came to see him, Pledged-Origin (Xu-You) asked, "What has Emperor Yao taught you?" "He has told me: You must learn to practice benevolence and righteousness and to speak clearly about right and wrong!" "Then why have you come here like this?" asked Pledged-Origin. "Yao has already tattooed you with benevolence and righteousness, and he's lopped off your nose with right and wrong. So how can you go wandering in any faraway, carefree, and as-you-like-it paths?"

"What you say may be true. But still, I might at least wander the borders of that realm." "Impossible," replied Pledged-Origin. "The blind never know the charms of a beautiful face. And the sightless never see silk lit with the embroidered colors of spring and autumn." "Never-Adorn losing her beauty, Buttress-Beam losing his strength, Yellow Emperor forgetting his knowledge—all these are possible if they are recast and remolded," countered Master Deliberation. "So how do you know that the Creator will not wipe away my tattoo, stick my nose back on again, and let me ride on the process of completion and follow after you, Master?" "Ah yes, it's true, there's no way of knowing," replied Pledged-Origin. "So I'll give you an outline: O my master! O my master! He makes the ten thousand things harmonize, but he doesn't think himself righteous; his bounty extends to ten thousand generations, but he doesn't think himself benevolent. He is older than the highest antiquity, but he doesn't think himself long-lived; he covers Heaven, bears up the earth, carves and fashions countless forms, but he doesn't think himself skilled. It is with him alone I wander."

顏回曰:"回益矣。"仲尼曰:"何謂也?"曰:"回忘仁義矣。"曰:"可矣,猶未也。"他日,復見,曰:"回益矣。"曰:"何謂也?"曰:"回忘禮樂矣。"曰:"可矣,猶未也。"他日,復見,曰:"回益矣。"曰:"何謂也?"曰:"回坐忘矣。"仲尼蹴然曰:"何謂坐忘?"顏回曰:"墮肢體,黜聰明,離形去知,同於大通,此謂坐忘。"仲尼曰:"同則无好也,化則无常也。而果其賢乎! 丘也請從而後也。"

Yan Hui said, "I am making progress." Confucius replied, "What do you mean?" "I have ceased to think of benevolence and righteousness," was the reply. "Very well; but that is not enough." Another day, Hui again saw Confucius, and said, "I am making progress." "What do you mean?" "I have lost all thought of ceremonies and music." "Very well, but that is not enough." A third day, Hui again saw the Master, and said, "I am making progress." "What do you mean?" "I sit quietly and forget everything." Confucius changed countenance, and said, "What do you mean by that?" Yan Hui replied, "I let the body fall away and the intellect fade. I cast off form, do away with knowledge, and make myself identical with the Great Thoroughfare. This is what I mean by sitting quietly and forgetting everything." Confucius said, "If you're identical with it, you are free of likes and dislikes! If you've been transformed, you do not stick to any principles! So you really are a worthy man after all! With your permission, I'd like to become your follower."

《荀子》/ Xunzi

勸學篇第一
Chapter 1   An Exhortation to Learning

君子曰:學不可以已。青,取之於藍,而青於藍;冰,水爲之而寒於水。木直中繩,輮以爲輪,其曲中規,雖有槁暴,不復挺者,輮使之然也。故木受繩則直,金就礪則利,君子博學而日參省乎己,則智明而行無過矣。

The gentleman says: Learning must never stop. Blue dye derives from the indigo plant, and yet it is bluer than the plant. Ice comes from water, and yet it is colder than water. A piece of wood as straight as a plumb line may be bent into a circle as true as any drawn with a compass and, even after the wood has dried, it will not straighten out again. The bending process has made it that way. Likewise, when wood comes under the plumb line, it becomes straight, and when metal is brought to the whetstone, it becomes sharp. The gentleman learns broadly and examines himself thrice daily, and then his mind is clear and his conduct is without fault.

故不登高山,不知天之高也;不臨深谿,不知地之厚也;不聞先王之遺言,不知學問之大也。干、越、夷、貉之子,生而同聲,長而異俗,教使之然也。

And so if you never climb a high mountain, you will not know the height of Heaven. If you never visit a deep ravine, you will not know the depth of the Earth. If you never hear the words passed down from the former kings, you will not know the magnificence of learning. The children of the Han, Yue, Yi, and Mo peoples all cry with the same sound at birth, but when grown they have different customs, because education makes them different.

吾嘗終日而思矣,不如須臾之所學也;吾嘗跂而望矣,不如登高之博見也。登高而招,臂非加長也,而見者遠;順風而呼,聲非加疾也,而聞者彰。假輿馬者,非利足也,而致千里。假舟楫者,非能水也,而絕江河。君子生非異也,善假於物也。

I once spent the whole day pondering, but it was not as good as a moment's worth of learning. I once stood on my toes to look far away, but it was not as good as the broad view from a high place. If you climb to a high place and wave, you have not lengthened your arms, but you can be seen from further away. If you shout from upwind, you have not made your voice stronger, but you can be heard more clearly. One who makes use of a chariot and horses has not thereby improved his feet, but he can now go a thousand miles (li). One who makes use of a boat and oars has not thereby become able to swim, but he can now cross rivers and streams. The gentleman is exceptional not by birth, but rather by being good at making use of things.

南方有鳥焉,名曰蒙鳩,以羽爲巢,而編之以髮,繫之葦苕。風至苕折,卵破子死。巢非不完也,所繫者然也。西方有木焉,名曰射干,莖長四寸,生於高山之上而臨百仞之淵。木莖非能長也,所立者然也。蓬生麻中,不扶而直;白沙在涅,與之俱黑。蘭槐之根是爲芷,其漸之滫,君子不近,庶人不服。其質非不美也,所漸者然也。故君子居必擇鄉,遊必就士,所以防邪僻而近中正也。

In the south there is a bird called the *mengjiu*. It makes its nest from feathers, weaving it together with hair, and attaches it to the slender branch of a reed. When the wind comes along, the branch snaps, the eggs break, and its young perish. This happens not because the nest itself is flawed, but rather because of what it is attached to. In the west there is a plant called the *ye gan*. Its trunk is no more than four inches tall and it grows on top of the high mountains, from whence it looks down into valleys a hundred fathoms deep. It is not a long trunk which affords the tree such a view, but simply the place where it stands. Likewise, when the peng vine grows among hemp plants, it will stand up straight without propping. If white sand is mixed with mud, it too will turn black. The root of the lan huai plant is sweet-smelling angelica, but if you soak it in foul water then the gentleman will not draw near it, and the common people will not wear it. This happens not because the original material is not fragrant, but rather because of what it is soaked in. Therefore, the gentleman is sure to select carefully the village where he dwells, and he is sure to associate with well-bred men when he travels. This is how he avoids corruption and draws near to what is correct.

物類之起，必有所始。榮辱之來，必象其德。肉腐生蟲，魚枯生蠹。怠慢忘身，禍災乃作。強自取柱，柔自取束。邪穢在身，怨之所構。施薪若一，火就燥也；平地若一，水就溼也。草木疇生，禽獸群居，物各從其類也。是故質的張而弓矢至焉，林木茂而斧斤至焉，樹成蔭而眾鳥息焉，醯酸而蜹聚焉。故言有召禍也，行有招辱也，君子慎其所立乎！

All the things and the kinds that come about surely have a point from which they start out. Honor or disgrace that comes unto you surely reflects your degree of virtue. In rotten meat bugs are generated. In fish that's spoiled maggots are created. Lazy, haughty men who forget their place shall have misfortune and ruin to face. Rigid things get themselves used for bracing. Pliant things get themselves used for lacing. If with corruption your person is filled, it's this upon which hate toward you will build.

The firewood you spread out look the same, but fire will move toward the dry pieces. The earth you work on appears all even, but water will move toward the lower place. Wherever grasses and trees grow together, birds and beasts will flock. This is because each thing follows its own class. For this reason, wherever an archery target is set out, bows and arrows will follow. Wherever wood grows in abundance, axes and hatchets will go. Wherever trees create shade, flocks of birds will rest. Wherever something turns sour, flies will gather. Likewise, there are words that summon misfortune, and there is conduct that beckons disgrace, so the gentleman is careful about where he takes his stand.

積土成山，風雨興焉；積水成淵，蛟龍生焉。積善成德，而神明自得，聖心備焉。故不積蹞步，無以至千里；不積小流，無以成江海。騏驥一躍，不能十步；駑馬十駕，功在不舍。鍥而舍之，朽木不折；鍥而不舍，金石可鏤。螾無爪牙之利、筋骨之強，上食埃土，下飲黃泉，用心一也。蟹六跪而二螯，非蛇蟺之穴無可寄託者，用心躁也。

If you accumulate enough earth to form a mountain, then wind and rain will arise from it. If you accumulate enough water to form a deep pool, then dragons will come to live in it. If you accumulate enough goodness to achieve virtue, then you will naturally attain spirit-like powers and enlightenment, and the heart of a sage is complete therein. And so, without accumulating tiny steps, you have no way to go a thousand li. Without accumulating little streams, you have no way to form river or sea. Let the fastest horse take a single leap, it still would go no farther than ten strides. Yet a horse that is old and in bad condition can run a thousand li in ten days because it never gives up. If you start carving and give up, you will not be able to break even rotten wood, but if you start carving and do not give up, then you can engrave even metal and stone. The earthworm does not have sharp teeth and claws, nor does it have strong bones and muscles. Yet, it eats of the earth above, and it drinks from the Yellow Springs below, because it acts with single-mindedness. In contrast, the crab has six legs and two pincers. Yet were it not for the abandoned holes of water snakes and eels, it would have no place to lodge, because it is frenetic-minded.

是故無冥冥之志者，無昭昭之明；無惛惛之事者，無赫赫之功。行衢道者不至，事兩君者不容。目不能兩視而明，耳不能兩聽而聰。螣蛇無足而飛，梧鼠五技而窮。《詩》曰："尸鳩在桑，其子七兮。淑人君子，其儀一兮。其儀一兮，心如結兮。"故君子結於一也。

For this reason, no great understanding can be achieved without perseverance in the dark. No impressive contribution can be made without doing boring work. One walking both forks of a road goes nowhere. One serving two lords is not viewed welcomely. Eyes focused on two things at once are not sharp. Ears tuned to two things at once don't hear clearly. Though footless, the *teng* snake moves quick as flying. By contrast, the *wu* rodent has five skills but still gets trapped. *The Odes* says:

    The *shijiu* bird is on the mulberry.

    Seven is the number of its offspring.

    As for the noble man and gentleman,

    Their standard is one and unwavering.

    Their standard is one and unwavering,

    Like their hearts were tied to it by binding.

Thus is the gentleman bound to one thing.

昔者，瓠巴鼓瑟而流魚出聽，伯牙鼓琴而六馬仰秣。故聲無小而不聞，行無隱而不形；玉在山而木潤，淵生珠而崖不枯。爲善不積邪？安有不聞者乎？

In ancient times, Hu Ba played the lute, and the swimming fish came up to listen. Bo Ya played the Qin, and the six kinds of horses all raised up their heads from grazing. There is no sound so small as not to be heard. There is no action so subtle as not to be manifest. When there are precious stones (jade) under the mountain, the grass and trees have a special sheen; where pearls grow in a pool, the banks are never parched. Do good and see if it does not pile up. If it does, how can it fail to be heard of?

學惡乎始？惡乎終？曰：其數則始乎誦經，終乎讀禮；其義則始乎爲士，終乎爲聖人。真積力久則入，學至乎沒而後止也，故學數有終，若其義則不可須臾舍也。爲之，人也，舍之，禽獸也。故書者，政事之紀也，詩者，中聲之所止也，禮者，法之大分，類之綱紀也，故學至乎禮而止矣。夫是之謂道德之極。禮之敬文也，樂之中和也，詩、書之博也，春秋之微也，在天地之閒者畢矣。

Where does learning begin and where does it end? I say that as to program, learning begins with the recitation of the classics and ends with the reading of the ritual texts; and as to objective, it begins with learning to be a man of breeding, and ends with learning to be a sage. If you truly pile up effort over a long period of time, you will enter into the highest realm. Learning continues until death and only then does it cease. Therefore we may speak of an end to the program of learning, but the objective of learning must never for an instant be given up. To pursue it is to be a man; to give it up is to become a beast.

The Documents is the record of government affairs. The Odes is the repository of balanced sound. The Rituals is about the maxims in the model (fa) and the general divisions of things. Therefore, learning reaches its completion with the rituals, for this is called the ultimate point in pursuit of the Dao and virtue. We can find reverence and refinement in The Rituals, the balance and harmony in The Music, the broad content of The Odes and The Documents, and the subtleties of The Spring and Autumn Annals. These are all the things between Heaven and Earth that we may learn.

君子之學也：入乎耳,箸乎心,布乎四體,形乎動靜。端而言,蝡而動,一可以爲法則。小人之學也：入乎耳,出乎口。口耳之間則四寸,曷足以美七尺之軀哉！古之學者爲己,今之學者爲人。君子之學也,以美其身；小人之學也,以爲禽犢。故不問而告謂之傲,問一而告二謂之囋。傲、囋,非也；君子如響矣。

The learning of the gentleman enters through his ears, fastens to his heart, spreads through his four limbs, and manifests itself in his actions. His slightest word, his most subtle movement, all can serve as a model for others. The learning of the petty person enters through his ears and passes out of his mouth. From mouth to ears it is only four inches—how could it be enough to improve a whole body much larger than that? Students in ancient times learned for their own sake, but the students of today learn for the sake of impressing others. Thus the learning of the gentleman is used to ennoble himself, while the learning of the petty man is used as a gift for others. To instruct without being asked is what people call being presumptuous, and to speak two things when asked only one is what people call being wordy. Being presumptuous is wrong, and being wordy is wrong. The gentleman is simply like an echo.

學莫便乎近其人。禮、樂法而不説，詩、書故而不切，春秋約而不速。方其人之習君子之説，則尊以遍矣，周於世矣。故曰：學莫便乎近其人。

In learning, nothing is more profitable than to associate with those who are learned. *The Rituals* and *The Music* present us with models but no explanations. *The Odes* and *The Documents* deal with ancient matters and are not always pertinent. *The Spring and Autumn Annals* is terse and cannot be quickly understood. However, if you imitate the right person and practice the doctrine of the gentleman, then you will become a respectable person of broad knowledge, being able to handle worldly affairs. Thus, in learning, nothing is more profitable than to associate with those who are learned.

學之經莫速乎好其人，隆禮次之。上不能好其人，下不能隆禮，安特將學雜識志、順詩、書而已爾，則没世窮年，不免爲陋儒而已。將原先王、本仁義，則禮正其經緯蹊徑也。若挈裘領，詘五指而頓之，順者不可勝數也。不道禮憲，以詩、書爲之，譬之猶以指測河也，以戈舂黍也，以錐餐壺也，不可以得之矣。故隆禮，雖未明，法士也；不隆禮，雖察辯，散儒也。

Of the paths to learning, none is quicker than to love the learned people, and honoring ritual comes second. If you are first of all unable to love such men and secondly are incapable of honoring ritual, then you will only be learning a mass of jumbled facts, blindly following *The Odes* and *The Dotuments*, and nothing more. In such a case you may study to the end of your days and you will never be anything but a vulgar pedant. If you want to become like the former kings and seek out benevolence and righteousness, then ritual is the very road by which you must travel. It is like picking up a fur coat by the collar: grasp it with all five fingers and the whole coat can easily be lifted. To lay aside the rules of ritual and try to attain your objective with *The Odes* and *The Documents* alone is like trying to measure the depth of a river with your finger, to pound millet with a spear point, or to eat a pot of stew with an awl. You will get nowhere. Therefore one who honors ritual, though he may not yet have full understanding, can be called a model man of breeding; while one who does not honor ritual, though he may have keen perception, is no more than a desultory pedant.

問楛者勿告也，告楛者勿問也，説楛者勿聽也，有爭氣者勿與辨也。故必由其道至，然後接之，非其道則避之。故禮恭而後可與言道之方，辭順而後可與言道之理，色從而後可與言道之致。故未可與言而言謂之傲，可與言而不言謂之隱，不觀氣色而言謂之瞽。故君子不傲、不隱、不瞽，謹慎其身。《詩》曰："匪交匪舒，天子所予。"此之謂也。

Do not answer one who asks about something improper. Do not ask questions of one who speaks on something improper. Do not listen to one who tries to persuade you of something improper. Do not debate with a person of combative demeanor. Only if people approach you in the proper way should you receive them. If they do not approach you in the proper way, then avoid them. And so, only if they follow ritual and are reverent should you discuss the highest aspects of the Dao with them. Only if their speech is calm should you discuss the pattern of the Dao with them. Only if their countenance is agreeable should you discuss the culmination of the Dao with them. To discuss these things with those unfit to discuss them is called being presumptuous. Not to discuss these things with those fit to discuss them is called being secretive. To discuss these things without first observing the person's manner and countenance is called being blind. The gentleman is neither presumptuous nor secretive nor blind; he carefully acts according to another person's character. *The Odes* says, "The gentlemen are

not indolent or haughty. Rewarded by the Son of Heaven shall they be."
This expresses my meaning.

百發失一，不足謂善射；千里蹞步不至，不足謂善御；倫類不通，仁義不一，不足謂善學。學也者，固學一之也。一出焉，一入焉，塗巷之人也。其善者少，不善者多，桀、紂、盜跖也。全之盡之，然後學者也。

He who misses one shot in a hundred cannot be called a really good archer; he who sets out on a thousand-mile journey and breaks down half a pace from his destination cannot be called a really good carriage driver; he who does not comprehend moral relationships and categories and who does not make himself one with benevolence (ren) and righteousness (yi) cannot be called a good scholar. Learning basically means learning to achieve this oneness. He who starts off in this direction one time and that direction another is only a commoner of the roads and alleys, while he who does a little that is good and much that is not good is no better than the tyrants Jie and Zhou or Robber Zhi.

君子知夫不全不粹之不足以為美也，故誦數以貫之，思索以通之，為其人以處之，除其害者以持養之，使目非是無欲見也，使耳非是無欲聞也，使口非是無欲言也，使心非是無欲慮也。及至其致好之也，目好之五色，耳好之五聲，口好之五味，心利之有天下。是故權利不能傾也，群眾不能移也，天下不能蕩也。生乎由是，死乎由是，夫是之謂德操。德操然後能定，能定然後能應；能定能應，夫是之謂成人。天見其明，地見其光，君子貴其全也。

The gentleman knows that whatever is imperfect and unrefined does not deserve praise. Therefore he reads and listens to explanations in order to penetrate the Dao, ponders in order to understand it, associates with men who embody it in order to make it part of himself, and shuns those who impede it in order to sustain and nourish it. He makes his eyes not want to see what is not right, makes his ears not want to hear what is not right, makes his mouth not want to speak what is not right, and makes his mind not want to think what is not right. When he has truly learned to love what is right, his eyes will take greater pleasure in it than in the five colors; his ears will take greater pleasure than in the five sounds; his mouth will take greater pleasure than in the five flavors; and his mind will feel keener delight than in the possession of the world. When he has reached this stage, he cannot be subverted by power or the love of profit; he cannot be swayed by the masses; he cannot be moved by the world. He lives by this, and he dies by this. This is called the state in which virtue has been grasped. He who has such constancy of virtue can order himself, and, having ordered himself, he can then respond to others. He who can order himself and respond to others is what is called the complete man. It is the characteristic of Heaven to manifest brightness, of Earth to manifest breadth, and of the gentleman to value completeness.

儒效篇第八
Chapter 8　The Achievements of the Confucian (*Ru*)

......

造父者，天下之善御者也，無輿馬則無所見其能。羿者，天下之善射者也，無弓矢則無所見其巧。大儒者，善調一天下者也，無百里之地，則無所見其功。輿固馬選矣，而不能以至遠，一日而千里，則非造父也。弓調矢直矣，而不能射遠中微，則非羿也。用百里之地，而不能以調一天下，制彊暴，則非大儒也。

...

Zao Fu was the best driver in the whole world, but without a chariot and horses, he would have had nowhere to display his abilities. Yi was the best archer in the world, but without a bow and arrows, he would have had nowhere to display his skill. The great ru (Confucian) is one who is good at aligning and unifying the whole world, but without a territory of a hundred li, he will have nowhere to display his merit. If the chariot is sturdy and the horses are of select quality but the man cannot use them to go as far as a thousand li in a single day, then he is not a Zao Fu. If the bow is properly adjusted and the arrows are straight but the man cannot use them to hit a fine point shooting from far away, then he is not a Yi. If the man has use of a territory of a hundred li but cannot use it to align and unify the whole world and put a stop to violence and tyranny, then he is not a great ru.

彼大儒者，雖隱於窮閻漏屋，無置錐之地，而王公不能與之爭名；在一大夫之位，則一君不能獨畜，一國不能獨容，成名況乎諸侯，莫不願得以爲臣。用百里之地，而千里之國莫能與之爭勝；笞棰暴國，齊一天下，而莫能傾也。是大儒之徵也。

The great ru is such that even if he hides himself in a leaky hut in a poor neighborhood and owns no land, kings and dukes cannot compete with his fame. If he were to occupy even so much as a grand minister's position, then no single lord could keep him, and no single state could contain him. He would be well-known to the feudal lords, all of whom would like to make him a minister. If he were to have use of a territory of a hundred li, then no state of a thousand li could compete with him for victory in battle. He would thrash the tyrannical states, bring concord and unity to the whole world, and no one could overthrow him. Such is the mark of a great ru.

其言有類，其行有禮，其舉事無悔，其持險應變曲當。與時遷徙，與世偃仰，千舉萬變，其道一也。是大儒之稽也。其窮也俗儒笑之；其通也英傑化之，嵬瑣逃之，邪說畏之，衆人媿之。通則一天下，窮則獨立貴名，天不能死，地不能埋，桀跖之世不能汙，非大儒莫之能立，仲尼、子弓是也。

His words accord with the proper categories of things, and his actions accord with ritual. In managing affairs, he leaves nothing to regret. In handling dangers and responding to changes, he does everything appropriately. He shifts and moves with the times. He bends and straightens with the age. Throughout a thousand acts and ten thousand changes, his way remains one and the same. Such is the test of a great ru. When he is in difficult circumstances, vulgar ru will mock him. When he is successful, then heroes and outstanding men will be transformed to follow him. Men of twisted and petty behavior will flee him. Men of perverse doctrines will fear him. The masses will be ashamed before him. When successful, then he unifies the whole world. When in difficult circumstances, then on his own he establishes a noble reputation for himself. Heaven cannot make it die. Earth cannot bury it. The ages of Jie and Robber Zhi cannot pollute it. None but a great *ru* can establish such a reputation. Just such men were Confucius and Zigong.

故有俗人者,有俗儒者,有雅儒者,有大儒者。不學問,無正義,以富利爲隆,是俗人者也。逢衣淺帶,解果其冠,略法先王而足亂世術,繆學雜舉,不知法後王而一制度,不知隆禮義而殺詩書;其衣冠行僞,已同於世俗矣,然而不知惡者;其言議談説已無以異於墨子矣,然而明不能別,呼先王以欺愚者而求衣食焉;得委積足以揜其口,則揚揚如也;隨其長子,事其便辟,舉其上客,億然若終身之虜而不敢有他志,是俗儒者也。法後王,一制度,隆禮義而殺詩書;其言行已有大法矣,然而明不能齊法教之所不及,聞見之所未至,則知不能類也;知之曰知之,不知曰不知,內不自以誣,外不自以欺,以是尊賢畏法而不敢怠傲,是雅儒者也。法先王,統禮義,一制度;以淺持博,以古持今,以一持萬;苟仁義之類也,雖在鳥獸之中,若別白黑;倚物怪變,所未嘗聞也,所未嘗見也,卒然起一方,則舉統類而應之,無所儗怍;張法而度之,則晻然若合符節,是大儒者也。

Thus, there are vulgar men, vulgar *ru*, refined *ru*, and great *ru*. One sort of person does not study or inquire. He has no correctness or *yi*. He takes wealth and profit as his exalted standards. Such a person is a vulgar man. Another sort of person wears large clothing with a slack belt. He wears his cap looking like split-open fruit. He only sketchily models himself on the former kings, but is capable enough to disorder the ways of the world. His learning is erroneous and his actions are haphazard. He does not know to model himself on the later kings and to pursue their regulations and measures single-mindedly. He does not know the significance of honoring ritual and *yi* and putting The Odes and The Documents second. His clothing, cap, and practice of deliberate effort are already the same as the vulgar customs of the age, but he does not recognize his own badness. His arguments and speech are already the same as Mozi, but his own understanding cannot make him see the difference. He calls upon the former kings so as to deceive the ignorant and seek clothing and food from them. If he gets enough provisions to stuff his mouth, then he is overjoyed. He follows his superiors, serves their attendants and favorites, and respects higher-ranking retainers in a manner like a contented lifelong slave who dares not have any other intentions. Such a person is a vulgar *ru*. Another sort of person models himself on the later kings. He pursues their regulations and measures single-mindedly. He honors ritual and *yi* and puts *The Odes* and *The Documents* second. His words and practices already hold to the grand model, but his own understanding cannot make them match up completely. Cases which the model and teachings do not cover, or where his experience does not reach, his own knowledge is unable to bring into conformity with the proper categories of things. If he knows, then he says he knows. If he does not know, then he says he does not know. On the inside, he does not delude himself about himself. On the outside, he does not deceive others about himself. In this manner, he honors the worthy, fearfully holds to the proper model, and dares not be lazy or arrogant. Such a person is a refined *ru*. Another sort of person models himself on the later kings. He gathers in himself all their rituals and *yi*. He pursues their regulations and measures single-mindedly. He uses what is shallow to manage what is broad, uses what is ancient to manage what is current, and uses what is one to manage what is myriad. As for the categories of ren and *yi*, even if he were dwelling among birds and beasts, he could distinguish them as easily as black and white. If at some point there suddenly arise deviant things and unusual changes that have never been heard of or seen before, then he takes up the comprehensive categories of things and responds to them without any hesitation or misgivings. He sets out the proper model and measures them, and then his response fits just like bringing together two halves of a tally. Such a person is a great *ru*.

故人主用俗人則萬乘之國亡，用俗儒則萬乘之國存，用雅儒則千乘之國安，用大儒則百里之地久，而後三年，天下爲一，諸侯爲臣；用萬乘之國，則舉錯而定，一朝而伯。

Thus, if a ruler of men employs vulgar men, then even a state of ten thousand chariots will perish. If he employs vulgar *ru*, then a state of ten thousand chariots can be made to survive. If he employs refined *ru*, then a state of a thousand chariots can be made secure. If he employs great *ru*, then even a territory of just a hundred li can be preserved for a long time, and after several years, all people under Heaven will be unified under him, and the feudal lords will be his ministers. If he should have use of a state of ten thousand chariots, then with a few orders all will be settled, and in a single day he will become renowned.

不聞不若聞之，聞之不若見之，見之不若知之，知之不若行之。學至於行之而止矣。行之，明也，明之爲聖人。聖人也者，本仁義，當是非，齊言行，不失豪釐，無它道焉，已乎行之矣。故聞之而不見，雖博必謬；見之而不知，雖識必妄；知之而不行，雖敦必困。不聞不見，則雖當，非仁也。其道百舉而百陷也。

......

Not having heard of it is not as good as having heard of it. Having heard of it is not as good as having seen it. Having seen it is not as good as knowing it. Knowing it is not as good as putting it into practice. Learning arrives at putting it into practice and then stops, because to put it into practice is to understand it, and to understand it is to be a sage. The sage bases himself on *ren* and *yi*, hits exactly on what is right and wrong, and makes his words and practices match up completely, all without the slightest misstep. There is no other way to this than simply to stop at putting it into practice. Thus, if you have heard of it but have not seen it, then even if you are broadly learned, you are sure to be mistaken. If you have seen it but do not know it, then even though you can recognize it, you are sure to act recklessly. If you know it but do not put it into practice, then even if you are thoroughly familiar with it, you are sure to find yourself trapped. If you have neither heard of it nor seen it, then even though you hit on what is fitting, that is not ren; such a way fails a hundred times for every hundred actions.

……

解蔽篇第二十一
Chapter 21 Dispelling Obsession

凡人之患,蔽於一曲,而闇於大理。治則復經,兩疑則惑矣。天下無二道,聖人無兩心。今諸侯異政,百家異說,則必或是或非,或治或亂。亂國之君,亂家之人,此其誠心,莫不求正而以自爲也。妒繆於道,而人誘其所迨也。私其所積,唯恐聞其惡也。倚其所私,以觀異術,唯恐聞其美也。是以與治雖走,而是己不輟也。豈不蔽於一曲,而失正求也哉！心不使焉,則白黑在前而目不見,雷鼓在側而耳不聞,況於使者乎？德道之人,亂國之君非之上,亂家之人非之下,豈不哀哉！

The thing that all men should fear is that they will become obsessed by a small corner of truth and fail to comprehend its overall principles. If they can correct this fault, they may return to correct standards, but if they continue to hesitate and be of two minds, then they will feel confused. There are not two Daos in the world; the sage is never of two minds. Nowadays the feudal lords follow different theories of government and the philosophers of the hundred schools teach different doctrines. Inevitably some teach what is right, and some what is wrong; some rulers govern well and others bring about disorder. Even the ruler of a chaotic state or the follower of a pernicious doctrine will undoubtedly in all sincerity seek what is proper and try to better his condition. But he is jealous and mistaken in his understanding of the Dao and hence allows other men to lead him astray. He clings to his familiar ways and is loath to hear them spoken ill of; he judges everything on the basis of his old prejudices; and when he encounters some different theory, he is loath to hear it praised. Thus he moves farther and farther away from a condition of order, and yet never ceases to believe that he is doing right. Is this not what it means to be obsessed by a small corner of truth and to fail in the search for proper ways? If one fails to use his mind, then black and white may be right before his eyes and he will not see them; thunder or drums may be sounding in his ear and he will not hear them. How much more so with a man whose mind is obsessed! The man who has truly attained the Dao is criticized from above by the rulers of chaotic states, and from below by men of pernicious doctrines. Is this not lamentable?

故爲蔽：欲爲蔽，惡爲蔽，始爲蔽，終爲蔽，遠爲蔽，近爲蔽，博爲蔽，淺爲蔽，古爲蔽，今爲蔽。凡萬物異則莫不相爲蔽，此心術之公患也。

What are the sources of obsession? One may be obsessed by desires or by hates, by the beginning of an affair or by the end, by those far away or those close by, by breadth of knowledge or by shallowness, by the past or by the present. When one makes distinctions among the myriad beings of creation, these distinctions all become potential sources of obsession. This is a danger in the use of the mind that is common to all men.

昔人君之蔽者，夏桀殷紂是也。桀蔽於末喜斯觀，而不知關龍逢，以惑其心，而亂其行。紂蔽於妲己、飛廉，而不知微子啟，以惑其心，而亂其行。故群臣去忠而事私，百姓怨非而不用，賢良退處而隱逃，此其所以喪九牧之地，而虛宗廟之國也。桀死於鬲山，紂縣於赤斾。身不先知，人又莫之諫，此蔽塞之禍也。

In ancient times there were rulers who were obsessed; Jie of the Xia Dynasty and Zhou of the Yin are examples. Jie was obsessed by his favorite concubine Mo Xi and his counselor Si Guan and did not recognize the worth of Guan Longfeng. Thus his mind became deluded and his conduct disorderly. Zhou was obsessed by his favorite concubine Da Ji and his counselor Fei Lian and did not recognize the worth of Qi, the prince of Wei, and thus his mind became deluded and his conduct disorderly. Therefore, the courtiers of these two rulers abandoned the principles of loyal service and thought only of selfish aims, the common people hated and spoke ill of them and refused to obey their commands, and men of true worth retired from the court and went into hiding. Thus they lost possession of the Nine Provinces and brought desolation to the ancestral temples of their dynasties. Jie was driven to his death on Mount Li and Zhou's head ended dangling from the red pennant of his attacker. They could not foresee the future for themselves and no one was willing to advise them. Such are the disasters that come from obsession and a closed mind.

成湯監於夏桀，故主其心而慎治之，是以能長用伊尹，而身不失道，此其所以代夏王而受九有也。文王監於殷紂，故主其心而慎治之，是以能長用呂望，而身不失道，此其所以代殷王而受九牧也。遠方莫不致其珍；故目視備色，耳聽備聲，口食備味，形居備宮，名受備號，生則天下歌，死則四海哭。夫是之謂至盛。……

Cheng Tang took warning from the fate of Jie and therefore he was careful to employ his mind correctly and to govern with circumspection. Accordingly, he was able to benefit from the good advice of Yi Yin over a long period of time and did not depart from the Dao. As a result he replaced Jie of the Xia as ruler and gained possession of the Nine Provinces. King Wen took warning from the fate of Zhou and therefore he was careful to employ his mind correctly and to govern with circumspection. Accordingly, he was able to benefit from the good advice of Lü Wang over a long period of time and did not depart from the Dao. As a result he replaced Zhou of the Yin as ruler and gained possession of the Nine Provinces. The men of distant regions all came with rare gifts, so that these wise rulers had everything they wished for to please the eye, the ear, the mouth, and the palate; fair were the palaces they lived in and the fame which they enjoyed. While they lived the world sang songs of praise and when they died all within the four seas wept. This is what it means to reach the height of glory. ...

……昔賓孟之蔽者，亂家是也。墨子蔽於用而不知文。宋子蔽於欲而不知得。慎子蔽於法而不知賢。申子蔽於埶而不知知。惠子蔽於辭而不知實。莊子蔽於天而不知人。故由用謂之道，盡利矣。由欲謂之道，盡嗛矣。由法謂之道，盡數矣。由執謂之道,盡便矣。由辭謂之道,盡論矣。由天謂之道,盡因矣。此數具者,皆道之一隅也。夫道者體常而盡變,一隅不足以舉之。曲知之人,觀於道之一隅,而未之能識也。故以爲足而飾之,內以自亂,外以惑人,上以蔽下,下以蔽上,此蔽塞之禍也。孔子仁知且不蔽,故學亂術足以爲先王者也。一家得周道,舉而用之,不蔽於成積也。故德與周公齊,名與三王並,此不蔽之福也。

... In past times, there were lobbyists who were obsessed, such as the pernicious schools. Mozi was obsessed by what is useful and did not understand the beauties of form. Songzi was obsessed by the need to lessen desires, for he did not understand the value of great achievements. Shenzi was obsessed with the concept of law and did not understand the part to be played by worthy men. Shen Buhai was obsessed by the power of circumstance and did not understand the role of the human intelligence. Huizi was obsessed by words and did not understand the truth that lies behind them. Zhuangzi was obsessed by thoughts of Heaven (i.e. Nature) and did not understand the importance of man.

He who thinks only of what is useful will take the Dao to be wholly a matter of material profit. He who thinks only of desires will take the Dao to be wholly a matter of avoiding dissatisfaction. He who thinks only of law will take the Dao to be wholly a matter of policy. He who thinks only of circumstance will take the Dao to be wholly a matter of expedience. He who thinks only of words will take the Dao to be wholly a matter of making arguments. He who thinks only of Heaven will take the Dao to be wholly a matter of harmonizing with natural forces. These various doctrines comprehend only one small corner of the Dao, but the true Dao must embody constant principles and be capable of embracing all changes. A single corner of it will not suffice. These men with their limited understanding saw one corner of the Dao, failing to understand that it was only a corner. So they considered it sufficient and proceeded to expound it in engaging terms. Such men bring chaos to themselves and delusion to others; if they are in a superior position, they inflict their obsessions upon their inferiors; and if in an inferior position, they inflict them upon their superiors. Such are the disasters that come from obsession and a closed mind.

Confucius, on the other hand, was benevolent, wise, and free from obsession. Thus, although he studied the doctrines of various other schools, he established his own school, taught the Dao of the Zhou, and showed how it could be put into practice, for he was not obsessed by old habits and prejudices. Hence his virtue is equal to that of the duke of Zhou, and his fame matches that of the sage-kings of the Three Dynasties. Such is the good fortune that comes from being free of obsession.

聖人知心術之患,見蔽塞之禍,故無欲、無惡、無始、無終、無近、無遠、無博、無淺、無古、無今,兼陳萬物而中縣衡焉。是故眾異不得相蔽以亂其倫也。

The sage understands the dangers involved in improper use of the mind, and sees the disasters that come from obsession and a closed mind. Therefore, he does not allow himself to be influenced by considerations of desire or hate, beginning or end, distance or nearness, breadth or shallowness, past or present, but searches and examines all things and weighs them impartially in a balance. As a result, the distinctions which exist in all things cannot inflict obsession upon him and bring disorder to his reason.

何謂衡? 曰:道。故心不可以不知道;心不知道,則不可道,而可非道。人孰欲得恣,而守其所不可,以禁其所可? 以其不可道之心取人,則必合於不道人,而不合於道人。以其不可道之心與不道人論道人,亂之本也。

And what is the balance that he uses? It is the Dao. The mind must understand the Dao, for if it does not, it will reject the Dao and give approval to that which is at variance with it. And what man, seeking to gratify his desires, will abide by what he has rejected and refuse to follow what he has given his approval to? Thus, if a man whose mind has rejected the Dao sets out to select helpers, he will invariably find himself drawn to men whose conduct is at variance with the Dao, and will not appreciate men who abide by it. When a man whose mind has rejected the Dao joins with similar men to criticize those who abide by the Dao, this is the beginning of disorder.

夫何以知？曰：心知道，然後可道；可道，然後守道以禁非道。以其可道之心取人，則合於道人，而不合於不道之人矣。以其可道之心與道人論非道，治之要也。何患不知？故治之要在於知道。

How will one know who follow the Dao? The mind must first understand the Dao before it can approve it, and it must first approve it before it can abide by it and reject what is at variance with it. If a man whose mind has given approval to the Dao sets out to select helpers, he will find himself drawn to men whose conduct is in accordance with the Dao and will feel no affinity for men whose conduct is at variance with it. And when a man whose mind has given approval to the Dao joins with similar men to criticize those whose conduct is at variance with the Dao, then this is the starting point of orderly government. Why should such a man need to worry about how true his understanding is? Therefore the beginning of good government lies in understanding the Dao.

人何以知道？曰：心。心何以知？曰：虛壹而靜。心未嘗不臧也，然而有所謂虛；心未嘗不兩也，然而有所謂壹；心未嘗不動也，然而有所謂靜。人生而有知，知而有志；志也者，臧也；然而有所謂虛；不以所已臧害所將受謂之虛。心生而有知，知而有異；異也者，同時兼知之；同時兼知之，兩也；然而有所謂一；不以夫一害此一謂之壹。心臥則夢，偷則自行，使之則謀；故心未嘗不動也；然而有所謂靜；不以夢劇亂知謂之靜。

How do we understand the Dao? Through mind. And how can the mind understand it? Through emptiness, single-mindedness, and stillness. The mind is always holding something. Yet, there is what is called being "empty". The mind is always two-fold. Yet, there is what is called being "single-minded". The mind is always moving. Yet, there is what is called being "still". Humans are born with awareness. With awareness, they have focus. To focus is to be holding something. Yet, there is something called being "empty". Not to let what one is already holding harm what one is about to receive is called being "empty". The mind has awareness when one is born. With awareness, there comes awareness of differences. These differences are known at the same time, and when they are known at the same time, this is to be two-fold. Yet, there is what is called being "single-minded". Not to let one idea harm another idea is called being "single-minded". When the mind sleeps, then it dreams. When it relaxes, then it goes about on its own. When one puts it to use, then it forms plans. Thus, the mind is always moving. Yet, there is what is called being "still". Not to let dreams and worries disorder one's understanding is called being "still".

未得道而求道者，謂之虛壹而靜。作之：則將須道者之虛則人，將事道者之壹則盡，盡將思道者靜則察。知道察，知道行，體道者也。虛壹而靜，謂之大清明。萬物莫形而不見，莫見而不論，莫論而失位。坐於室而見四海，處於今而論久遠。疏觀萬物而知其情，參稽治亂而通其度，經緯天地而材官萬物，制割大理而宇宙裏矣。恢恢廣廣，孰知其極？睪睪廣廣，孰知其德？涫涫紛紛，孰知其形？明參日月，大滿八極，夫是之謂大人。夫惡有蔽矣哉！

As for those who have not yet grasped the Dao but are seeking the Dao, I say to them: emptiness, single-mindedness, and stillness—make these your principles. If one who would search for the Dao achieves emptiness, then he may enter upon it. If one who would work at the Dao achieves single-mindedness, then he will exhaustively obtain it. If one who would ponder the Dao achieves stillness, then he will discern it keenly. He who understands the Dao and perceives its nature, he who understands the Dao and carries it out, may be said to embody the Dao. To be empty, and single-minded, and still—this is called great clarity and brilliance. For the person who achieves these things, none of the myriad things that take a form are not seen. None of the things that are seen are not assessed. None of the things that are assessed are misplaced. He sits in his chamber yet sees all within the four seas. He dwells in today yet assesses what is long ago and far away in time. He comprehensively observes the myriad things and knows their true nature. He inspects and examines both societies of order and societies of disorder and discerns the principles of governing. He sets straight Heaven and Earth, and arranges and makes useful the myriad things. He institutes great order, and the whole world is encompassed therein.

> So vast and broad is he! Who grasps his true limits?
> So lofty and broad is he! Who grasps his true virtue?
> So active and varied is he! Who grasps his true form?

His brilliance matches the sun and the moon. His greatness fills all the eight directions. Such is the Great Man. How could he become the victim of obsession?

心者，形之君也，而神明之主也，出令而無所受令。自禁也，自使也，自奪也，自取也，自行也，自止也。故口可劫而使墨云，形可劫而使詘申，心不可劫而使易意，是之則受，非之則辭。故曰：心容，其擇也無禁，必自現，其物也雜博，其情之至也不貳。《詩》云："采采卷耳，不盈傾筐。嗟我懷人，寘彼周行。"傾筐易滿也，卷耳易得也，然而不可以貳周行。故曰：心枝則無知，傾則不精，貳則疑惑。以贊稽之，萬物可兼知也。身盡其故則美。類不可兩也，故知者擇一而壹焉。

The mind is the lord of the body and the master of one's spirit and intelligence. It issues orders, but it takes orders from nothing: it restrains itself, and it employs itself; it lets itself go, and it takes itself in hand; it makes itself proceed, and it makes itself stop. The mouth can be compelled either to be silent or to speak, and the body can be compelled either to contract or to extend itself, but the mind cannot be compelled to change its thoughts. What it considers right, one accepts. What it considers wrong, one rejects. And so I say: when the mind selects its objects, it does so freely, according to its own view, without being constrained. While the objects it selects are broadly varying, the mind in its perfect state is able to concentrate on each of them. *The Odes* says:

> I pick and pick the juan-er leaves.
> But cannot fill my sloping basket.
> Oh for my cherished one!
> He is stationed on the Zhou campaign.

A sloping basket is easy to fill, and the juan-er leaves are easy to get, but if you think of the Zhou campaign when picking the juan-er leaves, you would not be able to fill your sloping basket. And so I say: if the mind is split, it will be unable to know. If it deviates, it will not be expertly refined. If it is divided, then it will be confused. If the mind is undivided in examining things, then everything can be known; and if the mind thoroughly understands what makes everything have their present form, then the person will be truly beautiful. There cannot be two fundamental principles of things. Hence, the person with understanding picks the one right principle and pursues it single-mindedly.

……人心譬如槃水，正錯而勿動，則湛濁在下，而清明在上，則足以見鬚眉而察理矣。微風過之，湛濁動乎下，清明亂於上，則不可以得大形之正也。心亦如是矣。故導之以理，養之以清，物莫之傾，則足以定是非決嫌疑矣。小物引之，則其正外易，其心內傾，則不足以決麤理矣。……

…The human mind can be compared to the water in a container. If you set it straight and do not move it, the muddy and turbid parts will settle to the bottom, and the clear and bright parts will be on the top, and then one can see one's whiskers and inspect the lines on one's face. But if a slight breeze passes over it, the muddy and turbid parts will be stirred up from the bottom, and the clear and bright parts will be disturbed on top, and then one cannot get a correct view of even large contours. The mind is just like this. Thus, if one guides it with good order, nourishes it with clarity, and nothing can make it deviate, then it will be capable of determining right and wrong and deciding what is doubtful. If it is drawn aside by even a little thing, then on the outside one's correctness will be altered, and on the inside one's mind will deviate, and then one will be incapable of discerning the multifarious patterns of things. ...

凡觀物有疑，中心不定，則外物不清。吾慮不清，未可定然否也。冥冥而行者，見寢石以爲伏虎也，見植林以爲後人也：冥冥蔽其明也。醉者越百步之溝，以爲蹞步之澮也；俯而出城門，以爲小之閨也：酒亂其神也。厭目而視者，視一爲兩；掩耳而聽者，聽漠漠而以爲哅哅：埶亂其官也。故從山上望牛者若羊，而求羊者不下牽也：遠蔽其大也。從山下望木者，十仞之木若箸，而求箸者不上折也：高蔽其長也。水動而景搖，人不以定美惡：水埶玄也。瞽者仰視而不見星，人不以定有無：用精惑也。有人焉以此時定物，則世之愚者也。彼愚者之定物，以疑決疑，決必不當。夫苟不當，安能無過乎？……

When you observe objects, doubts arise, and if your inner mind does not settle them, then your perception of external objects will become unclear. And if your thoughts themselves are unclear, then you cannot settle the doubts that arise. A person who walks in the dark sees a stone lying on the ground and mistakes it for a tiger lying in wait. He sees trees standing upright and mistakes them for people following behind him. This is because the darkness obscures his clarity of vision. A drunkard tries to leap over a gorge a hundred paces wide, mistaking it for a ditch a half step across. He bends down when exiting the city gate, mistaking it for a low doorway. This is because the wine has disordered his spirit. If you press your eyeball when you look at something, you will see two objects instead of one; if you cup your hands over your ears, dull noises will sound like a sharp din. This is because the actions you take disorder the functioning of the faculties. Thus, to people looking down on cows from on top of a mountain, they will look like sheep, but those seeking their sheep do not go down to lead them away, because [they understand that] the distance has obscured their true size. To people who from the foot of a mountain look at trees atop it, very tall trees will look like chopsticks, but those seeking chopsticks do not go up to pick among them, because [they understand that] the height has obscured their true length. When water is stirred up and its reflections waver, then people do not use it to determine the beautiful and the ugly, because the condition of the water is blurry. When a blind person looks up and does not see the stars, people do not rely on him to establish whether they are there or not, because they know that his faculties are impaired. If there is someone among them who uses such occasions to determine things, then he is the most foolish person in the world. Such a foolish person's way of determining things is to use one doubtful thing to decide another doubtful thing. In that case, his judgments are never accurate. And if his judgments are not accurate, how can he hope to escape error? ...

凡以知，人之性也；可以知，物之理也。以可以知人之性，求可以知物之理，而無所疑止之，則沒世窮年不能無也。其所以貫理焉雖億萬，已不足浹萬物之變，與愚者若一。學、老身長子，而與愚者若一，猶不知錯，夫是之謂妄人。

For everyone, the ability to know comes from human nature, and the ability to be known comes from the nature of things. If one takes the human ability to know what comes from human nature and uses it to seek the underlying patterns of things that can be known, but one has no point at which one will stop, then one may spend all the rest of one's life without being able to cover them all. Even if the things for which one has managed to string together their patterns are many million in number, but one is still unable to understand all the transformations which the countless beings undergo, one will be the same as a foolish person. Anyone who studies until he himself is old and his sons are full grown, and yet neither advances beyond the stage of the ignorant man nor has the sense to give up—such a man may be called a real fool.

故學也者，固學止之也。惡乎止之？曰：止諸至足。曷謂至足？曰：聖王。聖也者，盡倫者也；王也者，盡制者也；兩盡者，足以為天下極矣。故學者以聖王為師，案以聖王之制為法，法其法以求其統類，以務象效其人。嚮是而務，士也；類是而幾,君子也;知之,聖人也。故有知非以慮是,則謂之懼;有勇非以持是,則謂之賊;察孰非以分是,則謂之篡;多能非以脩蕩是,則謂之知;辯利非以言是,則謂之詌。

And so, learning is precisely learning to have a stopping point. Where should it stop? It should stop with the point of complete sufficiency. What do I mean by complete sufficiency? I mean the understanding of the sage and the king. The sage has complete mastery of all moral principles; the king has complete mastery of all regulations of society. Those who possess these two kinds of mastery are worthy to be called the pinnacles of the world. Hence the scholar should take the sage and the king as his teachers. He should take their regulations as his model and, on the basis of this model, seek to penetrate their reasoning and work to become like them. He who strives for this ideal is a man of breeding, he who comes close to realizing it is a gentleman, and he who truly understands it is a sage. He who has intelligence but does not think of striving for this ideal may be called timid. He who has bravery but fails to support this ideal may be called a brigand. He who has keen perception but fails to comprehend this ideal may be called mechanical minded. He who has much talent but fails to practice this ideal may be called wily.[①] He who is clever at talking but fails to speak of this ideal may be called a blabbermouth.

傳曰:"天下有二:非察是,是察非。"謂合王制不合王制也。天下不以是爲隆正也,然而猶有能分是非、治曲直者邪? 若夫非分是非,非治曲直,非辨治亂,非治人道,雖能之無益於人,不能無損於人;案直將治怪説,玩奇辭,以相撓滑也;案彊鉗而利口,厚顔而忍詬,無正而恣孳,妄辨而幾利;不好辭讓,不敬禮節,而好相推擠:此亂世姦人之説也,則天下之治説者,方多然矣。

A saying goes, "There are only two alternatives in the world: using what is wrong to investigate what is right, and using what is right to

---

[①] Scholars disagree on what these three sentences mean.

investigate what is wrong." This refers to whether one does or does not accord with the regulations of a true king. Is there anyone in the world who can fail to take these as his lofty standard of correctness and yet still be able to distinguish between right and wrong and master the crooked and the straight? If one's practice does not distinguish between right and wrong, does not master the crooked and the straight, does not differentiate order and chaos, and does not help govern human affairs, then being capable of it is of no benefit to people, and being incapable of it is no loss to people. One will simply master strange arguments and toy with bizarre claims so as to disturb and trip up others. Accordingly, such a person will vehemently maintain what is wrong and make his tongue slick; thick-skinned, he lacks any sense of correctness, engages in license and arrogance, argues recklessly and pursues profit. These people do not like deference and yielding, they do not respect ritual and proper measure, but instead they like only to jostle and hassle one another. This is the way cunning people make arguments in a disordered age, and now the number of those mastering this way of arguing has become many indeed.

傳曰："析辭而爲察，言物而爲辨，君子賤之。博聞彊志，不合王制，君子賤之。"此之謂也。爲之無益於成也，求之無益於得也，憂戚之無益於幾也，則廣焉能棄之矣，不以自妨也，不少頃干之胸中。不慕往，不閔來，無邑憐之心，當時則動，物至而應，事起而辨，治亂可否，昭然明矣。……

A saying goes, "The gentleman despises those who consider perception to consist merely in the analysis of words, or knowledge to consist merely in the description of objects. The gentleman despises men of broad learning and powerful memory who yet do not conform to the regulations of the king." This expresses my meaning. Things which are of no help to you in fulfilling your undertakings, no help to you in obtaining what you seek, no help to you in escaping from what you dread—put such things far away from yourself and reject them. Do not allow them to impede you; do not harbor them in your breast even for a moment. Do not long for the past, do not fret over the future, and do not allow your mind to be disturbed by anxiety or miserliness. Act when the time comes; respond to things as they appear; analyse events as they occur; and the distinction between order and disorder, proper and improper will become abundantly clear. ...

七、天人 / Part Ⅶ Heaven

　　季節更替、陰晴圓缺、生老病死……這些事情似乎是受到某個東西管控的。有人把這個東西稱之爲"上帝的意志",有人稱之爲"自然的規律"。中國古代哲學家則稱之爲"道"或"命"或"天志"。我們人類不能改變天道,天道界定了我們的活動範圍。逆天而行,注定會失敗。反之,順從天道,許多問題都會得到解決。所以,理解天道是非常重要的。

　　但我們能知道天道嗎? 如果可以,那麼發生在我們身上的一切事情是否都是由天道決定的,以至於自由選擇不過是個假象? 如果天道決定了一切,那麼這是否意味著我們就沒必要去做任何事情,只要平靜地接受任何發生在我們身上的事就好了? 如果天道沒有決定一切,那麼什麼是由它完全決定的,什麼不是? 它是否能完全決定一個人的壽命、政治地位,等等?

　　在這一部分,我們將會瞭解到儒家、墨家和道家對這個問題的論述。閱讀選文時,試著找出各家之間的差別,並思考他們的理論是否合理。

　　There seems to be something that governs the change of the seasons, the phases of the Moon, the birth and death of human beings, etc. Some call it the will of God. Some call it the laws of nature. Ancient Chinese philosophers call it the Way or the mandate or the will of Heaven. We humans cannot change the way of Heaven, which sets limits on what we can do. If we try to go against the way of Heaven, we are doomed to fail. However, if we follow the way of Heaven, we might be able to solve many problems. Thus it is important to grasp the way of Heaven.

　　But can we know the way of Heaven? If we can, is everything that happens to us determined by the way of Heaven so that free choice is just an illusion? If the way of Heaven determines everything, does it mean that we should not try to do anything except peacefully accept whatever happens to us? If the way of Heaven does not determine everything, then what are the limits? Does it completely determine when one will die, whether one can be the king or the president of a country, etc.?

In this part, we will see how the Confucians, the Mohists, and the Daoists address these questions. As you read the selections, try to figure out the differences between them. Ask yourself how plausible their theories are.

《論語》/ The Analects

2.4 子曰：" 吾十有五而志於學，三十而立，四十而不惑，五十而知天命，六十而耳順，七十而從心所欲，不踰矩。"

2.4 The Master said, "At fifteen, I set my mind upon learning; at thirty, I took my place in society; at forty, I became free of doubts; at fifty, I understood Heaven's Mandate; at sixty, my ear was attuned; and at seventy, I could follow my heart's desires without overstepping the bounds of propriety."

3.13 王孫賈問曰：" 與其媚於奧，寧媚於灶，何謂也？" 子曰：" 不然；獲罪於天，無所禱也。"

3.13 Wangsun Jia asked, "What do you think about the saying, 'It is better to pay homage to the kitchen stove than to the corner shrine.'" The Master replied, "This is not so. Once you have incurred the wrath of Heaven, there is no one to whom you can pray for help."

7.23 子曰：" 天生德於予，桓魋其如予何？"

7.23 The Master said, "It is Heaven itself that has endowed me with virtue. What have I to fear from the likes of Huan Tui?"

9.5　子畏於匡。曰："文王既没,文不在茲乎。天之將喪斯文也。後死者不得與於斯文也。天之未喪斯文也。匡人其如予何。"

9.5　The Master was ambushed in Kuang. He said, "Now that King Wen is gone, is not culture (wen) now invested here in me? If Heaven intended this culture to perish, it would not have given it to those of us who live after King Wen's death. Since Heaven did not intend that this culture should perish, what can the people of Kuang do to me?"

11.9　顏淵死。子曰:"噫! 天喪予! 天喪予!"

11.9　When Yan Hui died, the Master cried: "O, Heaven's killing me! It's killing me!"

14.36　公伯寮愬子路於季孫,子服景伯以告,曰:"夫子固有惑志於公伯寮,吾力猶能肆諸市朝。"子曰:"道之將行也與? 命也;道之將廢也與? 命也;公伯寮其如命何!"

14.36　Gongbo Liao submitted an accusation against Zilu to the head of the Ji Family. Zifu Jingbo reported this to Confucius, saying, "The master (i.e. the head of the Ji Family) has certainly been led astray by Gongbo Liao, but I still have the power to add Gongbo Liao's corpse to the market's display of criminals."
The Master said, "Whether or not the Way is to be put into action is a matter of fate. Whether or not the Way is to be discarded is also a matter of fate. What power does Gongbo Liao have to affect fate!"

16.8　孔子曰:"君子有三畏:畏天命,畏大人,畏聖人之言。小人不知天命而不畏也,狎大人,侮聖人之言。"

16.8　The Master said, "The gentleman stands in awe of three things:

the Mandate of Heaven, great men, and the teachings of the sages. The petty person does not understand the Mandate of Heaven, and thus does not regard it with awe; he shows disrespect to great men, and ridicules the teachings of the sages."

20.3　子曰:"不知命,無以爲君子也。不知禮,無以立也。不知言,無以知人也。"

20.3　The Master said, "Without recognizing fate, it is impossible to be a gentleman. Without an acquaintance with the rules of Propriety, it is impossible for the character to be established. Without knowing the force of words, it is impossible to know men."

《孟子》/ Mencius

5A.5　萬章曰:"堯以天下與舜,有諸?"孟子曰:"否,天子不能以天下與人。""然則舜有天下也,孰與之?"曰:"天與之。""天與之者,諄諄然命之乎?"曰:"否,天不言,以行與事示之而已矣。"曰:"以行與事示之者,如之何?"曰:"天子能薦人於天,不能使天與之天下;諸侯能薦人於天子,不能使天子與之諸侯;大夫能薦人於諸侯,不能使諸侯與之大夫。昔者堯薦舜於天而天受之,暴之於民而民受之。故曰:天不言,以行與事示之而已矣。"曰:"敢問薦之於天而天受之,暴之於民而民受之,如何?"曰:"使之主祭而百神享之,是天受之。使之主事而事治,百姓安之,是民受之也。天與之,人與之,故曰:天子不能以天下與人。舜相堯,二十有八載,非人之所能爲也,天也。堯崩,三年之喪畢,舜避堯之子於南河之南。天下諸侯朝覲者,不之堯之子而之舜;訟獄者,不之堯之子而之舜;謳歌者,不謳歌堯之子而謳歌舜;故曰'天'也。夫然後之中國,踐天子位焉。而居堯之宮,逼堯之子,是篡也,非天與也。《泰誓》曰:'天視自我民視,天聽自我民聽',此之謂也。"

5A.5　Wan Zhang said, "Was it the case that Yao gave the throne to Shun?"

Mencius said, "No. The sovereign cannot give the throne to another."

"Ok. But Shun had the throne. Who gave it to him?"

"Heaven gave it to him."

"If Heaven gave it to him, did Heaven confer its appointment on him with specific injunctions?"

Mencius replied, "No. Heaven does not speak. It reveals itself only through actions and events."

"How does it reveal itself through actions and events?"

Mencius replied, "The Son of Heaven can recommend someone to Heaven, but he cannot make Heaven give that man the throne. A prince can recommend a man to the Son of Heaven, but he cannot compel the Son of Heaven to make that man a prince. A minister can recommend a man to his prince, but he cannot compel the prince to make that man a minister. Yao recommended Shun to Heaven, and Heaven accepted him. He presented him to the people, and the people accepted him. Therefore I say, 'Heaven does not speak. It reveals itself only through actions and events.'"

"Yao recommended Shun to Heaven, and Heaven accepted him," repeated Wan Chang. "And Yao presented Shun to the people, and the people accepted him. But how did all this take place?"

"When he put Shun in charge of the sacrifices, the spirits welcomed them. This is how Heaven accepted him. When he put Shun in charge of the nation's affairs, they were well ordered and the people were at peace. This is how the people accepted him. So Heaven gave it to him, and the people gave it to him. This is what I mean when I say the Son of Heaven cannot give all beneath Heaven to another. Shun assisted Yao for twenty-eight years. People aren't capable of such things: only Heaven could have done it. And after Yao died and the three years of mourning had ended, Shun left for lands south of the South River in deference to Yao's son. Even still, when the princes of all beneath Heaven wanted an audience at court, they went to Shun, not Yao's son. When people had lawsuits to settle, they went to Shun, not Yao's son. When choruses sang ballads of praise, they sang of Shun, not Yao's son. This is what I mean when I say it was Heaven. For only after all this happened did Shun return to the Middle Kingdom and take his place as the Son of Heaven. If he'd just moved into Yao's palace and driven

Yao's son out, it would have been usurping the throne rather than receiving it from Heaven. That's why Emperor Wu says, in "The Great Declaration": Heaven sees through the eyes of the people; Heaven hears through the ears of the people."

5A.6 萬章問曰："人有言'至於禹而德衰,不傳於賢而傳於子',有諸?"孟子曰："否然也。天與賢則與賢,天與子則與子。昔者舜薦禹於天,十有七年;舜崩,三年之喪畢,禹避舜之子於陽城;天下之民從之,若堯崩之後不從堯之子而從舜也。禹薦益於天,七年,禹崩,三年之喪畢,益避禹子於箕山之陰;朝覲訟獄者,不之益而之啟,曰:'吾君之子也。'謳歌者不謳歌益而謳歌啟,曰:'吾君之子也。'丹朱之不肖,舜之子亦不肖;舜之相堯、禹之相舜也,歷年多,施澤於民久。啟賢,能敬承繼禹之道;益之相禹也,歷年少,施澤於民未久。舜、禹、益相去久遠,其子之賢不肖皆天也,非人之所能為也。莫之為而為者,天也;莫之致而至者,命也。匹夫而有天下者,德必若舜禹,而又有天子薦之者;故仲尼不有天下。繼世而有天下,天之所廢,必若桀紂者也;故益、伊尹、周公不有天下。伊尹相湯以王於天下,湯崩,太丁未立,外丙二年,仲壬四年。太甲顛覆湯之典刑,伊尹放之於桐三年;太甲悔過,自怨自艾,於桐處仁遷義,三年以聽伊尹之訓己也,復歸于亳。周公之不有天下,猶益之於夏、伊尹之於殷也。孔子曰:'唐虞禪,夏後、殷、周繼,其義一也。'"

5A.6 Wan Zhang asked. "People say 'Yu's virtue was inferior to that of Yao and Shun, because he allowed his son to succeed him rather than choose someone wise and worthy.' Is that true?"

"No," replied Mencius. "That isn't how it works. If Heaven wants to give all beneath Heaven to someone wise and worthy, Heaven gives it to someone wise and worthy. If Heaven wants to give it to a son, Heaven gives it to a son. In ancient times, Shun recommended Yu to Heaven. He died seventeen years later, and when the three years of mourning ended, Yu left for Yang Cheng in deference to Shun's son. However, the people throughout all beneath Heaven followed Yu the way they followed Shun after Yao's death, rather than follow Yao's son. Yu recommended Yi to Heaven. He died seven years later, and when the three years of mourning ended, Yi left for the north slope of the Ji Mountain in deference to Yu's son. But when people wanted an audience at court or they had a lawsuit to settle, they didn't go to Yi, they went to Yu's son Qi. And they said: He's the son of our sovereign. When choruses sang ballads of praise, they sang of Qi, not Yi. And they said: He's the son of our sovereign. Yao's son was depraved; so was Shun's. Meanwhile Shun was Yao's trusted assistant for many years, and Yu was Shun's, so their blessings had rained down on the people for a long time. Qi was wise and worthy, able to carry on Yu's Dao and honor it. Meanwhile Yi was Yu's trusted assistant for only a few years, so his blessings hadn't rained down on the people for long. Yi was far from another Shun or Yu, and there was a great difference in how wise and worthy the emperor's sons were. Such circumstances are all acts of Heaven: people aren't capable of such things. When something's done, but no one does it, it's an act of Heaven. When something happens, but no one makes it happen, it's the Mandate of Heaven. For a common man to rule all beneath Heaven, he needs the virtue of a Shun or Yu. But he also needs the Son of Heaven's recommendation. That's why Confucius never ruled all beneath Heaven. But if someone inherits all beneath Heaven, Heaven won't reject him unless he's a tyrant like Jie or Zhou. That's why Yi, Yi Yin and Duke Zhou never ruled all beneath Heaven. Because Yi Yin was his trusted assistant, Tang became emperor of all beneath Heaven. When Tang died, Tai Ding was no longer alive to succeed him. Wai Bing ruled for two years, and Zhong Ren four. Then Tai Jia overthrew the laws of Tang, so Yi Yin banished him to Tong. After three years, Tai Jia began to regret his crimes. He reproached himself and changed. There in Tong, he brought himself into righteousness and dwelled in benevolence. After another three years, having taken Yi Yin's admonitions to heart, he returned to Bo. Duke Zhou never ruled all beneath Heaven in the Zhou Dynasty, and it was for the same reason that Yi never ruled in the Xia and Yi Yin never ruled in the Shang. Confucius said, "With Yao and Shun, succession was through abdication to their chosen successors. With the founders of the Xia, Shang and Zhou Dynasties, succession was hereditary. But for all, the principle was the same."

7A.1　孟子曰："盡其心者,知其性也。知其性,則知天矣。存其心,養其性,所以事天也。夭壽不貳,修身以俟之,所以立命也。"

7A.1　Mencius said, "By fully developing one's mind, one knows one's nature. Knowing one's nature, one knows Heaven. Foster your mind, nurture your nature, then you are serving Heaven. Don't worry about dying young or living long. What will come will come. Cultivate yourself well and be patient in that perfection, let it come, and then you will stand firm in your destiny."

7A.2　孟子曰："莫非命也,順受其正。是故知命者,不立乎巖牆之下。盡其道而死者,正命也。桎梏死者,非正命也。"

7A.2　Mencius said, "There is, for everything, a destiny, but one should follow and accept only what is proper for oneself. Therefore, one who knows destiny does not stand under a wall in danger of collapsing. To die in the course of fulfilling the Dao is a proper destiny, while dying in manacles and fetters is not a proper destiny."

7A.3　孟子曰："'求則得之,舍則失之',是求有益於得也,求在我者也。'求之有道,得之有命',是求無益於得也,求在外者也。"

7A.3　Mencius said: "'What you seek you will find, and what you ignore you will lose.' Where this saying is right, such seeking is conducive to getting, for what I seek lies within myself. 'Though my seeking is in accordance with the Way, yet getting depends on destiny.' Where this is right, such seeking is not conducive to getting, for we're seeking something outside ourselves."

《墨子》/ Mozi

天志上第二十七
Chapter 27　Will of Heaven Ⅰ

见"義利"部分《墨子》选读

For the English translation of this chapter, see Part Ⅱ of this book.

非命上第三十五
Chapter 35　Anti-Fatalism Ⅰ

子墨子言曰：古者王公大人爲政國家者，皆欲國家之富，人民之衆，刑政之治。然而不得富而得貧，不得衆而得寡，不得治而得亂，則是本失其所欲，得其所惡，是故何也？子墨子言曰：執有命者以雜於民間者衆。執有命者之言曰："命富則富，命貧則貧，命衆則衆，命寡則寡，命治則治，命亂則亂，命壽則壽，命夭則夭。命雖強勁，何益哉？"上以説王公大人，下以駔百姓之從事。故執有命者不仁，故當執有命者之言，不可不明辨。

Mozi said: At present, in governing the states the rulers all desire to have their countries wealthy, their population large, and their administration orderly. But instead of wealth they obtain poverty, and instead of an increase they obtain a decrease in population, and instead of order they obtain chaos; i.e. they lose what they like but obtain what they dislike. What is the reason for this? Mozi said: It is due to the large number of fatalists among the people. The fatalists say, "When fate decrees that a man shall be wealthy he will be wealthy; when it decrees poverty, he will be poor; when it decrees a large population, it will be large; and when it decrees a small population, it will be small; if order is decreed, there will be order; if chaos, there will be chaos. If fate decrees old age, there will be old age; if untimely death, there will be untimely death. Even if a man sets himself against his fate, what is the use?" With this doctrine the rulers are urged above and the people are kept away from their work below. Hence the fatalists are unmagnanimous. And their doctrines must be clearly examined.

然則明辨此之說,將奈何哉?子墨子言曰:言必立儀。言而毋儀,譬猶運鈞之上而立朝夕者也,是非利害之辨,不可得而明知也。故言必有三表。何謂三表?子墨子言曰:有本之者,有原之者,有用之者。於何本之?上本之於古者聖王之事。於何原之?下原察百姓耳目之實。於何用之?廢以爲刑政,觀其中國家百姓人民之利。此所謂言有三表也。

Now, how is this doctrine to be examined? Mozi said: Some standard of judgment must be established. To expound a doctrine without regard to the standard is similar to determining the directions of sunrise and sunset on a revolving potter's wheel. By this means the distinction of right and wrong, benefit and harm, cannot be known. Therefore there must be three tests. What are the three tests? Mozi said: Its basis, its verifiability, and its applicability. How is it to be based? It should be based on the deeds of the ancient sage-kings. How is it to be verified? It is to be verified by the senses of hearing and sight of the common people. How is it to be applied? It is to be applied by adopting it in government and observing its benefits to the country and the people. This is what is meant by the three tests of every doctrine.

然而今天下之士君子,或以命爲有,蓋嘗尚觀於聖王之事。古者桀之所亂,湯受而治之。紂之所亂,武王受而治之。此世未易,民未渝,在於桀、紂則天下亂,在於湯、武則天下治。豈可謂有命哉!

Some of the gentlemen of the world assume there to be fate. Now let us examine the deeds of the sage-kings. In ancient times, the confusion produced by Jie was replaced by an orderly government by Tang, and the chaos of Zhou was turned into order by King Wu. The times did not alter and the people did not change, yet under Jie and Zhou the world was chaotic and under Tang and Wu it was orderly. Can it be said that there is fate?

然而今天下之士君子,或以命爲有,蓋嘗尚觀於先王之書。先王之書,所以出國家、佈施百姓者,憲也。先王之憲亦嘗有曰"福不可請,而禍不可諱,敬無益、暴無傷"者乎? 所以聽獄制罪者,刑也。先王之刑亦嘗有曰"福不可請,禍不可諱,敬無益、暴無傷"者乎? 所以整設師旅、進退師徒者,誓也。先王之誓亦嘗有曰"福不可請,禍不可諱,敬無益、暴無傷"者乎? 是故子墨子言曰:吾當未鹽數,天下之良書不可盡計數,大方論數,而五者是也。今雖毋求執有命者之言,不必得,不亦可錯乎?

But the gentlemen of the world still assume that there is fate. Now let us look at some of the writings of the early kings. The writings of the early kings that were issued to the whole country and distributed among the people were the laws. Did any of the laws of the early kings ever say "Blessing cannot be invoked and disaster cannot be avoided; reverence will not do any good and cruelty will not do any harm"? The standards according to which lawsuits were tried and punishments were meted out were the codes of punishment. Did any of the codes of punishment of the early kings say "Blessing cannot be invoked and disaster cannot be avoided; reverence will not do any good and cruelty will not do any harm"? The inspiration by which the armies were organized and the soldiers were commanded to advance or to retreat came from the declarations. Did any of the declarations of the early kings say "Blessing cannot be invoked and disaster cannot be avoided; reverence will do no good and cruelty will do no harm"? Mozi said: I have not enumerated the good books of the empire completely. As they cannot be exhaustively enumerated, I limit myself to the most prominent ones, namely, the three above mentioned. And try as we may, we cannot find any belief in the doctrine of fatalism. Should it not then be abandoned?

今用執有命者之言,是覆天下之義。覆天下之義者,是立命者也,百姓之誶也。説百姓之誶者,是滅天下之人也。然則所爲欲義在上者,何也? 曰:義人在上，天下必治，上帝、山川、鬼神必有幹主，萬民被其大利。何以知之？子墨子曰：古者湯封於亳，絕長繼短，方地百里，與其百姓兼相愛，交相利，移則分。率其百姓，以上尊天事鬼。是以天鬼富之，諸侯與之，百姓親之，賢士歸之，未殁其世而王天下，政諸侯。昔者文王封於岐周，絕長繼短，方地百里，與其百姓兼相愛，交相利，則，是以近者安其政，遠者歸其德。聞文王者皆起而趨之，罷不肖股肱不利者，處而願之，曰："奈何乎使文王之地及我吾，則吾利豈不亦猶文王之民也哉！"是以天鬼富之，諸侯與之，百姓親之，賢士歸之。未殁其世而王天下，政諸侯。鄉者言曰：義人在上，天下必治，上帝、山川、鬼神必有幹主，萬民被其大利。吾用此知之。

To adopt the fatalists' doctrine is to overthrow righteousness in the world. To overthrow righteousness in the world will establish fate, which is a temptation to the people. And to offer people temptation is to destroy the people. Now, why is it that we desire righteousness to be with the superiors? Because when the righteous are in authority, the world will have order, God, hills and rivers, and the spirits will have their chief sacrificer, and the people will be visited by the great blessings therefrom. How do we know? Mozi said: In ancient times, Tang was given a fief at Bo. Taking allowance for the irregular boundary lines, his land amounted to about a hundred li square. He worked with the people for mutual love and reciprocal benefit, and shared with them what was in abundance. And he led his people to reverence Heaven and worship the spirits. Thereupon, Heaven and the spirits enriched him, the feudal lords befriended him, the people loved him, and the virtuous came to him. Within a single generation he ruled over the empire and headed the feudal lords. Again in ancient times, King Wen was assigned to the state of Qi Zhou. Making allowance for the irregular boundary lines, his land amounted to about a hundred li square. He worked with his people for mutual love and reciprocal benefit. So those near him enjoyed his government and those distant submitted themselves to his virtues. All who heard of King Wen rose up and rushed over to him. The stupid and insolent and those weak in limbs remained where they were and complained, "Why not let the land of King Wen extend to this place. Wouldn't I then also be a subject of King Wen?" Thereupon Heaven and the spirits enriched him, the feudal lords befriended him, the people loved him and the virtuous came to him. Within a single generation he ruled over the whole empire and headed the feudal lords. As we have said: When the righteous are in authority the world will have order, God, hills and rivers, and the spirits will have their chief sacrificer, and the people will be visited by the great benefits therefrom. And this is how we know it to be so.

是故古之聖王,發憲出令,設以爲賞罰以勸賢。是以入則孝慈於親戚,出則弟長於鄉里,坐處有度,出入有節,男女有辨。是故使治官府則不盜竊,守城則不崩叛,君有難則死,出亡則送。此上之所賞,而百姓之所譽也。執有命者之言曰:"上之所賞,命固且賞,非賢故賞也。上之所罰,命固且罰,命固且罰,不暴故罰也。"是故入則不慈孝於親戚,出則不弟長於鄉里,坐處不度,出入無節,男女無辨。是故治官府則盜竊,守城則崩叛,君有難則不死,出亡則不送。此上之所罰,百姓之所非毀也。執有命者言曰:"上之所罰,命固且罰,不暴故罰也。上之所賞,命固且賞,非賢故賞也。"以此爲君則不義,爲臣則不忠,爲父則不慈,爲子則不孝,爲兄則不長,爲弟則不弟。而強執此者,此特凶言之所自生,而暴人之道也。

The ancient sage-kings published laws and issued orders to be standards of reward and punishment, and to encourage the virtuous and to obstruct the evil. And so the people were filial to their parents at home and respectful to the elders in the village or the district. They observed propriety in conduct, moderation in going out and coming in, and decency between men and women. And when they were made to look after the court they would not steal; when they were made to defend a city they would not raise an insurrection. When the lord met with death they would commit suicide, and when the lord was banished they would follow him. This is what the superior will reward and what the people will applaud. Now, the fatalists say, "Whoever is rewarded by the superior is destined to be rewarded. It is not because of his virtue that he is rewarded. Whoever is punished by the superior is destined to be punished. It is not because of his vice that he is punished." Under these conditions the people would not be filial to their parents at home, and respectful to the elders in the village or the district.

They would not observe propriety in conduct, moderation in going out and coming in, or decency between men and women. And, if they were made to look after the court they would steal; if they were made to defend a city they would raise an insurrection. If the lord met with death they would not commit suicide, and if the lord were banished they would not accompany him. This is what the superior will punish, and what the people will condemn. The fatalists say, "Whoever is punished by the superior is destined to be punished. It is not because of his vice that he is punished." Believing in this, the ruler would not be righteous, the minister would not be loyal, the father would not be affectionate, the son would not be filial, the elder brother would not be brotherly, and the younger brother would not be respectful. The unnatural adherence to this doctrine is responsible for pernicious ideas and is the way of the wicked.

然則何以知命之爲暴人之道？昔上世之窮民，貪於飲食，惰於從事，是以衣食之財不足，而饑寒凍餒之憂至。不知曰我罷不肖，從事不疾，必曰我命固且貧。昔上世暴王，不忍其耳目之淫，心塗之辟，不順其親戚，遂以亡失國家，傾覆社稷。不知曰我罷不肖，爲政不善，必曰吾命固失之。於《仲虺之告》曰："我聞於夏人，矯天命，布命於下。帝伐之惡，龔喪厥師。"此言湯之所以非桀之執有命也。於《太誓》曰："紂夷處，不肯事上帝鬼神，禍厥先神禔不祀，乃曰：'吾民有命。無廖排漏'。天亦縱棄之而弗葆。"此言武王所以非紂執有命也。今用執有命者之言，則上不聽治，下不從事。上不聽治，則刑政亂；下不從事，則財用不足。上無以供粢盛酒醴，祭祀上帝鬼神，下無以降綏天下賢可之士，外無以應待諸侯之賓客，內無以食饑衣寒，將養老弱。故命上不利於天，中不利於鬼，下不利於人。而强執此者，此特凶言之所自生，而暴人之道也！

Now how do we know fatalism is the way of the wicked? In ancient times, the miserable people indulged in drinking and eating and were lazy in their work. Thereupon their food and clothing became insufficient, and the danger of hunger and cold was approaching. They did not acknowledge, "I was stupid and insolent and was not diligent at work." But they would say, "It is but my lot to be poor." The ancient wicked kings did not control the sensuality of their ears and eyes and the passions of their mind. They did not follow their ancestors and so they lost their country and ruined their state. They did not know that they should confess, "I am stupid and insolent and was not diligent in attending to government." But they would say, "It is but my fate to lose it." "The Announcement of Zhong Hui" says, "I have heard that the man of Xia issued orders, pretending them to be fate of Heaven. God was displeased and destroyed his forces." This tells how Tang showed Jie's belief in fate to be wrong. "The Great Declaration" says, "Zhou became insolent and would not worship God and pushed away the ancestors and spirits without offering them sacrifices. And he said, 'Fortune is with my people,' and neglected and betrayed his duty. Heaven thereupon deserted him and withdrew its protection." This tells how King Wu showed Zhou's belief in fate to be wrong. If the doctrine of the fatalist were put to practice, the superiors would not attend to government and the subordinates would not attend to work. If the superior does not attend to government, jurisdiction and administration will be in chaos. If the subordinates do not attend to work, wealth will not be sufficient. Then, there will not be wherewith to provide for the cakes and wine to worship and do sacrifice to God, ghosts and spirits above, and there will not be wherewith to tranquillize the virtuous of the world below; there will not be wherewith to entertain the noble guests from without, and there will not be wherewith to feed the hungry, clothe the cold, and care for the aged and weak within. Therefore fatalism is not helpful to Heaven above, nor to the spirits in the middle sphere, nor to man below. The eccentric belief in this doctrine is responsible for pernicious ideas and is the way of the wicked.

是故子墨子言曰：今天下之士君子，忠實欲天下之富而惡其貧，欲天下之治而惡其亂，執有命者之言不可不非，此天下之大害也。

Therefore Mozi said: If the gentlemen in the world really desire to have the world rich and do not want to have it poor, desire to have it orderly and dislike to have it in confusion, the doctrine of fatalism must be rejected. It is a great calamity to the world.

《莊子》/ Zhuangzi

大宗師第六
Chapter 6   The Great and Most Honored Master

死生,命也,其有夜旦之常,天也。人之有所不得與,皆物之情也。彼特以天爲父,而身猶愛之,而況其卓乎！人特以有君爲愈乎己,而身猶死之,而況其真乎！

Life and death are fated—constant as the succession of dark and dawn, a matter of Heaven. There are some things that man can do nothing about—all are a matter of the nature of creatures. If a man is willing to regard Heaven as a father and to love it, then how much more should he be willing to do for that which is even greater! If he is willing to regard the ruler as superior to himself and to die for him, then how much more should he be willing to do for something truer than any ruler.

泉涸,魚相與處於陸,相呴以濕,相濡以沫,不如相忘於江湖。與其譽堯而非桀也,不如兩忘而化其道。

When the springs dry up and the fish are left stranded on the ground, they spew one another with moisture and wet one another down with spit, but it would be much better if they could forget one another in the rivers and lakes. Instead of praising Yao and condemning Jie, it would be better to forget both of them and transform yourself with the Way.

夫藏舟於壑,藏山於澤,謂之固矣。然而夜半有力者負之而走,昧者不知也。藏小大有宜,猶有所遯。若夫藏天下於天下而不得所遯,是恆物之大情也。……故聖人將遊於物之所不得遯而皆存。善夭善老,善始善終,人猶效之,又況萬物之所係,而一化之所待乎！

Suppose you hide your boat in the ravine and your fish net in the swamp. Suppose you tell yourself that they will be safe. But in the middle of the night, a strong man shoulders them and carries them off, and in your stupidity, you don't know why it has happened. You think you do right to hide little things in big ones, and yet they get away from you. Only if you hide all beneath Heaven inside all beneath Heaven, so there's nothing more into which it can vanish—only then have you reached the vast nature of the timeless thing. ... Therefore, the sage wanders in the realm where things cannot get away from him, and all are preserved. He delights in early death; he delights in old age; he delights in the beginning; he delights in the end. We might make such a person our teacher, but there's something the ten thousand things belong to, something all change depends upon—imagine making that your teacher!

夫道，有情有信，无爲无形；可傳而不可受，可得而不可見；自本自根，未有天地，自古以固存；神鬼神帝，生天生地；在太極之先而不爲高，在六極之下而不爲深，先天地生而不爲久，長於上古而不爲老。……

The Dao has its reality and its signs but is without action or form. You can hand it down, but you cannot receive it; you can get it, but you cannot see it. It is its own source, its own root. Before Heaven and Earth existed, it was there, firm from ancient times. It gave spirituality to the spirits and to God; it gave birth to Heaven and to Earth. It exists beyond the highest point, and yet you cannot call it lofty; it exists beneath the limit of the six directions, and yet you cannot call it deep. It was born before Heaven and Earth, and yet you cannot say it has been there for long; it is earlier than the earliest time, and yet you cannot call it old. ...

子祀、子輿、子犂、子來四人相與語曰：" 孰能以無爲首，以生爲脊，以死爲尻，孰知死生存亡之一體者，吾與之友矣。" 四人相視而笑，莫逆於心，遂相與爲友。

俄而子輿有病，子祀往問之。曰："偉哉夫造物者，將以予爲此拘拘也！曲僂發背，上有五管，頤隱於齊，肩高於頂，句贅指天。陰陽之氣有沴。"其心閒而无事，跰𨅖而鑑於井，曰："嗟乎！夫造物者又將以予爲此拘拘也。"

子祀曰："女惡之乎？"曰："亡，予何惡！浸假而化予之左臂以爲雞，予因以求時夜；浸假而化予之右臂以爲彈，予因以求鴞炙；浸假而化予之尻以爲輪，以神爲馬，予因以乘之，豈更駕哉！且夫得者，時也；失者，順也。安時而處順，哀樂不能入也。此古之所謂縣解也。而不能自解者，物有結之。且失物不勝天久矣，吾又何惡焉！"

俄而子來有病，喘喘然將死。其妻子環而泣之。子犁往問之，曰："叱！避！无怛化！"倚其户與之語曰："偉哉造化，又將奚以汝爲，將奚以汝適？以汝爲鼠肝乎？以汝爲蟲臂乎？"

子來曰："父母於子，東西南北，唯命之從。陰陽於人，不翅於父母；彼近吾死而我不聽，我則悍矣，彼何罪焉！夫大塊載我以形，勞我以生，佚我以老，息我以死。故善吾生者，乃所以善吾死也。今大冶鑄金，金踴躍曰'我且必爲鏌鋣'，大冶必以爲不祥之金。今一犯人之形，而曰'人耳人耳'，夫造化者必以爲不祥之人。今一以天地爲大爐，以造化爲大冶，惡乎往而不可哉！成然寐，蘧然覺。"

Zisi, Ziyu, Zili, and Zilai met one day. Talking together, they said, "Who can make non-being their head, life their spine, and death their butt? Who can understand that birth and death, living and dead are all one body? I will be his friend!" The four men looked at one another and smiled. There was no disagreement in their hearts, and so the four of them became friends.

All at once, Ziyu fell ill. Zisi went to ask how he was. "Amazing!" said Ziyu. "The Creator is making me all crooked like this! My back sticks up like a hunchback, and my vital organs are on top of me. My chin is hidden in my navel, my shoulders are up above my head, and my pigtail points at the sky. It must be some dislocation of the yin and yang!" Yet he seemed calm at heart and unconcerned. He hobbled over to a well, looked at himself in the water, and said, "My, my! So the Creator is making me all crooked like this!"

"Do you resent it?" asked Zisi. "No, what would I resent? If the process continues, perhaps in time he'll transform my left arm into a rooster. In that case I'll crow at the crack of dawn. Or perhaps in time he'll transform my right arm into a crossbow pellet, and I'll shoot down an owl for roasting. Or perhaps in time he'll transform my buttocks into cartwheels and my spirit into a horse, I'll just ride away. What need will I ever have for a carriage again? I received life because the time had come; I will lose it because the order of things passes on. Be content with this time and dwell in this order, and then neither sorrow nor joy can touch you. In ancient times this was called the 'freeing of the bound'. There are those who cannot free themselves because they are bound by things. But nothing can ever win against Heaven—that's the way it's always been. What would I have to resent?"

Suddenly Zilai grew ill. Gasping and wheezing, he lay at the point of death. His wife and children gathered round in a circle and began to cry. Zili, who had come to ask how he was, said, "Shoo! Get back! Don't disturb the process of change!" Then he leaned against the doorway and talked to Zilai. "How marvelous the Creator is! What is he going to make out of you next? Where is he going to send you? Will he make you into a rat's liver? Will he make you into a bug's arm?"

Zilai said, "A child, obeying his father and mother, goes wherever he is told, east or west, south or north. And the yin and yang—how much more are they to a man than father or mother! Now that they have brought me to the verge of death, if I should refuse to obey them, how perverse I would be! What fault is it of theirs? The Great Clod creates me with form, labors me with life, eases me in old age, and rests me in death. So if I think well of my life, for the same reason I must think well of my death. When a skilled smith is casting metal, if the metal should leap up and say, 'No, no, I must be one of those legendary Moye swords!' he would surely regard it as very inauspicious metal indeed. Now, having chanced upon the human form, if I should say, 'I don't want to be anything but a human! Nothing but a human!' the Creator would surely regard me as an inauspicious person. So now I think of Heaven and Earth as a great furnace, and the Creator as a skilled smith. Where could he send me that would not be all right? I will go off to sleep peacefully, and then with a start, I will wake up."

子桑户、孟子反、子琴張相與友，曰："孰能相與於无相與，相爲於无相爲？孰能登天遊霧，撓挑無極，相忘以生，無所終窮？"三人相視而笑，莫逆於心，遂相與爲友。

莫然有閒而子桑户死，未葬。孔子聞之，使子貢往侍事焉。或編曲，或鼓琴，相和而歌曰："嗟來桑户乎！嗟來桑户乎！而已反其真，而我猶爲人猗！"子貢趨而進曰："敢問臨尸而歌，禮乎？"二人相視而笑曰："是惡知禮意！"

子貢反，以告孔子，曰："彼何人者邪？修行無有，而外其形骸，臨尸而歌，顏色不變，無以命之，彼何人者邪？"孔子曰："彼，遊方之外者也；而丘，遊方之内者也。内外不相及，而丘使汝往弔之，丘則陋矣。彼方且與造物者爲人，而遊乎天地之一氣。彼以生爲附贅縣疣，以死爲決疯潰癰，夫若然者，又惡知死生先後之所在！假於異物，託於同體；忘其肝膽，遺其耳目，反覆終始，不知端倪；芒然彷徨乎塵垢之外，逍遥乎無爲之業。彼又惡能憒憒然爲世俗之禮，以觀衆人之耳目哉！"

子貢曰"然則，夫子何方之依？"孔子曰："丘，天之戮民也。雖然，吾與汝共之。"子貢曰："敢問其方。"孔子曰："魚相造乎水，人相造乎道。相造乎水者，穿池而養給；相造乎道者，無事而生定。故曰：魚相忘乎江湖，人相忘乎道術。"

子貢曰："敢問畸人。"曰："畸人者，畸於人而侔於天。故曰，天之小人，人之君子；人之君子，天之小人也。"

Zisanghu, Mengzi Fan, and Ziqinzhang, three friends, said to one another, "Who can make friends without the intention to make friends? Who can help each other without the intention to help each other? Who can climb up to Heaven and wander in the mists, roam the infinite, and forget life forever and forever?" The three men looked at one another and smiled. There was no disagreement in their hearts, and so they became friends.

Things went along quietly for a time. Zisanghu died. He had not yet been buried when Confucius, hearing of his death, sent Zigong to pay his respects at the funeral. When Zigong arrived, he found one of the dead man's friends weaving frames for silkworms, while the other played the Qin. Suddenly they broke into song together, " Ah, Zisanghu! Ah, Zisanghu! You have gone back to your true form while we remain as men, O!" Zigong hastened forward and said, "May I be so bold as to ask what sort of ceremony this is—singing in the very presence of the corpse?" The two men looked at each other and laughed. "What does this man know of the meaning of ceremony?" they said.

Zigong returned and reported to Confucius what had happened. "What sort of men are they, anyway?" he asked. "They pay no attention to proper behavior and disregard their personal appearance. They sing to their dead friend's corpse, not a trace of grief in their faces. There aren't words to describe them. What sort of men are they?"

"Such men as they," said Confucius, "wander beyond the realm; men like me wander within it. Beyond and within can never meet. It was stupid of me to send you to offer condolences. Even now they have joined with the Creator as men to wander in the single breath of Heaven and Earth. For them, life is a useless appendage, a swollen tumor, and death is like a boil breaking open or pus draining from a festering sore. To men such as these, how could there be any question of putting life first or death last? They borrow the forms of different creatures and house them in the same body. They forget liver and gall, cast aside ears and eyes, turning and revolving, ending and beginning again, unaware of where they start or finish. Idly they roam beyond the dust and dirt; they wander free and easy in the service of inaction. Why should they fret and fuss about the ceremonies of the vulgar world and make a display for the ears and eyes of the common herd?"

Zigong said, "Well then, Master, what is this 'realm' that you stick to?" Confucius said, "I am one of those men punished by Heaven. Nevertheless, I will share with you what I have." "Then may I ask about the realm?" said Zigong. Confucius said, "Fish thrive in water, man thrives in the Dao. For those that thrive in water, dig a pond, and they will find nourishment enough. For those that thrive in the Dao, don't bother about them, and their lives will be secure. So it is said, the fish forget one another in the rivers and lakes, and men forget one another in the arts of the Dao."

Zigong said, "May I ask about the singular man?" "The singular man is singular in comparison to other men, but a companion of Heaven. So it is said, the petty man in Heaven is a gentleman among men; the gentleman among men is a petty man in Heaven."

顏回問仲尼曰:"孟孫才,其母死,哭泣無涕,中心不戚,居喪不哀。無是三者,以善處喪蓋魯國。固有無其實而得其名者乎?回壹怪之。"

仲尼曰:"夫孟孫氏盡之矣,進於知矣。唯簡之而不得,夫已有所簡矣。孟孫氏不知所以生,不知所以死;不知就先,不知就後;若化爲物,以待其所不知之化已乎!且方將化,惡知不化哉?方將不化,惡知已化哉?吾特與汝,其夢未始覺者邪!且彼有駭形而无損心,有旦宅而无情死。孟孫氏特覺,人哭亦哭,是自其所以乃。且也相與吾之耳矣,庸詎知吾所謂吾之乎?且汝夢爲鳥而厲乎天,夢爲魚而沒於淵。不識今之言者,其覺者乎?其夢者乎?造適不及笑,獻笑不及排,安排而去化,乃入於寥天一。"

Yan Hui said to Confucius, "When Mengsun Cai's mother died, he wailed without shedding any tears; he did not grieve in his heart, and he conducted the funeral without any look of sorrow. In spite of these three failings, he is known all over the state of Lu for the excellent way he managed the funeral. Is it really possible to gain such a reputation when there are no facts to support it? This seems utterly bizarre to me!"

Confucius said, "Mengsun did all there was to do. He was advanced beyond ordinary understanding, and he would have simplified things even more, but that wasn't practical. However, there is still a lot that he simplified. Mengsun doesn't know why he lives and doesn't know why he dies. He doesn't know why he should go ahead; he doesn't know why he should fall behind. Like any other thing inhabiting change, he simply waits for whatever unfathomed transformation may come over him next. Moreover, when he is changing, how does he know that he really is changing? And when he is not changing, how does he know that he hasn't already changed? You and I, now—we are dreaming and haven't waked up yet. But in his case, though his body looks fearful, his mind remains unperturbed; though his body decays, his true nature never dies. Mengsun alone has waked up. Others wail and so he wails, too—that's the reason he acts like this. What's more, we go around telling one another, I do this, I do that—but how do we know that this 'I' we talk about has any 'I' to it? You dream you're a bird and soar up into the sky; you dream you're a fish and dive down in the pool. Do you know when you are speaking, you are awake or you are just dreaming? A pilgrimage can't compare to a good laugh, and a good laugh can't compare to simply letting yourself go. Once you're at peace, letting yourself go and leaving change behind, you can enter the mysterious oneness of Heaven."①

子輿與子桑友,而霖雨十日,子輿曰:"子桑殆病矣!"裹飯而往食之。至子桑之門,則若歌若哭,鼓琴曰:"父邪! 母邪! 天乎! 人乎!"有不任其聲而趨舉其詩焉。子輿入,曰:"子之歌詩,何故若是?"曰:"吾思夫使我至此極者而弗得也。父母豈欲吾貧哉? 天無私覆,地無私載,天地豈私貧我哉? 求其為之者而不得也。然而至此極者,命也夫!"

Ziyu and Zisang were friends. Once, after ten days of steady rain, Ziyu said to himself, "Zisang must be getting desperate by now." So he wrapped up some food and set out to comfort his friend. When he arrived at Zisang's gate, he heard a kind of song, or sob—someone plays the Qin and chanting, "Father? Mother? Heaven? Human?" It was as though the voice would not hold out and the singer were rushing to get through the words.

Ziyu went inside and asked, "Your song, its words—why are they like this?" "I was pondering what it is that has brought me to this extremity, but I couldn't find the answer. My father and mother surely wouldn't wish this poverty on me. Heaven covers all without partiality; Earth bears up all without partiality—Heaven and Earth surely wouldn't single me out to make me poor. I try to discover who is doing it, but I can't get the answer. Still, here I am—at the very extreme. It must be fate."

---

① Here I adopt Hinton's rendering of "造適不及笑,獻笑不及排", which is different from the standard interpretation offered by Chinese scholars. I think Hinton's rendering makes more sense.

《荀子》／ Xunzi

天論篇第十七
Chapter 17　Discourse on Heaven

　　天行有常，不爲堯存，不爲桀亡。應之以治則吉，應之以亂則凶。彊本而節用，則天不能貧；養備而動時，則天不能病；脩道而不貳，則天不能禍。故水旱不能使之飢，寒暑不能使之疾，祅怪不能使之凶。本荒而用侈，則天不能使之富；養略而動罕，則天不能使之全；倍道而妄行，則天不能使之吉。故水旱未至而飢，寒暑未薄而疾，祅怪未至而凶。受時與治世同，而殃禍與治世異，不可以怨天，其道然也。故明於天人之分，則可謂至人矣。

　　There is a constancy to the activities of Heaven. They do not persist because of Yao. They do not perish because of Jie. If you respond to them with good government, then you will have good fortune. If you respond to them with disorder, then you will have misfortune. If you strengthen agriculture and use resources carefully and wisely, then Heaven cannot make you poor. If you take care of your body and take action at the appropriate times, Heaven cannot make you ill. If you cultivate yourself in light of the Dao and do not deviate from it, then Heaven cannot ruin you. Thus, floods and drought cannot make you go hungry or thirsty, cold and heat cannot make you sick, and strange phenomena cannot make you misfortunate. If agriculture is neglected and resources are used extravagantly, then Heaven cannot make you wealthy. If you do not take care of your body and rarely take action, then Heaven cannot make you healthy. If you go against the Dao and act recklessly, then Heaven cannot make you fortunate. And so, although floods and drought have not yet come, you still will go hungry. Although heat and cold are not yet pressing, you will still become sick. Although strange phenomena have not yet come, you will still be misfortunate. The seasons will visit you as they do in a well-ordered age, but you will suffer misfortunes that a well-ordered age does not know. Yet you must not curse Heaven, for it is merely the natural result of your own actions. Therefore, those who understand that Heaven and man play different roles can be called a person of utmost achievement or a perfect person.

不爲而成,不求而得,夫是之謂天職。如是者,雖深,其人不加慮焉;雖大,不加能焉;雖精,不加察焉,夫是之謂不與天爭職。天有其時,地有其財,人有其治,夫是之謂能參。舍其所以參,而願其所參,則惑矣。

To bring to completion without acting, to obtain without seeking—this is the work of Heaven. Thus, although the sage has deep understanding, he does not attempt to exercise it upon the work of Heaven; though he has great talent, he does not attempt to apply it to the work of Heaven; though he has keen perception, he does not attempt to use it on the work of Heaven. This is called "not competing with Heaven". When Heaven has its proper seasons, Earth has its proper resources, and man has its proper order. Hence man may form a triad with the other two. If you give up what man can contribute, to envy what Heaven and Earth have contributed, you are confused.

列星隨旋,日月遞炤,四時代御,陰陽大化,風雨博施,萬物各得其和以生,各得其養以成,不見其事,而見其功,夫是之謂神。皆知其所以成,莫知其無形,夫是之謂天功。唯聖人爲不求知天。

The arrayed stars follow each other in their revolutions, the sun and the moon take turns shining, the four seasons proceed in succession, yin and yang undergo their great transformations, and winds and rain are broadly bestowed. Their harmony keeps the myriad things alive. Their nurturing helps the myriad things thrive. One does not see the process taking place, but sees only the results. Thus it is called spirit-like power. All men understand that the process has reached completion, but none understands the formless forces that bring it about. This is called the accomplishment of

Heaven. Only the sage does not seek to understand Heaven.

天職既立，天功既成，形具而神生，好惡喜怒哀樂臧焉，夫是之謂天情。耳目鼻口形能各有接而不相能也，夫是之謂天官。心居中虛，以治五官，夫是之謂天君。財非其類以養其類，夫是之謂天養。順其類者謂之福，逆其類者謂之禍，夫是之謂天政。暗其天君，亂其天官，棄其天養，逆其天政，背其天情，以喪天功，夫是之謂大凶。聖人清其天君，正其天官，備其天養，順其天政，養其天情，以全其天功。如是，則知其所爲，知其所不爲矣；則天地官而萬物役矣。其行曲治，其養曲適，其生不傷，夫是之謂知天。

When the work of Heaven has been established and its accomplishments brought to completion, when the form of man is whole and his spirit is born, then love and hate, delight and anger, sorrow and joy find lodging in him. These are called his Heavenly emotions. Ears, eyes, nose, mouth, and body all have that which they perceive, but they cannot substitute for one another. They are called the Heavenly faculties. The heart dwells in the center and governs the five faculties, and hence it is called the Heavenly lord. Food and provisions are not of the same species as man, and yet they serve to nourish him and are called Heavenly nourishment. To be in accordance with what is proper for one's kind is called happiness, and to go against what is proper for one's kind is called disaster—this is called one's Heavenly government. To becloud your Heavenly lord, disorder your Heavenly faculties, abandon your Heavenly nourishment, go against your Heavenly government, and turn your back on your Heavenly motions, so that you lose the accomplishments of Heaven—this is called the greatest misfortune. The sage keeps clear his Heavenly lord, sets straight his Heavenly faculties, makes complete his Heavenly nourishment, accords with his Heavenly government, and nurtures his Heavenly motions, so as to keep whole the accomplishment of Heaven. Thus he knows what he is to do and what he is not to do. Then Heaven and Earth will have their proper positions and the myriad things will all be servants to him. His conduct will be completely ordered, his nourishment will be completely appropriate, and his life will suffer no harm—this is called knowing Heaven.

故大巧在所不爲,大智在所不慮。所志於天者,已其見象之可以期者矣;所志於地者,已其見宜之可以息者矣;所志於四時者,已其見數之可以事者矣;所志於陰陽者,已其見和之可以治者矣。官人守天,而自爲守道也。

Hence the really skilled man has things which he does not do; the really wise man has things that he does not ponder. When he turns his thoughts to Heaven, he seeks to understand only those phenomena which can be regularly expected. When he turns his thoughts to Earth, he seeks to understand only those aspects that can be taken advantage of. When he turns his thoughts to the four seasons, he seeks to understand only the changes that will affect his undertakings. When he turns his thoughts to the yin and yang, he seeks to understand only the modulations which call for some action on his part. Let the officials keep watch over Heaven and yourself keep watch over the Dao.①

治亂,天邪? 曰:日月星辰瑞厤,是禹桀之所同也,禹以治,桀以亂;治亂非天也。時邪? 曰:繁啟蕃長於春夏,畜積收臧於秋冬,是禹桀之所同也,禹以治,桀以亂;治亂非時也。地邪? 曰:得地則生,失地則死,是又禹桀之所同也,禹以治,桀以亂;治亂非地也。《詩》曰:"天作高山,大王荒之。彼作矣,文王康之。"此之謂也。

Are social order/disorder caused by Heaven? I say: The sun, the moon, and the stars are wondrous calendrical phenomena. These things were the same for both Yu and Jie, but Yu brought order, while Jie brought disorder. So order and disorder are not caused by Heaven.

Are social order and disorder caused by the change of seasons? I say: In spring and summer things flourish, blossom, prosper, and grow. In fall and winter they are gathered, piled up, taken in, and stored. These things were

---

① According to Shipei Liu, "officials"(官人) here refers to those who are stupid.

the same for both Yu and Jie, but Yu brought order, while Jie brought disorder. So order and disorder are not caused by the change of seasons.

Are social order and disorder caused by Earth? I say: If one has the land, one will live, and if one loses the land, one will die. These things were the same for both Yu and Jie, but Yu brought order, while Jie brought disorder. So order and disorder are not caused by Earth. The Odes says, "Heaven made the high mountain. The Great King opened the land. These works were completed, and King Wen made them more grand." This expresses my meaning.

天不爲人之惡寒也輟冬，地不爲人之惡遼遠也輟廣，君子不爲小人之匈匈也輟行。天有常道矣，地有常數矣，君子有常體矣。君子道其常，而小人計其功。《詩》曰："禮義之不愆，何恤人之言兮！"此之謂也。

Heaven does not stop the coming of winter because humans dislike cold, Earth does not grow smaller because humans dislike huge distances, and the gentleman does not change his behavior because of the chatter of petty men. Heaven has its constant way; Earth has its constant dimensions; the gentleman has his constant demeanor. The gentleman follows what is constant whereas the petty man calculates what he can accomplish. The Odes says, "If you have not violated proper etiquette, then why care about the words of others!" This expresses my meaning.

楚王後車千乘，非知也；君子啜菽飲水，非愚也；是節然也。若夫志意脩，德行厚，知慮明，生於今而志乎古，則是其在我者也。故君子敬其在己者，而不慕其在天者；小人錯其在己者，而慕其在天者。君子敬其在己者，而不慕其在天者，是以日進也；小人錯其在己者，而慕其在天者，是以日退也。故君子之所以日進，與小人之所以日退，一也。君子小人之所以相縣者，在此耳。

If the king of Chu has a thousand chariots following behind him, this is not because he is wise. If the gentleman eats only crude greens and drinks only plain water, this is not because he is foolish. It is just because of the circumstances. As for the will to cultivate ourselves: be strong in virtue, have the clarity of wisdom, live in the present and yet set our will on the Dao of the ancient—this is what we can control. And so, the gentleman pays attention to what he can achieve and does not envy what only Heaven can do. The petty man gives up what he can achieve and instead envies what only Heaven can do. Since the gentleman pays attention to what he can achieve and does not envy what only Heaven can do, every day he makes progress. Since the petty man gives up what he can achieve and instead envies what only Heaven can do, every day he gets worse. Thus the reason why the gentleman makes progress every day and that why the petty man gets worse every day are one and the same. The reason why the gentleman and petty man are so far apart from each other lies in this.

星隊木鳴，國人皆恐。曰：是何也？曰：無何也！是天地之變，陰陽之化，物之罕至者也。怪之，可也；而畏之，非也。夫日月之有蝕，風雨之不時，怪星之黨見，是無世而不常有之。上明而政平，則是雖並世起，無傷也；上闇而政險，則是雖無一至者，無益也。……

If stars fall or trees groan, the people of the state are filled with fear and say, "What is this?" I say: It is nothing. These are simply rarely occurring things among the changes in Heaven and Earth and the transformations of yin and yang. To marvel at them is permissible, but to fear them is wrong. Eclipses of the sun and the moon, unseasonable winds and rain, unexpected appearances of strange stars—there is no age in which such things do not occur. If the superiors are enlightened and the government is stable, then even if several of these phenomena occur, there will be no harm. If the superiors are benighted and the government is unstable, then even if none of these things occur, it is of no benefit. ...

物之已至者，人祅則可畏也：楛耕傷稼，楛耨失歲，政險失民；田薉稼惡，糴貴民飢，道路有死人：夫是之謂人祅。政令不明，舉錯不時，本事不理，勉力不時，則牛馬相生，六畜作祅：夫是之謂人祅。禮義不脩，內外無別，男女淫亂，則父子相疑,上下乖離,寇難並至:夫是之謂人祅。祅是生於亂。三者錯,無安國。其說甚爾,其菑甚慘。……傳曰:"萬物之怪書不說。"無用之辯,不急之察,棄而不治。若夫君臣之義,父子之親,夫婦之別,則日切瑳而不舍也。

Among all such strange occurrences, the ones really to be feared are human portents. When the plowing is poorly done and the crops suffer, when the weeding is badly done and the harvest fails, when the government is evil and loses the support of the people, when the fields are neglected and the crops badly tended, when grain must be imported from abroad and sold at a high price, and the people are starving and die by the roadside—these are what I mean by human portents. "When government commands are unenlightened, when public works are undertaken at the wrong season, when agriculture is not properly attended to, when the people are called away for corvée labor at the wrong season, so that cows and horses are left to breed together and the six domestic animals produce prodigies—these too are human portents. When ritual principles are not obeyed, family affairs and outside affairs are not properly separated, and men and women mingle wantonly, so that fathers and sons begin to doubt each other, superior and inferior become estranged, and bands of invaders enter the state—these too are human portents. Portents such as these are born from disorder, and if all three types occur at once, there will be no safety for the state. The reasons for their occurrence may be found very close at hand; the suffering they cause is great indeed. …A saying goes, "As for anomalies among the myriad things, *The Documents* does not explain them." As for unnecessary debates and unimportant investigations, abandon them and do not study them. As for the *yi* of lord and minister, the intimate relations of father and son, and the differentiation of husband and wife, polish and refine them daily and do not let them go.

雩而雨,何也? 曰:無何也,猶不雩而雨也。日月食而救之,天旱而雩,卜筮然後決大事,非以爲得求也,以文之也。故君子以爲文,而百姓以爲神。以爲文則吉,以爲神則凶也。

One prays for rain, and it rains. Why? I say: the reason why it rains has nothing to do with the prayer. If one did not pray for rain, it would rain anyway. When the sun and the moon eclipse, we take action to save them; when Heaven causes drought, we pray for rain; when great decisions of state must be made, we perform augury. We do not think that we will get what we seek by performing divination; we do all these as a "decoration". So the gentleman does this for decoration, and the common man thinks it is the work of the supernatural. To think it is decoration is fortune, and to think it is divine is misfortune.

在天者莫明於日月,在地者莫明於水火,在物者莫明於珠玉,在人者莫明於禮義。故日月不高,則光明不赫;水火不積,則暉潤不博;珠玉不睹乎外,則王公不以爲寶;禮義不加於國家,則功名不白。故人之命在天,國之命在禮。君人者,隆禮尊賢而王,重法愛民而霸,好利多詐而危,權謀傾覆幽險而亡矣。

In Heaven, nothing is brighter than the sun and the moon. On the Earth, nothing is brighter than water and fire. Among things, nothing is brighter than pearls and jade. For human beings, nothing is brighter than ritual and yi. If the sun and the moon are not high above, their light is not radiant. If water and fire do not accumulate, their gleam and shimmer does not spread far. If pearls and jade are not visible on the outside, then kings and dukes do not treasure them. If ritual and yi are not applied to the state and family, then accomplishments and fame do not shine. And so, a person's fate rests with Heaven. The fate of the state rests with ritual. If the lord of men exalts ritual and honors the worthy, he will become a true king. If he relies heavily on law and has concern for the people, he will become a hegemon. If he cares only for profit and frequently engages in deception, he will be endangered. If he is scheming, debauched, unpredictable and dangerous, he will get himself killed.

大天而思之,孰與物畜而制之! 從天而頌之,孰與制天命而用之! 望時而待之，孰與應時而使之！因物而多之，孰與騁能而化之！思物而物之，孰與理物而勿失之也！願於物之所以生，孰與有物之所以成！故錯人而思天，則失萬物之情。

    Compared with exalting Heaven and thinking of it, isn't it much better to treat it as cattle to be raised and controlled! Compared with obeying Heaven and praising it, isn't it much better to grasp the mandate of Heaven and make use of it! Compared with watching the change of time and waiting for the good things to happen to you, isn't it much better to seize the opportunity and act! Compared with waiting for things to increase themselves, isn't it much better to develop their potentials and transform them! Compared with thinking of things but regarding them as outside you, isn't it much better to control things and not let them slip your grasp? Compared with longing for the source from which things are born, isn't it much better to possess the means to bring them to completion! Therefore if a person neglects what humans can do and seeks for what Heaven does, he fails to understand the nature of things.

附錄：哲學家小傳 /
Appendix: Biographies of Chinese philosophers

（以下內容參考維基百科[Wikipedia]、斯坦福哲學百科全書[Stanford Encyclopedia of Philosophy]和哲學網絡百科全書[Internet Encyclopedia of Philosophy]相關詞條彙編而成，編者做了一些修訂。）

孔子 Confucius

Confucius (September 28, 551 BC-479 BC) was a Chinese teacher, editor, politician, and philosopher of the Spring and Autumn period of Chinese history.

Confucius was born into the class of shi (士), between the aristocracy and the common people. He is said to have worked in various government jobs during his early twenties, and also worked as a bookkeeper and a caretaker of sheep and horses, from which he used the proceeds to give his mother a proper burial. When his mother died, Confucius (aged 23) is said to have mourned for three years, as was the tradition.

Confucius' home state, Lu, was headed by a ruling ducal house. Under the duke were three aristocratic families, whose heads bore the title of viscount and held hereditary positions in the Lu bureaucracy. In 501 BC, Confucius came to be appointed to the minor position of governor of a town. Eventually, he rose to the position of Minister of Crime.

Confucius desired to return the authority of the state to the duke by dismantling the fortifications of the city—strongholds belonging to the three families. In this way, he could establish a centralized government.

Later in 498 BC, Duke Ding personally went with an army to lay siege to Cheng in an attempt to raze its walls to the ground, but he did not succeed. Thus, Confucius could not achieve the idealistic reforms that he wanted including restoration of the legitimate rule of the duke. He had made powerful enemies within the state, especially with Viscount Ji Huan. So he departed his homeland in 497 BC after his support for the failed attempt of dismantling the fortified city walls of the three families. He left the state of Lu without resigning, remaining in self-exile and unable to return as long as Viscount Ji Huan was alive.

After Confucius' resignation, he began a long journey or a set of journeys around the small kingdoms of north-east and central China. At the courts of these states, he expounded his political beliefs but did not see them implemented.

According to *Zuo Zhuan*, Confucius returned home to his native Lu when he was 68, after he was invited to do so by Ji Kangzi, the chief minister of Lu. *The Analects* depicts him spending his last years teaching 72 or 77 disciples and transmitting the old wisdom via a set of texts called the Five Classics. During his return, Confucius sometimes acted as an advisor to several government officials in Lu, including Ji Kangzi, on matters including governance and crime. Burdened by the loss of both his son and his favorite disciples, he died at the age of 71 or 72.

Confucius is traditionally credited with having authored or edited many Chinese classic texts including all of the Five Classics, but modern scholars are cautious of attributing specific assertions to Confucius himself. Aphorisms concerning his teachings were compiled in *The Analects*, but only many years after his death.

韩非 Han Fei

Han Fei(c. 280 BC-233 BC), also known as Han Feizi, was an influential political philosopher of the "Chinese Legalist" school in the Warring States period (403 BC-221 BC). He is often considered to be the greatest representative of Chinese Legalism.

Unlike other famed philosophers of the time, Han Fei was a member of the ruling aristocracy, having been born into the ruling family of the state of Han during the end phase of the Warring States period. In this context, his works have been interpreted by some scholars as being directed to his cousin, the king of Han. Seeing Han was on the decline, he often remonstrated with the king of Han by submitting papers, but the king did not agree to employ him.

According to the historian Sima Qian, Han Fei studied together with the future Qin chancellor Li Si under the Confucian philosopher Xunzi. It is said that because of his stutter, Han Fei could not properly present his ideas in court. His advice otherwise being ignored, but observing the slow decline of his Han state, he developed "one of the most brilliant [writing] styles in ancient China".

The works of Han Fei ultimately ended up in the hands of the thrilled King of Qin (i.e. the future first emperor of China, Qin Shi Huang). The King of Qin commented, "If I can make friend with this person (Han Fei), I may die without regrets." He invited Han Fei to Qin. Han Fei presented the essay "Preserving the Han" to the King of Qin, asking the king not to attack his homeland. But his ex-friend and rival Li Si, who was jealous of Han Fei, used that essay to convince the King of Qin to imprison Han Fei on account of his loyalty to Han. Han Fei responded by writing another essay named "At the First Time of Meeting the King of Qin", hoping to use his writing talent to win the king's heart. Han Fei did win the king's heart, but not before Li Si forced him to commit suicide by drinking poison.

老子 Laozi

Laozi (also Lao-Tzu or Lao-Tze, meaning "Old Master") was an ancient Chinese philosopher and writer. He is known as the reputed author of *Dao De Jing* and the founder of philosophical Daoism, and as a deity in religious Daoism and traditional Chinese religions.

According to traditional accounts, Laozi was a scholar who worked as the Keeper of the Archives for the royal court of Zhou. This allowed him broad access to the works of the Yellow Emperor and other classics of the time. The stories assert that Laozi never opened a formal school but nonetheless attracted a large number of students and loyal disciples. There are many variations of the story retelling his encounter with Confucius, most famously in Zhuangzi.

According to Sima Qian, Laozi grew weary of the moral decay of the life in Zhou and noted the kingdom's decline. He ventured west to live as a hermit in the unsettled frontier at the age of 80. At the western gate of the kingdom, he was recognized by the guard Yinxi. The sentry asked the old master to record his wisdom for the good of the country before he would be permitted to pass. The text Laozi wrote was said to be Dao De Jing. In some versions of the tale, the sentry was so touched by the work that he became a disciple and left with Laozi, never to be seen again. In others, the "Old Master" journeyed all the way to India and was the teacher of Siddartha Gautama, the Buddha. Others say he was the Buddha himself.

孟子 Mencius

Mencius or Mengzi (372 BC-289 BC; alt. 385 BC-303/ 302 BC), also known by his birth name Meng Ke or Meng Ko (孟軻), was a Chinese philosopher who is the most famous Confucian after Confucius himself.

Mencius was born in a state only thirty kilometres (eighteen miles) south of Confucius' birthplace. Mencius's mother is often held up as an exemplary female figure in Chinese culture. One of the most famous traditional Chinese four-character idioms is 孟母三遷 (pinyin: mèngmǔ-sānqiān; literally: "Mencius's mother, three moves"); this saying refers to the legend that Mencius's mother moved houses three times before finding a location that she felt was suitable for the child's upbringing.

Mencius was an itinerant Chinese philosopher and sage, and one of the principal interpreters of Confucianism. Supposedly, he was a pupil of

Confucius' grandson, Zisi. Like Confucius, according to the legend, he travelled throughout China for forty years to offer advice to rulers for reform. During the Warring States period, Mencius served as an official and scholar at the Jixia Academy in the state of Qi (1046 BC-221 BC) from 319 BC to 312 BC. He expressed his filial devotion when he took three years' leave of absence from his official duties for Qi to mourn his mother's death. Disappointed at his failure to effect any political changes, he finally retired from public life.

墨子 Mozi

Mozi, (ca. 468 BC-ca. 391 BC), original name Mo Di (墨翟), was a Chinese philosopher during the Hundred Schools of Thought period (early Warring States period). A book named after him, Mozi, contains material ascribed to him and his followers.

Most historians believe that Mozi was a member of the lower artisan class who managed to climb his way to an official post. It is known, however, that his parents were not affectionate towards him and showed him very little love. Like Confucius, Mozi was a native of the state of Lu, although for a time he served as a minister in the state of Song. Like Confucius, Mozi was known to have maintained a school for those who desired to become officials serving in the different ruling courts of the Warring States.

Mozi was a carpenter and was extremely skilled in creating devices, designing everything from mechanical birds to wheeled, mobile "cloud ladders" used to besiege city walls. Though he did not hold a high official position, Mozi was sought out by various rulers as an expert on fortification. He was schooled in Confucianism in his early years, but he viewed Confucianism as being too fatalistic and emphasizing too much on elaborate celebrations and funerals which he felt were detrimental to the livelihood and productivity of common people. He managed to attract a large following during his lifetime which rivaled that of Confucius. His followers—mostly technicians and craftspeople—were organized in a disciplined order that studied both Mozi's philosophical and technical writings.

荀子 Xunzi

Xunzi, also widely known as Xun Kuang, was a Chinese Confucian philosopher who lived during the Warring States period and contributed to the Hundred Schools of Thought. A book known as *Xunzi* is traditionally attributed to him.

The early years of Xunzi's life are enshrouded in mystery. Nothing is known of his lineage. According to Sima Qian, he was born in the state of Zhao (now Shanxi, China). Xunzi was first known at the age of fifty, around 264 BC, when he went to the state of Qi to study and teach at the Jixia Academy. Xunzi was well respected in Qi.

It was around this time that Xunzi visited the state of Qin and praised its governance, and debated military affairs with Lord Linwu (臨武君) in the court of King Xiaocheng of Zhao. Later, Xunzi was slandered in the Qi court, and he retreated south to the state of Chu, where Lord Chunshen, the prime minister, gave him a position as Magistrate of Lanling (蘭陵令). In 238 BC, Lord Chunshen was assassinated by a court rival, and Xunzi subsequently lost his position. He remained in Lanling for the rest of his life and was buried there. The year of his death is unknown.

莊子 Zhuangzi

Zhuangzi (Chuang-Tze), often known as Zhuang Zhou, was an influential Chinese philosopher who lived around the 4th century BC during the Warring States period, a period corresponding to the summit of Chinese philosophy, the Hundred Schools of Thought. He is credited with writing—in part or in whole—a work known by his name, *Zhuangzi*.

We know very little about Zhuangzi's life. According to Sima Qian's *Records of the Grand Historian*, which draws heavily on the anecdotes in

Zhuangzi itself, Zhuangzi was a minor official from the town of Meng (in Anhui) in the state of Song. He had made himself well acquainted with all the literature of his time, but preferred the views of Laozi. King Wei of Chu, having heard of the ability of Zhuangzi, sent messengers with large gifts to bring him to his court, promising that he would make him his chief minister. Zhuangzi, however, declined the offer.

術語 / Glossary

道(dao): the way; the road; the truth; the invisible principle; the unifying principle; the first cause

德(de): virtue; power; acquired thing

法(fa): law; rule; model

君子(junzi): the gentleman; the noble-minded; sometimes the person of high social status

利(li): profit; interests; utility; money

禮(li): rituals; etiquette; proprieties

名(ming): name; title

命(ming): fate; mandate of Heaven

氣(qi): air; material energy; life force; energy flow

仁(ren): benevolence; magnanimity; goodness

弟(同"悌";ti): to love and respect one's elder brothers; to do one's duty as a younger brother

天(tian): Heaven; God; the sky

天下(tianxia): All-Under-Heaven; the world

無(wu): nothingness; the unoccupied; the invisible

孝(xiao): filial piety; to love and respect one's parents

性(xing): nature; essence; innate quality

義(yi): righteousness; justice; obligation; duty

陰陽(yin-yang): dark-bright; negative-positive; female-male; covert-overt

知(zhi): knowledge; wisdom

參考書目 / Bibliography

Bloom, I. (2009). Mencius. Columbia University Press.

Dubs, H. H. (1928). The works of Hsüntze. Arthur Probsthain.

Feng, Y-L. (2016). Chuang-Tzu a New Selected Translation with an Exposition of the Philosophy of Kuo Hsiang. Foreign Language Teaching and Research Publishing Co., Ltd and Springer.

Graham, A. C., 1981. Chuang-tzu: The Seven Inner Chapters and Other Writings from the Book Chuang-tzu. London:George Allen and Unwin.

Hinton, D., 2013. The Four Chinese Classics: Tao Te Ching, Analects, Chuang Tzu, Mencius. Berkeley:Counterpoint.

Hutton, E. L., 2014. Xunzi: The Complete text. Princeton: Princeton University Press.

Ivanhoe, P. J., 2003. The Daodejing of Laozi. Zndianapolis: Hackett Publishing.

Johnston, I., 2004. "The Gongsun Longzi: A translation and an analysis of its relationship to later Mohist writings". Journal of Chinese Philosophy, 31(2), pp.271-295.

Johnston, I., 2010. The Mozi: A Complete Translation. New York: Columbia University Press.

Knoblock, J., 1988-1994. Xunzi: A Translation and Study of the Complete Works, 3 vols., Stanford: Stanford University Press.

Lau, D.C., 1970. Mencius. New York: Penguin.

Lau, D. C., 1979. Confucius: The Analects. London: Penguin Books.

Lau, D. C., 1982. Chinese Classics: Tao Te Ching. Hong Kong: Chinese

University Press.

Liao, W. K. 1939. *The Complete Works of Han Fei Tzu*. London: A. Probsthain.

Legge, J., 1865. *The Chinese Classics*. London: Trubner & Company.

Mei, Y., 1929. *The Ethical and Political Works of Motse*. London: Probsthain.

Ni, P., 2017. *Understanding the Analects of Confucius: A New Translation of Lunyu with Annotations*. Albany: SUNY Press.

Palmer, M., Elizabeth B., Wai-ming C., and Jay R., 1996. *The Book of Chuang Tzu*, London: Penguin Books.

Rosemont, H. and Ames, R. T., 2009. *The Chinese Classic of Family Reverence: A Philosophical Translation of the Xiaojing*. Honolulu: University of Hawaii Press.

Slingerland, E., 2003. *Confucius: Analects*, Indianapolis: Hackett Publishing.

Van Norden, B. W., 2008. *Mengzi: With Selections from Traditional Commentaries*, Indianapolis: Hackett Publishing.

Watson, B., 1963. *Mo Tzu: Basic Writings*. New York: Columbia University Press.

Watson, B., 1963. *Hsün Tzu: Basic Writings*. New York: Columbia University.

Watson, B., 1964. *Han Fei Tzu: Basic Writings*. New York: Columbia University Press.

Watson, B., 1968. *The Complete Works of Chuang Tzu*. New York: Columbia University Press.

Ziporyn, B., 2009. *Zhuangzi: The Essential Writings (With Selections from Traditional Commentaries)*. Indianapolis: Hackett Publishing.

图书在版编目(CIP)数据

中国古典哲学原著选读:汉英对照 / 胡星铭编著.
—南京:南京大学出版社,2018.9
 ISBN 978-7-305-20924-6

Ⅰ.①中… Ⅱ.①胡… Ⅲ.①古典哲学-著作-介绍-中国-汉、英 Ⅳ.①B211

中国版本图书馆 CIP 数据核字(2018)第 207615 号

出版发行	南京大学出版社
社　　址	南京市汉口路 22 号　　邮　编 210093
出 版 人	金鑫荣
书　　名	中国古典哲学原著选读(汉英对照)
编　　著	胡星铭
责任编辑	付　裕　沈卫娟
封面设计	清　早
照　　排	南京紫藤制版印务中心
印　　刷	常州市武进第三印刷有限公司
开　　本	718×1000　1/16　印张 22.25　字数 400 千
版　　次	2018 年 9 月第 1 版　2018 年 9 月第 1 次印刷
ISBN	978-7-305-20924-6
定　　价	68.00 元

网　　址:http://www.njupco.com
官方微博:http://weibo.com/njupco
官方微信:njupress
销售咨询热线:(025)83594756

* 版权所有,侵权必究

* 凡购买南大版图书,如有印装质量问题,请与所购
　图书销售部门联系调换